HORSE RACING

Records · Facts and Champions

HORSE RACING

RECORDS · FACTS AND CHAMPIONS

Tony Morris and
John Randall

GUINNESS BOOKS

Tony Morris, born in the same year as Tudor Minstrel, fell under the spell of the Turf in the year of Ribot's second Prix de l'Arc de Triomphe.

He joined the racing staff of the Press Association on leaving school two months before Relko's Derby and transferred to the *Sporting Life* when Mill Reef and Brigadier Gerard were three-year-olds. He moved in Oh So Sharp's Triple Crown year to the *Racing Post*, and is the Bloodstock Editor of that journal.

He was for seven seasons Editor of the annual *Bloodstock Breeders' Review* (1971-7) and his other published works, as author or co-author, include *Great Moments in Racing* (1976), *The Stallion Guide* (1983, 1984) and *Notable English and Irish Thoroughbreds* (1984).

John Randall was born in Beckenham, Kent in the year of Sir Ken's second Champion Hurdle and, at the age of six, had the course of his life changed by seeing the first televised Grand National.

After gaining a law degree he found the lure of the Turf too strong and spent nine years with Raceform, three of them as Editor of *The Racehorse*. He is now on the editorial staff of the *Racing Post*.

As well as writing four quiz books and contributing to the *Bloodstock Breeders' Review*, *Notable English and Irish Thoroughbreds* and other books, he has since 1976 been responsible for compiling the racing section in the *Guinness Book of Records*. He has never bet on a horse in his life.

Editor: Simon Duncan
Picture Editor: Alex Goldberg
Design and Layout: Alan Hamp

© Tony Morris & John Randall
and Guinness Publishing Ltd, 1985, 1988, 1990

First published in 1985
Second edition 1988
Third edition 1990
Published in Great Britain by Guinness Publishing Ltd,
33 London Road, Enfield, Middlesex

Typeset in Century Schoolbook and Helvetica
Typeset by Ace Filmsetting Ltd, Frome, Somerset
Printed and bound in Great Britain by
The Bath Press, Bath

'Guinness' is a registered trade mark of
Guinness Superlatives Ltd

British Library Cataloguing in Publication Data

Randall, John, *1953–*
Horse racing: records, facts and champions.
1. Racehorses. Racing. Records of
achievement
I. Title II. Morris, Tony, *1944–*
789.4'009

ISBN 0–85112–902–1

Contents

Introduction

If you have ever tried to trace your family tree, you will know how difficult it can be. Usually only the most aristocratic of the human race find it possible to progress beyond a few generations, and even when records enable us to identify our antecedents, we generally remain ignorant about how they lived their lives.

By contrast, the pedigree of the humblest Thoroughbred racehorse in any part of the world can be readily traced to its roots, in many cases for more than 30 generations, and we have access to the performance and breeding records of all its ancestors. No other animal species is better documented than the Thoroughbred horse; no other organized sport has a longer recorded history than horse racing.

The wealth of material available to the researcher is prodigious, and the following pages are the product of countless hours spent examining, checking and re-checking official and unofficial records, wherever possible from contemporary archives. Much of the data set out here has never been published before in this form, and in many instances our researches have enabled us to correct erroneous versions of events traditionally accepted as fact. It is our hope that *Horse Racing – Records, Facts and Champions* will entertain, educate and settle many arguments about the history of the Sport of Kings.

Tony Morris & John Randall

Front cover: *Desert Orchid, the popular grey steeplechaser who has won more prize-money than any other jumper in racing history. (All-Sport)*

Page 1: *Peter Scudamore urges the grey Pukka Major over the second-last fence on his way to victory in the 1989 Cheltenham Grand Annual Handicap Chase. This was Scudamore's only success at the National Hunt meeting in a season in which he won 221 races, easily a record for a jump jockey. (Alan Johnson)*

Page 2: *Mandarin in retirement with Fred Winter. In 1962 the partnership gained a unique double in the championship races for steeplechasers in England and France – the Cheltenham Gold Cup and the Grand Steeple-Chase de Paris respectively. (Gerry Cranham)*

Abbreviations

colour		sex		a	age unknown	Fav	favourite
b	bay	c	colt	yr	years	Jt-Fav	joint-favourite (of 2)
bl	black	f	filly	m	mile	Co-Fav	co-favourite (of 3)
br	brown	g	gelding	f	furlong	gns	guineas (1 guinea =
ch	chestnut	h	horse	yd	yard		£1.05)
gr	grey	m	mare	sp	starting price	st, lb	stones, pounds
ro	roan					kg	kilogrammes

1. HISTORICAL MILESTONES

1540 Racing is recorded for the first time on the Roodee at Chester, the oldest surviving course in England.

1580s Queen Elizabeth attends the races on Salisbury Plain.

1595 A racecourse appears on a map of Doncaster Town Moor.

1605 James I is the first monarch to visit Newmarket.

1619 The earliest known rules of racing are drawn up at Kiplingcotes, Yorkshire.

1640s Racing at Epsom is recorded for the first time.

1665 North America's first formal racecourse is laid out on Long Island, New York.

1660s Charles II's patronage makes Newmarket the main centre of racing in England.

1689 The Byerley Turk, earliest of the 3 male-line ancestors of the Thoroughbred, is imported into England.

*c***1704** The Darley Arabian, male-line ancestor of over 90 per cent of modern Thoroughbreds, is imported into England.

1709 York holds the first fully-reported race meeting.

1711 The first meeting at Ascot takes place at Queen Anne's instigation.

1713 First use of the term 'thro-bred' to describe horses.

1727 Death of Tregonwell Frampton, the Father of the Turf and controller of the royal horses at Newmarket during 4 reigns.

John Cheny of Arundel publishes the first annual racing calendar.

1730 The Godolphin Arabian, last of the 3 male-line ancestors of the Thoroughbred, is imported into England.

1731 Racing at York is transferred to the Knavesmire.

Bedale, Yorkshire stages the first race for 3-year-olds.

1740 In order to check the growth of the sport, Parliament outlaws nearly all races worth less than £50.

*c***1750** The Jockey Club is founded at the Star and Garter in Pall Mall, London.

1751 John Pond's first *Sporting Kalendar* contains regulations destined to evolve into the modern Rules of Racing.

1752 The earliest recorded steeplechase takes place when Mr Edmund Blake and Mr O'Callaghan ride a match of 4½ miles from the Church of Buttevant to St Leger Church, Co Cork.

1758 The Jockey Club passes its first resolution, requiring all riders at Newmarket to weigh in after a race.

1762 Racing colours are first registered at Newmarket.

1764 Birth of Eclipse, the greatest racehorse of the 18th century.

1766 Richard Tattersall starts to organize bloodstock sales at Hyde Park Corner, London.

1769 Newmarket sees the first appearance on a racecourse of a 2-year-old.

1770 The Orders of the Jockey Club, applicable only at Newmarket, are published for the first time.

1773 James Weatherby, Keeper of the Match-Book at Newmarket, publishes the first volume of his *Racing Calendar*.

1774 Birth of Highflyer, the greatest sire of the 18th century.

1776 Inaugural running at Doncaster of the sweepstakes which became the St Leger in 1778.

The first organized meeting in France is held near Paris.

1779 The Oaks Stakes at Epsom is run for the first time.

1780 Inaugural running of the Derby Stakes at Epsom.

*c***1790** The first bookmaker appears on a racecourse.

1790 Formation of the Turf Club, the governing body of racing in Ireland.

1791 James Weatherby publishes the first volume of the *General Stud Book*.

The Oatlands Stakes at Ascot is the first important handicap in England.

The Prince of Wales withdraws from Newmarket after a Jockey Club enquiry into the inconsistent running of his horse Escape.

1792 The earliest recorded steeplechases in England take place in Leicestershire.

1802 Goodwood holds its first recognized meeting.

1807 Inaugural running of the Gold Cup at Ascot.

1809 Inaugural running of the 2000 Guineas at Newmarket.

1810 The first recorded meeting in Australia is held in Sydney.

1811 Bedford stages the first steeplechase over an artificial course.

1814 Inaugural running of the 1000 Guineas at Newmarket.

1816 A trailer is used to convey a horse to the races for the first time.

1821 Death of Sir Charles Bunbury, permanent steward of the Jockey Club and the first dictator of the Turf.

The Jockey Club issues its first warning-off notice.

The first artificial dirt track comes into use at the Union Course on Long Island, New York.

1822 The first organized meeting in Germany is held at Doberan, Mecklenburg.

1827 Pest stages the first organized meeting in Hungary.

1828 Retirement of Robert Robson of Newmarket,

Previous page The Byerley Turk, one of the founding stallions of the Thoroughbred horse, was Captain Byerley's charger at the Battle of the Boyne in 1690. (BBC Hulton Picture Library)

credited with being the first trainer to refrain from 'sweating' his horses, i.e. wrapping them in heavy sheets and subjecting them to long gallops.

1829 Liverpool's new course at Aintree holds its first meeting.

1830 Thomas Coleman, the father of steeplechasing, organizes the first St Albans steeplechase.

1831 Cheltenham races are held at Prestbury Park for the first time; they find a permanent home there in 1902.

The Jockey Club refuses to resolve any more disputes arising at meetings where its Rules are not in force.

1833 Randwick, Sydney holds its first meeting.

Formation of the Société d'Encouragement pour l'amélioration des races de chevaux en France; Lord Henry Seymour is its first president.

1834 Horses at Newmarket take their ages from 1 January instead of 1 May; horses elsewhere in Great Britain follow suit in 1858.

Chantilly holds its first meeting.

1836 Inaugural running of the Prix du Jockey-Club at Chantilly.

1837 Florence and Naples stage the first organized meetings in Italy.

1838 The first recorded meeting in Victoria is held in Melbourne.

1839 Inaugural running at Liverpool of the race which became the Grand National Steeple Chase in 1847.

1840 Flemington, Melbourne holds its first meeting.

1842 The first formal meeting in New Zealand is held in Auckland.

Formation of the Australian Jockey Club, the governing body of racing in New South Wales.

The Jockey Club refuses to settle any more disputes over betting.

1843 Inaugural running of the Prix de Diane at Chantilly.

1844 'Running Rein' wins the Derby but is exposed as a 4-year-old.

1848 Death of Lord George Bentinck, administrator, reformer and the second dictator of the Turf.

1850 Birth of Lexington, America's greatest sire.

1851 California's first formal racecourse opens near San Francisco.

Fairyhouse holds its first meeting.

The Flying Dutchman beats Voltigeur in a match at York.

1853 West Australian becomes the first Triple Crown winner.

1855 Admiral Henry Rous, author of the weight-for-age scale, is appointed handicapper to the Jockey Club.

Inaugural running of the Victoria Derby at Flemington.

1857 Ellerslie (Auckland) and Longchamp hold their first meetings.

1858 Baden-Baden holds its first meeting.

1860 Yearlings may no longer race in Great Britain. The Queen's Plate, Canada's premier classic, is run for the first time.

1861 The first organized meeting in Japan is held in Yokohama.

The AJC Derby at Randwick and the Melbourne Cup at Flemington are both run for the first time.

1863 Inaugural running of the Grand Prix de Paris at Longchamp.

Formation of the Société des Steeple-Chases de France.

1864 Formation of the Victoria Racing Club, the governing body of racing in Victoria.

Saratoga and Deauville hold their first meetings.

1865 Parisian Pierre Oller devises the first system of pari-mutuel betting.

Gladiateur, the 'Avenger of Waterloo', becomes the first foreign-bred Derby winner.

1866 Formation of the Grand National Steeple Chase Committee, renamed the National Hunt Committee in 1889.

1867 The Belmont Stakes in New York is run for the first time.

Hoppegarten, Berlin holds its first meeting.

Formation of the Union-Klub, the governing body of racing in Germany until World War II.

1869 The Norddeutsches Derby in Hamburg, forerunner of the Deutsches Derby, is staged for the first time.

The Marquess of Drogheda founds the Irish National Hunt Steeplechase Committee.

1870 The Jockey Club restricts the length of the Flat season and no longer recognizes meetings which are not subject to its Rules.

1873 Inaugural running of the Preakness Stakes at Pimlico, Maryland.

Auteuil holds its first meeting.

1874 Birth of Kincsem, Hungary's champion racemare.

1875 Sandown Park, the first enclosed course in Great Britain, holds its inaugural meeting.

The Kentucky Derby at Churchill Downs and the Great Northern Derby (renamed the New Zealand Derby in 1973) at Ellerslie are both run for the first time.

1877 The Rules of Racing provide for a draw for starting positions.

1878 At Palo Alto, California, English-born photographer Eadweard Muybridge reveals in detail the gait of a galloping horse.

1879 Jockeys in Great Britain are required to be licensed.

1881 Formation of the Jockey Club Italiano.

Birth of St Simon, the greatest sire of the 19th century.

Woodbine, Toronto holds its first meeting; the new track there opens in 1956.

1882 Racing at Newcastle is transferred to Gosforth Park.

Suffragette Emily Davison lies fatally injured after bringing down the King's horse Anmer at Tattenham Corner in the 1913 Derby. (Syndication International)

Minimum requirements are laid down for the number and size of fences or hurdles in a race.

1883 Birth of Ormonde, the greatest racehorse of the 19th century.

1884 The Derby Reale, forerunner of the Derby Italiano, and the Gran Premio Nacional (Argentine Derby) are both staged for the first time.

1886 Inaugural running of the Eclipse Stakes, the first £10,000 race in England, at Sandown Park on 23 July.

Champion jockey Fred Archer shoots himself in a fit of depression on 8 November.

1887 First meeting of the body which became the New Zealand Racing Conference in 1897.

The Gran Premio Internacional in Buenos Aires, forerunner of the Gran Premio Carlos Pellegrini, is staged for the first time.

1888 Leopardstown holds its first meeting.

1890 Sheepshead Bay, New York pioneers the use of the camera to decide the finish of races.

Lingfield Park holds its first meeting.

1891 A pari-mutuel betting monopoly is established in France.

1894 Formation of the Jockey Club of New York, parent body of the American Turf.

Aqueduct, New York holds its first meeting; the new track there opens in 1959.

1895 American Willie Simms is the first to use the modern jockeys' seat in England.

The Derby is the first race to be recorded on film.

1897 The starting gate is introduced on British courses at Newmarket.

1898 Federico Tesio founds the Razza Dormello on the shores of Lake Maggiore.

1899 Haydock Park holds its first meeting.

1902 Sceptre wins all the Classics except the Derby. Phoenix Park holds its first meeting.

1903 Doping is banned by the Jockey Club in response to the practices of some American trainers.

1905 The Jockey Club requires trainers to be licensed.

Belmont Park and Newbury hold their first meetings.

1909 Anti-betting legislation causes racing in California to be abandoned.

1910 The National Hunt Committee makes number-cloths compulsory, requires trainers to be licensed and bans doping.

Anti-betting legislation suspends racing in New York until 1913.

1911 The National Hunt meeting settles permanently at Cheltenham.

1913 The Jockey Club no longer allows races to be shorter than 5 furlongs or horses older than 2 to run unnamed.

The favourite is disqualified after the 'Suffragette Derby.'

The 'Jersey Act' bars many American-breds from the *General Stud Book*; the success of horses thus excluded causes its repeal in 1949.

1916 The National Stud is founded at Tully, Co

Kildare; it is moved to England in 1943.

1917 Birth of Man o' War, America's champion racehorse.

*c*1920 American William Murray designs the first starting stalls.

1920 The Jockey Club no longer allows owners to use assumed names or amateur riders to compete against professionals.

Inaugural running of the Prix de l'Arc de Triomphe at Longchamp.

1922 Number-cloths are carried for the first time on the Flat in Great Britain.

1924 Inaugural running of the Cheltenham Gold Cup.

Skull caps are made compulsory under National Hunt Rules.

1925 Hialeah Park, Florida holds its first meeting.

1926 Chancellor of the Exchequer Winston Churchill introduces betting tax in his Budget but its failure forces him to abandon it in 1929.

The sporting papers agree on a combined return of starting prices.

Birth of Phar Lap, Australasia's champion racehorse.

1927 Inaugural running of the Champion Hurdle at Cheltenham.

The Grand National and the Derby are the first races in England to be broadcast on radio.

The Jockey Club requires all horses to be run on their merits; hitherto one horse could be stopped in favour of another in the same ownership.

Arlington Park, Chicago holds its first meeting.

1928 Formation of the Racecourse Betting Control Board, reconstituted as the Horserace Totalisator Board in 1961.

1929 A new type of starting gate is introduced on British courses at Lincoln.

Abolition of the 'void nominations' rule whereby the death of an owner rendered void all entries for his horses.

Totalisator betting is tried out at Newmarket and Carlisle on 2 July.

1930 Most American tracks adopt starting stalls.

1931 Dead-heats in Great Britain may no longer be run off.

1932 The Derby is the first race to be televised.

Inaugural running of the Japanese Derby.

1933 Racing with pari-mutuel betting is legalized in California.

1934 Santa Anita, California holds its first meeting.

1935 Hyperion starts his stud career in Newmarket.

1936 Most American tracks adopt the photo-finish camera.

1938 Hollywood Park, California holds its first meeting.

Nearco is imported from Italy to stand at stud in Newmarket.

1942 National Hunt racing in Great Britain is suspended for 2 seasons due to the war.

1945 California pioneers the air transport of racehorses.

1946 No horse in Great Britain may run unnamed. Nearly all French races are opened to foreign-bred horses.

1947 The photo-finish camera is introduced on British courses at Epsom on 22 April.

The first evening meeting in Great Britain is held at Hamilton Park on 18 July.

1949 The first East European international meeting is staged in Prague.

1950 Nasrullah is exported from Ireland to stand at stud in Kentucky.

1951 Citation becomes the first equine dollar millionaire.

Inaugural running of the King George VI and Queen Elizabeth Stakes at Ascot.

1952 Birth of Ribot, Italy's champion racehorse.

Electrical timing and loudspeaker commentaries are introduced on British courses at Newmarket and Goodwood respectively.

1954 The pari-mutuel tiercé bet is introduced, greatly increasing the flow of revenue into French racing.

Formation of the Japan Racing Association.

1957 Birth of champion steeplechaser Arkle.

1960 The patrol camera is introduced on British courses at Newmarket on 30 June.

1961 The Jockey Club introduces overnight declarations.

Betting shops become legal on 1 May.

The Horserace Betting Levy Board, the controlling body of British racing finances, comes into being on 1 September.

1962 Birth of Sea-Bird, France's champion racehorse.

Inaugural running of the Irish Sweeps Derby at The Curragh.

1963 France is the first major racing nation in Europe to adopt starting stalls.

1965 Starting stalls are introduced on British courses at Newmarket on 8 July; they are first used in the Classics in 1967.

1966 The Jockey Club is forced to grant trainers' licences to women.

Chancellor of the Exchequer James Callaghan reintroduces betting tax in his Budget; it comes into effect on 24 October.

1968 The Jockey Club and the National Hunt Committee amalgamate on 12 December.

1971 Introduction of Pattern Race classifications in Europe.

Inaugural year of the Eclipse Awards in America.

1972 The Jockey Club permits races for women riders.

Australian racing goes metric on 1 August.

1973 Introduction of Graded Stakes classifications in North America.

The Jockey Club adopts computer-assisted centralized handicapping.

Secretariat becomes the first American Triple Crown winner for 25 years.

New Zealand racing goes metric on 1 August.

1975 Introduction of graded handicaps on the Flat in Great Britain.

1978 Sha Tin, Hong Kong's £100 million racecourse, holds its first meeting.

1981 The Arlington Million in Chicago and the Japan Cup in Tokyo are both run for the first time.

1984 All the English Classics are sponsored.

Inaugural year of the European Breeders' Fund, whereby half the maiden 2-year-old races in Great Britain, Ireland and France are open only to the progeny of nominated stallions.

Inaugural year of the Breeders' Cup programme in North America, culminating in Breeders' Cup Day at Hollywood Park on 10 November with $10 million in prize money.

1987 The first Festival of British Racing Day is held at Ascot on 26 September.

1989 Great Britain's first meeting on an all-weather racing surface takes place at Lingfield Park on 30 October.

2. EQUINE ACHIEVEMENTS

Most Successful Horses: Races Won

Most wins in a career

The holder of the world record for races won in a career is Galgo Jr, a Puerto Rican-bred horse, foaled in 1928 on Vieques Island. The product of parents imported from the USA, he did all his racing at the Quintana and Las Monjas tracks in Puerto Rico between 1930 and 1936. He ran 159 times, recording 137 wins, 18 second places, one third and two fourths. He finished 'out of the money' only once, and his earnings of $31,738 constituted a then-record for Puerto Rican racing. Galgo Jr was still in training when he died of a heart attack in his box at Las Monjas Racing Park on 21 December 1936, and at the time of his death he was the holder, or joint-holder, of eight track records for native Puerto Rican-breds, from 5½ furlongs to 9 furlongs. Inevitably, Galgo Jr enjoyed the status of a local hero, but his merit was never tested at international level and the times he achieved suggested that he was not an outstanding runner by comparison with contemporary champions in more prominent racing nations. But if his class was suspect, his consistency and durability made him a worthy record holder.

Galgo Jr's career record

	won	$
1930	21	7,757
1931	30	9,244
1932	19	6,109
1933	15	2,209
1934	18	2,771
1935	25	2,700
1936	9	949
Total	137	31,739

The record for races won in a career by a British-bred horse is 79, achieved by the mare Catherina between 1832 and 1841. She ran only once against top-class opposition, when unplaced as third favourite for the 1833 Oaks, but thereafter proved markedly successful in lesser company all over the North of England, the Midlands and Wales. In all she contested 176 races, but her record is all the more impressive for the fact that many of those events were run in heats. She actually faced the starter 298 times and came home first on 136 occasions, including two dead-heats, two heats in which she was disqualified from first place, and one walk-over. As a 9-year-old she ran six 2-mile heats in the course of an afternoon at Welshpool, finishing fresh enough to come back and win another race in three 1½-mile heats on the following day. Her most important win came in the Tradesmen's Cup at Manchester in 1838.

Previous page *Provideo* (far side) *was more than a stone below top class, but his toughness and consistency enabled him to win a record-equalling 16 races as a 2-year-old in Great Britain in 1984. (Gerry Cranham)*

Catherina, foaled in 1830, was a daughter of 1815 Derby winner Whisker out of a mare called Alecto who was herself tough enough to win three races in an afternoon at Heaton Park as a pregnant 7-year-old.

Confounding the theory that hard-trained mares retain no vitality for their stud careers, Catherina became the dam of two above-average runners in Sweetheart, winner of the 1849 July Stakes at Newmarket, and Phaeton, who won both the 1853 Criterion Stakes at Newmarket and the 1854 Ascot Derby. The mare was destroyed at the age of 28 in 1858.

Catherina's career record

	ran	won	2nd	3rd	£
1832	2	–	2	–	–
1833	10	4	2	1	200
1834	17	10	3	–	790
1835	19	9	6	–	685
1836	20	11	4	1	948
1837	18	6	7	2	305
1838	12	5	4	2	575
1839	25	10	8	5	463
1840	25	12	5	3	579
1841	28	12	7	3	464
Total	176	79	48	17	5,009

Most wins in a season

The world record for races won in a single season is 30, registered in 1931 by the Puerto Rican-bred 3-year-old Galgo Jr, also holder of the record for most races won in a career. Galgo Jr, whose other seasonal tallies included 25 wins as a 7-year-old and 21 at two, also boasted a winning streak of 39 races, between July 1930 and July 1931.

The record for races won in a British season is 23, attained by the 3-year-old colt Fisherman in 1856.

Trained by his owner, Tom Parr, Fisherman was an unfashionably-bred son of Heron and Mainbrace. He started 34 times between 12 February and 30 October, also notching five second places and three thirds. Many of his races were uncompetitive in terms of numbers of rivals – he walked over three times and had only one or two opponents on eight other occasions – but he did prove victorious over a wide range of distances, from ½-mile to 3 miles, and among his victims were the winners of that season's Derby, Oaks and St Leger. His most important win that year came in the Gold Vase at Ascot.

The nearest approach to Fisherman's 1856 record was the same horse's tally of 22 wins in 1857. He won the Ascot Gold Cups of 1858 and 1859, his score in the former year being 21 wins. In all he won 69 of 119 starts.

The 5-year-old mare Lilian won 21 races in 1874, and in 1844 the 6-year-old mare Alice Hawthorn had 20 outright wins plus a dead-heat.

The record number of wins by a British 2-year-old is 16, set by The Bard (including one walkover) in 1885 and equalled by Provideo in 1984. Provideo's 16 wins are a British 20th-century record for a horse of any age in one season.

Most wins in one race

The only horse to win the same race 7 consecutive times is Doctor Syntax (foaled 1811), who won the Preston Gold Cup every year from 1815 to 1821 inclusive. Run over distances between 3 and 4 miles, the race never had more than 4 runners during that period but Doctor Syntax beat some top-class horses in it, notably St Leger winners Filho da Puta, The Duchess and Reveller. In 1822 he attempted an eighth victory at the Lancashire course but the previous year's runner-up, Reveller, reversed the placings with him. Doctor Syntax had a career total of 35 wins and went on to sire champion racemare Beeswing, who was prevented only by one second place (in 1840) from winning the Gold Cup at Newcastle every year from 1836 to 1842. At the age of 9, in 1842, she also won the Ascot Gold Cup.

The only other horse to win the same race 7 times was Franc Picard (foaled 1846), the most famous French steeplechaser of the 19th century. He won the Grand Steeple-Chase at Dieppe from 1853 to 1857 inclusive and also in 1859 and 1861; he did not contest the race in 1858 and was beaten in 1860.

The 20th-century record is held by Brown Jack, who won at Royal Ascot every year from 1928 to 1934; on the last 6 occasions he won the Queen Alexandra Stakes (Alexandra Stakes before 1931) over 2¾ miles 85 yards.

The only horses to win the same championship race 5 times are Golden Miller and Kelso. Golden Miller monopolized the Cheltenham Gold Cup from 1932 to 1936, and though the race had not attained its present status, he was certainly the best steeplechaser of his time in England. Kelso was America's Horse of the Year from 1960 to 1964 and each time he clinched the title with victory in the 2-mile Jockey Club Gold Cup. At the time the race was the most important weight-for-age prize in the country.

Most stake and Pattern wins

The most stake races won in North America is 34 by Exterminator. This remarkable gelding landed the Kentucky Derby in 1918 but did not reach his peak until the age of 7, becoming one of America's greatest and most popular champions. 'Old Bones' usually carried heavy weights in handicaps, but he was almost unbeatable over long distances and won America's premier prize for stayers, the Saratoga Cup, 4 times (1919–22). He was also successful 3 times in the Pimlico Cup (1919–21) and Toronto

Autumn Cup (1920–22) and his other triumphs included the Latonia Cup in 1918 and Brooklyn Handicap in 1922. He won exactly half his career total of 100 starts over 8 seasons.

Exterminator's 34 stake wins were:

1918
Kentucky Derby (1m 2f) Churchill Downs
Carrollton Handicap (1m 110yd) Laurel
Ellicott City Handicap (1m 1f) Laurel
Pimlico Autumn Handicap (1m 2f) Pimlico
Latonia Cup Handicap (2m 2f) Latonia
1919
Ben Ali Handicap (1m 110yd) Lexington
Camden Handicap (1m 2f) Lexington
Saratoga Cup (1m 6f) Saratoga
Pimlico Cup Handicap (2m 2f) Pimlico
1920
Long Beach Handicap (1m 1f) Jamaica
Brookdale Handicap (1m 1f) Aqueduct
Windsor Jockey Club Handicap (1m 1f) Windsor
George Hendrie Memorial Cup Handicap (1m 110yd) Windsor
Saratoga Cup Handicap (1m 6f) Saratoga
Autumn Gold Cup Handicap (2m) Belmont Park
Toronto Autumn Cup Handicap (1m 2f) Woodbine
Ontario Jockey Club Cup Handicap (2m 2f) Woodbine
Pimlico Cup Handicap (2m 2f) Pimlico
1921
Long Beach Handicap (1m 1f) Jamaica
Independence Handicap (1m 4f) Latonia
Merchants' and Citizens' Handicap (1m 1½f) Saratoga
Saratoga Cup Handicap (1m 6f) Saratoga (walk-over)
Autumn Gold Cup Handicap (2m) Belmont Park
Toronto Autumn Cup Handicap (1m 2f) Woodbine
Pimlico Cup Handicap (2m 2f) Pimlico
1922
Harford Handicap (6f) Havre de Grace
Pimlico Spring Handicap (1m 110yd) Pimlico
Clark Handicap (1m 1f) Churchill Downs
Kentucky Handicap (1m 2f) Churchill Downs
Brooklyn Handicap (1m 1f) Aqueduct
Saratoga Cup Handicap (1m 6f) Saratoga
Toronto Autumn Cup Handicap (1m 2f) Woodbine
Laurel Stakes (1m) Laurel
1923
Philadelphia Handicap (1m 110yd) Havre de Grace

Exterminator's record of 34 stakes is one more than the number achieved by Kingston. The latter won more races than any other horse in American history, with a total of 89 wins from 138 starts in a career of 9 seasons from 1886 to 1894.

The most Graded-stake wins in North America is 25 by John Henry, who won 16 Grade I races, 3 Grade II races and 6 Grade III races:

1978
Round Table Handicap (Gr III) Arlington Park (1m 110yd)
1980
San Gabriel Handicap (Gr III) Santa Anita (1m 1f)
San Marcos Handicap (Gr III) Santa Anita (1m 2f)
Hialeah Turf Cup Handicap (Gr II) Hialeah (1m 4f)
San Luis Rey Stakes (Gr I) Santa Anita (1m 4f)
San Juan Capistrano Invitational Handicap (Gr I) Santa Anita (1m 6f)
Hollywood Invitational Handicap (Gr I) Hollywood Park (1m 4f)
Brighton Beach Handicap (Gr III) Belmont Park (1m 2f)
Oak Tree Invitational Stakes (Gr I) Santa Anita (1m 4f)
1981
San Luis Obispo Handicap (Gr II) Santa Anita (1m 4f)
Santa Anita Handicap (Gr I) Santa Anita (1m 4f)
San Luis Rey Stakes (Gr I) Santa Anita (1m 4f)
Hollywood Invitational Handicap (Gr I) Hollywood Park (1m 4f)
Sword Dancer Stakes (Gr III) Belmont Park (1m 4f)
Jockey Club Gold Cup Stakes (Gr I) Belmont Park (1m 4f)
Oak Tree Invitational Stakes (Gr I) Santa Anita (1m 2f)

1982
Santa Anita Handicap (Gr I) Santa Anita (1m 2f)
Oak Tree Invitational Stakes (Gr I) Santa Anita (1m 4f)
1983
American Handicap (Gr II) Hollywood Park (1m 1f)
Hollywood Invitational Turf Cup Stakes (Gr I) Hollywood Park
    (1m 3f)
1984
Golden Gate Handicap (Gr III) Golden Gate (1m 3f)
Hollywood Invitational Handicap (Gr I) Hollywood Park (1m 4f)
Sunset Handicap (Gr I) Hollywood Park (1m 4f)
Arlington Million (Gr I) Arlington Park (1m 2f)
Turf Classic Stakes (Gr I) Belmont Park (1m 4f)

John Henry's Graded-stake wins were all on turf except the San Marcos Handicap (1980), Jockey Club Gold Cup Stakes (1981) and Santa Anita Handicap (1981 and 1982), which were run on dirt. He won 5 non-Graded stakes, including the 1981 Arlington Million and the last and richest prize of his career, the 1984 Ballantine's Scotch Classic Handicap.

Ardross (Lester Piggott) wins the 1982 Ascot Gold Cup, the 11th of his record-equalling 13 Pattern-race victories in Europe. (Gerry Cranham)

The most Pattern-race wins in Europe is 13 by Brigadier Gerard, who was a 3-year-old when the Pattern-race system was introduced in 1971, and Ardross (foaled 1976), the champion stayer and Prix de l'Arc de Triomphe runner-up, and Acatenango (foaled 1982), the Deutsches Derby winner who gained all but one of his victories (the 1986 Grand Prix de Saint-Cloud) in uncompetitive events in his native West Germany.

Brigadier Gerard won 6 Group I races, 6 Group II races and 1 Group III race:

1971
2000 Guineas (Gr I) Newmarket (1m)
St James's Palace Stakes (Gr II) Ascot (1m)
Sussex Stakes (Gr I) Goodwood (1m)
Goodwood Mile (Gr II) Goodwood (1m)
Queen Elizabeth II Stakes (Gr II) Ascot (1m)
Champion Stakes (Gr I) Newmarket (1m 2f)

1972
Lockinge Stakes (Gr II) Newbury (1m)
Westbury Stakes (Gr III) Sandown Park (1m 2f)
Prince of Wales's Stakes (Gr III) Sandown Park (1m 2f)
Eclipse Stakes (Gr I) Sandown Park (1m 2f)
King George VI and Queen Elizabeth Stakes (Gr I) Ascot (1m 4f)
Queen Elizabeth II Stakes (Gr II) Ascot (1m)
Champion Stakes (Gr I) Newmarket (1m 2f)

If the Pattern-race system had been introduced a year earlier, Brigadier Gerard's score in such races would have been 14, for he won the Middle Park Stakes (subsequently Gr I) in 1970. He retired with 17 wins and one second from 18 starts.

Ardross won 3 Group I races, 6 Group II races and 4 Group III races:

1979
Gallinule Stakes (Gr II) The Curragh (1m 4f)
1980
Jockey Club Cup (Gr III) Newmarket (2m)
1981
Yorkshire Cup (Gr II) York (1m 6f)
Ascot Gold Cup (Gr I) Ascot (2m 4f)
Goodwood Cup (Gr II) Goodwood (2m 5f)
Geoffrey Freer Stakes (Gr II) Newbury (1m 5f 60yd)
Prix Royal-Oak (Gr I) Longchamp (3,100 metres)
1982
Jockey Club Stakes (Gr III) Newmarket (1m 4f)
Yorkshire Cup (Gr II) York (1m 6f)
Henry II Stakes (Gr III) Sandown Park (2m)
Ascot Gold Cup (Gr I) Ascot (2m 4f)
Geoffrey Freer Stakes (Gr II) Newbury (1m 5f 60yd)
Doncaster Cup (Gr III) Doncaster (2m 2f)

Ardross won only one non-Pattern race in his career, the Saval Beg Stakes at Leopardstown in 1980. He retired with 14 wins, 4 seconds and 2 thirds from 24 starts.

Acatenango won 7 Group I races, 4 Group II races and 2 Group III races:

1985
Grosser Hertie-Preis (Gr II) Munich (2,200 metres)
Union-Rennen (Gr II) Cologne (2,200 metres)
Deutsches Derby (Gr I) Hamburg (2,400 metres)
Aral-Pokal (Gr I) Gelsenkirchen (2,400 metres)
1986
Gerling-Preis (Gr III) Cologne (2,400 metres)
Grosser Preis der Badischen Wirtschaft (Gr II) Baden-Baden (2,200 metres)
Grand Prix de Saint-Cloud (Gr I) Saint-Cloud (2,500 metres)
Grosser Preis von Berlin (Gr I) Dusseldorf (2,400 metres)
Aral-Pokal (Gr I) Gelsenkirchen (2,400 metres)
Grosser Preis von Baden (Gr I) Baden-Baden (2,400 metres)
1987
Gerling-Preis (Gr III) Cologne (2,400 metres)
Grosser Hansa Preis (Gr II) Hamburg (2,200 metres)
Grosser Preis von Baden (Gr I) Baden-Baden (2,400 metres)

Most active careers

The lack of comprehensive information on racing in most parts of the world makes it impossible to determine which horse has run most times in a career or in one season, though America in the late 19th and early 20th centuries boasted some of the busiest campaigners. For instance, George de Mar (foaled 1922) raced 333 times for 60 wins and another gelding, Seth's Hope (foaled 1924), 327 times for 62 wins. In 1890 the 5-year-old gelding John Jay S. started in 76 races, gaining 4 victories, at a time when some tracks raced all year round. Another American horse, Blitzen, had 18 races in 37 days in 1893; he won 10 of them, came second 6 times and third once, and was only once unplaced. Imp ran 50 times as a 3-year-old in 1897, winning 14, and blossomed in her next 3 seasons to become one of America's greatest racemares. Donau won 15 of his 41 races as a juvenile before triumphing in the Kentucky Derby of 1910.

Most Successful Horses: Money Earned

Most money earned in a career

The most prize money earned in a career is $6,679,242 by Alysheba, the 1987 Kentucky Derby winner and 1988 Horse of the Year in America, from 26 races in 3 seasons (1986–88).

Alysheba, a bay colt by Alydar out of Bel Sheba, was foaled on 3 March 1984 and sold by his breeder, Preston Madden, for $500,000 at the Keeneland July Select Yearling Sale to the Scharbauer family – Texas rancher Clarence, his wife Dorothy and daughter Pamela.

He won only once as a 2-year-old but was rated just 4 lb below the top in the Experimental Free Handicap, and he became America's champion 3-year-old in 1987 thanks mainly to victories in the Kentucky Derby and Preakness Stakes. He would probably also have been voted Horse of the Year had he won the Breeders' Cup Classic instead of being beaten a nose by Ferdinand.

As a 4-year-old Alysheba gained his revenge on Ferdinand in the Santa Anita and San Bernardino Handicaps, though the results confirmed that the two champions were almost identical in ability. After a couple of defeats Alysheba won his last 4 races, on his final start, at Churchill Downs on 5 November 1988, clinching Horse of the Year honours with victory in the world's richest race, the Breeders' Cup Classic. The first prize of $1,350,000 took his career earnings past the world record of $6,597,947 held by John Henry, America's Horse of the Year in 1981 and 1984.

Alysheba was not a great champion, winning only 11 of his 26 races, but he was tough and consistent, and clearly the best of his year in America. He was also the best horse ever trained by Jack Van Berg, who has trained the winners of more races than anyone else in racing history. He is now a stallion at Lane's End Farm, near Versailles, Kentucky.

Alysheba's 10 stakes wins were:
1987
Kentucky Derby (Gr I) Churchill Downs (1m 2f)
Preakness Stakes (Gr I) Pimlico (1m 1½f)
Super Derby Invitational (Gr I) Louisiana Downs (1m 2f)
1988
Charles H. Strub Stakes (Gr I) Santa Anita (1m 2f)
Santa Anita Handicap (Gr I) Santa Anita (1m 2f)
San Bernardino Handicap (Gr II) Santa Anita (1m 1f)
Philip H. Iselin Handicap (Gr I) Monmouth Park (1m 1f)
Woodward Handicap (Gr I) Belmont Park (1m 2f)
Meadowlands Cup Handicap (Gr I) The Meadowlands (1m 2f)
Breeders' Cup Classic (Gr I) Churchill Downs (1m 2f)

Alysheba's career summary

	ran	won	2nd	3rd	$
1986	7	1	4	1	359,486
1987	10	3	3	1	2,511,156
1988	9	7	1	–	3,808,600
Total	26	11	8	2	6,679,242

Below *John Henry (Bill Shoemaker) noses out The Bart in the world's first million-dollar race, the inaugural Arlington Million at Arlington Park, Chicago, in August 1981. (Gerry Cranham)*

Right *Time Charter (nearest camera, Joe Mercer) wins the 1983 King George VI and Queen Elizabeth Stakes – the richest prize in a career which saw the champion filly become the leading earner in the British Isles. (Gerry Cranham)*

Current leading earners

In November 1989, among horses who had raced at least once in North America, the following 52 had amassed career earnings of more than $1.8 million:

	$
Alysheba (colt, 1984)	6,679,242
John Henry (gelding, 1975)	6,597,947
Sunday Silence (colt, 1986)	4,600,154
Easy Goer (colt, 1986)	4,534,650
Spend a Buck (colt, 1982)	4,220,689
Creme Fraiche (gelding, 1982)	4,024,727
Ferdinand (colt, 1983)	3,777,978
Slew o' Gold (colt, 1980)	3,533,534
Precisionist (colt, 1981)	3,485,398
Snow Chief (colt, 1983)	3,383,210
Cryptoclearance (colt, 1984)	3,376,327
Bet Twice (colt, 1984)	3,308,599
Gulch (colt, 1984)	3,095,521
Lady's Secret (filly, 1982)	3,021,325
All Along (filly, 1979)	3,018,420
Theatrical (colt, 1982)	2,943,552
Symboli Rudolf (colt, 1981)	2,909,593
Great Communicator (colt, 1983)	2,870,840
Spectacular Bid (colt, 1976)	2,781,607
Forty Niner (colt, 1985)	2,726,000
Triptych (filly, 1982)	2,706,175
Manila (colt, 1983)	2,692,799
Broad Brush (colt, 1983)	2,656,793
Trinycarol (filly, 1979)	2,647,141
Gate Dancer (colt, 1981)	2,501,705
Steinlen (colt, 1983)	2,401,172
Affirmed (colt, 1975)	2,393,818
Seeking The Gold (colt, 1985)	2,307,000
Life's Magic (filly, 1981)	2,252,218
Skywalker (colt, 1982)	2,226,750
Waquoit (colt, 1983)	2,225,360
Wild Again (colt, 1980)	2,204,829
Proud Truth (colt, 1982)	2,198,895
Chief's Crown (colt, 1982)	2,191,168
Nostalgia's Star (colt, 1982)	2,154,827
Turkoman (colt, 1982)	2,146,924
Miesque (filly, 1984)	2,096,517
Lost Code (colt, 1984)	2,085,396
Sunshine Forever (colt, 1985)	2,084,800
Majesty's Prince (colt, 1979)	2,075,200
Risen Star (colt, 1985)	2,029,812
Kelso (gelding, 1957)	1,977,896
Greinton (colt, 1981)	1,940,294
Forego (gelding, 1970)	1,938,957
Estrapade (filly, 1980)	1,924,588
Prized (colt, 1986)	1,910,305
Java Gold (colt, 1984)	1,908,832
Open Mind (filly, 1986)	1,844,372
Little Bold John (gelding, 1982)	1,842,928
Skip Trial (colt, 1982)	1,837,451
Yankee Affair (colt, 1982)	1,830,466
With Approval (colt, 1986)	1,819,700

All these leading earners were trained in North America for most of their careers except All Along, Triptych, and Miesque (France), Symboli Rudolf (Japan) and Trinycarol (Venezuela).

The first horse to pass $1 million in earnings was 6-year-old Citation when winning the Hollywood Gold Cup at Hollywood Park, California on 14 July 1951. Despite injury problems the American Triple Crown hero was kept in training solely in order to achieve this target, which had been the ambition of his late owner Warren Wright. Having succeeded, Citation was promptly retired to stud.

Most money earned in a year

The most money earned in one year is $4,578,454 by Sunday Silence in the USA in 1989. The 3-year-old colt won 7 of his 9 races that year including 6 Graded stakes – the San Felipe Handicap, Santa Anita Derby, Kentucky Derby, Preakness Stakes, Super Derby Invitational and the world's richest race, the Breeders' Cup Classic. His earnings included a $1 million bonus for having the best record in the Triple Crown races (won Kentucky Derby and Preakness Stakes, second in Belmont Stakes). In the Breeders' Cup Classic at Gulfstream Park on 4 November 1989, the first prize of $1,350,000 took Sunday Silence's seasonal earnings past the world record of $3,808,600 set by Alysheba in 1988.

Most money earned in one race

The most money earned in one race is $2,600,000 by Spend a Buck in the Jersey Derby at Garden State Park, New Jersey, on 27 May 1985. This consisted of the $600,000 first prize plus a $2,000,000 bonus offered by the Garden State executive to a horse who won a series of 4 races comprising the Cherry Hill

Mile Handicap, Garden State Stakes, Kentucky Derby and Jersey Derby. There was controversy when Spend a Buck, owned by the Hunter Farm of Dennis Diaz and trained by Cam Gambolati, was pointed at this rich bonus instead of attempting the Triple Crown after winning the Kentucky Derby. The 3-year-old colt, ridden by Laffit Pincay, won the Jersey Derby by a neck from Creme Fraiche and was later voted America's Horse of the Year for 1985.

The most 'regular' prize money earned in one race is $1,350,000 by the winners of the world's richest race, the Breeders' Cup Classic, which was inaugurated in 1984.

Below are lists of horses who have held a world or British record for the amount of money earned in a career. In all cases the earnings include place money, and official exchange rates have been used where appropriate. The date on the left is the year in which each horse broke the record but the other figures reflect complete racing careers.

Progressive list of world financial champions

Since Zev surpassed the earnings of English champion Isinglass in 1923, all holders of the world earnings record have been trained in North America.

		Ran	Won	2nd	3rd	$
1923	Zev (1920)	43	23	8	5	313,639
1930	Gallant Fox (1927)	17	11	3	2	328,165
1931	Sun Beau (1925)	74	33	12	10	376,744
1940	Seabiscuit (1933)	89	33	15	13	437,730
1942	Whirlaway (1938)	60	32	15	9	561,161
1947	Assault (1943)	42	18	6	7	675,470
	Armed (1941)	81	41	20	10	817,475
	Stymie (1941)	131	35	33	28	918,485
1950	Citation (1945)	45	32	10	2	1,085,760
1956	Nashua (1952)	30	22	4	1	1,288,565
1958	Round Table (1954)	66	43	8	5	1,749,869
1964	Kelso (1957)	63	39	12	2	1,977,896
1979	Affirmed (1975)	29	22	5	1	2,393,818
1980	Spectacular Bid (1976)	30	26	2	1	2,781,607
1981	John Henry (1975)	83	39	15	9	6,597,947
1988	Alysheba (1984)	26	11	8	2	6,679,242

Female world financial champions

Since 2-year-old Top Flight surpassed the earnings of English champion Sceptre in 1931, all holders of the world earnings record for fillies and mares have raced in North America, though Trinycarol earned all her prize money in her native Venezuela and All Along was trained in France throughout her career.

		Ran	Won	2nd	3rd	$
1931	Top Flight (1929)	16	12	–	–	275,900
1945	Busher (1942)	21	15	3	1	334,035
1947	Gallorette (1942)	72	21	20	13	445,535
1951	Bewitch (1945)	55	20	10	11	462,605
1962	Cicada (1959)	42	23	8	6	783,675
1971	Shuvee (1966)	44	16	10	6	890,445
1974	Dahlia (1970)	48	15	4	6	1,535,443
1982	Trinycarol (1979)	29	18	3	1	2,647,141
1984	All Along (1979)	21	9	4	2	3,018,420
1987	Lady's Secret (1982)	45	25	9	3	3,021,325

English and Irish financial champions

The following have held the record for the most money earned in a career by a horse trained in the British Isles. Donovan and Isinglass also held the world record.

		Ran	Won	2nd	3rd	£
1889	Donovan (1886)	21	18	2	1	55,443
1895	Isinglass (1890)	12	11	1	–	58,655
1952	Tulyar (1949)	13	9	1	1	76,577
1958	Ballymoss (1954)	17	8	5	1	114,150
1963	Ragusa (1960)	12	7	1	2	148,955
1964	Santa Claus (1961)	7	4	2	–	153,646
1967	Ribocco (1964)	14	5	3	3	155,669
1968	Royal Palace (1964)	11	9	–	1	166,063
1968	Sir Ivor (1965)	13	8	3	1	227,100
1970	Nijinsky (1967)	13	11	2	–	282,223
1972	Mill Reef (1968)	14	12	2	–	314,212
1975	Grundy (1972)	11	8	2	–	326,421
1977	The Minstrel (1974)	9	7	1	1	333,197
1978	Alleged (1974)	10	9	1	–	336,784
1979	Troy (1976)	11	8	2	1	450,428
1982	Glint of Gold (1978)	17	10	6	1	472,760
1984	Time Charter (1979)	20	9	4	1	526,910
1985	Teleprompter (1980)	36	11	11	4	758,483
1985	Pebbles (1981)	15	8	4	–	1,182,140

Female English and Irish financial champions

The following have held the record for the most money earned by a filly or mare trained in the British Isles. La Flèche and Sceptre also held the world record.

		Ran	Won	2nd	3rd	£
1892	La Flèche (1889)	24	16	3	2	35,003
1903	Sceptre (1899)	25	13	5	3	39,583
1955	Meld (1952)	6	5	1	–	43,162
1959	Petite Etoile (1956)	19	14	5	–	72,624
1969	Park Top (1964)	24	13	6	2	137,414
1978	Dunfermline (1974)	12	3	3	3	138,830
1978	Fair Salinia (1975)	8	4	2	–	139,354
1980	Mrs Penny (1977)	16	9	4	2	281,379
1983	Time Charter (1979)	20	9	4	1	526,910
1985	Pebbles (1981)	15	8	4	–	1,182,140

English and Irish financial champions: geldings on the Flat

		Ran	Won	2nd	3rd	£
1899	Democrat (1897)	17	8	3	–	14,037
1901	Epsom Lad (1897)	8	3	1	–	19,712
1933	Brown Jack (1924)	55	18	8	4	23,526
1959	Morecambe (1953)	33	11	8	6	25,584
1965	Grey of Falloden (1959)	55	13	12	12	31,119
1970	Morris Dancer (1961)	90	25	14	12	38,198
1973	Petty Officer (1967)	44	12	10	3	56,330
1976	Boldboy (1970)	45	14	10	10	131,073
1984	Bedtime (1980)	16	10	3	–	214,645
1985	Teleprompter (1980)	36	11	11	4	758,483

Right, above Pebbles (Pat Eddery), the leading earner among horses trained in the British Isles, scores a spectacular victory in the 1985 Champion Stakes at Newmarket. (All-Sport)

Right All Along (Walter Swinburn) gets the better of Sun Princess in the 1983 Prix de l'Arc de Triomphe on her way to becoming the world's leading earner among fillies and mares (Gerry Cranham)

English and Irish financial champions: jumpers

(The following figures do not include Flat or National Hunt Flat races)

		Ran	Won	2nd	3rd	£
1950	**Freebooter** (1941)	61	18	15	7	24,725
1961	**Nicolaus Silver** (1952)	55	9	9	6	28,973

		Ran	Won	2nd	3rd	£
1962	**Mandarin** (1951)	52	19	13	5	51,496
1965	**Arkle** (1957)	32	26	2	2	78,464
1975	**Comedy of Errors** (1967)	49	23	12	4	111,633
1977	**Red Rum** (1965)	100	24	14	21	145,234
1981	**Night Nurse** (1971)	64	32	14	7	181,770
1983	**Silver Buck** (1972)	48	34	2	3	196,053
1985	**Wayward Lad** (1975)	55	28	12	7	278,064
1986	**Dawn Run** (1978)	28	18	4	1	278,837
1988	**Desert Orchid** (1979)	55	27	9	5	408,108

Triple Crown Winners

English Triple Crown Champions

For more than a century it has been generally acknowledged that the highest status attainable by a Thoroughbred on the British Turf is that of Triple Crown winner. Few horses are capable of excelling over a variety of courses and distances, and only a truly exceptional athlete possesses all the necessary gifts to achieve dominance over his or her contemporaries over Newmarket's straight mile in the first week in May, around Epsom's switchback mile and a half a month later, and again over the flat, extended mile and three-quarters of the galloping Doncaster course in September.

Only 15 colts have managed to win all three of the Classics open to them, and three of those (Pommern, Gay Crusader and Gainsborough) were not required to display the degree of adaptability shown by the others, recording their trebles in wartime substitute events at Newmarket. There have been nine winners of the Fillies' Triple Crown, including one, Sun Chariot, whose victories were all achieved at Newmarket. As racing becomes ever-more competitive and as breeding seems to be increasingly geared to the production of specialists, rather than all-round performers, the emergence of future Triple Crown champions can be by no means guaranteed.

West Australian, a bay colt bred and raced by John Bowes, became the first horse to collect the 2000 Guineas, the Derby and the St Leger in 1853. Trained at Malton by John Scott, he suffered one surprising reverse at two, but was otherwise unbeaten, his 4-year-old campaign including a victory in the Ascot Gold Cup. He stood at stud in both England and France, but his achievements as a stallion did not match his exceptional merit as a runner. He died in France on 2 May 1870.

Gladiateur earned the nickname 'Avenger of Waterloo' when he became the first French-bred winner of the Derby in 1865. He had been a narrow winner of the 2000 Guineas, but his Epsom and Doncaster triumphs were achieved with complete authority, and, unique among Triple Crown heroes, he also had victories to his credit in the Grand Prix de Paris and the Ascot Gold Cup. Though bred in France by his owner, Comte Frédéric de Lagrange, he raced from the Newmarket stable of Tom Jennings. His record as a sire was extremely disappointing, and he died at stud in Essex when only 14 years old.

Lord Lyon, bred by Mark Pearson and leased for racing purposes to Richard Sutton, had the Triple Crown of 1866 among his 17 career victories. His reputation was never particularly exalted, largely because the rest of his generation appeared to be moderate, and in both the Derby and the St Leger he scraped home by only a head. Trained at East Ilsley by James Dover (who always rated the colt in lower esteem than his younger sister, Achievement), he went on to sire two top-class runners in Placida (Oaks) and Minting (Grand Prix de Paris), but his overall record at stud was not impressive. He was destroyed at the age of 24, on 11 April 1887.

Formosa, who became the first winner of the Fillies' Triple Crown in 1868, set a notable record by racing unbeaten in four Classics. She shared the 2000 Guineas in a desperate finish with Moslem, but took the other three – she did not run in the Derby – by clear-cut margins, including the Oaks by 10 lengths. Bred by James Cookson, she was sold as a yearling for only 700 gns and was trained at Beckhampton by Henry Woolcott. She died at the Haras de Dangu in December 1880, having failed to distinguish herself as a broodmare.

Hannah, bred and raced by Baron Meyer de Rothschild and trained at Newmarket by Joe Hayhoe, was the dominant 3-year-old filly of 1871. She scored by three lengths in both the 1000 Guineas and the Oaks, and in the St Leger she had a length to spare over Albert Victor, one of the dead-heaters for second place in the Derby. She was a stable-companion of the Derby winner, Favonius, and many compared her favourably with the colt. Sadly, her form tailed off badly at four and she died on 24 November 1875 after having slipped twins.

Apology, winner of the 1874 Fillies' Triple Crown, was bred and raced by a clergyman, the Rev John King, who raced under the *nom de course* of 'Mr Launde' in a vain attempt to avoid the censure of his Bishop. The filly may have been a little lucky in that her generation was not conspicuously rich in talent, but she went on to win the Ascot Gold Cup as a 5-year-old, by which time she was the property of

Gladiateur, the second Triple Crown winner, was widely regarded as the greatest champion of the 19th century until the advent of Ormonde. (BBC Hulton Picture Library)

King's widow, his former kitchen-maid whom he had married when he was 74 and she was 22. Apology left William Osborne's Middleham stable for stud at the end of 1876 and in due course became the dam of winners of the Gimcrack and Craven Stakes. She was destroyed in April 1888, aged 17.

Ormonde was the first Triple Crown winner to be hailed as such at the time of his success in 1886, the term having gained currency some time after Lord Lyon's feat of 20 years before. Unquestionably one of the true giants of racing history, he was trained at Kingsclere by John Porter for his owner-breeder, the 1st Duke of Westminster, and he raced unbeaten through three campaigns. Unfortunately, he developed a wind infirmity as a 3-year-old, and in his second stud season he contracted a severe illness which left him sub-fertile. He served as a stallion in England, Argentina and the USA, his relatively few foals including the dual Eclipse Stakes winner Orme at home and the Futurity winner Ormondale in the States. He was destroyed at stud in California on 21 May 1904.

Common, winner of the 1891 Triple Crown, was said to have been aptly named in view of his looks, but he was something out of the ordinary as a runner, as he indicated when he won the 2000 Guineas in a canter on his racecourse début. But he was to prove the most lightly-campaigned of all Triple Crown winners, his only other races producing a bloodless victory over a solitary rival in the St James's Palace Stakes and a third place in the Eclipse Stakes behind Surefoot, the previous season's vanquished Derby favourite. Partners Lord Alington and Sir Frederick Johnstone, who bred and raced Common, sold him for £15,000 after his hard-fought neck victory in the St Leger and he left John Porter's stable for an unexciting term at stud. He died on 17 December 1912.

La Flèche, a record-priced yearling at 5,500 gns, proved a tremendous bargain for Baron Maurice de Hirsch. Bought out of the Hampton Court Stud (and thus officially bred by Queen Victoria), she was undefeated in four starts as a 2-year-old and at three, in 1892, collected eight out of nine, her sole loss coming in the Derby, when she was the victim of an incompetent ride and finished second to Sir Hugo. She settled matters with Sir Hugo decisively in the St Leger in the most conclusive of her Classic triumphs, then proceeded to win the Cambridgeshire under 8 st 10 lb. At the end of her 3-year-old campaign La Flèche moved from John Porter's stable to that of Richard Marsh at Newmarket. She was never quite so dominant again, but she did win the Ascot Gold Cup and the Champion Stakes at five, when carrying her first foal. Her best son was John o' Gaunt, who ran second in the Derby and became the sire of the outstanding Swynford. She died at Sledmere Stud, in Yorkshire, on 22 April 1916.

Isinglass, bred and raced by sometime Member of Parliament for Newmarket, Harry McCalmont, was more than just the leader of his generation by a wide margin. Having won his Triple Crown in 1893, he proved himself decidedly superior to the following season's 2000 Guineas and Derby victor, Ladas, and at five he ran away with the Ascot Gold Cup. He suffered only one defeat in four seasons, when narrowly failing to concede 10 lb to Derby third Raeburn at Manchester, and when he quit Jimmy Jewitt's Newmarket stable for a successful stud career, he took with him an earnings record unsurpassed in England for 57 years. He died at Cheveley Park Stud on 5 December 1911.

Galtee More, who was trained by Sam Darling at Beckhampton, carried the colours of Co Limerick owner-breeder John Gubbins. He compiled a two-season record of 11 wins from 13 starts, failing only when dead-heating for second with Glencally, a short head behind Brigg, in a valuable juvenile contest at Liverpool, and on his final appearance at three, when anchored by 9 st 6 lb in the Cambridgeshire. He consistently overwhelmed Velasquez, himself a thoroughly top-class horse, hinting that he might well have been one of the very best Triple Crown winners. The shame is that, apart from Velasquez, there was

Emil Adam's portrait of Isinglass (Tommy Loates), the Triple Crown winner of 1893 who was beaten only once in a career of 12 races.

nothing capable of testing him on anything like level terms. Sold to Russia at the end of his Classic season (1897), he later moved to Germany; he did well as a sire in both countries and died at Hoppegarten, near Berlin, on 30 January 1917.

Flying Fox, the fourth Triple Crown champion trained by John Porter, represented the same owner-breeder as Ormonde and was a grandson of that great horse. He did not always get his act together as a 2-year-old, but all the promises were delivered in 1899, when he proved himself easily the best of his generation. The only moment of doubt came in the straight at Epsom, when Holocauste seemed to be going every bit as well as Flying Fox, but the French-trained challenger then broke a fetlock, leaving the favourite to win at his leisure. On the death of the 1st Duke of Westminster in 1900, Flying Fox was submitted to auction at Kingsclere, where he fetched the unprecedented sum of 37,500 gns. The price seemed outlandish, but the buyer, French breeder Edmond Blanc, eventually profited handsomely from the deal. Flying Fox became an important sire at Blanc's Haras de Jardy, where he died on 21 March 1911. His sale price remained a British auction record for a horse in training until Vaguely Noble changed hands for 136,000 gns 67 years later.

Diamond Jubilee was, by general consent, nothing like as good a racehorse as his elder brother Persimmon. But, whereas Persimmon was slow to come

to hand at three, missing the 2000 Guineas (in which, in any case, he might not have beaten St Frusquin), Diamond Jubilee was able to go one better and take the 1900 Triple Crown. Diamond Jubilee had no adversary of St Frusquin's merit to contend with, the chief threat to his Classic campaign coming from his own temperament. The problem was solved by the allocation of race-riding duties to Herbert Jones, his regular work-jockey. The partnership flourished to the extent of victories in the Triple Crown, the Newmarket Stakes and the Eclipse Stakes, but after the St Leger his form deteriorated and he did not win again. Diamond Jubilee, bred and owned by the Prince of Wales (later King Edward VII), was trained by Richard Marsh at Newmarket. He subsequently headed the sires' list in Argentina on four occasions. He was found dead in his box at stud in that country on 10 July 1923.

Sceptre holds the distinction of being the only outright winner of four Classic races, a feat she achieved in 1902. Like Flying Fox, she was a product of the 1st Duke of Westminster's Eaton Stud, and she came up for sale at Newmarket as a result of the Duke's death. Her price, 10,000 gns, constituted a world record for an auction yearling, but it proved a good deal less than her value. Her buyer was Bob Sievier, a notoriously heavy gambler, who turned her over to Wantage trainer Charles Morton. She showed abundant promise in her first season, winning the Woodcote and July Stakes, but the accomplished Morton then accepted the post of private trainer to Jack Joel, and Sievier decided that he would train the filly himself. With an amateur trainer and, for several races, a jockey who had only just turned professional, the filly was patently grossly misused. But she overcame the treatment famously, bouncing back from a narrow defeat in the Lincolnshire Handicap to contest all five Classics. She won the 2000 Guineas in record time, readily added the 1000, finished fourth as even-money favourite for the Derby, then proved easily best in both the Oaks and the St Leger. Sceptre was restored to professional hands after her first start at four, when Sievier sold her to William Bass and she joined Alec Taylor's Manton string. In due course she came into her own with a crushing defeat of the year-younger Triple Crown victor Rock Sand in the Jockey Club Stakes, and she added the Champion Stakes by 10 lengths. Sceptre was evidently 'over the top' at five, when she failed to win in three efforts, but she subsequently became a successful broodmare, both her first two foals – Maid of the Mist and Maid of Corinth – winning the Cheveley Park Stakes. She died at the Exning Stud, near Newmarket, on 5 February 1926.

Rock Sand, who raced for owner-breeder Sir James Miller, was trained at Newmarket by George Blackwell. As a 2-year-old he suffered one surprising defeat in the Middle Park Plate, but overall his form suggested that he was a worthy favourite for the 1903

Classics. So it proved. Nothing emerged as a serious challenger to him for the Triple Crown, which he collected with the minimum of fuss. But he was possibly lucky to have avoided competition from Zinfandel, whose Classic entries had been rendered void by the death of his owner. Zinfandel might have proved his match at three; he was more than Rock Sand's match at four in the Coronation Cup. There was also abundant evidence to indicate that Rock Sand's best form was inferior to that of Sceptre and Ard Patrick, leaders of the previous generation. Rock Sand stood in England and the USA before transferring to France, where he died on 20 July 1914, aged only 14. He did quite well as a sire, his best son being Tracery, while one of his daughters produced Man o' War.

Pretty Polly, who raced for owner-breeder Eustace Loder and was trained by Peter Purcell Gilpin at Newmarket, burst on the scene with an amazing début display at Sandown Park in 1903. She raced clear of her rivals almost throughout and finished so far in front that many observers imagined there must have been a false start. She became a public idol almost from that moment on, and success was piled on success. Her other juvenile performances included easy victories in the National Breeders' Produce, Champagne and Cheveley Park Stakes and Middle Park Plate, and at three she collected the 1000 Guineas, Oaks and St Leger, all by emphatic three-length margins. After 15 consecutive wins she carried an air of invincibility, but her triumphant sequence was ended in sensational style, when Presto beat her in the Prix du Conseil Municipal at Longchamp. The result did not truly reflect her merit, and she proceeded to provide ample evidence that she had not permanently lost her form. In the following year she won the Coronation Cup in devastating fashion, establishing a course record (2:33.8) for the Epsom mile and a half which was not matched until Mahmoud's 1936 Derby and remained unbroken until 1973. Pretty Polly retired after her defeat by Bachelor's Button in the 1906 Ascot Gold Cup – only her second loss in 24 races. At stud she produced two talented daughters in Molly Desmond (Cheveley Park Stakes) and Polly Flinders (National Breeders' Produce Stakes). She died in Ireland in August 1931, aged 30.

Pommern, first of the 'substitute Triple Crown' winners, was bred and raced by Solly Joel, who gave only 500 gns for the dam, Merry Agnes, when she was carrying him. He was a good, rather than outstanding, 2-year-old, but at three in 1915 he proved easily best of a generation which seemed otherwise undistinguished. Trained at Newmarket by Charley Peck, he failed to give 15 lb to Rossendale in the Craven Stakes, but thereafter he was unbeaten, and his victories in the 2000 Guineas, New Derby and September Stakes were all achieved by clear margins. He proved a disappointing sire and was destroyed on 26 June 1935.

Sun Chariot, the 1942 fillies' Triple Crown winner, displays some of the temperament which taxed the patience of trainer Fred Darling (left). (BBC Hulton Picture Library)

Gay Crusader, bred and raced by Alfred Cox and trained at Manton by Alec Taylor, developed into a formidable 3-year-old in 1917. After failing honourably to give 11 lb to Coq d'Or in the Column Produce Stakes in the spring, he proved invincible, picking up all the substitute Classics open to him, in addition to Newmarket's version of the Gold Cup and the Champion Stakes. He was injured before he could start at four and retired to a stud career which did not come up to expectations. He was destroyed on 14 September 1932.

Gainsborough failed to reach a 2,000 gns reserve when offered for sale as a yearling, so his breeder, Lady James Douglas, put him into training with Alec Taylor. He turned out to be a colt of similar merit to Gay Crusader, and he emulated his year-older stable-companion with successes in the substitute Triple Crown and Gold Cup in 1918. But he did not dominate his contemporaries to any great extent and lost by a length when asked to concede 3 lb to Prince Chimay in the Jockey Club Stakes. He became champion sire on two occasions, with Solario and Hyperion his most celebrated sons, and he died at the age of 30 on 5 June 1945.

Bahram became only the second Triple Crown winner (after Ormonde) to retire undefeated. He was the undisputed champion of his generation at two and three years, and there was general disappointment when his owner-breeder, Aga Khan III, decided to retire him after he had completed his sweep of the 1935 Triple Crown events. He looked better than ever when he took the St Leger (his ninth start) by five lengths, and his Newmarket trainer, Frank Butters, would dearly have loved to keep him for a third season. Instead, Bahram went to stud, where he was to sire such as Big Game and Persian Gulf before his controversial sale to America for £40,000. He was not a success in the States, and he did no better in Argentina, where he died on 24 January 1956.

Sun Chariot, bred at the National Stud and leased for racing purposes to King George VI, was a popular heroine of the Turf during World War II. But for one temperamental lapse at Salisbury, she would never have been beaten, and she proved herself manifestly superior to the colts of her generation at both two and three. In 1942 she won the New 1000 Guineas by four lengths, the New Oaks by a length (after losing a lot of ground at the start and again at the turn), and the New St Leger emphatically by three lengths over Watling Street, the New Derby winner. Her career comprised only nine races, but Beckhampton trainer Fred Darling was not totally sorry to see her leave on account of the frequently mulish behaviour which made her a problem to handle. Her first foal was the highly-gifted, but unsound, unbeaten colt Blue Train, and she produced other good winners in Gigantic, Landau, Persian Wheel and Pindari. She was destroyed at the National Stud in June 1963.

Meld, bred by her owner, Lady Zia Wernher, at the Someries Stud, was trained at Newmarket by Cecil (later Sir Cecil) Boyd-Rochfort. Her career was anything but exacting, as it consisted of only six races, but she won both 1955 fillies-only Classics in decisive fashion, then overcame the colts in the St Leger while sickening for the cough. She was never required to tackle the kind of formidable male opposition which such as Sceptre, Pretty Polly and Sun Chariot had to encounter, but she was unquestionably a high-class performer. Her only defeat came on her début, when she started as an unfancied outsider and went under by a length to a stable-companion. Uniquely among Triple Crown heroines, Meld became the dam of a Classic winner, a distinction she achieved by Charlottown's Derby of 1966. She died in Ireland on 14 September 1983 at the age of 31 – a record for longevity among English Classic winners.

Nijinsky became the first Triple Crown-winning colt to have been purchased at auction. Bred in Canada by Eddie Taylor, he was acquired for $84,000 by Charles Engelhard, who put him into training with Vincent O'Brien. Comfortably best of the 2-year-olds in Ireland and England in 1969, he proceeded to stride majestically through a second campaign which had many referring to him as 'the horse of the century'. His Triple Crown victories were all emphatically achieved, and he took in the Irish Derby and Ascot's King George VI and Queen Elizabeth Stakes (beating the previous year's Derby winner Blakeney with scarcely an effort) along the way. He came to the Prix de l'Arc de Triomphe still unbeaten in 11 races, but Sassafras deprived him of that prize by a head, and on his only subsequent outing Nijinsky turned in a dull display to finish second to Lorenzaccio in the Champion Stakes. Sent to stud in Kentucky, he swiftly established himself among the world's leading sires, with Derby-winning sons Golden Fleece (1982) and Shahrastani (1986) among his progeny.

Oh So Sharp was bred and raced by Sheikh Mohammed, who acquired her dam, Oh So Fair, in his purchase of Jim Philipps's Dalham Hall Stud and breeding stock in 1981. Unbeaten in three efforts as a 2-year-old, when officially rated second-best of her sex in England, she went on to win four out of six in a 1985 Classic campaign noted as much for her competitive attitude as for her class and versatility. She came from a seemingly impossible position to take

Nijinsky (Lester Piggott) beats Meadowville in the 1970 St Leger to become the only colt to win England's Triple Crown since Bahram in 1935. (Gerry Cranham)

Secretariat

When Secretariat won the US Triple Crown in 1973, he was the first to record that feat in a quarter of a century. It was taken as one of the measures of his greatness that he had achieved what had seemed to be beyond the powers of the modern Thoroughbred.

When, in the course of the next five years, both Seattle Slew and Affirmed also became Triple Crown heroes, their perform-ances might have served to remove a little of the gloss from Secretariat's shining image. In fact, the inevitable reappraisals produced no such result; the consensus was that Secretariat's Triple Crown retained its unique glitter, that among all the American champions of the modern era, he reigned supreme.

Secretariat was foaled, just after midnight on 30 March 1970, at Meadow Stud in Virginia. In the eyes of the public, both the stud and its highly-successful racing arm, Meadow Stable, had long been identified with their founder, self-made millionaire Christopher Chenery, but his health had collapsed in 1967 and the management of both ventures had been taken over by his daughter, (then) Mrs Penny Tweedy. Chenery, who had bred Secretariat's dam, Something-royal, and had bought his grand-dam, Imperatrice, for $30,000 in 1947, never knew about his stud's greatest product, and he died between the colt's two racing seasons.

A bright chestnut with three socks and a diamond-shaped star between his eyes, the last and greatest champion son of the outstanding sire Bold Ruler epitomised all that the word 'Thoroughbred' implies. He was all power and symmetry, so much the *beau idéal* of his species that Charlie Hatton, the most gifted and experienced racing journalist of his day, was moved to write that 'trying to fault Secretariat's conformation was like dreaming of dry rain'.

It is almost a rule of racing that the best-looking horses do not make the best runners. Secretariat broke it, while utilising his 25-foot stride to break records galore as well. But he did not begin with a win. On his first outing, at Aqueduct, he was caught flat-footed when the gate opened, then impeded when another runner cut across him; 10 lengths off the lead at the quarter pole, he finished just over a length behind the winner. He had eight more starts that year and was first home every time.

In his first three races Secretariat just looked good, a lack of quality in his competition preventing a proper assessment of his merit. Then came an encounter with the highly-regarded Linda's Chief in the Sanford Stakes at Saratoga. When Secretariat trounced that colt, all New York knew he was good.

Thereafter he always competed in top stakes company, and though he did not always win, it was never his fault when he did not. He won the Hopeful and the Futurity, both with complete authority, and treated stronger opposition much the same in the Champagne, only to forfeit his win on account of his jockey's wayward riding. In the Laurel Futurity and the Garden State Stakes he overwhelmed his rivals. Although it was not the done thing to name a two-year-old 'Horse of the Year', there was no other option.

Secretariat dominated his class completely at two, and so obviously threatened to repeat the performance at three that a syndication deal put together following Christopher Chenery's death valued him at $6.08 million – an unheard-of price for any horse, let alone one who had yet to prove his mettle as a three-year-old. The only way the colt could justify the price-tag was to accomplish what none had accomplished for 25 years, and *en route* to the Triple Crown the sceptics and cynics sat back and waited for things to go wrong.

First time out at three, in the Bay Shore Stakes, Secretariat proved nothing he had not proved before. The company was no better in the Gotham Stakes, but there seemed a need to prove something, so he equalled the Aqueduct track record for the mile. Then came the moment for the doubters to say 'I told you so'.

Racing for the first time over nine furlongs in the Wood Memorial Stakes, 'Big Red' came back a well-beaten third, four lengths behind his own barn companion Angle Light and that colt's head victim, Sham. 'He's a non-stayer, like all the other Bold Rulers' the know-alls declared – and even some of Secretariat's most ardent followers feared that to be the case.

In fact, trainer Lucien Laurin had sent the champion into the Wood ill-prepared for the test. It was neither the first nor the last time that Secretariat's human connections let him down; granted better luck in that department, he would probably never have known defeat.

But all went spectacularly well in the Triple Crown series. Ron Turcotte did not make it easy for him in the Kentucky Derby, dropping him back to last soon after the start, then having to steer wide when it became apparent that the only clear path would be on the outside. The supposed doubtful stayer, made to run via the longest route,

The greatest performance in a modern Classic: Secretariat wins the 1973 Belmont Stakes by 31 lengths. (Associated Press)

thought nothing of the inconvenience. He flashed home to an easy victory in track record time of 1:59.4. After 16 subsequent Derbys, Secretariat's remains the only one completed in less than two minutes.

Sham and Our Native, second and third in the Derby, filled the same positions, and by the same margins, in the Preakness. The only differences were that Secretariat led much earlier in the Pimlico contest, and that this time he was not credited with a track record. He set one, as every timing device bar one confirmed, but the exception was the official apparatus, and Pimlico declined to correct its obvious error.

No matter. In the Belmont, Secretariat not only lowered the 12-furlong track record by more than two seconds, but was also clocked inside the world record for 13 furlongs while Turcotte tried to pull him up. This was acknowledged as the greatest performance in any Classic race, with Secretariat first disposing of Sham in a furious battle at top sprinting pace, then opening out to register a winning margin of 31 lengths. It is hard to conceive how any horse in history could have lived with him, at any distance, on that magic afternoon of 9 June 1973.

There came four more victories, one in world record time for nine furlongs in the Marlboro Cup, another in course record time for a mile and a half in the Man o' War Stakes, his first effort on grass. There were even a couple of shock defeats, for which his trainer was patently to blame.

At the end of his second season, when he retired to Claiborne Farm, he was an automatic choice for 'Horse of the Year' again. The three-year-old Secretariat was the only horse to whom the award came as an insult; the application of the same term for his outstanding form at two and his monumental achievements at three seemed inappropriate. Those who were present on Belmont day will always insist that 'Horse of the Century' was a more fitting description.

the 1000 Guineas in a finish of short heads with Al Bahathri (subsequent winner of the Irish 1000 Guineas) and Bella Colora, and in the Oaks she stormed home by six lengths from Triptych, previously conqueror of the colts in the Irish 2000 Guineas. By St Leger time she was patently 'over the top', but she did not need to be at her best to account for rather modest opposition. She left Henry Cecil's Newmarket stable for stud after her Doncaster triumph, having recorded seven wins and two second places (in the King George VI and Queen Elizabeth Stakes and the Benson & Hedges Gold Cup) from nine starts.

US Triple Crown Winners

For many years the nearest equivalents to the English Triple Crown races were a trio of events at New York's Belmont Park – the Withers Stakes (founded 1874) over a mile in May, the Belmont Stakes (1867) at .1 mile 3 furlongs in June, and the Lawrence Realization Stakes (1889) over 1 mile 5 furlongs in September. This treble was achieved twice, by the celebrated Man o' War in 1920 and three years later by Zev, best known for his match-race victory over England's Derby winner Papyrus.

However, Americans rightly did not consider themselves bound by English convention, and when the term 'Triple Crown' gained currency in the 1930s, after an article by renowned Turf writer Charles Hatton, the designated races were the Kentucky Derby, the Preakness Stakes and the Belmont Stakes. They were (and still are) the most important races contested by 3-year-olds in Kentucky, Maryland and New York respectively, but they form a combination which has little in common with the English series, being closer together both in distance and in the calendar, and thus much less demanding in terms of versatility and durability. To date there have been 11 US Triple Crown champions.

Sir Barton, first to complete the treble, came into the 1919 Kentucky Derby a maiden after six efforts, there merely to set the pace for his owner's proven performer Billy Kelly. As it happened, Billy Kelly could never get in a blow against Sir Barton, who won by five lengths. Four days later he collected the Preakness by four lengths and within a month he completed his Classic set, establishing an American record for 11 furlongs as he stormed clear of his only two Belmont rivals. Having won the Kentucky Derby claiming a maiden allowance (though carrying 2½ lb overweight), Sir Barton had rapidly become a champion for owner John Ross and trainer Guy Bedwell. In 1920 he was trounced by Man o' War in a famous match race in Canada, but he accumulated career earnings of $116,857, with 13 wins from 31 starts. An extremely disappointing sire, he was sold, when 17 years old, to the US Remount Service, and he died in Wyoming in 1937.

Gallant Fox, bred and raced by William Woodward of Belair Stud and trained by 'Sunny Jim' Fitzsimmons, was nothing special as a 2-year-old, but from the moment he went into training his preparation was geared towards fulfilment of his potential at three. He proved unquestionably the best horse around in 1930, when he won nine of 10 starts, including the Preakness by three-quarters of a length, the Kentucky Derby by two lengths and the Belmont Stakes by three. His other victories included the Wood Memorial, the Dwyer Stakes and the Jockey Club Gold Cup, and his sole defeat (in the Travers Stakes at Saratoga) is still regarded as one of the shock results of the century. He went to stud at four, having won 11 of his 17 races and earned $328,165, and from his first crop of foals the second Triple Crown winner sired Omaha, the third to gain that distinction. He died at the age of 27 in November 1954.

Omaha, who represented the same owner-breeder and trainer as his sire Gallant Fox, won only one of his nine races at two in 1934, and only when second in the Sanford Stakes at Saratoga gave a hint of what was to come. Omaha's Triple Crown was remarkable in that after winning the Kentucky Derby handily by a length and a half and the Preakness a week later by six lengths, he was beaten by Rosemont in the Withers Stakes *en route* to the Belmont Stakes. But all came right on the big day, when he left Rosemont toiling in third place, almost 10 lengths in arrears. By the end of July he had added triumphs in the Dwyer Stakes and the Arlington Classic, and he was expected to enhance his reputation still further at Saratoga. But when he got there he fell lame, and he never raced in America again. However, when he was restored to fitness, Omaha was sent to England, where Cecil Boyd-Rochfort took charge of him. He won both his prep races for the Ascot Gold Cup, but lost by a short head a thrilling battle with Quashed for the Cup itself and afterwards went under narrowly to Taj Akbar in the Princess of Wales's Stakes at Newmarket. Omaha won nine of his 22 career starts and earned $154,755. A sire of strictly limited influence, he died on 24 April 1959.

War Admiral, the Triple Crown hero of 1937, was remarkable for courage as well as class. Trained by George Conway for owner-breeder Sam Riddle (who had also raced his sire Man o' War), he swept unbeaten through his 3-year-old campaign, notching eight successes. At Churchill Downs he scored comfortably by nearly two lengths from Pompoon, but that rival gave him a far tougher time at Pimlico a week later, so that the Preakness was won by only a head. Pompoon tried again at Belmont Park, but could never get into contention with War Admiral, who equalled the American record for a mile and a half, stringing his field out impressively. War Admiral was almost as dominant again at four, when he took the Widener Handicap and Jockey Club Gold Cup among nine triumphs. He would have been Horse of the Year for a second time if he had won his match race against Seabiscuit, but the result and the title went the other way. He retired after a solitary (winning) run at five, bringing his record to 21 wins from 26 starts, with earnings of $273,240. He died on 30 October 1959 after a long and quite successful stud career.

Whirlaway, son of Epsom Derby winner Blenheim, was bred and raced by Warren Wright of Calumet Farm and had Ben Jones as trainer. He had toughness and consistency to match his class, as his career record of 32 wins and 14 minor placings from 60 starts testifies. He headed the Experimental Handicap at two in 1940, and he was voted Horse of the Year at both three and four. His domination of the Triple Crown events was total. He ran away with the Kentucky Derby by eight lengths, overcame a sluggish start to take the Preakness by more than five, then toyed with the three no-hopers who dared to challenge him in the Belmont. Although he was beaten almost as often as he won, he was undoubtedly a true champion. Many of his losses resulted from his habit of veering to the right under pressure. He retired with earnings of $561,161 and proved a total disaster as a sire, both in America and France, where he died on 6 April 1953.

Count Fleet raced for his breeder, Mrs Frances Hertz and was trained by a Scotsman, Don Cameron. He was comfortably the best 2-year-old of 1942, when he won 10 of his 15 starts, and at three he was invincible. Six races brought six victories, all by clear margins, including the Kentucky Derby by three lengths, the Preakness by eight and the Belmont by 25 – a record until Secretariat came along. Unfortunately, he suffered an injury in the Belmont which caused his retirement from racing. He had won 16 of 21 races and earned $250,300. He soon became a leading sire and died on 3 December 1973, less than a month before what would have been his 34th official birthday.

Assault, bred and raced by Texan breeder Bob Kleberg of King Ranch, was trained by Max Hirsch. He was not one of the foremost 2-year-olds of 1945, winning only twice that season, once as a 71/1 shot in the Flash Stakes at Saratoga. But he proved altogether more formidable at three, when a campaign of 15 starts brought him eight victories and five minor placings. He streaked home by eight lengths in the Kentucky Derby, held on bravely by a neck when Lord Boswell's late bid threatened him in the Preakness, and impressively put three lengths between himself and Natchez in the last furlong of the Belmont. Assault later won the Dwyer Stakes and beat Stymie in the Pimlico Special. At four he collected the Suburban and Brooklyn Handicaps, giving weight to Stymie on both occasions, as he compiled a winning streak of five, but thereafter he was only intermittently sound. He was retired from racing after a single start in 1948, but a routine test on his arrival at stud showed that he was sterile. In due

course he was put back into training and he won a second Brooklyn Handicap at six. He finally bowed out of racing at seven, having won 18 of 42 starts and earned $675,470. He died at the age of 28 on 1 September 1971.

Citation, a second Triple Crown winner for owner-breeder Warren Wright, seemed to be the second coming of Man o' War – at least until the end of his second season in training. He won 9 out of 10 as a juvenile and 19 out of 20 at three, dominating at all distances from 4½ furlongs to 2 miles. He took the Belmont Stakes by 3½ lengths, the Preakness by 5½ and the Belmont by eight. He acquired a sky-high reputation early, with the result that he often faced few rivals, and on one occasion at Pimlico he was accorded the honour of a walk-over. But whatever challenged him was ruthlessly shrugged aside as he piled prestige victory on prestige victory. At the end of 1948 he suffered a fetlock injury, tendon trouble followed, and he was away from the races for over a year. He was never so formidable thereafter, but was kept in training with Ben Jones with the objective of becoming the first horse to earn a million dollars. The target was reached with victory in the 1951 Hollywood Gold Cup Handicap, and Citation went to stud, winner of 32 out of 45 races, with $1,085,760 in the bank. He proved a disappointing sire and died on 8 August 1970.

Secretariat became the first Triple Crown winner for 25 years in 1973 and in doing so became a national hero. Much the best of his crop at two, when he finished first in eight consecutive races, he confirmed his status emphatically at three, in spite of three uncharacteristic lapses. There were no mistakes in the Triple Crown. He set a track record time in the Kentucky Derby, just missed the track record in the Preakness, then annihilated the track record in the Belmont, which he won by a record 31 lengths – the most one-sided Classic in history. His subsequent victories included the Marlboro Cup Handicap, the Man o' War Stakes and the Canadian International Championship, after which race he was retired as winner of 16 of 21 starts, with earnings of $1,316,808. Though syndicated for stud duties at the end of his first season, he raced throughout his career in the colours of his breeder, Meadow Stud, whose trainer was Lucien Laurin. Secretariat found it rather more difficult to excel as a sire, but he did get Lady's Secret, Horse of the Year in 1986. He died on 4 October 1989.

Seattle Slew, who fetched only $17,500 as a yearling, became the first American Triple Crown winner to have been sold at public auction, and the first to complete the Triple Crown series while still unbeaten. He achieved that feat in 1977 and the Belmont was only the ninth start of his career. He was named champion 2-year-old on the strength of an impressive victory in the Champagne Stakes, and his second title was assured by his Classic campaign, which produced authoritative displays in the Kentucky Derby and Preakness and a comprehensive four-length triumph in the Belmont. Surprisingly, Seattle Slew finished only fourth in his next race, but he returned to take a third divisional title as a 4-year-old, when he twice beat the year-younger Triple Crown winner, Affirmed. Seattle Slew, trained in his Classic season by Billy Turner for Mrs Karen Taylor, retired with career earnings of $1,208,726 after 14 wins from 17 starts. He became America's champion sire, with record progeny earnings, in 1984 and in the following year his stud fee stood at an amazing $750,000.

Affirmed, the latest Triple Crown hero, was bred and raced by Louis Wolfson's Harbor View Farm and trained by Laz Barrera. He was named the best of his crop at two and repeated the performance at three in 1978 in a season which featured several memorable duels between him and Alydar. To Alydar fell the unique distinction of being a Triple Crown runner-up, as he was Affirmed's closest pursuer in the Kentucky Derby (beaten 1½ lengths), the Preakness (a neck) and the Belmont (a head). Affirmed later went under by three lengths to Seattle Slew in the first-ever encounter between Triple Crown winners – in the Marlboro Cup – and was considerably further behind in their second meeting, when both were beaten by Exceller. But that occasion was marred by the slipping of Affirmed's saddle. After a couple of defeats as a 4-year-old, Affirmed renewed his winning ways and concluded his career with a seven-victory sequence which included the Santa Anita Handicap, the Hollywood Gold Cup, the Woodward Stakes and the Jockey Club Gold Cup. His final score was 22 wins and six minor placings from 29 starts, with earnings of $2,393,818. His stud career to date has been disappointing.

Other Triple Crown Winners

IRELAND

The Irish Triple Crown consists of the Irish 2000 Guineas (inaugurated 1921) over a mile, the Irish Derby (1866) over 1½ miles and the Irish St Leger (1915) over 1¾ miles, all run at The Curragh. However, these classics contained penalty clauses before 1946 and the Irish St Leger was opened to older horses in 1983. The two Triple Crown winners have been Museum (1935), who also won the Ebor Handicap as a 3-year-old, and unbeaten Windsor Slipper (1942), who started in no other race that year.

FRANCE

There is no such thing as the French Triple Crown, though for many years the nearest French equivalents to the English Triple Crown races were the Poule d'Essai des Poulains (Poule d'Essai before 1883), Prix du Jockey-Club and Prix Royal-Oak (open to older horses from 1979). This treble was achieved by Zut in 1879 and Perth in 1899.

ITALY

There is no such thing as the Italian Triple Crown, though the Italian equivalents to the English Triple Crown races are the Premio Parioli (inaugurated 1907) over 1,600 metres in Rome, the Derby Italiano (1884) over 2,400 metres in Rome and the St Leger Italiano (1890) over 2,900 metres in Turin. This treble was achieved by Niccolo dell'Arca (1941), Gladiolo (1946) and Botticelli (1954).

WEST GERMANY

The West German Triple Crown consists of the Mehl-Mülhens-Rennen (formerly Henckel-Rennen, inaugurated 1871) over 1,600 metres at Gelsenkirchen, the Deutsches Derby (1869) over 2,400 metres at Hamburg and the Deutsches St Leger (1881) over 2,800 metres at Dortmund. The only horse to win all 3 races was Königsstuhl in 1979.

CANADA

The Canadian Triple Crown consists of the premier classic, the Queen's Plate over 1¼ miles on dirt at Woodbine, followed by the Prince of Wales Stakes over 1 mile 1½ furlongs on dirt at Fort Erie and the Breeders' Stakes over 1½ miles on turf at Woodbine. All three have been won by New Providence (1959), Canebora (1963) and With Approval (1989).

JAPAN

The Japanese Triple Crown consists of the Satsuki Shou (2000 Guineas) over 2,000 metres at Nakayama, the Tokyo Yuushun (Derby) over 2,400 metres in Tokyo and the Kikuka Shou (St Leger) over 3,000 metres at Kyoto. The 4 Triple Crown winners have been St Lite (1941), Shinzan (1964), Mr C. B. (1983) and Symboli Rudolf (1984).

ARGENTINA

The Argentine Triple Crown consists of the Polla de Potrillos (2000 Guineas) over 1,600 metres at the Hipodromo Argentino, the Gran Premio Jockey Club over 2,000 metres at San Isidro and the Gran Premio Nacional (Derby) over 2,500 metres at the Hipodromo Argentino. The most recent Triple Crown winner is El Serrano (1986).

The Quadruple Crown consists of these 3 races plus Argentina's premier weight-for-age prize, the Gran Premio Internacional Carlos Pellegrini over 2,400 metres at San Isidro. The 10 Quadruple Crown winners have been Pippermint (1902), Old Man (1904), Botafogo (1917), Rico (1922), Mineral (1931), Yatasto (1951), Tatan (1955), Manantial (1958), Forli (1966) and Telescopico (1978).

ENGLISH STAYERS

In England the stayers' Triple Crown consists of the 3 principal Cup events: the Ascot Gold Cup (inaugurated 1807) over 2½ miles, the Goodwood Cup (1812) over 2 miles 5 furlongs and the Doncaster Cup (1766)

over 2¼ miles. These have been won in the same year
by Isonomy (1879), Alycidon (1949), Souepi (1953),
Le Moss (1979 and 1980) and Longboat (1986),
though Souepi could only dead-heat at Doncaster.
Rock Roi was first past the post in all 3 races in 1971
but was disqualified in the Ascot Gold Cup.

AMERICAN FILLIES

The American Triple Crown races for fillies were
once recognized as the distaff equivalents to the
colts' Triple Crown races, namely the Kentucky Oaks

*Omaha, perhaps the least distinguished of all American Triple
Crown winners and the only one of that select band to race in
England. (W. W. Rouch)*

over 1 mile 1 furlong at Churchill Downs, the Black-
Eyed Susan Stakes (Pimlico Oaks before 1952) over
1 mile 110 yards at Pimlico, and the Coaching Club
American Oaks over 1½ miles at Belmont Park.
These three have been won by Wistful (1949), Real
Delight (1952) and Davona Dale (1979).

A more modern fillies' Triple Crown (renamed the

Triple Tiara in 1988), established by the New York Racing Association in 1961, consists of the Acorn Stakes over a mile, the Mother Goose Stakes over 1 mile 1 furlong, and the Coaching Club American Oaks over 1½ miles, all at Belmont Park. These three have been won by Dark Mirage (1968), Shuvee (1969), Chris Evert (1974), Ruffian (1975), Davona Dale (1979), Mom's Command (1985) and Open Mind (1989).

AMERICAN HANDICAPPERS

The American Handicap Triple Crown consists of the Metropolitan Handicap (inaugurated 1891) over a mile, the Suburban Handicap (1884) over 1¼ miles and the Brooklyn Handicap (1887) over 1½ miles, all run at Belmont Park, though their distances and venues have varied. All three have been won in the same year by Whisk Broom (1913), Tom Fool (1953), Kelso (1961) and Fit to Fight (1984).

Horses of the Year

Great Britain: Flat

From 1959 to 1965 the *Bloodstock Breeders' Review* asked 20 racing journalists to name their Horse of the Year. The champions, with their age and sex, the number of votes they received and their most important wins that season, were as follows:

1959 **Petite Etoile** (3yr filly) 18
  Free Handicap, 1000 Guineas, Oaks, Sussex Stakes, Yorkshire Oaks, Champion Stakes.
1960 **St Paddy** (3yr colt) 11
  Dante, Derby, Great Voltigeur and St Leger Stakes.
1961 **Right Royal** (3yr colt) 10
  Poule d'Essai des Poulains, Prix Lupin, Prix du Jockey-Club, King George VI and Queen Elizabeth Stakes, Prix Henri Foy.
1962 **Match** (4yr colt) 9
  Prix Boïard, Grand Prix de Saint-Cloud, King George VI and Queen Elizabeth Stakes, Washington DC International.
1963 **Exbury** (4yr colt) 15
  Prix Ganay, Coronation Cup, Grand Prix de Saint-Cloud, Prix de l'Arc de Triomphe.
1964 **Santa Claus** (3yr colt) 10
  Irish 2000 Guineas, Derby, Irish Derby.
1965 **Sea-Bird** (3yr colt) 19
  Prix Greffulhe, Prix Lupin, Derby, Grand Prix de Saint-Cloud, Prix de l'Arc de Triomphe.

In 1965 an official Racehorse of the Year award was established, determined by ballot among racing journalists; any horse who has run in Great Britain during the season is eligible. The Racecourse Association presented the award from 1965 to 1977, since when the Racegoers' Club has been responsible. In 1965 and 1966 the 40 voters gave points to their top 6 horses in order of preference. The champions, with their age and sex, the number of votes they received, the total number of votes cast and their most important wins that season, have been as follows:

1965 **Sea-Bird** (3yr colt) 228/240
  Prix Greffulhe, Prix Lupin, Derby, Grand Prix de Saint-Cloud, Prix de l'Arc Triomphe.

1966 **Charlottown** (3yr colt) 176/240
  Derby, Oxfordshire Stakes.
1967 **Busted** (4yr colt) 18/40
  Coronation, Eclipse and King George VI and Queen Elizabeth Stakes, Prix Henri Foy.
1968 **Sir Ivor** (3yr colt) 26/40
  2000 Guineas Trial, 2000 Guineas, Derby, Champion Stakes, Washington DC International.
1969 **Park Top** (5yr mare) 20/40
  Prix de la Seine, Coronation Cup, Hardwicke Stakes, King George VI and Queen Elizabeth Stakes, Prix Foy.
1970 **Nijinsky** (3yr colt) 38/40
  Gladness Stakes, 2000 Guineas, Derby, Irish Derby, King George VI and Queen Elizabeth Stakes, St Leger.
1971 **Mill Reef** (3yr colt) 30/37
  Greenham, Derby, Eclipse and King George VI and Queen Elizabeth Stakes, Prix de l'Arc de Triomphe.
1972 **Brigadier Gerard** (4yr colt) 40/40
  Lockinge, Westbury, Prince of Wales's, Eclipse, King George VI and Queen Elizabeth, Queen Elizabeth II and Champion Stakes.
1973 **Dahlia** (3yr filly) 29/39
  Prix de la Grotte, Prix Saint-Alary, Irish Oaks, King George VI and Queen Elizabeth Stakes, Prix Niel, Washington DC International.
1974 **Dahlia** (4yr filly) 32/36
  Grand Prix de Saint-Cloud, King George VI and Queen Elizabeth Stakes, Benson and Hedges Gold Cup, Man o' War Stakes, Canadian International Championship.
1975 **Grundy** (3yr colt) 38/40
  Irish 2000 Guineas, Derby, Irish Derby, King George VI and Queen Elizabeth Stakes.
1976 **Pawneese** (3yr filly) 21/40
  Prix La Camargo, Pénélope and Cléopâtre, Oaks, Prix de Diane, King George VI and Queen Elizabeth Stakes.
1977 **The Minstrel** (3yr colt) 26/37
  Ascot 2000 Guineas Trial, Derby, Irish Derby, King George VI and Queen Elizabeth Stakes.
1978 **Shirley Heights** (3yr colt) 21/35
  Heathorn Stakes, Dante Stakes, Derby, Irish Derby.
1979 **Troy** (3yr colt) 27/32
  Classic Trial, Predominate Stakes, Derby, Irish Derby, King George VI and Queen Elizabeth Stakes, Benson and Hedges Gold Cup.

1980 **Moorestyle** (3yr colt)   23/31
Free Handicap, Norwest Holst Trophy
Handicap, July Cup, Vernons Sprint
Cup, Prix de l'Abbaye de Longchamp,
Challenge Stakes, Prix de la Forêt.

1981 **Shergar** (3yr colt)   22/31
Classic Trial, Chester Vase, Derby, Irish
Derby, King George VI and Queen
Elizabeth Stakes.

1982 **Ardross** (6yr horse)   17/30
Jockey Club Stakes, Yorkshire Cup,
Henry II Stakes, Ascot Gold Cup,
Geoffrey Freer Stakes, Doncaster Cup.

1983 **Habibti** (3yr filly)   23/26
July Cup, William Hill Sprint
Championship, Vernons Sprint Cup,
Prix de l'Abbaye de Longchamp.

1984 **Provideo** (2yr colt)   17/30
Brocklesby, Cock of the North, Star,
Champion 2-Y-O Trophy and Doncaster
Stakes.

1985 **Pebbles** (4yr filly)   28/30
Trusthouse Forte Mile, Eclipse Stakes,
Champion Stakes, Breeders' Cup Turf.

1986 **Dancing Brave** (3yr colt)   27/27
Craven, 2000 Guineas, Eclipse, King
George VI and Queen Elizabeth and
Select Stakes, Prix de l'Arc de
Triomphe.

1987 **Reference Point** (3yr colt)   12/20
Dante, Derby, King George VI and
Queen Elizabeth, Great Voltigeur and St
Leger Stakes.

1988 **Mtoto** (5yr horse)   20/21
Prince of Wales, Eclipse, King George
VI and Queen Elizabeth and Select
Stakes.

*Mtoto (Michael Roberts) beats
Unfuwain in the King George VI and
Queen Elizabeth Stakes – the most
important victory in his 1988 Horse of
the Year campaign. (Sporting Pictures)*

Double champion

Dahlia (1973, 1974)

Elected unanimously

Brigadier Gerard (1972), Dancing Brave
(1986)

Closest decision

Charlottown (1966) received just 2 points
more than Sodium, who had twice
beaten him on merit.

Oldest

6 years – Ardross (1982)
5 years – Park Top (1969), Mtoto (1988)

Youngest

2 years – Provideo (1984)

Fillies and mares

Petite Etoile (1959), Park Top (1969),
Dahlia (1973, 1974), Pawneese (1976),
Habibti (1983), Pebbles (1985)

Fillies monopolized the voting in 1983
through Habibti (23 votes), Sun
Princess (2) and Time Charter (1), and
in 1985 through Pebbles (28 votes) and
Oh So Sharp (2)

Grey

Petite Etoile (1959)

Most wins in championship season

16 – Provideo (1984)
7 – Brigadier Gerard (1972), Moorestyle
(1980)

Unbeaten in championship season

6 races – Petite Etoile (1959)
5 races – Exbury (1963), Sea-Bird (1965)
4 races – Busted (1967)

Least successful

Charlottown won only 2 of his 5 races in
1966

Most active

24 races – Provideo (1984)
10 races – Dahlia (1973 and 1974)

Least active

4 races – Busted (1967).
Right Royal (1961), Match (1962), Exbury
(1963), Sea-Bird (1965) and Dahlia
(1973) won on their only appearance in
Great Britain that year.

Earliest retirements

1 July – Shirley Heights (1978)
23 July – The Minstrel (1977)

Trained in Ireland

Santa Claus (1964), Sir Ivor (1968),
Nijinsky (1970), The Minstrel (1977)

Trained in France

Right Royal (1961), Match (1962), Exbury (1963), Sea-Bird (1965), Dahlia (1973, 1974), Pawneese (1976)

Most successful owner

2 wins – Nelson Bunker Hunt: Dahlia (twice)

Most successful breeders

2 wins – Nelson Bunker Hunt: Dahlia (twice)
Eddie Taylor: Nijinsky, The Minstrel

Most successful trainers

3 wins – Noel Murless: Petite Etoile, St Paddy, Busted
Vincent O'Brien: Sir Ivor, Nijinsky, The Minstrel

Most successful sires

2 wins – Vaguely Noble: Dahlia (twice)
Northern Dancer: Nijinsky, The Minstrel
Great Nephew: Grundy, Shergar
Mill Reef: Shirley Heights, Reference Point

Great Britain: Jumping

From 1958/59 to 1964/65 the *Bloodstock Breeders' Review* asked 20 racing journalists to name the best hurdler and the best steeplechaser of the season. The champions, with their age and sex (if entire horse or mare), the number of votes they received and their most important wins that season, were as follows:

Best hurdler

1958/59 **Fare Time** (6yr)   15
Oteley Hurdle, Champion Hurdle.
1959/60 **Another Flash** (6yr)   15
Champion Hurdle, (2nd) Scalp Hurdle.
1960/61 **Eborneezer** (6yr horse)   8
Oteley Hurdle, Champion Hurdle, (2nd) Grande Course de Haies d'Auteuil.
1961/62 **Anzio** (5yr)   20
Wyld Court, Berkshire Handicap, Greenham Handicap and Champion Hurdles, (2nd) Imperial Cup.
1962/63 **Anzio** (6yr)   14
Nuneaton Hurdle, (4th) Schweppes Gold Trophy.
1963/64 **Magic Court** (6yr)   16
Punch Bowl Handicap, Waterloo Handicap, Princess Royal Handicap and Champion Hurdles.
1964/65 **Salmon Spray** (7yr)   13
Tote Investors' Handicap Hurdle, Ovaltine Cup, National Spirit Challenge Trophy, Liverpool Handicap Hurdle.

Best steeplechaser

1958/59 **Mandarin** (8yr)   5
Sandown Handicap Chase, (2nd) Whitbread Gold Cup, (2nd) Grand Steeple-Chase de Paris.
1959/60 **Pas Seul** (7yr)   14
Cheltenham Gold Cup, (2nd) Whitbread Gold Cup.
1960/61 **Pas Seul** (8yr)   15
Westminster Handicap, Star and Garter Handicap, Manifesto Handicap and Farnborough Chases, Whitbread Gold Cup, (2nd) Cheltenham Gold Cup.
1961/62 **Mandarin** (11yr)   10
Clun Chase, Hennessy Gold Cup, Walter Hyde Handicap Chase, Cheltenham Gold Cup, Grand Steeple-Chase de Paris.
1962/63 **Mill House** (6yr)   20
Walton Green Handicap Chase, Sandown Handicap Chase, Cheltenham Gold Cup, Mandarin Handicap Chase.

1963/64 **Arkle** (7yr)   20
Carey's Cottage, Christmas, Thyestes and Leopardstown Handicap Chases, Cheltenham Gold Cup, Irish Grand National.
1964/65 **Arkle** (8yr)   20
Carey's Cottage, Hennessy Gold Cup and Leopardstown Handicap Chases, Cheltenham Gold Cup, Whitbread Gold Cup.

Right *Monksfield (Tommy Kinane) leads Sea Pigeon, his successor as champion hurdler and Horse of the Year, over the final flight on his way to victory in the 1978 Champion Hurdle at Cheltenham. (All-Sport)*

In 1965/66 an official National Hunt Horse of the Year award for the overall champion jumper was established, run on the same lines as the Racehorse of the Year award on the Flat. For the first two seasons the 40 voters gave points to their top 6 horses in order of preference. The champions, with the age and sex (if entire horse or mare), the number of votes they received, the total number of votes cast and their most important wins that season, have been as follows:

1965/66 **Arkle** (9yr)   239/240
Gallaher Gold Cup, Hennessy Gold Cup, King George VI Chase, Leopardstown Handicap Chase, Cheltenham Gold Cup.
1966/67 **Mill House** (10yr)*   197/240
Gainsborough Chase, Whitbread Gold Cup.
1967/68 **Persian War** (5yr)   36/40
Wyld Court Hurdle, Schweppes Gold Trophy, Champion Hurdle.
1968/69 **Persian War** (6yr)   39/40
Lonsdale Handicap, Champion and Welsh Champion Hurdles.
1969/70 **Persian War** (7yr)   33/38
Champion Hurdle, (3rd) Sweeps Hurdle, (3rd) Welsh Champion Hurdle.
1970/71 **Bula** (6yr)   36/40
Osborne, Jane Drewery Memorial, Benson and Hedges Handicap, Mill House, Kingwell Pattern, Champion and Welsh Champion Hurdles.

* in 1966/67 some voters mistakenly thought that Arkle's injury had rendered the Irish champion ineligible for the award.

1971/72 **Bula** (7yr)   37/39
Ackermann Skeaping Trophy, Kingwell Pattern Hurdle, Champion Hurdle.
1972/73 **Pendil** (8yr)   12/38
Black and White Gold Cup, Benson and Hedges Handicap, King George VI, Newbury Spring Handicap and Yellow Pages Pattern Handicap Chases, (2nd) Cheltenham Gold Cup.
1973/74 **Red Rum** (9yr)   38/38
Windermere, Joan Mackay, John Eustace Smith Trophy, Brettanby, Grand National and Scottish Grand National Handicap Chases, (2nd) Hennessy Cognac Gold Cup.
1974/75 **Comedy of Errors** (8yr)   34/39
Fighting Fifth, Cheltenham Trial, Sweeps, Wolverhampton Champion Trial, Champion and Scottish Champion Hurdles.
1975/76 **Night Nurse** (5yr)   37/40
Free Handicap, William Hill, Fighting Fifth, Sweeps, Corporation Challenge Trophy, Champion, Scottish Champion and Welsh Champion Hurdles.
1976/77 **Night Nurse** (6yr)   23/39

William Hill, John Skeaping, Champion, Templegate and Welsh Champion Hurdles.
1977/78 **Midnight Court** (7yr)   20/37
Embassy Premier Chase Qualifier, Baxter Gate, Kirk and Kirk Handicap, SGB Handicap and Geoffrey Gilbey Memorial Handicap Chases, Aynsley China Cup, Cheltenham Gold Cup.
1978/79 **Monksfield** (7yr horse)   33/34
A R Soudavar Memorial Trial, Champion, Colt Sigma and Welsh Champion Hurdles, (2nd) Royal Doulton Handicap Hurdle.
1979/80 **Sea Pigeon** (10yr)   29/31
Holsten Diat Pils, Champion and Welsh Champion Hurdles.
1980/81 **Sea Pigeon** (11yr)   17/33
Holsten Diat Pils, Fighting Fifth and Champion Hurdles.
1981/82 **Silver Buck** (10yr)   25/31
Terry Biddlecombe Challenge Trophy, Edward Hanmer Memorial Handicap Chase, Cox Moore Sweaters Handicap Chase, Cheltenham Gold Cup.
1982/83 **Gaye Brief** (6yr)   17/30

Cambridgeshire, Tom Masson Trophy, Fred Rimell, City Trial Handicap, Champion and Sun Templegate Hurdles.

1983/84 **Dawn Run** (6yr mare) 14/30
A R Soudavar Memorial Trial, VAT Watkins, Christmas, Wessel Cable Champion, Champion and Sandeman Aintree Hurdles, Prix La Barka, Grande Course de Haies d'Auteuil.

1984/85 **Burrough Hill Lad** (9yr) 16/27
Silver Buck Handicap, Hennessy Cognac Gold Cup Handicap, Charlie Hall Memorial Wetherby Pattern, King George VI and Gainsborough Handicap Chases.

1985/86 **Dawn Run** (8yr mare) 21/30
Punchestown Chase, Sean P Graham Chase, Cheltenham Gold Cup, Match with Buck House.

1986/87 **Desert Orchid** (8yr) 16/26
Holsten Export Lager Handicap, Frogmore Handicap, King George VI, Gainsborough Handicap, Jim Ford Challenge Cup and Peregrine Handicap Chases.

1987/88 **Desert Orchid** (9yr) 21/25
Terry Biddlecombe Challenge Trophy, Boxing Day Trial Chase, Chivas Regal Cup, Whitbread Gold Cup.

1988/89 **Desert Orchid** (10yr) 28/28
Terry Biddlecombe Challenge Trophy, Tingle Creek Handicap, King George VI, Victor Chandler Handicap and Gainsborough Handicap Chases, Cheltenham Gold Cup.

Triple champions

Arkle, Persian War, Desert Orchid

Elected unanimously

Anzio (1961/62), Mill House (1962/63), Arkle (1963/64 and 1964/65), Red Rum (1973/74), Desert Orchid (1988/89)

Closest decisions

Mandarin was elected champion steeplechaser of 1958/59 by one vote. Pendil received just 2 votes more than Crisp in 1972/73.

Oldest

11 years – Mandarin (1961/62), Sea Pigeon (1980/81)

Youngest

5 years – Anzio (1961/62), Persian War (1967/68), Night Nurse (1975/76)

Mare

Dawn Run (1983/84, 1985/86)

Entires

Eborneezer (1960/61), Monksfield (1978/79)

Grey or roan

Anzio, Desert Orchid

Most wins in championship season

8 – Night Nurse (1975/76)

Unbeaten in championship season

8 races – Night Nurse (1975/76)
7 races – Bula (1970/71), Midnight Court (1977/78)
5 races – Mandarin (1961/62), Arkle (1965/66)

Least successful

Mandarin (1958/59) and Pas Seul (1959/60) won only one of their 8 races in those championship seasons.

Most active

10 races – Red Rum (1973/74)

Earliest retirement

2 March – Burrough Hill Lad (1985)

Trained in Ireland

Another Flash, Arkle, Monksfield, Dawn Run

Most successful owners

3 wins – Anne, Duchess of Westminster: Arkle (3 times)
Henry Alper: Persian War (3 times)
Richard Burridge: Desert Orchid (3 times)

Most successful trainers

6 wins – Fulke Walwyn: Mandarin, Anzio and Mill House (twice each)
4 wins – Fred Winter: Bula (twice), Pendil, Midnight Court
Peter Easterby: Night Nurse and Sea Pigeon (twice each)

Phar Lap

When talk among racing people turns to the identity of the greatest horses of all time, the only Australasian champions to merit serious consideration are Carbine and Phar Lap. Of all the outstanding geldings in racing history none ranks higher than Phar Lap, who achieved unprecedented status as a national hero in Australia before being sent to America and dying in mysterious circumstances.

Phar Lap was bred by Alick Roberts and was foaled on 26 October 1926 at Seadown Stud, near Timaru on New Zealand's South Island. His sire Night Raid (a descendant of Carbine) failed to win at all in England and did not fare much better when exported to Australia, while his dam Entreaty was unplaced on her only start.

The rich chestnut colt had little to commend him on pedigree or looks when offered at Trentham Yearling Sales in January 1928 but Harry Telford, a minor trainer in Sydney, persuaded American David Davis to buy him and the purchase was duly made for 160 guineas. When the big, ungainly youngster arrived in Australia Davis was reluctant to pay to have him in training so Telford took a 3-year lease on him.

Phar Lap, named after the Thai word for lightning, was gelded and took plenty of time to mature. In fact he lost nine of his first ten races, being unplaced in eight of them, but once he found his form he soon asserted his supremacy. As a 3-year-old in 1929–30 he won the premier classics in both Sydney and Melbourne, the AJC and Victoria Derbys, but could finish only third in Australia's greatest race, the two-mile Melbourne Cup.

However, he swept unbeaten through his last nine starts of that campaign including the VRC and AJC St Legers. The pattern of his career had been set: classics, handicaps and weight-for-age races all came alike to him and he displayed a remarkable blend of speed and stamina, often crushing top-class opposition in effortless style by a wide margin.

As a 4-year-old in 1930–31, Phar Lap set the seal on his greatness, finishing a close second on his first and last outings of the season but in between running up a sequence of 14 wins including the Melbourne Cup. This, the most celebrated victory of his career, was preceded by an attempt by gunmen, presumably in the pay of underworld bookmakers, to shoot him on his way back to his stable from morning exercise.

The shots missed their target and Phar Lap, an exceptionally placid individual, won the Melbourne Stakes that very afternoon. Three days later, on 4 November 1930, came the Cup itself; the champion, despite being handicapped at 9 st 12 lb and conceding at least a stone all round, started at odds-on and turned the race into a procession, winning by three lengths with regular jockey Jim Pike sitting motionless.

His other victories that season included Australia's premier weight-for-age prize, the W S Cox Plate at Moonee Valley, and the Futurity Stakes against top sprinters. Among those left toiling in his wake at various times were Amounis and Nightmarch, both of whom were outstanding champions by any standard except his own. Trainer Telford's lease ended in February 1931 but Davis allowed him to buy a half-share in the champion very cheaply.

Phar Lap remained almost invincible in late 1931, winning his first eight races as a 5-year-old including the Spring Stakes, Randwick Plate, W S Cox Plate and Melbourne Stakes for the second time and the Craven Plate for the third time. However, he was jaded when the Melbourne Cup came round again and in any case had the impossible burden of 10 st 10 lb, 5 lb more than Carbine's record for the race.

In finishing eighth, conceding 54 lb to the winner, Phar Lap ran his last race in Australia, for David Davis had already decided to send him to North America for the ten-furlong Agua Caliente Handicap, billed as the richest race in the world. He travelled by ship to California via his native New Zealand, where he had never raced, and arrived in January 1932 in the charge of Tommy Woodcock, the young man who had been his constant attendant throughout his career and was now promoted to trainer.

Betting had been outlawed in California and the race was run at Caliente, just over the border in Mexico, on 20 March. The prize money had been halved, so Phar Lap could not become the world's leading earner as planned, and he had to overcome a hoof injury, but by winning decisively in record time he did enough to persuade some hard-headed judges that he was the greatest Thoroughbred ever to race in North America.

Immediately afterwards the champion was moved to Menlo Park, near San Francisco, where he fell ill on the morning of 5 April 1932. His stomach became distended and he died in agony soon after midday, leaving a mystery that has never been explained satisfactorily.

The news was regarded as a national disaster in Australia and there were wild rumours of deliberate poisoning. The generally-accepted explanation was that he had eaten grass accidentally contaminated by arsenic from an insecticide, though another theory blamed swelling of the abdomen caused by eating damp lucerne. The medical evidence was inconclusive and the true cause of his tragic death will never be known for sure.

Phar Lap won 37 of his 51 races over four seasons, including 32 of his last 35; he was campaigned rigorously and it is likely that at his death his best years were already behind him. For toughness, durability and soundness as well as sheer brilliance, few champions of any country or any era can be considered his equal. His mounted hide is on display in the National Museum in Melbourne and still attracts more visitors than any other exhibit, while his skeleton stands in the National Museum, Wellington.

Phar Lap in action with regular partner Jim Pike in the saddle.

Timeform Champions

From 1969 the Timeform organization in Halifax, Yorkshire has named a Horse of the Year in its *Racehorses of 19—* annual, which contains ratings for all the best horses in Europe. The Timeform champion has always been the horse with the highest rating except in 1969 (Habitat rated 134), 1982 (Assert and Green Forest rated level with Ardross), 1984 (El Gran Senor rated 136) and 1985 (Slip Anchor rated 136).

		Rating
1969	**Levmoss** (4yr colt)	133
1970	**Nijinsky** (3yr colt)	138
1971	**Mill Reef** (3yr colt)	141
	Brigadier Gerard (3yr colt)	141
1972	**Brigadier Gerard** (4yr colt)	144
1973	**Rheingold** (4yr colt)	137
	Apalachee (2yr colt)	137
1974	**Allez France** (4yr filly)	136
1975	**Grundy** (3yr colt)	137
1976	**Youth** (3yr colt)	135
1977	**Alleged** (3yr colt)	137
1978	**Alleged** (4yr colt)	138
1979	**Troy** (3yr colt)	137
1980	**Moorestyle** (3yr colt)	137
1981	**Shergar** (3yr colt)	140
1982	**Ardross** (6yr horse)	134
1983	**Habibti** (3yr filly)	136
1984	**Provideo** (2yr colt)	112
1985	**Pebbles** (4yr filly)	135
1986	**Dancing Brave** (3yr colt)	140
1987	**Reference Point** (3yr colt)	139
1988	**Warning** (3yr colt)	136

From 1975/76 the Timeform organization has named a Champion Jumper in its *Chasers & Hurdlers* annual, which contains ratings for all the best jumpers in the British Isles. The Timeform champion has always been the jumper with the highest rating except in 1975/76 (Captain Christy rated 182), 1983/84 (Badsworth Boy rated 177) and 1985/86 (Burrough Hill Lad rated 183).

		Rating
1975/76	**Night Nurse** (5yr gelding)	178
1976/77	**Night Nurse** (6yr gelding)	182
1977/78	**Monksfield** (6yr horse)	177
1978/79	**Monksfield** (7yr horse)	180
1979/80	**Sea Pigeon** (10yr gelding)	175
1980/81	**Little Owl** (7yr gelding)	176
1981/82	**Silver Buck** (10yr gelding)	175
1982/83	**Badsworth Boy** (8yr gelding)	179
1983/84	**Dawn Run** (6yr mare)	173
1984/85	**Burrough Hill Lad** (9yr gelding)	184
1985/86	**Dawn Run** (8yr mare)	167
1986/87	**Desert Orchid** (8yr gelding)	177
1987/88	**Desert Orchid** (9yr gelding)	177
1988/89	**Desert Orchid** (10yr gelding)	182

United States

Between 1936 and 1970 Triangle Publications (publishers of the newspaper *Daily Racing Form*) and the magazine *Turf and Sports Digest* conducted separate Horse of the Year polls among journalists, and in 1950 a third poll was established among racing secretaries at Thoroughbred Racing Associations tracks. The results were usually the same but in some years two champions were acclaimed. From 1971 the Thoroughbred Racing Associations, *Daily Racing Form* and the National Turf Writers' Association have conducted their own polls, with the results combined to determine the recipient of the official Eclipse Award for the Horse of the Year. The champions, with their age, sex and most important wins that season, have been as follows:

1936 **Granville** (3yr colt)
BELMONT, Classic, Kenner and Travers Stakes, Saratoga Cup, Lawrence Realization.

1937 **War Admiral** (3yr colt)
Chesapeake Stakes, KENTUCKY DERBY, PREAKNESS Stakes, BELMONT Stakes, Washington Handicap, Pimlico Special.

1938 **Seabiscuit** (5yr horse)
Agua Caliente Handicap, Bay Meadows Handicap, Hollywood Gold Cup, Match with Ligaroti, Havre de Grace Handicap, Pimlico Special (Match with War Admiral).

1939 **Challedon** (3yr colt)
PREAKNESS Stakes, Yankee Handicap, Classic Stakes, Narragansett Special, Hawthorne Gold Cup, Havre de Grace Handicap, Tranter Stakes, Maryland Handicap, Pimlico Special.

1940 **Challedon** (4yr colt)
Hollywood Gold Cup, Whitney Stakes, Havre de Grace Handicap, Pimlico Special.

1941 **Whirlaway** (3yr colt)
A J Joyner Handicap, KENTUCKY DERBY, PREAKNESS, BELMONT and Dwyer Stakes, Saranac Handicap, Travers Stakes, American Derby, Lawrence Realization.

1942 **Whirlaway** (4yr colt)
Clark, Dixie, Brooklyn, Massachusetts and Trenton Handicaps, Narragansett Special, Jockey Club Gold Cup, Washington Handicap, Pimlico Special, Governor Bowie Handicap, Louisiana Handicap.

1943 **Count Fleet** (3yr colt)
Wood Memorial, KENTUCKY DERBY, PREAKNESS, Withers and BELMONT Stakes.

1944 **Twilight Tear** (3yr filly)
Rennert Handicap, Pimlico Oaks, Acorn Stakes, Coaching Club American Oaks, Princess Dorren Stakes, Skokie Handicap, Classic Stakes, Meadowview Handicap, Queen Isabella Handicap, Pimlico Special.

1945 **Busher** (3yr filly)
Santa Susana Stakes, San Vicente, Santa Margarita, Cleopatra and Arlington Handicaps, Match with Durazna, Washington Park Handicap, Hollywood Derby, Vanity Handicap.

1946 **Assault** (3yr colt)
Experimental Free Handicap No. 1, Wood Memorial, KENTUCKY DERBY, PREAKNESS, BELMONT and Dwyer Stakes, Pimlico Special, Westchester Handicap.

1947 **Armed** (6yr gelding)
Florida, McLennan, Widener, Gulfstream Park, Stars and Stripes and Arlington Handicaps, Whirlaway Stakes, Washington Park Handicap, Match with Assault, Sysonby Mile.

1948 **Citation** (3yr colt)
Seminole Handicap, Everglades Handicap, Flamingo, Chesapeake, Derby Trial, KENTUCKY DERBY,

PREAKNESS, Jersey and BELMONT Stakes, Stars and Stripes Handicap, American Derby, Sysonby Mile, Jockey Club Gold Cup, Gold Cup, Pimlico Special, Tanforan Handicap.

1949 **Capot** (3yr colt)
Chesapeake, PREAKNESS and BELMONT Stakes, Jerome Handicap, Sysonby Mile, Pimlico Special.
   Coaltown (4yr colt)
McLennan, Widener, Gulfstream Park, Edward Burke, Gallant Fox, Roger Williams, Stars and Stripes and Arlington Handicaps, Whirlaway Stakes, Washington Park Handicap.

1950 **Hill Prince** (3yr colt)
Experimental Free Handicap No. 1, Wood Memorial, Withers and PREAKNESS Stakes, American Derby, Jerome Handicap, Jockey Club Gold Cup, Sunset Handicap.

1951 **Counterpoint** (3yr colt)
Peter Pan Handicap, BELMONT Stakes, Lawrence Realization, Jockey Club Gold Cup, Empire Gold Cup, Empire City Handicap.

1952 **One Count** (3yr colt)
BELMONT Stakes, Travers Stakes, Jockey Club Gold Cup, Empire Gold Cup.
   Native Dancer (2yr colt)
Youthful, Flash, Saratoga Special, Grand Union Hotel, Hopeful, Anticipation, Futurity and East View Stakes.

1953 **Tom Fool** (4yr colt)
Sation, Joe H Palmer, Metropolitan, Suburban, Carter and Brooklyn Handicaps, Wilson, Whitney and Sysonby Stakes, Pimlico Special.

1954 **Native Dancer** (4yr colt)
Metropolitan Handicap, Oneonta Handicap.

1955 **Nashua** (3yr colt)
Flamingo, Florida Derby, Wood Memorial, PREAKNESS, BELMONT and Dwyer Stakes, Arlington Classic, Match with Swaps, Jockey Club Gold Cup.

1956 **Swaps** (4yr colt)
L A County Fair, Broward, Argonaut, Inglewood, American, Hollywood Gold Cup, Sunset and Washington Park Handicaps.

1957 **Bold Ruler** (3yr colt)
Bahamas, Flamingo, Wood Memorial and PREAKNESS Stakes, Times Square, Jerome, Vosburgh, Queens County, Benjamin Franklin and Trenton Handicaps.
   Dedicate (5yr horse)
John B Campbell Memorial Handicap, Monmouth Handicap, Woodward Stakes.

1958 **Round Table** (4yr colt)
San Fernando Stakes, Santa Anita Maturity, San Antonio, Santa Anita, Gulfstream Park, Caliente, Argonaut, Arch Ward Memorial, Laurence Armour Memorial, Arlington and Hawthorne Gold Cup Handicaps.

1959 **Sword Dancer** (3yr colt)
Metropolitan Handicap, BELMONT Stakes, Monmouth Handicap, Travers Stakes, Woodward Stakes, Jockey Club Gold Cup.

1960 **Kelso** (3yr gelding)
Choice Stakes, Jerome Handicap, Discovery Handicap, Lawrence Realization, Hawthorne Gold Cup, Jockey Club Gold Cup.

1961 **Kelso** (4yr gelding)
Metropolitan Handicap, Whitney Stakes, Suburban Handicap, Brooklyn Handicap, Woodward Stakes, Jockey Club Gold Cup.

1962 **Kelso** (5yr gelding)
Stymie Handicap, Woodward Stakes, Jockey Club Gold Cup, Governor's Plate Stakes.

1963 **Kelso** (6yr gelding)
Seminole, Gulfstream Park and John B Campbell Handicaps, Nassau County Stakes, Suburban Handicap, Whitney, Aqueduct and Woodward Stakes, Jockey Club Gold Cup.

1964 **Kelso** (7yr gelding)
Straight Face Handicap, Aqueduct Stakes, Jockey Club Gold Cup, Washington DC International

1965 **Roman Brother** (4yr gelding)
Woodward Stakes, Manhattan Handicap, Jockey Club Gold Cup.
   Moccasin (2yr filly)
Spinaway, Matron, Alcibiades, Selima and Gardenia Stakes.

1966 **Buckpasser** (3yr colt)
Everglades, Flamingo and Leonard Richards Stakes, Arlington Classic, Chicagoan Stakes, Brooklyn Handicap, American Derby, Travers Stakes, Woodward Stakes, Lawrence Realization, Jockey Club Gold Cup, Malibu Stakes.

1967 **Damascus** (3yr colt)
Bay Shore, Wood Memorial, PREAKNESS, BELMONT and Leonard Richards Stakes, Dwyer Handicap, American Derby, Travers, Aqueduct and Woodward Stakes, Jockey Club Gold Cup.

1968 **Dr Fager** (4yr colt)
Roseben Handicap, Californian Stakes, Suburban Handicap, Whitney Stakes, Washington Park, United Nations and Vosburgh Handicaps.

1969 **Arts and Letters** (3yr colt)
Everglades Stakes, Blue Grass Stakes, Metropolitan Handicap, BELMONT, Jim Dandy, Travers and Woodward Stakes, Jockey Club Gold Cup.

1970 **Fort Marcy** (6yr gelding)
Dixie, Bowling Green and United Nations Handicaps, Man o' War Stakes, Washington DC International.
   Personality (3yr colt)
Wood Memorial, PREAKNESS, Jersey Derby, Jim Dandy and Woodward Stakes.

1971 **Ack Ack** (5yr horse)
San Carlos Handicap, San Pasqual Handicap, San Antonio Stakes, Santa Anita, Hollywood Express, American and Hollywood Gold Cup Invitational Handicaps.

1972 **Secretariat** (2yr colt)
Sanford, Hopeful, Futurity, Laurel Futurity and Garden State Stakes.

1973 **Secretariat** (3yr colt)
Bay Shore, Gotham, KENTUCKY DERBY, PREAKNESS, BELMONT and Arlington Invitational Stakes, Marlboro Cup, Man o' War Stakes, Canadian International Championship.

1974 **Forego** (4yr gelding)

5-times champion

Kelso (1960 to 1964)

Triple champion

Forego (1974, 1975, 1976)

Donn, Gulfstream Park, Widener, Carter and Brooklyn Handicaps, Woodward Stakes, Vosburgh Handicap, Jockey Club Gold Cup.

1975 **Forego** (5yr gelding)
Seminole, Widener, Carter, Brooklyn and Suburban Handicaps, Woodward Stakes.

1976 **Forego** (6yr gelding)
Metropolitan, Nassau County, Brooklyn, Woodward and Marlboro Cup Handicaps.

1977 **Seattle Slew** (3yr colt)
Flamingo, Wood Memorial, KENTUCKY DERBY, PREAKNESS and BELMONT Stakes.

1978 **Affirmed** (3yr colt)
San Felipe Handicap, Santa Anita Derby, Hollywood Derby, KENTUCKY DERBY, PREAKNESS, BELMONT and Jim Dandy Stakes.

1979 **Affirmed** (4yr colt)
Charles H Strub Stakes, Santa Anita Handicap, Californian Stakes, Hollywood Gold Cup, Woodward Stakes, Jockey Club Gold Cup.

1980 **Spectacular Bid** (4yr colt)
Malibu, San Fernando and Charles H Strub Stakes, Santa Anita Handicap, Mervyn Le Roy Handicap, Californian Stakes, Washington Park Stakes, Amory L Haskell Handicap, Woodward Stakes.

1981 **John Henry** (6yr gelding)
San Luis Obispo Handicap, Santa Anita Handicap, San Luis Rey Stakes, Hollywood Invitational Handicap, Sword Dancer Stakes, Arlington Million, Jockey Club Gold Cup, Oak Tree Invitational Stakes.

1982 **Conquistador Cielo** (3yr colt)
Metropolitan Handicap, BELMONT, Dwyer and Jim Dandy Stakes.

1983 **All Along** (4yr filly)
Prix de l'Arc de Triomphe, Rothmans International, Turf Classic, Washington DC International.

1984 **John Henry** (9yr gelding)
Golden Gate, Hollywood Invitational and Sunset Handicaps, Arlington Million, Turf Classic, Ballantine's Scotch Classic.

1985 **Spend a Buck** (3yr colt)
Cherry Hill Mile, Garden State Stakes, KENTUCKY DERBY, Jersey Derby, Monmouth Handicap.

1986 **Lady's Secret** (4yr filly)
El Encino Stakes, La Canada Stakes, Santa Margarita, Shuvee, Molly Pitcher and Whitney Handicaps, Maskette Stakes, Ruffian Handicap, Beldame Stakes, Breeders' Cup Distaff.

1987 **Ferdinand** (4yr colt)
Hollywood Gold Cup, Cabrillo and Goodwood Handicaps, Breeders' Cup Classic.

1988 **Alysheba** (4yr colt)
Charles H Strub Stakes, Santa Anita, San Bernardino, Philip H Iselin, Woodward and Meadowlands Cup Handicaps, Breeders' Cup Classic.

Champion each year he raced

Secretariat (1972, 1973)

Closest decision

One vote for Slew o' Gold instead of John

The grey Lady's Secret ranks among the best American fillies of recent years after winning 10 races in her 1986 Horse of the Year campaign. (All-Sport)

Henry in 1984, and for Theatrical instead of Ferdinand in 1987, would have given them the title.

Oldest

9 years – John Henry (1984)
7 years – Kelso (1964)

Youngest

2 years – Native Dancer (1952), Moccasin (1965), Secretariat (1972)

Fillies

Twilight Tear (1944), Busher (1945), Moccasin (1965), All Along (1983), Lady's Secret (1986).

Geldings

Armed (1947), Kelso (1960 to 1964), Roman Brother (1965), Fort Marcy (1970), Forego (1974, 1975, 1976), John Henry (1981, 1984)

Grey

Native Dancer (1952, 1954), Spectacular Bid (1980), Lady's Secret (1986)

Most wins in championship season

19 – Citation (1948)
14 – Twilight Tear (1944), Round Table (1958)

Unbeaten in championship season

10 races – Tom Fool (1953)
 9 races – Native Dancer (1952), Spectacular Bid (1980)
 8 races – War Admiral (1937), Moccasin (1965)
 6 races – Count Fleet (1943)
 3 races – Native Dancer (1954)

Least successful

Dedicate won only 4 of his 12 races in 1957.

Most active

22 races – Whirlaway (1942)
20 races – Whirlaway (1941), Citation (1948), Round Table (1958)

Least active

3 races – Native Dancer (1954)

Earliest retirements

5 June – Count Fleet (1943)
3 July – Seattle Slew (1977)

Most versatile

Dr Fager (1968) was also voted champion on grass and champion sprinter

Campaigned exclusively in California

Ack Ack (1971)

Campaigned exclusively on grass

All Along (1983)

Trained in France

All Along (1983)

Most successful owners

6 wins – Calumet Farm (Warren Wright): Whirlaway (twice), Twilight Tear, Armed, Citation, Coaltown
5 wins – Bohemia Stable (Mrs Allaire duPont): Kelso (5 times)

Most successful breeders

6 wins – Calumet Farm (Warren Wright): Whirlaway (twice), Twilight Tear, Armed, Citation, Coaltown
5 wins – Mrs Allaire duPont: Kelso (5 times)

Most successful trainers

5 wins – Carl Hanford: Kelso (5 times)
3 wins – Ben Jones: Whirlaway (twice), Twilight Tear
Jimmy Jones: Armed, Citation, Coaltown
Jim Fitzsimmons: Granville, Nashua, Bold Ruler
Elliott Burch: Sword Dancer, Arts and Letters, Fort Marcy

Most successful sires

5 wins – Your Host: Kelso (5 times)
4 wins – Bull Lea: Twilight Tear, Armed, Citation, Coaltown

Australia

There are two Horse of the Year polls in Australia. In 1968/69 the Victoria Racing Club inaugurated a poll among officials of the major racing clubs, and in 1976/77 the Ansett award was established, determined by members of the Australian Racing Writers' Association. The Horses of the Year, with their age, sex and most important wins that season, have been as follows, with the VRC champion preceding the Ansett champion where the two polls have disagreed:

1968/69 Vain (2yr colt)
Maribyrnong Plate, Merson Cooper, VRC Sires' Produce, Golden Slipper and Champagne Stakes.
1969/70 Rain Lover (5yr horse)
Craiglee Stakes, Underwood Stakes, Melbourne Cup, St George Stakes, Queen's Plate, Autumn Stakes.
1970/71 Gay Icarus (3yr gelding)
Werribee Intermediate Handicap, Burwood Handicap, Blamey Stakes, St George Stakes, Australian Cup, Chipping Norton Stakes, Australasian Champion Stakes, AJC Queen Elizabeth Stakes, (2nd) Victoria Derby.
1971/72 Gunsynd (4yr colt)
Flying, Epsom, Toorak and George Adams Handicaps, Sandown Cup, Frederick Clissold Handicap, Futurity Stakes, Queen's Plate, VRC Queen Elizabeth Stakes, Doncaster Handicap.
1972/73 Dayana (3yr gelding)
Advanced Handicap, Graduation Stakes, Royal Park Graduation Stakes, South Australian Derby, Geelong Derby Trial, Victoria Derby, West Australian Derby, Australian Derby, Perth Cup.
1973/74 Taj Rossi (3yr colt)
Ascot Vale Stakes, Carrum Handicap, Moonee Valley Stakes, WS Cox Plate, Victoria Derby, George Adams Handicap, Sandown Guineas.
1974/75 Leilani (4yr filly)
Turnbull Stakes, Toorak Handicap, Caulfield Cup, LKS Mackinnon Stakes, Queen's Cup, CF Orr Stakes, St George Stakes, Queen's Plate, Australian Cup, (2nd) Melbourne Cup.
1975/76 Lord Dudley (3yr colt)
Freeway, William Reid and Blamey Stakes, Australian Cup, VRC St Leger.
1976/77 Surround (3yr filly)
Ailsa Handicap, Ascot Vale Stakes, Moonee Valley Stakes, Caulfield Guineas, WS Cox Plate, VRC Oaks, CF Orr, Blamey and Alister Clark Stakes, AJC Oaks, Queensland Oaks, Grand Prix Stakes.
1977/78 Maybe Mahal (5yr mare)

Strawberry Road, Australia's Horse of the Year in 1982/83, parades before the 1984 Prix de l'Arc de Triomphe, in which he finished fifth. (Gerry Cranham)

Lightning Stakes, Newmarket Handicap, Doncaster Handicap.
1978/79 Manikato (3yr gelding)
Ascot Vale Stakes, Marlboro Cup, Caulfield Guineas, William Reid, CF Orr, Futurity and George Ryder Stakes, Rothmans Hundred Thousand.
1979/80 Kingston Town (3yr gelding)
Commissionaire Handicap, Peter Pan, Gloaming, Spring Champion, Express and Heritage Stakes, Rosehill Guineas, HE Tancred Stakes, AJC Derby, Sydney Cup, Grand Prix Stakes, Queensland Derby, (2nd) Victoria Derby.
1980/81 Hyperno (7yr gelding)
Caulfield Stakes, Queen Elizabeth Stakes, St George Stakes, Blamey Quality Handicap, Australian Cup, Rawson Stakes, (2nd) Caulfield Cup.
1981/82 Rose of Kingston (3yr filly)
Ascot Vale Stakes, VRC Oaks, Tauto Handicap, Queen of the South Stakes, Australasian Oaks, AJC Derby.
1982/83 Strawberry Road (3yr colt)
Show Ego Improvers', Bob Readings Novice and Governor Hunter Transition Handicaps, Prestbury Graduation Stakes, Rosehill Guineas, AJC Derby, Channel 7 Stakes, Power Hotels Quality Handicap, Queensland Derby.
Gurner's Lane (4yr gelding)

Winfield Gold Cup, Caulfield Cup, Melbourne Cup.
1983/84 Emancipation (4yr filly)
Premiere, Chelmsford, Hill, George Main, Apollo, Chipping Norton, Rosemount Wines Classic, George Ryder and All Aged Stakes.
1984/85 Red Anchor (3yr colt)
Roman Consul Stakes, Moonee Valley Stakes, Caulfield Guineas, WS Cox Plate, Victoria Derby, Apollo Stakes.
1985/86 Bounding Away (2yr filly)
Sledmere Handicap, Blue Diamond Prelude, Blue Diamond, Magic Night, Golden Slipper and Champagne Stakes.
1986/87 Bonecrusher (4yr gelding)
Underwood Stakes, Caulfield Stakes, WS Cox Plate, Australian Cup.
Placid Ark (3yr gelding)
Landcruiser Graduation Stakes, City Belmont Quality Sprint Handicap, Ansett Air Freight-Quality Handicap, Sir Ernest Lee-Steere Classic, Lightning Stakes, Oakleigh Plate, Newmarket Handicap, Canterbury Stakes.
1987/88 Beau Zam (3yr colt)
Hill, Spring Champion, Segenhoe, H E Tancred, AJC Derby, AJC St Leger and Queen Elizabeth Stakes.
1988/89 Research (3yr filly)
Flight Stakes, Wakeful Stakes, VRC Oaks, Storm Queen Stakes, AJC Derby, AJC Oaks.

France

France's Horses of the Year are chosen in a poll of racing journalists conducted by the magazine *Courses & Elevage.*

Flat

1979 **Three Troikas** (3yr filly)	1984 **Northern Trick** (3yr filly)
1980 **Detroit** (3yr filly)	1985 **Sagace** (5yr horse)
1981 **Bikala** (3yr colt)	1986 **Dancing Brave** (3yr colt)
1982 **Saint Cyrien** (2yr colt)	1987 **Miesque** (3yr filly)
1983 **All Along** (4yr filly)	1988 **Miesque** (4yr filly)

Jumping

1979 **Chinco** (7yr gelding)
1980 **Paiute** (7yr gelding)
1981 **Metatero** (8yr gelding)
1982 **Metatero** (9yr gelding)
1983 **Bayonnet** (4yr colt)
1984 **Le Pontif** (7yr gelding)
1985 **Sir Gain** (6yr gelding)
1986 **Gacko** (5yr gelding)
1987 **Marly River** (4yr colt)
1988 **Katko** (5yr gelding)

West Germany

Flat

1957 **Thila** (3yr filly)
1958 **Orsini** (4yr colt)
1959 **Obermaat** (5yr horse)
1960 **Waidmann** (4yr colt)
1961 **Baalim** (3yr colt)
1962 **Windbruch** (5yr horse)
1963 **Mercurius** (3yr colt)
1964 **Mercurius** (4yr colt)
1965 **Kronzeuge** (4yr colt)
1966 **Ilix** (3yr colt)
1967 **Luciano** (3yr colt)
1968 **Luciano** (4yr colt)
1969 **Hitchcock** (3yr colt)
1970 **Alpenkönig** (3yr colt)
1971 **Lombard** (4yr colt)
1972 **Lombard** (5yr horse)
1973 **Athenagoras** (3yr colt)
1974 **Marduk** (3yr colt)
1975 **Star Appeal** (5yr horse)
1976 **Windwurf** (4yr colt)
1977 **Windwurf** (5yr horse)
1978 **Esclavo** (2yr colt)
1979 **Königsstuhl** (3yr colt)
1980 **Nebos** (4yr colt)
1981 **Orofino** (3yr colt)
1982 **Orofino** (4yr colt)
1983 **Orofino** (5yr horse)
1984 **Las Vegas** (3yr filly)
1985 **Acatenango** (3yr colt)
1986 **Acatenango** (4yr colt)
1987 **Acatenango** (5yr horse)
1988 **Kondor** (4yr colt)

Jumping

1980 **Romping To Work** (8yr gelding)
1981 **Bonito** (7yr horse)
1982 **Yolly Boy** (5yr gelding)
1983 **Ariporo** (5yr gelding)
1984 **Stragon** (4yr gelding)
1985 **Ottilie** (8yr mare)
1986 **Ottilie** (9yr mare)
1987 **Constantin** (7yr horse)
1988 **Cognac** (6yr gelding)

Canada

Canada's Horse of the Year is chosen in a poll of racing journalists conducted by the Toronto edition of *Daily Racing Form*.

1951 **Bull Page** (4yr colt)
1952 **Canadiana** (2yr filly)
1953 **King Maple** (2yr colt)
1954 **Queen's Own** (3yr colt)
1955 **Ace Marine** (3yr colt)
1956 **Canadian Champ** (3yr colt)
1957 **Hartney** (6yr gelding)
1958 **Nearctic** (4yr colt)
1959 **Wonder Where** (3yr filly)
1960 **Victoria Park** (3yr colt)
1961 **Hidden Treasure** (4yr colt)
1962 **Crafty Lace** (3yr gelding)
1963 **Canebora** (3yr colt)
1964 **Northern Dancer** (3yr colt)
1965 **George Royal** (4yr colt)
1966 **Victorian Era** (4yr colt)
1967 **He's a Smoothie** (4yr colt)
1968 **Viceregal** (2yr colt)
1969 **Jumpin Joseph** (3yr colt)

1970 **Fanfreluche** (3yr filly)
1971 **Lauries Dancer** (3yr filly)
1972 **La Prévoyante** (2yr filly)
1973 **Kennedy Road** (5yr horse)
1974 **L'Enjoleur** (2yr colt)
1975 **L'Enjoleur** (3yr colt)
1976 **Norcliffe** (3yr colt)
1977 **L'Alezane** (2yr filly)
1978 **Overskate** (3yr colt)
1979 **Overskate** (4yr colt)
1980 **Glorious Song** (4yr filly)
1981 **Deputy Minister** (2yr colt)
1982 **Frost King** (4yr gelding)
1983 **Travelling Victor** (4yr colt)
1984 **Dauphin Fabuleux** (2yr colt)
1985 **Imperial Choice** (3yr gelding)
1986 **Ruling Angel** (2yr filly)
1987 **Afleet** (3yr colt)
1988 **Play The King** (5yr gelding)

New Zealand

1973/74 **Battle Heights** (6yr gelding)
1974/75 **Show Gate** (5yr mare)
1975/76 **Balmerino** (3yr colt)
1976/77 **Show Gate** (7yr mare)
1977/78 **Uncle Remus** (3yr colt)
1978/79 **La Mer** (5yr mare)
1979/80 **Little Brown Jug** (3yr colt)
1980/81 **Drum** (5yr gelding)

1981/82 **Altitude** (3yr colt)
1982/83 **Our Flight** (3yr filly)
1983/84 **Kiwi** (6yr gelding)
1984/85 **Hunterville** (9yr gelding)
1985/86 **Bonecrusher** (3yr gelding)
1986/87 **Tidal Light** (4yr filly)
1987/88 **Courier Bay** (5yr gelding)
1988/89 **Poetic Prince** (4yr gelding)

Divisional Champions

European Champions: Official Ratings

In 1977 the official Handicappers in Great Britain, Ireland and France jointly compiled the first International Classifications, handicaps of the best horses aged 3 and above who had raced in those countries during the season. The first International Classification of 2-year-olds was published in 1978 and the

European Champions: Official Ratings

	2-Y-O Colt	2-Y-O Filly	3-Y-O Colt	3-Y-O Filly
1977	—	—	**Alleged** Ireland 138	**Dunfermline** GB 130
				Madelia France 130
1978	**Tromos** GB 131	**Sigy** France 129	**Ile de Bourbon** GB 135	**Swiss Maid** GB 131
1979	**Dragon** France 123	**Mrs Penny** GB 121	**Troy** GB 136	**Three Troikas** France 137
	Monteverdi Ireland 123	**Princesse Lida** France 121		
1980	**Storm Bird** Ireland 128	**Marwell** GB 122	**Moorestyle** GB 131	**Detroit** France 128
		Tolmi GB 122		
1981	**Green Forest** France 128	**Circus Ring** GB 119	**Shergar** GB 140	**Marwell** GB 130
		Height of Fashion GB 119		
		Play It Safe France 119		
1982	**Diesis** GB 127	**Ma Biche** France 121	**Golden Fleece** Ireland 134	**Akiyda** France 129
1983	**El Gran Senor** Ireland 128	**Almeira** France 120	**Shareef Dancer** GB 133	**Habibti** GB 131
1984	**Kala Dancer** GB 124	**Triptych** France 122	**El Gran Senor** Ireland 138	**Northern Trick** France 127
1985	**Bakharoff** GB 123	**Baiser Volé** France 120	**Slip Anchor** GB 135	**Oh So Sharp** GB 130
1986	**Reference Point** GB 127	**Forest Flower** GB 125	**Dancing Brave** GB 141	**Sonic Lady** GB 127
1987	**Warning** GB 125	**Ravinella** France 125	**Reference Point** GB 135	**Miesque** France 132
1988	**High Estate** GB 125	**Tersa** France 118	**Warning** GB 133	**Diminuendo** GB 128
		Tessla GB 118		

handicaps were extended to include Italy and West Germany in 1985.

The ratings express racing merit in pounds and all horses with the same rating are deemed to be of equal merit regardless of age, sex or distance requirements. The ratings are calculated on an unvarying scale so that champions of different years can be compared. In 1986 the ratings were raised by 40 lb all round so, for the sake of comparison, the ratings for 1977–85 in the table below have been raised accordingly. The official European champions in each age and sex category, with the country in which they were trained and their rating, have been as follows:

Older Male	*Older Female*	*Best Horse*	
Balmerino (5) NZ/USA/GB 134	**Flying Water** (4) France 131	**Alleged**	1977
Orange Bay (5) GB 134			
Alleged (4) Ireland 140	**Sanedtki** (4) France 131	**Alleged**	1978
	Trillion (4) France 131		
Ile de Bourbon (4) GB 135	**Trillion** (5) France 127	**Three Troikas**	1979
		Moorestyle	1980
Ela-Mana-Mou (4) GB 130	**Three Troikas** (4) France 127		
Northjet (4) France 132	**Gold River** (4) France 130	**Shergar**	1981
Kalaglow (4) GB 133	**April Run** (4) France 128	**Golden Fleece**	1982
Diamond Shoal (4) GB 129	**All Along** (4) France 132	**Shareef Dancer**	1983
Teenoso (4) GB 135	**Cormorant Wood** (4) GB 128	**El Gran Senor**	1984
Rainbow Quest (4) GB 133	**Pebbles** (4) GB 132	**Slip Anchor**	1985
Sagace (5) France 133			
Shardari (4) GB 132	**Triptych** (4) France 130	**Dancing Brave**	1986
Mtoto (4) GB 134	**Triptych** (5) France 128	**Reference Point**	1987
Mtoto (5) GB 131	**Miesque** (4) France 132	**Warning**	1988
Tony Bin (5) Italy 131			

Above *Warning (Pat Eddery) spreadeagles his rivals in the Queen Elizabeth II Stakes over Ascot's round mile, and proves himself the best horse to race on the Flat in Europe in 1988. (Gerry Cranham)*

European Champions: Timeform Ratings

In 1947 the Timeform organization in Halifax, Yorkshire, started to publish, in its *Racehorses of 19—* annual, comments and ratings for each horse that had run on the Flat in Great Britain during the year, and for the best horses in Ireland and France. For a full explanation of Timeform ratings and symbols, see pages 85 and 98.

European Champions: Timeform Ratings

	2-Y-O Colt	2-Y-O Filly	3-Y-O Colt	3-Y-O Filly
1947	**My Babu** GB 136	**Masaka** GB 126	**Tudor Minstrel** GB 144	**Port Blanc** GB 122
1948	**Abernant** GB 133	**Musette** France 124? / **Starry Scene** GB 121	**Black Tarquin** GB 134	**Careless Nora** GB 131
1949	**Masked Light** GB 132	**Diableretta** GB 132	**Abernant** GB 138	**Coronation** France 135
1950	**Big Dipper** GB 133	**Djelfa** France 126 / **Sanguine** France 126	**Tantième** France 136	**Diableretta** GB 132
1951	**Windy City** Ireland 142	**Zabara** GB 134	**Arctic Prince** GB 135 / **Sicambre** France 135 / **Supreme Court** GB 135 / **Tulyar** GB 134	**Belle of All** GB 124 / **Djelfa** France 124 / **Neasham Belle** GB 124 / **Lady Sophia** GB 130
1952	**Dragon Blanc** France 132 / **Nearula** GB 132	**Neemah** GB 131		
1953	**The Pie King** Ireland 132	**Cordova** France 129	**Pinza** GB 137	**La Sorellina** France 128
1954	**Beau Prince** France 131 / **Hugh Lupus** Ireland 131 / **Our Babu** GB 131	**Gloria Nicky** GB 127	**Never Say Die** GB 137	**Philante** France 125
1955	**Philius** France 131 / **Verrières** France 131	**Star of India** GB 138	**Pappa Fourway** GB 139	**Meld** GB 128
1956	**Skindles Hotel** Ireland 134	**Sarcelle** GB 131	**Gilles de Retz** GB 132 / **Philius** France 132	**Apollonia** France 132
1957	**Major Portion** GB 128 / **Tarquin** France 128	**Texana** France 136	**Crepello** GB 136	**Refined** Ireland 131
1958	**Carnoustie** GB 132	**Rosalba** GB 132	**Alcide** GB 135	**Bella Paola** France 131
1959	**Sing Sing** GB 134	**Never Too Late** France 130	**Herbager** France 136	**Petite Etoile** GB 134
1960	**Floribunda** Ireland 135	**Kathy Too** Ireland 131	**Charlottesville** France 135	**Marguerite Vernaut** Italy 129
1961	**Abdos** France 134p	**La Tendresse** Ireland 135	**Molvedo** Italy 137	**Sweet Solera** GB 127
1962	**Le Mesnil** France 131? / **Crocket** GB 130	**Hula Dancer** France 133	**Arctic Storm** Ireland 134 / **Hethersett** GB 134	**Gay Mairi** GB 131 / **Secret Step** GB 131
1963	**Santa Claus** Ireland 133+ / **Showdown** GB 133	**Texanita** France 128	**Ragusa** Ireland 137	**Hula Dancer** France 133 / **Noblesse** Ireland 133
1964	**Grey Dawn** France 132	**Fall In Love** France 126	**Prince Royal** Italy/France 134	**La Bamba** France 129
1965	**Soleil** France 133 / **Young Emperor** Ireland 133	**Soft Angels** GB 124	**Sea-Bird** France 145	**Aunt Edith** GB 128
1966	**Bold Lad** Ireland 133	**Silver Cloud** France 125	**Danseur** France 134	**Caterina** GB 124
1967	**Petingo** GB 135	**Sovereign** GB 129	**Reform** GB 132	**Casaque Grise** France 126
1968	**Ribofilio** GB 130 / **Yelapa** France 130	**Saraca** France 125	**Vaguely Noble** France 140	**Roselière** France 127
1969	**Nijinsky** Ireland 131	**Mange Tout** GB 125	**Habitat** GB 134	**Flossy** France 129
1970	**My Swallow** GB 134	**Cawston's Pride** GB 131	**Nijinsky** Ireland 138	**Highest Hopes** GB 129 / **Miss Dan** France 129
1971	**Deep Diver** GB 134	**First Bloom** France 129	**Mill Reef** GB 141 / **Brigadier Gerard** GB 141	**Pistol Packer** France 133
1972	**Simbir** France 130 / **Targowice** France 130	**Jacinth** GB 133	**Deep Diver** GB 134 / **Sallust** GB 134	**San San** France 133
1973	**Apalachee** Ireland 137	**Hippodamia** France 130	**Thatch** Ireland 136	**Allez France** France 132 / **Dahlia** France 132
1974	**Grundy** GB 134	**Broadway Dancer** France 131	**Caracolero** France 131 / **Dankaro** France 131 / **Nonoalco** France 131 / **Sagaro** France 131	**Comtesse de Loir** France 131
1975	**Manado** France 130	**Theia** France 128	**Grundy** GB 137	**Rose Bowl** GB 133
1976	**Blushing Groom** France 131	**Cloonlara** Ireland 130	**Youth** France 135	**Pawneese** France 131
1977	**Try My Best** Ireland 130p	**Cherry Hinton** GB 125	**Alleged** Ireland 137	**Dunfermline** GB 133
1978	**Tromos** GB 134	**Sigy** France 132	**Ile de Bourbon** GB 133	**Swiss Maid** GB 129
1979	**Monteverdi** Ireland 129	**Aryenne** France 120	**Troy** GB 137	**Three Troikas** France 133
1980	**Storm Bird** Ireland 134	**Marwell** GB 124	**Moorestyle** GB 137	**Detroit** France 131

The 7-year-old Marsyas was the best older horse in Europe in 1947, for he decisively beat Souverain when winning the Prix du Cadran for the fourth consecutive time, but he was not included in the first Timeform annual. Timeform's European champions in each age and sex category, with the country in which they were trained and their rating, have been as follows:

Older Male	Older Female	Best Horse	
Chanteur (5) France 135 **Souverain** (4) France 135 **The Bug** (4) GB 135	**Ann Denise** (4) GB 119	**Tudor Minstrel**	1947
Arbar (4) France 135 **Tenerani** (4) Italy 135	**Port Blanc** (4) GB 119	**Arbar** and **Tenerani**	1948
Alycidon (4) GB 138	**High Beacon** (5) GB 113	**Alycidon** and **Abernant**	1949
Abernant (4) GB 142	**Coronation** (4) France 132	**Abernant**	1950
Tantième (4) France 135	**Val d'Assa** (4) GB 121	**Windy City**	1951
Dynamiter (4) France 133 **Nuccio** (4) France 133 **Zucchero** (4) GB 133	**Wayside Singer** (5) GB 117	**Tulyar**	1952
Silnet (4) France 131 **Zucchero** (5) GB 131 §	**Fairy Flax** (4) GB 127	**Pinza**	1953
Aureole (4) GB 132	**Banassa** (4) France 128	**Never Say Die**	1954
Princely Gift (4) GB 137	**Rosa Bonheur** (6) France 124	**Pappa Fourway**	1955
Ribot (4) Italy 142	**Ephemeral** (4) GB 126	**Ribot**	1956
Oroso (4) France 133	**Midget** (4) France 128	**Crepello** and **Texana**	1957
Ballymoss (4) Ireland 136	**Gladness** (5) Ireland 131	**Ballymoss**	1958
Right Boy (5) GB 137	**Gladness** (6) Ireland 128	**Right Boy**	1959
Bleep-Bleep (4) GB 134	**Petite Etoile** (4) GB 134	**Charlottesville** and **Floribunda**	1960
Pandofell (4) GB 132 **St Paddy** (4) GB 132	**Petite Etoile** (5) GB 131	**Molvedo**	1961
Match (4) France 135	**Crisper** (4) GB 126	**Match**	1962
Exbury (4) France 138	**Secret Step** (4) GB 128	**Exbury**	1963
Relko (4) France 136	**Matatina** (4) GB 124	**Relko**	1964
Free Ride (4) France 129 **Indiana** (4) GB 129	**Astaria** (4) France 123	**Sea-Bird**	1965
Diatome (4) France 132	**Aunt Edith** (4) GB 126	**Danseur**	1966
Busted (4) GB 134	**Parthian Glance** (4) France 119	**Petingo**	1967
Royal Palace (4) GB 131	**Bamboozle** (4) GB 114 **Secret Ray** (4) GB 114 **Park Top** (4) GB 114	**Vaguely Noble**	1968
Levmoss (4) Ireland 133	**Park Top** (5) GB 131	**Habitat**	1969
Balidar (4) GB 133	**Park Top** (6) GB 129	**Nijinsky**	1970
Caro (4) France 133	**Miss Dan** (4) France 124	**Mill Reef** and **Brigadier Gerard**	1971
Brigadier Gerard (4) GB 144	**Abergwaun** (4) Ireland 128	**Brigadier Gerard**	1972
Rheingold (4) GB 137	**Attica Meli** (4) GB 125	**Rheingold** and **Apalachee**	1973
Admetus (4) France 133 **Margouillat** (4) France 133	**Allez France** (4) France 136	**Allez France**	1974
Bustino (4) GB 136	**Lianga** (4) France 133	**Grundy**	1975
Trepan (4) France 133? **Lochnager** (4) GB 132	**Ivanjica** (4) France 132	**Youth**	1976
Balmerino (5) NZ/USA/GB 133 **Sagaro** (6) France 133 **Alleged** (4) Ireland 138	**Flying Water** (4) France 132	**Alleged**	1977
	Sanedtki (4) France 129 **Trillion** (4) France 129	**Alleged**	1978
Ile de Bourbon (4) GB 133	**Trillion** (5) France 124	**Troy**	1979
Le Moss (5) GB 135	**Three Troikas** (4) France 128	**Moorestyle**	1980

	2-Y-O Colt	2-Y-O Filly	3-Y-O Colt	3-Y-O Filly
1981	**Wind and Wuthering** GB 132	**Circus Ring** GB 122	**Shergar** GB 140	**Marwell** GB 133
1982	**Diesis** GB 133	**Ma Biche** France 123	**Assert** Ireland 134	**Akiyda** France 131
			Green Forest France 134	**Time Charter** GB 131
1983	**El Gran Senor** Ireland 131	**Treizième** France 121	**Shareef Dancer** GB 135	**Habibti** GB 136
1984	**Kala Dancer** GB 129	**Triptych** France 125	**El Gran Senor** Ireland 136	**Northern Trick** France 131
	Law Society Ireland 129			
1985	**Huntingdale** GB 132	**Femme Elite** France 124	**Slip Anchor** GB 136	**Oh So Sharp** GB 131
1986	**Reference Point** GB 132	**Forest Flower** GB 127	**Dancing Brave** GB 140	**Darara** France 129
				Sonic Lady GB 129
1987	**Warning** GB 127p	**Ravinella** France 121p	**Reference Point** GB 139	**Indian Skimmer** GB 132
1988	**Prince of Dance** GB 128	**Pass the Peace** GB 116p	**Warning** GB 136	**Diminuendo** GB 126
	Scenic GB 128	**Tessla** GB 116p		

British Champions: Free Handicaps

The Free Handicap is an official assessment of the best 2-year-olds in Great Britain. In 1924, and every year from 1928, the handicap has been published at the end of the season, so the top-weight is recognized as the champion 2-year-old. In 1980 the handicap became the European Free Handicap, as it was opened to all horses included in the International Classification of 2-year-olds even if they had not run in Great Britain; champions Green Forest, Play It Safe, Almeira, Triptych, Baiser Volé and Tersa qualified on that count. The Free Handicap top-weights with their margin of superiority expressed in pounds and the best of the opposite sex, with the number of pounds they were rated below the champion, have been as follows:

	Top weight	Best of opposite sex
1924	**Saucy Sue** (filly) (1)	**Picaroon** (colt) (1)
1928	**Tiffin** (filly) (1)	**Costaki Pasha** (colt) (1)
		Mr Jinks (colt) (1)
1929	**Diolite** (1)	**Fair Isle** (4)
1930	**Jacopo**	**Turtle Soup** (6)
	Portlaw	
1931	**Mannamead**	**Gela** (14)
	Orwell	
1932	**Myrobella** (filly) (3)	**Manitoba** (colt) (6)
1933	**Colombo** (7)	**Campanula** (7)
1934	**Bahràm** (1)	**Caretta** (12)
1935	**Bala Hissar** (1)	**Sansonnet** (6)
1936	**Foray** (1)	**Carissa** (8)
1937	**Portmarnock** (1)	**Radiant** (4)
1938	**Foxbrough** (4)	**Scenery** (8)
1939	**Tant Mieux*** (1)	**Golden Penny** (3)
1940	**Poise** (gelding) (3)	**Keystone** (3)
1941	**Sun Chariot** (filly) (1)	**Big Game** (colt) (1)
1942	**Lady Sybil** (filly) (1)	**Nasrullah** (colt) (1)
1943	**Orestes** (2)	**Fair Fame** (3)
1944	**Dante** (1)	**Isle of Capri** (4)
1945	**Gulf Stream** (2)	**Neolight** (3)
1946	**Tudor Minstrel** (2)	**Missolonghi*** (12)
1947	**My Babu** (2)	**Fair Dinah** (10)
1948	**Abernant** (2)	**Ballisland** (10)
		Integrity (10)
1949	**Masked Light** (2)	**Diabletta*** (6)
1950	**Big Dipper** (2)	**Belle of All** (8)
		Gamble in Gold (8)
1951	**Windy City** (5)	**Zabara** (5)
1952	**Nearula** (2)	**Bebe Grande** (2)
		Neemah (2)
1953	**The Pie King** (2)	**Sixpence** (7)
1954	**Our Babu** (1)	**Gloria Nicky** (3)
1955	**Star of India** (filly) (4)	**Buisson Ardent** (colt) (4)
1956	**Sarcelle** (filly) (2)	**Pipe of Peace** (colt) (2)
1957	**Major Portion** (1)	**Rich and Rare** (3)
1958	**Tudor Melody** (2)	**Lindsay** (5)
		Rosalba (5)

	Top weight	Best of opposite sex
1959	**Sing Sing** (3)	**Paddy's Sister** (6)
1960	**Opaline** (filly) (1)	**Typhoon** (colt) (1)
1961	**La Tendresse** (filly) (4)	**Miralgo** (colt) (6)
1962	**Crocket** (3)	**Noblesse** (3)
1963	**Talahasse** (1)	**Mesopotamia** (5)
1964	**Double Jump** (2)	**Night Off** (9)
1965	**Young Emperor** (4)	**Soft Angels** (7)
1966	**Bold Lad** (3)	**Fleet** (11)
1967	**Petingo** (1)	**Sovereign** (6)
1968	**Ribofilio** (2)	**Folle Rousse** (4)
1969	**Nijinsky** (2)	**Humble Duty** (7)
1970	**My Swallow** (1)	**Cawston's Pride** (3)
1971	**Crowned Prince** (2)	**Rose Dubarry** (6)
1972	**Jacinth** (filly) (3)	**Noble Decree** (colt) (3)
1973	**Apalachee** (5)	**Bitty Girl** (13)
		Gentle Thoughts (13)
		Melchbourne (13)
1974	**Grundy** (1)	**Cry of Truth** (2)
1975	**Wollow** (5)	**Pasty** (8)
1976	**J O Tobin** (5)	**Durtal** (13)
1977	**Try My Best** (3)	**Cherry Hinton** (4)
1978	**Tromos** (5)	**Devon Ditty** (6)
		Formulate (6)
1979	**Monteverdi** (1)	**Mrs Penny** (2)
1980	**Storm Bird** (1)	**Marwell** (6)
		Tolmi (6)
1981	**Green Forest** (3)	**Circus Ring** (9)
		Height of Fashion (9)
		Play It Safe (9)
1982	**Diesis** (1)	**Ma Biche** (6)
1983	**El Gran Senor** (1)	**Almeira** (8)
1984	**Kala Dancer** (1)	**Triptych** (2)
1985	**Bakharoff** (1)	**Baiser Volé** (3)
1986	**Reference Point** (2)	**Forest Flower** (2)
1987	**Ravinella** (filly)	
	Warning	
1988	**High Estate** (1)	**Tersa** (7)
		Tessla (7)

* 3 French-trained champions were omitted from the Free Handicap: Djebel, who beat Tant Mieux in the 1939 Middle Park Stakes; Djerba, who beat Missolonghi in the 1946 Cheveley Park Stakes; and Corejada, who beat Diableretta in the 1949 Cheveley Park Stakes.

Biggest margin of superiority: Colombo was rated 7 lb clear of the second-best, champion filly Campanula, in 1933. In the days when the handicap was published before the end of the season, Tetratema was rated 12 lb clear in 1919 and his sire The Tetrarch was rated 10 lb clear in 1913.

Fillies dominant: Myrobella, Betty and Brown Betty were all rated above champion colt Manitoba in 1932.

Best guide: Sun Chariot, Big Game and Watling Street, the first 3 in the 1941 Free Handicap, won all 5 Classics between them in 1942.

Older Male	Older Female	Best Horse	
Northjet (4) France 136	**Gold River** (4) France 132	**Shergar**	1981
Ardross (6) GB 134	**April Run** (4) France 130	**Ardross, Assert** and **Green Forest**	1982
Diamond Shoal (4) GB 130	**All Along** (4) France 134	**Habibti**	1983
Sagace (4) France 135	**Cormorant Wood** (4) GB 130	**El Gran Senor**	1984
Teenoso (4) GB 135			
Never So Bold (5) GB 135	**Pebbles** (4) GB 135	**Slip Anchor**	1985
Shardari (4) GB 134	**Triptych** (4) France 132	**Dancing Brave**	1986
Mtoto (4) GB 134	**Triptych** (5) France 133	**Reference Point**	1987
Mtoto (5) GB 134	**Indian Skimmer** (4) GB 133	**Warning**	1988
Tony Bin (5) Italy 134	**Miesque** (4) France 133		

El Gran Senor (Pat Eddery) proves himself the best horse of 1984 in Europe with a scintillating victory in the 2000 Guineas at Newmarket. (All-Sport)

The Free Handicap for 3-year-olds, originally confined to middle-distance performers, was opened to horses of all distance requirements in 1972, and an equivalent handicap for older horses was established in 1974. These domestic British handicaps were subsumed in the International Classifications in 1977.

3-Year-Olds

	Top weight	Best of opposite sex
1972	**Deep Diver**	**Attica Meli**
1973	**Dahlia** (filly)	
	Thatch	
1974	**Take a Reef**	**Dibidale**
1975	**Grundy**	**May Hill**
		Rose Bowl
1976	**Vitigès**	**Pawneese**

Older horses

1974	**Dahlia** (4) (filly)	**Admetus** (4) (gelding)
1975	**Bustino** (4)	**Lianga** (4)
	Flirting Around (4)	
1976	**Sagaro** (5)	**Rose Bowl** (4)

British Champion Jumpers: Official Ratings

FREE HANDICAP HURDLE

The Free Handicap Hurdle is the jumping equivalent of the Free Handicap on the Flat. At the end of each season since 1968/69, the best 4-year-old hurdlers in Great Britain have been assessed for a handicap run at Chepstow in the autumn. The following horses have been awarded top weight:

1968/69	**Coral Diver**	1980/81	**Broadsword**
1969/70	**Frozen Alive**	1981/82	**Shiny Copper**
1970/71	**Boxer**	1982/83	**Sabin du Loir**
1971/72	**Official**	1983/84	**Clarinbridge**
1972/73	**Moonlight Bay**		**Fealty**
1973/74	**Attivo**		**Northern Game**
1974/75	**Royal Epic**	1984/85	**Out of the Gloom**
1975/76	**Peterhof**	1985/86	**Dark Raven**
1976/77	**Decent Fellow** *	1986/87	**Alone Success**
1977/78	**Connaught Ranger**	1987/88	**Kribensis**
1978/79	**Pollardstown**	1988/89	**Royal Derbi**
1979/80	**Heighlin**		

* In 1977 the Irish-trained Meladon beat Decent Fellow in the Triumph Hurdle but was not included in the Free Handicap.

Biggest margin of superiority: 14 lb by Dark Raven (1985/86).

British Champion Jumpers: Timeform Ratings

In 1975/76 Timeform started to publish, in its *Chasers & Hurdlers* annual, comments and ratings for each jumper in Great Britain, and for the best in Ireland. Timeform's British champion jumpers in each category, with their age, the country in which they were trained and their rating, have been as follows:

British Champion Jumpers: Timeform Ratings

	4-Y-O Hurdler	Novice Hurdle	Hurdler	Novice Chaser
1975/76	**Valmony** GB 157	**Grand Canyon** (6) GB 159	**Night Nurse** (5) GB 178	**Bannow Rambler** (7) Ireland 152p
1976/77	**Meladon** Ireland 149	**Outpoint** (7) GB 154	**Night Nurse** (6) GB 182	**Tree Tangle** (8) GB 159 § / **Bunker Hill** (7) Ireland 157
1977/78	**Major Thompson** GB 144	**Golden Cygnet** (6) Ireland 176	**Monksfield** (6) Ireland 177	**The Dealer** (8) GB 145
1978/79	**Pollardstown** GB 141	**Venture To Cognac** (4) GB 162	**Monksfield** (7) Ireland 180	**Silver Buck** (7) GB 151
1979/80	**Hill of Slane** GB 144	**Hill of Slane** (4) GB 144 / **Slaney Idol** (5) Ireland 143	**Sea Pigeon** (10) GB 175	(f) **Anaglogs Daughter** (7) Ireland 156
1980/81	**Broadsword** GB 144	**Dunaree** (6) Ireland 159	**Sea Pigeon** (11) GB 175	**Clayside** (7) GB 145
1981/82	**Shiny Copper** GB 141	**Angelo Salvini** (6) GB 149	**For Auction** (6) Ireland 174	**Brown Chamberlin** (7) GB 147p
1982/83	**Sabin du Loir** GB 147p	(f) **Dawn Run** (5) Ireland 168	**Gaye Brief** (6) GB 175	**Righthand Man** (6) GB 150
1983/84	**Northern Game** Ireland 142	**Desert Orchid** (5) GB 158	(f) **Dawn Run** (6) Ireland 173	**Bobsline** (8) Ireland 161p
1984/85	**Out of the Gloom** GB 151	**Out of the Gloom** (4) GB 151 / **Asir** (5) GB 148p	**Browne's Gazette** (7) GB 172	**Drumadowney** (7) GB 159
1985/86	**Dark Raven** Ireland 153p	**River Ceiriog** (5) GB 158p	**See You Then** (6) GB 173	**Pearlyman** (7) GB 150
1986/87	**Aldino** GB 154	**Aldino** (4) GB 154 / **The West Awake** (6) GB 153p	**See You Then** (7) GB 173	**Kildimo** (7) GB 151p
1987/88	**Kribensis** GB 143p	**Carvill's Hill** (6) Ireland 157p	**Celtic Shot** (6) GB 170	**Danish Flight** (9) GB 156p
1988/89	**Royal Derbi** GB 144	**Wishlon** (6) GB 152+ / **Sondrio** (8) GB 152p	**Beech Road** (7) GB 172	**Carvill's Hill** (7) Ireland 169p

American Champions

Between 1936 and 1970 Triangle Publications (publishers of the newspaper *Daily Racing Form*) and the magazine *Turf and Sports Digest* conducted separate polls among journalists to determine the United States champions in each age and sex category, and in 1950 a third poll was established among racing secretaries at Thoroughbred Racing Associations tracks. In the Triangle Publications poll, a 3-year-old who beat older rivals was eligible for the Handicap Male or Female award. In many years the standard in the grass and sprint divisions did not justify a champion being elected.

American Champions

	2-Y-O Male	2-Y-O Filly	3-Y-O Male	3-Y-O Filly	Handicap Male
1936	**Pompoon**	**Apogee**	**Granville**	—	**Discovery** (5)
1937	**Menow**	**Jacola**	**War Admiral**	—	**Seabiscuit** (4)
1938	**El Chico**	**Inscoelda**	**Stagehand**	—	**Seabiscuit** (5)
1939	**Bimelech**	**Now What**	**Challedon**	**Unerring**	**Kayak** (4)
1940	**Our Boots** / **Whirlaway**	**Level Best**	**Bimelech**	—	**Challedon** (4)
1941	**Alsab**	**Petrify**	**Whirlaway**	**Painted Veil**	**Mioland** (4) / **Big Pebble** (5)
1942	**Count Fleet**	**Askmenow**	**Alsab**	**Vagrancy**	**Whirlaway** (4)
1943	**Platter** / **Occupy**	**Durazna** / **Twilight Tear**	**Count Fleet**	**Stefanita**	**Market Wise** (5) / **Devil Diver** (4)
1944	**Pavot**	**Busher**	**By Jimminy**	**Twilight Tear**	**Devil Diver** (5)
1945	**Star Pilot**	**Beaugay**	**Fighting Step**	**Busher**	**Stymie** (4)
1946	**Double Jay** / **Education**	**First Flight**	**Assault**	**Bridal Flower**	**Armed** (5)
1947	**Citation**	**Bewitch**	**Phalanx**	**But Why Not**	**Armed** (6)
1948	**Blue Peter**	**Myrtle Charm**	**Citation**	**Miss Request**	**Citation** (3) / **Shannon** (7)
1949	**Hill Prince** / **Oil Capitol**	**Bed o' Roses**	**Capot**	**Two Lea** / **Wistful**	**Coaltown** (4)
1950	**Battlefield**	**Aunt Jinny**	**Hill Prince**	**Next Move**	**Noor** (5)
1951	**Tom Fool**	**Rose Jet**	**Counterpoint**	**Kiss Me Kate**	**Hill Prince** (4) / **Citation** (6)
1952	**Native Dancer**	**Sweet Patootie**	**One Count**	**Real Delight**	**Crafty Admiral** (4)
1953	**Porterhouse** / **Hasty Road**	**Evening Out**	**Native Dancer**	**Grecian Queen**	**Tom Fool** (4)
1954	**Nashua**	**High Voltage**	**High Gun**	**Parlo**	**Native Dancer** (4)

2-Mile Chaser	*Staying Chaser*	*Best Horse*	
Lough Inagh (9) Ireland 167	**Captain Christy** (9) Ireland 182	**Captain Christy**	1975/6
Tree Tangle (8) GB 159 § **Skymas** (12) Ireland 156 **Tingle Creek** (12) GB 154	**Bannow Rambler** (8) Ireland 163	**Night Nurse**	1976/77
Siberian Sun (8) GB 151	**Midnight Court** (7) GB 164	**Monksfield**	1977/78
I'm a Driver (9) GB 163	**Gay Spartan** (8) GB 166	**Monksfield**	1978/79
(f) **Anaglogs Daughter** (8) Ireland 171	**Silver Buck** (8) GB 171	**Sea Pigeon**	1979/80
Rathgorman (10) GB 170	**Little Owl** (7) GB 176	**Little Owl**	1980/81
Badsworth Boy (8) GB 179	**Silver Buck** (10) GB 175	**Silver Buck**	1981/82
Badsworth Boy (9) GB 177	**Bregawn** (9) GB 177	**Badsworth Boy**	1982/83
	Wayward Lad (9) GB 175 **Burrough Hill Lad** (8) GB 175	**Badsworth Boy**	1983/84
Bobsline (9) Ireland 164+	**Burrough Hill Lad** (9) GB 184	**Burrough Hill Lad**	1984/85
(f) **Dawn Run** (8) Ireland 167	**Burrough Hill Lad** (10) GB 183	**Burrough Hill Lad**	1985/86
Pearlyman (8) GB 171	**Desert Orchid** (8) GB 177	**Desert Orchid**	1986/87
Pearlyman (9) GB 174	**Desert Orchid** (9) GB 177	**Desert Orchid**	1987/88
Desert Orchid (10) GB 182	**Desert Orchid** (10) GB 182	**Desert Orchid**	1988/89

Handicap Female	*Grass Horse*	*Sprinter*	*Jumper*	*Horse of the Year*	
—	—	(f) **Myrtlewood** (4)	**Bushranger** (6)	**Granville**	1936
—	—	—	**Jungle King** (7)	**War Admiral**	1937
Marica (5)	—	—	—	**Seabiscuit**	1938
Lady Maryland (5)	—	—	—	**Challedon**	1939
War Plumage (4)	—	—	—	**Challedon**	1940
Fairy Chant (4)	—	—	**Speculate** (5)	**Whirlaway**	1941
Vagrancy (3)	—	—	**Elkridge** (4)	**Whirlaway**	1942
Mar-Kell (4)	—	—	**Brother Jones** (7)	**Count Fleet**	1943
Twilight Tear (3)	—	—	**Rouge Dragon** (6)	**Twilight Tear**	1944
Busher (3)	—	—	**Mercator** (6)	**Busher**	1945
Gallorette (4)	—	—	**Elkridge** (8)	**Assault**	1946
But Why Not (3)	—	**Polynesian** (5)	**War Battle** (6)	**Armed**	1947
Conniver (4)	—	**Coaltown** (3)	**American Way** (6)	**Citation**	1948
Bewitch (4)	—	**Delegate** (5) **Royal Governor** (5)	**Trough Hill** (7)	**Capot** **Coaltown**	1949
Two Lea (4)	—	**Sheilas Reward** (3)	**Oedipus** (4)	**Hill Prince**	1950
Bed o' Roses (4)	—	**Sheilas Reward** (4)	**Oedipus** (5)	**Counterpoint**	1951
Real Delight (3) **Next Move** (5)	—	**Tea-Maker** (9)	**Jam** (5) **Oedipus** (6)	**One Count** **Native Dancer**	1952
Sickle's Image (5)	**Iceberg** (5)	**Tom Fool** (4)	**The Mast** (6)	**Tom Fool**	1953
Parlo (3) **Lavender Hill** (5)	**Stan** (4)	**White Skies** (5)	**King Commander** (5)	**Native Dancer**	1954

	2-Y-O Male	2-Y-O Filly	3-Y-O Male	3-Y-O Filly	Handicap Male
¹1955	Needles Nail	Doubledogdare Nasrina	Nashua	Misty Morn	High Gun (4)
1956	Barbizon	Leallah Romanita	Needles	Doubledogdare	Swaps (4)
1957	Nadir Jewel's Reward	Idun	Bold Ruler	Bayou	Dedicate (5)
1958	First Landing	Quill	Tim Tam	Idun	Round Table (4)
1959	Warfare	My Dear Girl	Sword Dancer	Royal Native Silver Spoon	Sword Dancer (3) Round Table (5)
1960	Hail to Reason	Bowl of Flowers	Kelso	Berlo	Bald Eagle (5)
1961	Crimson Satan Ridan	Cicada	Carry Back	Bowl of Flowers	Kelso (4)
1962	Never Bend	Smart Deb Affectionately	Jaipur	Cicada	Kelso (5)
1963	Hurry To Market Raise a Native	Tosmah Castle Forbes	Chateaugay	Lamb Chop	Kelso (6)
1964	Bold Lad	Queen Empress	Northern Dancer	Tosmah	Kelso (7)
1965	Buckpasser	Moccasin	Tom Rolfe	What a Treat	Roman Brother (4)
1966	Successor	Regal Gleam Mira Femme	Buckpasser	Lady Pitt	Buckpasser (3) Bold Bidder (4)
1967	Vitriolic	Queen of the Stage	Damascus	Furl Sail Gamely	Damascus (3) Buckpasser (4)
1968	Top Knight	Gallant Bloom Process Shot	Stage Door Johnny Forward Pass	Dark Mirage	Dr Fager (4)
1969	Silent Screen	Fast Attack Tudor Queen	Arts and Letters	Gallant Bloom	Arts and Letters (3) Nodouble (4)
1970	Hoist the Flag	Forward Gal	Personality	Office Queen Fanfreluche	Fort Marcy (6) Nodouble (5)

From 1971 the Thoroughbred Racing Associations, *Daily Racing Form* and the National Turf Writers' Association have conducted their own polls, with the results combined to determine the recipients of the official Eclipse Awards for the divisional champions as well as the overall Horse of the Year. From 1979 the grass horse category has had separate male and female champions.

American Champions: Eclipse Awards

	2-Y-O Male	2-Y-O Filly	3-Y-O Male	3-Y-O Filly	Older Male
1971	Riva Ridge	Numbered Account	Canonero	Turkish Trousers	Ack Ack (5)
1972	Secretariat	La Prévoyante	Key To the Mint	Susan's Girl	Autobiography (4)
1973	Protagonist	Talking Picture	Secretariat	Desert Vixen	Riva Ridge (4)
1974	Foolish Pleasure	Ruffian	Little Current	Chris Evert	Forego (4)
1975	Honest Pleasure	Dearly Precious	Wajima	Ruffian	Forego (5)
1976	Seattle Slew	Sensational	Bold Forbes	Revidere	Forego (6)
1977	Affirmed	Lakeville Miss	Seattle Slew	Our Mims	Forego (7)
1978	Spectacular Bid	Candy Eclair It's In the Air	Affirmed	Tempest Queen	Seattle Slew (4)
1979	Rockhill Native	Smart Angle	Spectacular Bid	Davona Dale	Affirmed (4)
1980	Lord Avie	Heavenly Cause	Temperence Hill	Genuine Risk	Spectacular Bid (4)
1981	Deputy Minister	Before Dawn	Pleasant Colony	Wayward Lass	John Henry (6)
1982	Roving Boy	Landaluce	Conquistador Cielo	Christmas Past	Lemhi Gold (4)
1983	Devil's Bag	Althea	Slew o' Gold	Heartlight No. One	Bates Motel (4)
1984	Chief's Crown	Outstandingly	Swale	Life's Magic	Slew o' Gold (4)
1985	Tasso	Family Style	Spend a Buck	Mom's Command	Vanlandingham (4)
1986	Capote	Brave Raj	Snow Chief	Tiffany Lass	Turkoman (4)
1987	Forty Niner	Epitome	Alysheba	Sacahuista	Ferdinand (4)
1988	Easy Goer	Open Mind	Risen Star	Winning Colors	Alysheba (4)

Handicap Female	Grass Horse	Sprinter	Jumper	Horse of the Year	
Misty Morn (3) **Parlo** (4)	**St Vincent** (4)	**Berseem** (5)	**Neji** (5)	**Nashua**	1955
Blue Sparkler (4)	**Career Boy** (3)	**Decathlon** (3)	**Shipboard** (6)	**Swaps**	1956
Pucker Up (4)	**Round Table** (3)	**Decathlon** (4)	**Neji** (7)	**Bold Ruler Dedicate**	1957
Bornastar (5)	**Round Table** (4)	**Bold Ruler** (4)	**Neji** (8)	**Round Table**	1958
Tempted (4)	**Round Table** (5)	**Intentionally** (3)	**Ancestor** (10)	**Sword Dancer**	1959
Royal Native (4)	—	—	**Benguala** (6)	**Kelso**	1960
Airmans Guide (4)	**TV Lark** (4)	—	**Peal** (5)	**Kelso**	1961
Primonetta (4)	—	—	**Barnaby's Bluff** (4)	**Kelso**	1962
Cicada (4)	**Mongo** (4)	—	**Amber Diver** (9)	**Kelso**	1963
Tosmah (3) **Old Hat** (5)	—	—	**Bon Nouvel** (4)	**Kelso**	1964
Old Hat (6) **Affectionately** (5)	**Parka** (7)	(f) **Affectionately** (5)	**Bon Nouvel** (5)	**Roman Brother Moccasin**	1965
Open Fire (5) **Summer Scandal** (4)	**Assagai** (3)	**Impressive** (3)	**Mako** (6) **Tuscalee** (6)	**Buckpasser**	1966
Straight Deal (5)	**Fort Marcy** (3)	**Dr Fager** (3)	**Quick Pitch** (7)	**Damascus**	1967
Gamely (4) **Politely** (5)	**Dr Fager** (4)	**Dr Fager** (4)	**Bon Nouvel** (8)	**Dr Fager**	1968
Gallant Bloom (3) **Gamely** (5)	**Hawaii** (5)	(f) **Ta Wee** (3)	**L'Escargot** (6)	**Arts and Letters**	1969
Shuvee (4)	**Fort Marcy** (6)	(f) **Ta Wee** (4)	**Top Bid** (6)	**Fort Marcy Personality**	1970

Most Eclipse Awards

8 **Forego**
7 **John Henry**
5 **Secretariat**
  Affirmed
4 **Seattle Slew**
  Spectacular Bid
  Flatterer

Older Female	Grass Horse	Sprinter	Jumper	Horse of the Year	
Shuvee (5)	**Run the Gantlet** (3)	**Ack Ack** (5)	**Shadow Brook** (7)	**Ack Ack**	1971
Typecast (6)	**Cougar** (6)	(f) **Chou Croute** (4)	**Soothsayer** (5)	**Secretariat**	1972
Susan's Girl (4)	**Secretariat** (3)	**Shecky Greene** (3)	**Athenian Idol** (5)	**Secretariat**	1973
Desert Vixen (4)	(f) **Dahlia** (4)	**Forego** (4)	**Gran Kan** (8)	**Forego**	1974
Susan's Girl (6)	**Snow Knight** (4)	**Gallant Bob** (3)	(f) **Life's Illusion** (4)	**Forego**	1975
Proud Delta (4)	**Youth** (3)	(f) **My Juliet** (4)	**Straight and True** (6)	**Forego**	1976
Cascapedia (4)	**Johnny D** (3)	(f) **What a Summer** (4)	**Café Prince** (7)	**Seattle Slew**	1977
Late Bloomer (4)	**Mac Diarmida** (3)	**Dr Patches** (4) **J O Tobin** (4)	**Café Prince** (8)	**Affirmed**	1978
Waya (5)	(m) **Bowl Game** (5) (f) **Trillion** (5)	**Star de Naskra** (4)	**Martie's Anger** (4)	**Affirmed**	1979
Glorious Song (4)	(m) **John Henry** (5) (f) **Just a Game** (4)	**Plugged Nickle** (3)	**Zaccio** (4)	**Spectacular Bid**	1980
Relaxing (5)	(m) **John Henry** (6) (f) **De La Rose** (3)	**Guilty Conscience** (5)	**Zaccio** (5)	**John Henry**	1981
Track Robbery (6)	(m) **Perrault** (5) (f) **April Run** (4)	(f) **Gold Beauty** (3)	**Zaccio** (6)	**Conquistador Cielo**	1982
Ambassador of Luck (4)	(m) **John Henry** (8) (f) **All Along** (4)	**Chinook Pass** (4)	**Flatterer** (4)	**All Along**	1983
Princess Rooney (4)	(m) **John Henry** (9) (f) **Royal Heroine** (4)	**Eillo** (4)	**Flatterer** (5)	**John Henry**	1984
Life's Magic (4)	(m) **Cozzene** (5) (f) **Pebbles** (4)	**Precisionist** (4)	**Flatterer** (6)	**Spend a Buck**	1985
Lady's Secret (4)	(m) **Manila** (3) (f) **Estrapade** (6)	**Smile** (4)	**Flatterer** (7)	**Lady's Secret**	1986
North Sider (5)	(m) **Theatrical** (5) (f) **Miesque** (3)	**Groovy** (4)	**Inlander** (6)	**Ferdinand**	1987
Personal Ensign (4)	(m) **Sunshine Forever** (3) (f) **Miesque** (4)	**Gulch** (4)	**Jimmy Lorenzo** (6)	**Alysheba**	1988

Dancing Brave

Dancing Brave is officially regarded as the best racehorse of his time in Europe. The International Classifications, annual assesments compiled by the official Handicappers in Great Britain, Ireland and France, were introduced in 1977, and since then this versatile champion has achieved a higher rating than any other horse.

Dancing Brave, supreme at both a mile and a mile and a half, dominated racing in Europe in 1986, and his 8 wins in 10 career starts included the 2000 Guineas, Eclipse Stakes, King George VI and Queen Elizabeth Stakes and Prix de l'Arc de Triomphe; he was also a most unlucky Derby runner-up.

With a calm temperament and relaxed style of racing, he was always held up in order to make best use of his brilliant finishing speed, so that he rarely won by a wide margin, but when that rapier thrust was timed correctly, as it was against a top-class international field in the 'Arc', the manner of his victory left no doubt that he was a truly great champion.

Dancing Brave, a bay colt standing 16 hands, was bred by Glen Oak Farm, Kentucky, and was foaled on 11 May 1983. His sire Lyphard, a son of Northern Dancer, was a top-class miler in France, and his dam Navajo Princess was a tough, Grade II-winning American racemare. He was offered at the Fasig-Tipton Keeneland Summer Yearling Sale and was bought for $200,000 by James Delahooke on behalf of Saudi Arabian Prince Khalid bin Abdullah.

He was not a precocious colt and West Sussex trainer Guy Harwood ran him only twice as a juvenile, resulting in easy wins in minor events at Sandown Park and Newmarket in the autumn. It was enough to earn him 8 st 10 lb in the European Free Handicap (11 lb below the top) and winter favouritism for the first colts' Classic in England, the 2000 Guineas.

Dancing Brave breezed home on his 1986 reappearance in the Craven Stakes at Newmarket and returned there in May for the 2000 Guineas over a mile. The slow pace did not inconvenience him at all, and he quickened away up the final hill to score by 3 lengths from Green Desert, a subsequent Group I-winning sprinter.

It seemed Dancing Brave had only to stay the extra half-mile in order to win the Derby, but circumstances dictated

Dancing Brave wins the 1986 Prix de l'Arc de Triomphe in the style of a great champion. (All-Sport)

otherwise. Greville Starkey used exaggerated waiting tactics on him but it was his inability to handle the unique gradients of Epsom which proved his downfall. Like so many horses before him, he became badly unbalanced coming down Tattenham Hill and was still nearly last, about 10 lengths in arrears, by the time he found his stride two furlongs out. He then unleashed a spectacular burst but at the line Shahrastani was still a fast-diminishing half-length in front. Shahrastani was an above-average Derby winner who went on to land the Irish Derby by 8 lengths, but Dancing Brave should have beaten him.

No excuses were needed a month later when, meeting older horses for the first time, he romped away with the Eclipse Stakes over Sandown Park's 10 furlongs. He beat the top French filly Triptych by 4 lengths with Arlington Million hero Teleprompter third.

Dancing Brave emphasized his supremacy when gaining his revenge on Shahrastani in England's premier weight-for-age race, the King George VI and Queen Elizabeth Stakes over 1½ miles at Ascot. Pat Eddery, substituting for the injured Starkey, delivered Dancing Brave's finishing burst rather early, for he led over a furlong out and allowed Shardari, the best older horse in Europe, enough time to rally and be beaten only three-quarters of a length in the end. Triptych was well behind in third place with a below-par Shahrastani fourth.

After a brief mid-summer rest Dancing Brave had little more than an exercise canter when breaking Goodwood's 10-furlong record in the Select Stakes – a warm-up for the stiffest test of his career, the Prix de l'Arc de Triomphe. The 'Arc', over 2,400 metres at Longchamp, Paris, is the most important inter-age contest in Europe, and in October 1986 it attracted its

Trainer Guy Harwood and jockey Pat Eddery after Dancing Brave's Arc victory. (All-Sport)

strongest field since Sea-Bird triumphed in 1965.

The 15 runners included the 3 best horses in England – Dancing Brave, Shahrastani and Shardari – French champion Bering (unbeaten in 4 races that year including the Prix du Jockey-Club), West German champion Acatenango (winner of his last 12 races), champion fillies Triptych and Darara, and champions from Japan and Chile.

Ridden by Eddery for the second time, Dancing Brave raced towards the rear and was switched to the wide outside as the leaders fanned out early in the straight. Receiving only a couple of taps of encouragement, he produced an exceptional turn of foot to cut down Bering 100 yards from home and win by an official but conservative margin of 1½ lengths. Triptych was a further half-length behind in third place, just in front of Shahrastani and Shardari. Dancing Brave, relishing the firm ground, beat the record Arc time by 0.3 sec and became only the fourth horse to achieve the King George–Arc double, following Ribot (1956), Ballymoss (1958) and Mill Reef (1971).

That performance set the seal on the colt's greatness but he raced once more. He was sent to California to contest the

Breeders' Cup Turf at Santa Anita in November, but his arduous campaign and long journey to run in unfamiliar conditions proved too much and he trailed in fourth behind Manila, Theatrical and Estrapade.

That defeat took nothing away from Dancing Brave's achievements and he was unanimously elected Horse of the Year. He was also awarded a rating of 141 in the 1986 International Classifications, making him officially the best horse of the decade in Europe – 1 lb above both Alleged (1978) and Shergar (1981). Timeform gave him a rating of 140, equal with Shergar and 2 lb above Alleged.

During the summer Dancing Brave had been syndicated for a sum which placed a valuation of £14 million on him, with several shares being taken by Sheikh Mohammed, and he retired to the latter's Dalham Hall Stud in Newmarket at a fee of £120,000. In November 1987 he was found to be suffering from the rare Marie's Disease and he suffered an infertility problem in 1988, but was restored to full fitness for the 1989 covering season.

Australasian Champions

In 1979/80 the first combined Australia–New Zealand Classifications were published. These handicaps, compiled by a panel of representatives of Australian and New Zealand racing clubs, contain ratings for the best horses to have raced in those two countries during the season. The official Australasian champions in each age and sex category, with the country in which they were trained and their rating, have been as follows:

Australasian Champions

	2-Y-O Male	2-Y-O Filly	3-Y-O Male	3-Y-O Filly
1979/80	**Paddy Boy** NZ 54	**Shaybisc** Aus 56	**Kingston Town** Aus 64	**Lowan Star** Aus 57
1980/81	**Crown Jester** Aus 56	**Black Shoes** Aus 56	**Paddy Boy*** Aus 60	**Shaybisc** Aus 56.5
1981/82	**Rancher** Aus 60	**Vaindarra** Aus 54.5	**Best Western** Aus 58.5	**Rose of Kingston** Aus 58
1982/83	**Sir Dapper** Aus 59	**Love a Show** Aus 56	**McGinty*** NZ 58.5	**Emancipation** Aus 60
			Strawberry Road Aus 58.5	
1983/84	**Inspired** Aus 58	**Vin d'Amour** NZ 58	**Sir Dapper** Aus 61.5	**Burletta** NZ 58.5
1984/85	**Rory's Jester** Aus 58.5	**Speed Check** Aus 56.5	**Red Anchor** Aus 62.5	**Spirit of Kingston** Aus 57.5
1985/86	**Precocious Lad** NZ 57	**Bounding Away** Aus 60.5	**Bonecrusher** NZ 63	**Heat of the Moment** Aus 59
	Shannon NZ 57			
1986/87	**Marauding** Aus 58	**Midnight Fever** Aus 56	**Placid Ark** Aus 61	**Tidal Light** Aus 59.5
	Snippets Aus 58			
1987/88	**Star Watch** Aus 59	**Comely Girl** Aus 56.5	**Beau Zam** Aus 63	**Bravery** Aus 56
				Candide* NZ 56
				Savana City Aus 56

Longest Winning Sequences

56 – Camarero (1951)

The world record for the most wins in succession is held by Camarero, who was unbeaten in the first 56 races of his career in Puerto Rico from April 1953 to August 1955. Owned by José Coll Vidal, he won 18 races as a juvenile in 1953, notably the Clasico Munoz Rivera Memorial, and 19 at 3 years including the local Triple Crown. Camarero scored on his first 19 outings in 1955, thus breaking Kincsem's record of 54 races without defeat, but finished fourth on his next start. He eventually won 29 out of 32 at the age of four and a further seven out of eight before falling fatally ill in August 1956. Overall, Camarero won 73 of his 77 races at Quintana and Las Casas over distances from 5 to 9 furlongs; he came second twice, fourth once and sixth once. Although both his parents were Thoroughbreds imported from America, he was no more than pony-sized and ran only in races for Puerto Rican native-breds. He was too good for his local rivals but not good enough for open competition.

54 – Kincsem (1874)

In many respects the most remarkable career record in Turf history is that of Kincsem, a Hungarian-bred mare who raced 54 times and never knew defeat. She was in training for 4 seasons, winning 10 races as a 2-year-old, 17 at 3 years, 15 at 4 years and 12 at 5 years. A renowned international traveller, she took the train to wherever she could find competition, contesting many of the top races in Hungary, Austria, Germany, Czechoslovakia, France and, on one occasion, England. At the time of her visit to England, in the summer of 1878, she had already won 36 races, including the Austrian versions of the 2000 Guineas and Derby, the Hungarian equivalents of the 2000 Guineas and Oaks, and the top German all-aged race, the Grosser Preis von Baden. In spite of that formidable record, she started as the outsider of three for the Goodwood Cup, but she won easily. On her way home she collected the Grand Prix de Deauville and a second Grosser Preis von Baden, this one after the only close call she ever experienced. She won that by five lengths after being taken to a deciding heat by Prince Giles the First. A third victory in the Grosser Preis von Baden provided the feature of her final racing campaign, and she retired with an unblemished record, having been tested at all distances from under 5 furlongs to 2½ miles, with as much as 76½ kg in the saddle.

39 – Galgo Jr (1928)

Galgo Jr, who raced exclusively on two tracks in Puerto Rico, set world records for the number of races won in a season and in a career. Another remarkable feat was his tally of 39 consecutive victories, recorded between July 1930 and July 1931.

23 – Leviathan (1793)

Leviathan was the first gelding to become a champion in America and the grey still holds the record for the longest winning sequence by any American horse. Owned in turn by Edmund Brooke and John Tayloe III, he campaigned almost exclusively in Virginia and swept unchallenged through 23 consecutive

* New Zealand-breds Paddy Boy, Blue Denim, Gold Hope, McGinty
and Candide raced in Australia under the names Our Paddy Boy,
My Blue Denim, My Gold Hope, Mr McGinty and It's Candide
respectively.

Older Male	Older Female	Best Horse	
Dulcify (4) Aus 63	**Mellseur** (5) NZ 56	**Kingston Town**	1979/80
Kingston Town (4) Aus 64	**Blue Denim*** (5) Aus 57.5	**Kingston Town**	1980/81
Kingston Town (5) Aus 63.5	**Gold Hope*** (4) NZ 56	**Kingston Town**	1981/82
Gurner's Lane (4) Aus 62	**Rose of Kingston** (4) Aus 56	**Gurner's Lane**	1982/83
McGinty* (4) NZ 59.5	**Emancipation** (4) Aus 60.5	**Sir Dapper**	1983/84
Trissaro (5) Aus 59.5			
Alibhai (4) Aus 59.5	**Nouvelle Star** (4) Aus 57	**Red Anchor**	1984/85
Lockley's Tradition (4) Aus 57.5	**Tristarc** (4) Aus 58	**Bonecrusher**	1985/86
Rising Prince (5) Aus 57.5			
Tanalyse (5) NZ 57.5			
Bonecrusher (4) NZ 62.5	**Kosha** (6) NZ 56	**Bonecrusher**	1986/87
Rubiton (4) Aus 62.5	**Special** (4) Aus 57	**Beau Zam**	1987/88

races from 1797 to 1801, nine of them in 4-mile heats. In the spring of 1801, at the age of eight, he won a 5-mile match under 180 lb, conceding 70 lb to his rival, but his sequence ended the following autumn. He never scored again, retiring with 24 wins in 30 races.

22 – Pooker T (1958)

Pooker T, who competed in claiming races in Puerto Rico, had only modest ability but enjoyed a remarkable run of success as a 4-year-old in 1962. He won a total of 24 races that season, 22 of them in succession.

22 – Miss Petty (1981)

On the very day when the career of Picnic in the Park (see below) ended at one minor Queensland meeting, the filly who would eventually top his record Australian sequence had her first race at another small track in the same State. Miss Petty won three of her seven races as a four-year-old and began her skein of 22 victories with the last of three (from eight starts) at five. As a six-year-old she won all her 14 races, and after her seventh triumph at seven, in which she set a record for 1100 metres at the July 1989 Longreach fixture, she was retired to stud. She was a proficient sprinter, up to carrying high weights, but was never tested in high-class company.

21 – Meteor (1783)

The record for the most wins in succession by a horse trained in Great Britain is held by Meteor, who won his last 4 races as a 3-year-old in 1786 and was unbeaten in 5 outings in 1787 and 12 in 1788, most of them at Newmarket. Bred and owned by the 1st Earl Grosvenor, this son of Eclipse came second in the Derby but then developed into such an outstanding champion that he scared away nearly all opposition. During his record sequence he walked over 5 times and had a solitary rival on 9 occasions, though most of those were matches against top-class rivals. Sir Peter Teazle was the horse who finally ended his run. Meteor was small in stature, but he won 30 of his 33 starts over 5 seasons and came second in the other three.

21 – Bond's First Consul (1798)

Bond's First Consul was champion of the northern states of America in the early 1800s. From 1801 to 1806 Joshua Bond's horse won the first 21 races of his career, mostly in 4-mile heats and meeting the best horses in training at courses from New York to Maryland, but he lost his remaining 4 races.

21 – Lottery (1803)

Lottery was an outstanding American mare who lost only the first of her 22 races. Owned by Richard Singleton, she won the Jockey Club purse in 4-mile heats at Charleston, South Carolina in 1808 and 1810, and she also picked up similar prizes over shorter distances at the same venue. She became an influential broodmare.

21 – Picnic in the Park (1979)

Picnic in the Park broke the Australasian record of 19 consecutive wins which had been held by Desert Gold and Gloaming for more than 60 years. He won 21 consecutive sprint races at humble 'bush' tracks in Queensland between August 1984 and March 1985, and was injured and beaten when attempting to extend his sequence. He never won on a metropolitan track.

20 – Filch (1773)

Filch, a grey Irish horse, won his last 9 races of 1778, notably the Jockey Club Purse and a King's Plate at The Curragh. He was unbeaten in 7 outings as a 6-year-old, including a walk-over for his second Jockey Club Purse, and added 4 more prizes in 1780, among them another King's Plate, before his sequence ended. During that time he had a total of 12 races in heats and 3 walk-overs.

20 – Fashion (1837)

Fashion, perhaps the greatest of all American race-mares, won 32 of her 36 races over 9 seasons and came second in the other 4; most of them were run in 4-mile heats. She won her last 3 starts in 1841 and was undefeated in 4 races in 1842, seven in 1843 and six in 1844 at courses from New York to Maryland. For her most famous victory she represented the North in a match with the great but ageing southern champion Boston at the Union Course, Long Island in May 1842.

Sweetmeat, unbeaten in 19 races as a 3-year-old in 1845, and sire of 1863 Derby winner Macaroni. (BBC Hulton Picture Library)

20 – Kentucky (1861)

Kentucky dominated racing in America at the end of the Civil War together with unbeaten Asteroid and Norfolk; all three were sons of Lexington. Eastern champion Kentucky suffered his only defeat when fourth to Norfolk in the 1864 Jersey Derby. He numbered the Travers Stakes at Saratoga's inaugural meeting and the Jersey St Leger among his 6 victories later that year, and was unbeaten in 7 races in both 1865 and 1866 including the first 2 runnings of the Saratoga Cup. He had 2 walk-overs and 8 races in heats.

19 – Skiff (1821)

Skiff, running only at minor Scottish meetings, won his last 9 races in 1825 and all 11 in 1826, though on the final occasion he was disqualified for carrying too little weight. He picked up Gold Cups at Inverness and Montrose and a King's Plate at Perth; his sequence included 3 walk-overs and 5 races in heats.

19 – Boston (1833)

Boston was perhaps the best horse to race in America before the Civil War and no American champion except Kelso has dominated the sport for so long. He won 40 of his 45 starts over 8 seasons, mostly in 4-mile heats, and in 37 consecutive races from 1836 to 1841 he lost only when unfit on his début in 1839. He won his remaining 8 races that year, all 7 (including a walk-over) in 1840 and, after a season at stud, his first

four in 1841 at courses from New York to Georgia. Boston became champion sire 3 times and his offspring included Lexington.

19 – Sweetmeat (1842)

Sweetmeat did not contest the Classics but was unbeaten in 19 outings as a 3-year-old in 1845 including the Gold Vase at Ascot, the Doncaster Cup (beating Alice Hawthorn) and 9 races in which he walked over after scaring away all opposition. He won 22 of his 25 career starts and became an influential sire.

19 – The Hero (1843)

The Hero was the first horse to win all three of England's premier Cup events. John Barham Day's colt took his last 11 races in 1846, including the Doncaster Cup, and his first 8 in 1847, notably the Gold Vase, Emperor of Russia's Plate (Ascot Gold Cup) and Goodwood Cup; he also had 5 walk-overs and 2 races in heats.

19 – Desert Gold (1912)

Desert Gold was the greatest racemare ever produced in New Zealand and, together with Gloaming, she holds the New Zealand record of 19 consecutive victories. Having won on her last start at 2 years, she swept unbeaten through her 14-race campaign as a 3-year-old in 1915–16 including the New Zealand Derby and Oaks at Riccarton and the Great Northern Derby, Oaks and St Leger at Ellerslie; she also won her first 4 races the following season. Desert Gold usually dominated her rivals from the start, and set several time records.

19 – Gloaming (1915)

Gloaming ranks second only to Phar Lap among New Zealand geldings and he shares with Desert Gold the New Zealand record of 19 wins in succession. Having landed 3 Derbys in his first season, this remarkable champion won his last 5 races at 4 years, all 12 as a 5-year-old in 1920–21 including the Islington, Auckland and Kelburn Plates, and his first 2 at 6 years. Gloaming, who never ran in a handicap or beyond 12 furlongs, retired with 57 wins and 9 seconds from 67 starts over 7 seasons; he fell in his only other race.

18 – Eclipse (1764)

Eclipse was the greatest racehorse of the 18th century and has become almost a legendary figure. He won all his 18 races, 9 of them as a 5-year-old in 1769 and 9 in 1770, and though eight of them were walk-overs, that was merely because his overwhelming superiority frightened away nearly all opposition.

Seven of his other races were run in heats of up to 4 miles each and he was a frequent competitor in King's Plates, winning 11 of those prestige prizes altogether including two at Newmarket. Bred by William, Duke of Cumberland, Eclipse ran at first in the name of William Wildman but was later bought by Dennis O'Kelly, who had correctly predicted on the champion's début that the result would be 'Eclipse first and the rest nowhere'. He died in 1789. Over 90 per cent of all modern Thoroughbreds descend from him in the male line.

18 – Sally Hope (1822)

American racemare Sally Hope won her last 18 races, most of them in heats of up to 4 miles. Running almost exclusively in Virginia, she took her last 7 races in 1827 and all 10 in 1828, including 4 Jockey Club purses, but she broke down when winning another such prize on her reappearance the following spring.

18 – Light (1856)

Light was not a champion but set a French record for consecutive victories which still stands. He won his last 7 races in 1859 and 11 more in 1860 including the Prix Biennal and Prix de Suresnes at Longchamp, though he usually ran in the provinces. He sired classic winners Bigarreau and Sornette.

18 – Hindoo (1878)

Hindoo, perhaps the greatest American champion of the 19th century, won 30 of his 35 races including the first 18 of a brilliant 3-year-old campaign in 1881. Trained by James Rowe for the brothers Phil and Mike Dwyer, he romped away with the Kentucky Derby before moving to New York and winning the Tidal, Coney Island Derby, Lorillard, Travers, United States Hotel, Kenner, Champion, Jersey St Leger and other stakes. He walked over once and had one race in heats.

18 – Ajax (1934)

Ajax, one of Australia's greatest champions, was a brilliant miler and held the record for the most consecutive wins in that country until Picnic in the Park's feat in 1984/85. They comprised his last 6 races at 3 years, notably the Newmarket Handicap and All Aged Plate, and his first 12 as a 4-year-old in 1938–39, all but one of them at weight-for-age including the W S Cox Plate and the Underwood, Melbourne, Caulfield and L K S Mackinnon Stakes. He retired with 36 wins from 46 starts.

18 – Karayel (1970)

Karayel was the best horse ever to race in Turkey and was never extended in any of his 18 races. Sadik Eliyesil's colt won 5 times as a juvenile and his tally of 11 in 1973 included the Triple Crown – Erkek Tay Deneme Kosusu (2000 Guineas), Gazi Kosusu (Derby) and Ankara Kosusu (St Leger) – as well as Turkey's premier weight-for-age race, the Cumhurbaskanligi Kupasi Kosusu over 2,400 metres, by a distance. Karayel, a son of 2000 Guineas runner-up Prince Tudor, won twice more in the spring of 1974 but then fractured a cannon-bone in a training gallop, though he was saved for stud duty.

17 – Careless (1751)

Careless won the first 17 races of his career in England from 1755 to 1758 including 10 King's Plates, the only ones he ever started for. He had 7 walk-overs and 7 races in heats.

17 – Boston (1833)

When American champion Boston won 19 races in succession (see above) he already had a sequence of 17 to his credit. In 1836 this bad-tempered horse refused to race on his first public appearance, but he won his remaining 2 starts that year, all 4 in 1837 and all 11 in 1838.

17 – Harkaway (1834)

Harkaway disputes with Barcaldine the distinction of being the greatest Irish racehorse of the 19th century. He won on 17 consecutive outings at The Curragh between April 1837 and June 1838, including 7 Royal Plates, and later became the first Irish horse to prove himself a champion in England, winning the Goodwood Cups of 1838 and 1839. He would have achieved even greater glory but for being mismanaged by his owner, Tom Ferguson.

17 – Beeswing (1835)

The American Beeswing, foaled 2 years after her more famous English namesake, won 17 in a row before breaking down at New Orleans in 1840. This was during a race run in heats and the Louisiana mare had to be withdrawn after winning the first heat.

17 – Alice Hawthorn (1838)

Alice Hawthorn, one of the toughest of English racemares, won her last 16 races as a 6-year-old in 1844 and her first at 7 years. In that time this great stayer recorded her second success in the Doncaster Cup and also picked up the Gold Cups at York and Richmond, and 7 Queen's Plates; she walked over 7 times, had one race in heats and dead-heated once.

17 – Hanover (1884)

Hanover, based in New York, was unbeaten in 3 juvenile starts – the Hopeful, July and Sapling Stakes – and was the best horse in America as a 3-year-old in 1887. He won his first 14 races and 20 in all that year, adding the Brooklyn Derby, Withers, Belmont, Swift, Tidal, Coney Island Derby and Lorillard Stakes to his tally before his first defeat. He became champion sire 4 times.

17 – Dudley (1914)

Dudley was perhaps the best 2-mile steeplechaser of his time in England and this tough, versatile gelding won his first 17 contests as an 11-year-old in 1925, comprising 6 steeplechases, 4 hurdle races, one Flat race and 6 National Hunt Flat races. They included the Victory Chase at Manchester, the Cheltenham Grand Annual Chase (both handicaps) and a walk-over.

17 – Mainbrace (1947)

Mainbrace is one of the very greatest champions in New Zealand racing history. He won 23 of his 25

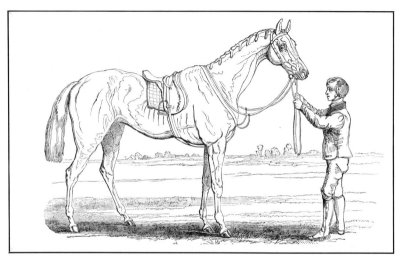

Alice Hawthorn, the champion racemare of the 1840s who recorded 17 of her 51 victories in succession. (Mary Evans Picture Library)

starts, the last 17 of them consecutively, and his 15 victories as a 3-year-old in 1950–51 constitute a New Zealand record for one season. Among them were 4 Guineas races, the Great Northern Derby and the New Zealand and Great Northern St Legers. He had 2 further races at 4 before injury ended his career.

17 – Sir Ken (1947)

Sir Ken was a great hurdler who failed to win in his native France but was unbeaten in 16 races over timber and one on the Flat during his first 3 seasons in England. He won the Lancashire Hurdle in 1951 and the Champion Hurdle in each of the next 2 years before his sequence ended. He added a third title in 1954.

17 – Gradisco (1957)

Gradisco won the first 17 races of his career in Venezuela during 1959 and 1960 before fracturing a sesamoid. He attempted a come-back in 1961 but broke down, thus spoiling an unbeaten record.

16 – Master Bagot (1787)

Master Bagot won his last 4 starts in 1790 and was Ireland's leading earner in 1791 thanks to an unbeaten campaign of 11 races (three of them in heats) in which he added 2 more King's Plates and the Lord Lieutenant's Plate at The Curragh to his score; he also won on his reappearance at 5 years. He became champion sire a record 8 times in Ireland.

16 – Luke Blackburn (1877)

Luke Blackburn was one of the greatest American champions of the 19th century. Based in New York, he won 22 of his 24 races as a 3-year-old in 1880, the last 15 of them in succession including the United States Hotel, Grand Union Prize, Kenner, Champion and Great Challenge Stakes and the Long Island and Kentucky St Legers. He scored on his reappearance in 1881 but his crown then passed to his stablemate Hindoo.

16 – Miss Woodford (1880)

Miss Woodford is probably the greatest filly or mare to race in America since the Civil War and she succeeded stablemate Hindoo as the best horse in the country. Her long sequence of victories included all nine of her starts at the age of four in 1884 and she later became the first horse of either sex to earn $100,000 in America. She was unplaced only twice in a career of 48 races, winning 37 of them.

16 – The Bard (1883)

The Bard set a British record with an unbeaten campaign of 16 races as a 2-year-old including the Brocklesby Stakes at Lincoln, New Biennial Stakes at Ascot, Tattersall Sale Stakes at Doncaster and a walk-over. On his reappearance he came second to mighty Ormonde in the Derby; he later won the Doncaster Cup.

16 – Ormonde (1883)

Ormonde may well have been the greatest of all English champions, for he never looked likely to be beaten in any of his 16 races. This brilliant colt numbered the Criterion Stakes and Dewhurst Plate among his 3 outings as a juvenile and in 1886 his triumphant progress took in the Triple Crown events plus the St James's Palace, Hardwicke, Great Foal and Champion Stakes, the Free Handicap and 2 walk-overs. He then became a roarer but added the Rous Memorial Stakes, Hardwicke Stakes and Imperial Gold Cup (July Cup) to his tally at 4. He died in 1904.

16 – Prestige (1903)

Prestige was easily the best of his generation in France but was not entered for the major 3-year-old events. This unbeaten champion won 7 races as a juvenile, notably the Critérium de Maisons-Laffitte, Grand Critérium and Prix de la Forêt, and 9 in 1906, including the Prix Eugène Adam and 2 walk-overs. Trained by William Duke for William K Vanderbilt, he was far superior to his stablemate and contemporary Maintenon, who won the Prix du Jockey-Club. Prestige sired Sardanapale, one of France's greatest champions, and died in 1924.

16 – Citation (1945)

Citation ranks among the very greatest American champions. During a magnificent 3-year-old campaign in 1948 his sole conqueror was Saggy, and he swept unchallenged through his remaining 15 races (including a walk-over) that season over distances from 6 furlongs to 2 miles and at tracks across the USA, winning the Triple Crown plus the American Derby and Jockey Club Gold Cup. Sidelined by injury throughout 1949, he won on his reappearance at 5 years but the longest winning sequence in North America this century was then ended by Miche. Citation was trained by Jimmy Jones for Calumet Farm and usually ridden by Eddie Arcaro.

16 – Ribot (1952)

Ribot, a product of the Italian breeding genius Federico Tesio, was never beaten in 16 races and disputes with Sea-Bird the distinction of being the greatest middle-distance horse in Europe since World War II. Having taken 3 prizes as a juvenile, including the Gran Criterium, he had 5 races in Italy in 1955, among them the Gran Premio del Jockey Club, and also romped away with the Prix de l'Arc de Triomphe. His 7-race campaign in 1956 featured the Gran Premio di Milano, the King George VI and Queen Elizabeth Stakes and his second Arc by a record margin of 6 lengths. Ribot spent most of his stud career in America and died in 1972.

16 – Minimo (1968)

Turkish champion Minimo lost her first race but won her next 16. Her unblemished 1971 record included the Disi Tay Deneme Kosusu (1000 Guineas), Kisrak Kosusu (Oaks), Gazi Kosusu (Derby), Ankara Kosusu (St Leger) and Turkey's premier weight-for-age prize, the Reisi Cumhur Kupasi Kosusu, all in effortless style.

15 – Rattler (1816)

Rattler, also known as Thornton's Rattler, was an American horse who won his first 15 races including the Jockey Club purse at Charleston, South Carolina in 1820. He was injured when suffering his first defeat.

15 – Thebais (1878)

Thebais, England's champion 2-year-old of 1880, won her last 10 races that season, among them the Ham Produce, Great Challenge and Criterion Stakes and 3 walk-overs, and her first five in 1881, including the 1000 Guineas, Oaks, Nassau Stakes and Yorkshire Oaks. Her brother Clairvaux was an unbeaten champion sprinter and her sister St Marguerite won the 1000 Guineas.

15 – Carbine (1885)

Carbine disputes with Phar Lap the distinction of being the greatest horse ever to race in Australasia. Bred in New Zealand but trained in Australia after the age of two by Walter Hickenbotham for Donald Wallace, he won his last 7 races as a 4-year-old in 1889–90, including the Sydney Cup, and his first 8 at 5 years, notably the Melbourne Cup under 10 st 5 lb, a weight which is still a record for the winner of Australia's greatest prize. Carbine, who started twice on the same afternoon several times, won 33 of his 43 races and spent most of his successful stud career in England.

15 – Pretty Polly (1901)

Pretty Polly dominated her contemporaries and set the standard by which all English champion fillies are measured. Her 9 victories as a juvenile included the National Breeders' Produce, Champagne, Cheveley Park, Middle Park and Criterion Stakes, and in 1904 she breezed through the 1000 Guineas, Oaks, Coronation Stakes, Nassau Stakes, St Leger and Park Hill Stakes before suffering her first defeat on her only visit to France.

15 – Colin (1905)

Colin is one of a handful of American champions who can be compared with Man o' War. Trained by James Rowe for James R Keene and racing only in the state of New York, this unbeaten colt swept in brilliant style through his 12 races as a juvenile including the Saratoga Special, Futurity, Matron and Champagne Stakes. In 1908 he won the Withers, Belmont and Tidal Stakes before a leg injury ended his career, though he was sent to trainer Sam Darling in England before his retirement was announced. Colin died in 1932.

15 – Bayardo (1906)

Bayardo, the greatest horse of his time in England, was a champion in each of his 3 seasons. He was not fit when unplaced in the 2000 Guineas and Derby of 1909, but won his remaining 11 races that year including the Prince of Wales's, Eclipse, St Leger and Champion Stakes. He also took his first four in 1910, highlighted by a magnificent victory in the Ascot Gold Cup, and retired with 22 wins from 25 starts.

15 – Macon (1922)

Macon was the best horse of his time in Argentina. His 9 wins in 1925 included the Polla de Potrillos (2000 Guineas), Gran Premio Nacional (Derby) and Argentina's premier weight-for-age prize, the Gran Premio Carlos Pellegrini. In 1926 the unbeaten colt won 6 more races, notably the Gran Premio de Honor (stayers' championship) and a second Gran Premio Carlos Pellegrini.

15 – Vander Pool (1928)

Vander Pool, an American colt, won all his 11 races as a juvenile and his first 4 at 3 years, but on the only occasion he met top-class opposition he was lucky to be awarded the Youthful Stakes (his seventh race) on the disqualification of Equipoise.

15 – Bernborough (1939)

Bernborough was probably the best racehorse ever bred in Australia. Until he was 6, controversy over his ownership restricted him to a country meeting in Queensland but at that age, in 1945–46, he entered major competition and won his last 10 races, notably the Newmarket Handicap, Rawson Stakes, All Aged Stakes, Doomben Ten Thousand and Doomben Cup. This great weight-carrier also won his first 5 races at 7 years, including the Melbourne and Caulfield Stakes.

15 – Buckpasser (1963)

Buckpasser was the champion of his generation in America in each of his 3 seasons. In 1966 he won the last 13 races of his brilliant Horse of the Year campaign including the Flamingo, Arlington Classic, Brooklyn Handicap, American Derby, Travers, Woodward and Jockey Club Gold Cup, though injury made him miss the Triple Crown series. He took his first 2 starts in 1967, notably the Metropolitan Handicap, but then lost his only race on grass

15 – Brigadier Gerard (1968)

Brigadier Gerard won 17 of his 18 races and is rivalled only by Tudor Minstrel as the greatest miler to race in England since World War II. The Middle Park Stakes was the most important of his 4 juvenile victories and on his reappearance in 1971 he decisively beat Mill Reef for the 2000 Guineas. The Sussex and Champion Stakes were among his other 5 races that year, and in 1972 he extended his brilliant unbeaten sequence to 15, culminating in the Eclipse and the King George VI and Queen Elizabeth Stakes, before Roberto defeated him at York.

15 – Squanderer (1973)

Indian champion and Triple Crown hero Squanderer won 18 of his 19 races. After losing on his fourth start, he won the Bangalore Derby and Indian 2000 Guineas in 1976, while at 4 years his 8 victories included the Indian Derby and St Leger, and the President of India Gold Cup, a race which also figured among his 5 successes in 1978.

14 – Lucifer (1813)

Lucifer was a Scottish horse who won his last 9 races in 1817 and first 5 in 1818, notably the Gold Cup and King's Plate at Edinburgh. He had 2 walk-overs and 8 races in heats.

14 – Friponnier (1864)

Friponnier was the most prolific winner in Great Britain in 1867, when he lost on only the fifth of his 19 starts. Thereafter he walked over in 7 races, including the Goodwood Derby, and twice beat Derby winner Hermit, notably in the Grand Duke Michael Stakes.

Brigadier Gerard (Joe Mercer) gains the last of his 15 consecutive wins in the 1972 King George VI and Queen Elizabeth Stakes, in which class rather than stamina enabled him to beat Parnell and Riverman over 1½ miles. (Syndication International)

14 – Harry Bassett (1868)

Harry Bassett, the best horse of his generation in America, lost the first race of his career but won the next 14. These comprised his last 3 as a juvenile, all 9 in 1871 including the Belmont, Jersey Derby, Travers, Kenner and Champion Stakes, and his first 2 as a 4-year-old. He was then beaten by the great champion Longfellow.

14 – Prince Charlie (1869)

Prince Charlie, the 2000 Guineas hero of 1872, was one of the fastest and most popular horses ever to run in England. He won his last race at 3 years, all 10 at 4 years, including the Queen's Stand Plate at Ascot and a walk-over, and his first 3 in 1874. He won 25 of his 29 career starts, mostly over sprint distances, and was never beaten at Newmarket.

14 – Springfield (1873)

Springfield won 17 of his 19 races and was probably the best specialist sprinter-miler of the 19th century in England. He swept unbeaten through his last 2 seasons and numbered the Fern Hill Stakes, inaugural July Cup and 2 walk-overs among his tally of nine in 1876. He won 5 more races in 1877 including the Queen's Stand Plate, July Cup and inaugural Champion Stakes.

14 – Man o' War (1917)

Man o' War is widely regarded as the greatest of all American champions, having won 20 of his 21 races over 2 seasons. Trained by Louis Feustel for Samuel Riddle, he was unluckily beaten by Upset on his seventh juvenile start, the Sanford Memorial Stakes at Saratoga, and had 3 more races that year, notably the Hopeful Stakes and Belmont Futurity. He did not contest the Kentucky Derby but his 11 races in 1920 included the Preakness, Withers, Belmont, Dwyer, Travers, Lawrence Realization and Jockey Club Stakes; he set 5 American record times during that all-conquering campaign. 'Big Red' proved a successful stallion and died in 1947.

14 – Phar Lap (1926)

Phar Lap's claims to being regarded as the greatest of all Australasian Thoroughbreds are challenged only by Carbine. This New Zealand-bred gelding proved himself overwhelmingly the best 3-year-old in Australia in 1929–30 and recorded 14 consecutive wins in a brilliant campaign at 4 years, highlighted by an easy victory under 9 st 12 lb in the Melbourne Cup and also including the W S Cox Plate and Melbourne and Futurity Stakes. In early 1932 he was sent to North America and won in Mexico for his 37th win in 51 starts before falling victim to a sudden, mysterious and fatal illness.

14 – Nearco (1935)

Nearco, bred, owned and trained by Federico Tesio, was an outstanding Italian champion who went unbeaten through a career of 14 starts. His 7 races as a juvenile included the Gran Criterium, Premio Tevere and Premio Chiusura, and in 1938 he added seven more, notably the Premio Parioli, Derby Italiano, Gran Premio di Milano and Grand Prix de Paris. He stood at stud in Newmarket and became perhaps the most influential sire of the 20th century, dying in 1957.

13 – Hippolitus (1767)

Hippolitus was an Irish gelding who won his last 12 races in 1773, nearly all of them run in heats at minor meetings, and then scored at The Curragh on his reappearance as a 7-year-old.

13 – Phoenomenon (1780)

Phoenomenon won his last 2 races in 1783, gaining a narrow success in the St Leger, all 10 in 1784, notably a victory over Dungannon in the Doncaster Cup, and his only start as a 5-year-old before being retired. He had 4 walk-overs and one race in heats.

13 – Dungannon (1780)

Dungannon came second in the Derby and developed into a champion in his last 2 campaigns, being unbeaten in 9 races in 1785 and 4 in 1786. Most of them, including a King's Plate, were at Newmarket, and he had 3 walk-overs and 2 contests in heats. He won 26 of his 29 career starts and was second in the other three.

13 – Rockingham (1781)

Rockingham was a top-class English horse who won his last 3 races in 1786 and 16 out of 17 in 1787, the first 10 of them consecutively. These included the Jockey Club Plate at Newmarket and 5 King's Plates, three of them run in heats.

13 – Timoleon (1813)

Timoleon, the best horse of his day in America, was based in Virginia and enjoyed his long run of success in 1816 and 1817, often walking over for Jockey Club purses after frightening away the opposition. He sired the great champion Boston.

Six mid-Victorian Classic-winning jockeys are pictured on the cover of a music sheet. Top: *Harry Custance.* Centre: *Jemmy Grimshaw, George Fordham, Harry Grimshaw.* Bottom: *John Wells, Tom Chaloner. (Mary Evans Picture Library)*

Left, above *Flying Childers (foaled 1715), who was never beaten and is widely regarded as the first great racehorse. (Fine Art Photographic Library)*

Left *Lynwood Palmer's portrait of St Simon, who was unbeaten in 9 races including the 1884 Ascot Gold Cup, and became the greatest sire of the 19th century. (Jockey Club)*

Above *Diamond Jubilee (Herbert Jones), who in 1900 became the ninth winner of the Triple Crown, and the only one of that élite company to carry the royal colours.*

Right *Mill Reef (Geoff Lewis) enters the winner's circle after the 1971 Derby – the seventh of his 12 victories in a brilliant career in which only My Swallow and Brigadier Gerard beat him. (Gerry Cranham)*

Above *The 'Race of the Century': Derby hero Grundy (Pat Eddery) beats champion older horse Bustino (Joe Mercer) by half a length after a duel up the Ascot straight in the 1975 King George VI and Queen Elizabeth Stakes. (Gerry Cranham)*

Right, above *Bregawn (Graham Bradley) returns in triumph after the 1983 Cheltenham Gold Cup, in which the first 5 horses were all trained by Michael Dickinson. Runner-up Captain John follows his stablemate back. (Gerry Cranham)*

Right *Dahlia (Lester Piggott) after winning at York in 1975. The dual British Horse of the Year later became the world's leading money-winning racemare. (Gerry Cranham)*

Habibti (Willie Carson) wins the 1983 July Cup at Newmarket. The champion sprinter was, according to Timeform, the best 3-year-old filly to race in Europe in the post-war era. (Gerry Cranham)

Time Charter (Steve Cauthen) has just won the 1984 Coronation Cup – the last victory in a career in which she became Britain's leading money-winning racemare. (All-Sport)

Lester Piggott and Commanche Run after winning the 1984 St Leger – a victory which took Piggott past the record of 27 English Classic wins by 19th-century jockey Frank Buckle. (All-Sport)

Longboat (Willie Carson) wins the 1986 Ascot Gold Cup, the first of 3 Cup victories which made the 5-year-old the most recent winner of the stayers' Triple Crown. (Gerry Cranham)

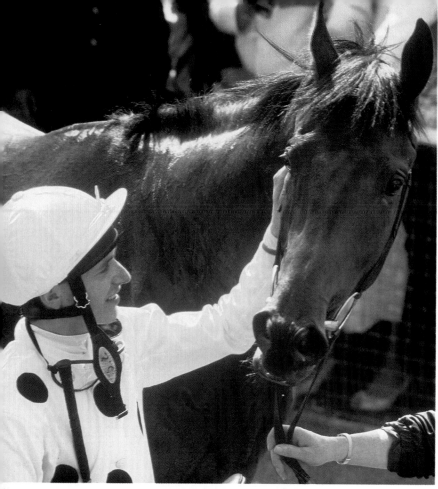

Left *Reference Point, Europe's champion racehorse of 1987, with Steve Cauthen after their victory in the Derby. (Gerry Cranham)*

Right *Triptych (Tony Cruz) wins the Champion Stakes at Newmarket for the second time in 1987. This tough performer was, according to Timeform, the best 5-year-old mare to race in Europe in the post-war era. (Gerry Cranham)*

Below *Mtoto (Michael Roberts), Europe's champion older horse, wins the 1987 Eclipse Stakes by three-quarters of a length from Horse of the Year Reference Point, for whom the distance of 10 furlongs was too short. (Gerry Cranham)*

Right, below *Ravinella (Gary Moore), seen here winning the 1988 1000 Guineas, was the first filly to head the 2-year-old Free Handicap since Jacinth in 1972. (Gerry Cranham)*

Left *Celtic Shot (Peter Scudamore)
about to jump the final flight on his way
to victory in the 1988 Champion Hurdle.
Classical Charm (left) was second.
(Sporting Pictures)*

Right *Indian Skimmer (Michael
Roberts), the best filly ever trained by
Henry Cecil, wins the 1988 Sun Chariot
Stakes at Newmarket. (Alan Johnson)*

Below *The crowd at the 1988 Kentucky
Derby at Churchill Downs, Louisville. A
world record paying attendance of
163,628 watched the 100th running of
America's premier Classic in 1974.
(All-Sport)*

Right, below *Minster Son with jockey
Willie Carson and trainer Neil Graham
after winning the 1988 St Leger – a
victory which made Carson the only
man ever to ride an English Classic
winner he had bred himself. (Gerry
Cranham)*

Peter Scudamore with Strands of Gold after winning the 1988 Hennessy Cognac Gold Cup at Newbury – the 83rd of the champion jump jockey's record 221 wins in the 1988/89 season. (Gerry Cranham)

Right *Record-breaking trainer Martin Pipe with Corporal Clinger and jockey Mark Perrett after their triumph in the 1988 Mecca Bookmakers' Handicap Hurdle at Sandown Park. (Gerry Cranham)*

Right, below *The grey Sayfar's Lad (Mark Perrett) on his way to victory in the 1989 Sun Alliance Novices' Hurdle at Cheltenham. This was the 162nd of trainer Martin Pipe's record 208 wins in a British season in 1988/89. (Gerry Cranham)*

Left *Desert Orchid (Simon Sherwood) parades before the 1989 Cheltenham Gold Cup, in which the champion steeplechaser put the seal on his third Horse of the Year campaign. (All-Sport)*

Right *Nashwan's sire: Blushing Groom in the parade before the 1977 Derby, in which he failed to stay and finished third. Europe's champion 2-year-old of 1976 is now among the world's most successful stallions. (Gerry Cranham)*

Below *Nashwan's dam: Height of Fashion, Europe's joint-champion 2-year-old filly of 1981. She was later sold by the Queen to Sheikh Hamdan al Maktoum, for whom she produced the 1989 Derby hero. (Sporting Pictures)*

Nashwan (Willie Carson) passes the post 5 lengths clear in the 1989 Derby to notch his second Classic success. (Gerry Cranham)

Right Nashwan in the winner's circle at Epsom with, at his head, owner Sheikh Hamdan al Maktoum, the first member of the ruling family of Dubai to win the Derby. (Gerry Cranham)

13 – Effie Deans (1815)

Effie Deans graduated from selling plates to become the most prolific winner of the season in Great Britain in 1819, when she took her last 13 races including 10 in heats (notably the King's Plate at Salisbury) and 2 walk-overs.

13 – The Flying Dutchman (1846)

The Flying Dutchman was one of the greatest champions of the 19th century. He won 5 races as a juvenile, notably the July and Champagne Stakes, 6 in 1849, including the Derby, St Leger and 3 walk-overs, and added the Emperor of Russia's Plate (Ascot Gold Cup) and one other prize in 1850 before being upset by Voltigeur in the Doncaster Cup, the only defeat of his 15-race career.

13 – Planet (1855)

Planet was the best horse in America just before the Civil War, winning 27 of his 31 starts. He raced throughout the southern states and his long spell of success in 1859 and 1860 included victories in the Great Post and Planet Post Stakes, both in 4-mile heats at New Orleans.

13 – Mollie McCarthy (1873)

Champion American mare Mollie McCarthy won the first 13 races of her career in California but was then distanced in the first heat of a match with Ten Broeck at Churchill Downs in July 1878.

13 – Tremont (1884)

Tremont's career was a brief flash of brilliance, his 13 races all coming within 10 weeks in New York and New Jersey in the summer of 1886, and in that time he proved himself by far the best 2-year-old in America. Trained by Frank McCabe for the brothers Phil and Mike Dwyer, he was a phenomenally fast starter and was never headed for a single stride. His victories included the Juvenile, Great Post, Atlantic, Tyro and Junior Champion Stakes, but he could not stand further training.

13 – Kingston (1884)

Kingston won a career total of 89 races, which still stands as an American record; they included his last 13 as a 5-year-old in 1889, when he was just about the best older horse in the country. He was unplaced only 4 times in 138 starts and before his retirement at the age of 10 had become America's leading earner, his most valuable victory coming in the Select Stakes as a juvenile. He became champion sire twice.

13 – Polar Star (1904)

Polar Star was England's champion 2-year-old of 1906, winning all his 12 races including the Gimcrack and Criterion Stakes. On his reappearance at 3 he took the Kempton Park Great Jubilee Handicap, but then lost his form.

13 – Limerick (1923)

New Zealand champion Limerick won 4 races in his native land, notably the Canterbury Cup, as a 4-year-old in 1927–28 and numbered the All Aged Stakes and King's Cup in Sydney among 5 further victories that season. At 5 years the gelding extended his sequence to 13, the last of them a dead-heat.

13 – Sweet Wall (1925)

Sweet Wall, the best filly of her generation in Ireland, won her last 6 races as a 3-year-old, culminating in the Irish Cambridgeshire under top weight, and all 7 in her farewell season of 1929, including 2 walk-overs.

13 – Grano de Oro (1937)

Grano de Oro was successful in Ireland in 1940 under his original name of Roe, and when exported to Venezuela the gelding won his first 13 races in Caracas.

13 – Bula (1965)

Bula never ran on the Flat and was unbeaten in his first 2 seasons over timber. In 1970 he won a division of the Gloucestershire Hurdle and the following year took the first of his 2 Champion Hurdles, dethroning Persian War, as well as the Welsh Champion Hurdle.

13 – Weimar (1968)

Italian champion Weimar won his first 13 races, comprising 3 as a juvenile, 8 in 1971 – notably the Gran Premio d'Italia, Gran Premio di Milano, St Leger Italiano and Gran Premio del Jockey Club – and his first 2 in 1972, but he never won again.

13 – Personal Ensign (1984)

Champion American filly Personal Ensign was unbeaten in a career of 13 races including 8 Grade I stakes – the Frizette Stakes, Beldame Stakes (twice), Shuvee, Hempstead, Whitney and Maskette Handicaps and, by a short head, the 1988 Breeders' Cup Distaff.

Breeders' Cup

The Breeders' Cup programme, inaugurated in 1984, is the richest and most ambitious scheme ever devised in Thoroughbred racing. Founded and administered by breeders, it offers more than $20 million in prize money each year to horses in North America, $10 million of it in the 7 races run on Breeders' Cup Event Day in November, the richest day's racing anywhere in the world.

The Breeders' Cup was the brainchild of John Gaines, owner of Gainesway Farm near Lexington, Kentucky, who announced his plan on 23 April 1982. Gaines was concerned about the possible decline of racing in America, and with the help of television he wanted to stimulate public interest and thus ensure the long-term health of the sport.

The principal means to this end would be Breeders' Cup Event Day, consisting of 7 extremely valuable races in which the best horses in each age, sex and distance category would compete to decide the seasonal championships. America's racing year would have a climax, an equivalent to the Super Bowl and the World Series.

Gaines persuaded other major breeders to join him in founding Breeders' Cup Limited to organize the project, and in 1984 it came to fruition. The first Event Day took place at Hollywood Park on 7 November 1984 – and from that day there has been little doubt about the scheme's success. Helped by a special telecast and many celebrity guests, racing has become the focus of media attention in America to an extent it had never achieved before.

The huge amounts needed to fund the Breeders' Cup are raised from two main sources. Stallions are nominated by an annual payment of a sum equal to their stud fee; and their offspring are made eligible as foals at a cost of $500.

The money thus raised is allocated to three different funds. In 1989, $10 million went to the races on Event Day; $8 million to the Premium Award Fund, which boosts the prizes of about 500 existing stakes races at tracks throughout North America; and $4 million to the Special Stakes Fund (initiated in 1986), which finances about 50 new sponsored stakes races.

The 7 races on Event Day are:
• *Breeders' Cup Classic:* total purse $3 million ($1.35 million to the winning owner) over 1¼ miles – the world's richest race.
• *Breeders' Cup Turf:* $2 million ($900,000) 1½ miles on grass.
• *Breeders' Cup Mile:* $1 million ($450,000) 1 mile on grass.
• *Breeders' Cup Sprint:* $1 million ($450,000) 6 furlongs.
• *Breeders' Cup Distaff:* $1 million ($450,000) 1 mile 1 furlong, fillies and mares.
• *Breeders' Cup Juvenile:* $1 million ($450,000) 1 mile 110 yards, 2-year-old colts and geldings.
• *Breeders' Cup Juvenile Fillies:* $1 million ($450,000) 1 mile 110 yards, 2-year-old fillies.

The venues have been:
1984 Hollywood Park, California
1985 Aqueduct, New York
1986 Santa Anita, California
1987 Hollywood Park, California
1988 Churchill Downs, Kentucky
1989 Gulfstream Park, Florida
1990 Belmont Park, New York
1991 Churchill Downs, Kentucky

In addition the Breeders' Cup Steeplechase, worth $250,000

Manila (outside) beats Theatrical (rails) and Estrapade in the 1986 Breeders' Cup Turf, with European champion Dancing Brave well behind. Theatrical won the race the following year. (All-Sport)

Ferdinand and Bill Shoemaker (centre) hold on by a nose from Alysheba and Chris McCarron (left) in the 1987 Breeders' Cup Classic. Alysheba won the race the following year. (All-Sport)

($125,000 to the winner), had its inaugural running in 1986, but it is held at a different track (Fair Hill, Maryland 1986–88; Far Hills, New Jersey 1989) and, from 1987, on a different day to the other races.

Perhaps the biggest supporter of the Breeders' Cup is champion trainer D Wayne Lukas, who gears the preparation of his best horses towards Event Day. In the first five years he led all other trainers with nine winners, and in the same period Pat Day and Laffit Pincay were the most successful jockeys with four winners.

However, no single day's racing can provide a definitive series of championships because some horses are inevitably missing through injury, or are past their best for the season. This is especially true when Event Day is as late as 21 November, as it was in 1987 because of the demands of television.

In addition, European horses must make a long journey to race in unfamiliar conditions, a handicap which proved too much for the most distinguished transatlantic challenger to date, Dancing Brave, who finished only fourth in the 1986 Breeders' Cup Turf. Even so, on the first five Event Days, five of the races were won by horses trained in Europe – Lashkari (1984 Turf), Pebbles (1985 Turf), Last Tycoon (1986 Mile) and Miesque (1987 and 1988 Mile). Indeed, Miesque was the first horse to win two Breeders' Cup races.

A more serious objection is the fact that the Breeders' Cup diminishes the significance of other major prizes, with the emphasis on one race rather than a season-long campaign and an unworthy winner like Smile (1986 Sprint) being acclaimed as a champion.

But above all, the integrity of the entire programme is in doubt over the issue of medication. If Event Day is held in a State which allows horses to run on drugs, the Breeders' Cup executive allow it in their races. This means that unless Event Day is held in New York (the only American State which bans race-day medication), European horses compete against rivals who would fail a dope test.

Nevertheless, the Breeders' Cup races have quickly established themselves as the ultimate targets for all top-class horses in North America and some in Europe. Twenty-five of the 35 winners on the first five Event Days (1984–88) picked up Eclipse Awards, the premier awards in American racing, which are decided by ballot among racing writers and officials and given to the champions in each age and sex category. Some owed their title almost entirely to their Breeders' Cup victory.

The Breeders' Cup has changed the pattern of the sport in the world's most powerful racing nation, acts as a showcase for the best talent available, both human and equine, and attracts enough European horses to make it an international occasion. Future generations will wonder how American racing managed before John Gaines had his vision.

LONGEST LOSING SEQUENCES

It is a well-established fact that most horses are incapable of winning a race, and usually owners are quite swift to recognize the futility of persevering with animals of no evident merit. But there have been instances of remarkable reluctance to admit defeat.

The all-time record for consistent failure probably belongs to Ouroene, a mare bred and raced in Australia by George and Lorraine Chiotis. Foaled in 1974, this daughter of Farnworth became a figure of fun on Sydney tracks over a long period, racing 124 times without a single victory between December 1976 and November 1983. But the sequence was not all gloom, being punctuated with two second and seven third places, which contributed $14,605 towards the mare's upkeep. The saga ended when Ouroene's owners took her home after the 124th failure, and though she was put back into training in December 1984, mercifully she did not run again.

Britain's nearest equivalent to Ouroene was Elsich, a gelding of uncertain breeding who worked between the shafts down on the farm as part of his preparation for steeplechasing. Foaled in 1936, Elsich had to make a late start to his jumping career because National Hunt racing was suspended for much of World War II. He made up for lost time by having his first two races on the same afternoon at Cheltenham in February 1945. He fell in both. For more than two years his intrepid and eccentric owner-trainer Charles Edwards ran him all over the country, including three times in the Cheltenham Gold Cup (ran out, fell, pulled up) and once in the Grand National (fell at the first fence). He completed the course in less than a third of his 50 races, sometimes even then only after being remounted. Edwards was keen to persevere and was highly indignant when, in June 1947, the authorities informed him that they would accept no further entries for Elsich. The gelding had never been nearer than second – and that when beaten a distance in a two-horse race.

On the other hand, there are cases of horses coming good after promising little. Perhaps the most remarkable concerns Reckless, an Australian-bred son of Better Boy who had only a couple of seconds and a couple of thirds to show for 30 efforts in his first three seasons. He finally got his head in front in his 33rd start, when already five years old, and the following season improved out of all recognition. Before being retired at the age of seven he had won the Sydney, Adelaide and Brisbane Cups – all Group I events – and finished second, beaten a length, in the Melbourne Cup. He began duties as a stallion in Victoria in 1978.

Unbeaten Horses

The following 148 horses (colts unless otherwise specified) were never beaten during their racing careers. They are ranked according to the number of races they had, together with the country in which they were trained, their year of birth and their most important victories.

54
Kincsem (Austria-Hungary 1874: filly)
Zukunfts-Preis, Preis des Jockey Club, Grosser Preis von Hannover, Grosser Preis von Baden (3 times), Pesti St Leger, Kancza-dij (3 times), Goodwood Cup, Grand Prix de Deauville, Silberner Schild.

18
Eclipse (GB 1764)
King's Plates at Winchester, Salisbury, Canterbury, Lewes, Lichfield, Newmarket (2), Guildford, Nottingham, York and Lincoln, Match with Bucephalus.
Karayel (Turkey 1970)
Queen Elizabeth II Kupasi, Caldiran Kosusu, Erkek Tay Deneme Kosusu, Gazi Kosusu (Turkish Derby), Ankara Kosusu, Cumhurbaskanligi Kupasi Kosusu, Basbakanlik Kupasi Kosusu, Senatobaskanligi Kupasi Kosusu, Bogazici Kosusu.

16
Ormonde (GB 1883)
Criterion Stakes, Dewhurst Plate, 2000 Guineas, Derby, St James's Palace, Hardwicke (twice), St Leger, Great Foal, Newmarket St Leger, Champion and Rous Memorial Stakes, Imperial Gold Cup (July Cup).
Prestige (France 1903)
Critérium de Maisons-Laffitte, Grand Critérium, Prix de la Forêt, Prix Lagrange, Prix Eugène Adam.
Ribot (Italy 1952)

Criterium Nazionale, Gran Criterium, Premio Emanuele Filiberto, Prix de l'Arc de Triomphe (twice), Gran Premio del Jockey Club, Gran Premio di Milano, King George VI and Queen Elizabeth Stakes, Premio Piazzale.

15
Colin (USA 1905)
National Stallion, Eclipse, Great Trial, Brighton Junior, Saratoga Special, Grand Union Hotel, Futurity, Flatbush, Produce, Matron, Champagne, Withers, Belmont and Tidal Stakes.
Macon (Argentina 1922)
Polla de Potrillos, Gran Premio Nacional, Gran Premio Carlos Pellegrini (twice), El Comparacion (twice), Gran Premio de Honor.

14
Nearco (Italy 1935)
Criterium Nazionale, Gran Criterium, Premio Tevere, Premio Chiusura, Premio Parioli, Premio Principe Emanuele Filiberto, Gran Premio del Re (Italian Derby), Gran Premio dell'Impero, Gran Premio di Milano, Grand Prix de Paris.

13
Tremont (USA 1884)
Juvenile, Sequence, Foam, Surf, Zephyr, Paddock, Spring, June, Great Post, Good-Bye, Atlantic, Tyro and Junior Champion Stakes.
Personal Ensign (USA 1984: filly)
Frizette Stakes, Rare Perfume Stakes, Beldame Stakes (twice), Shuvee, Hempstead, Molly Pitcher, Whitney and Maskette Handicaps, Breeders' Cup Distaff.

12
Highflyer (GB 1774)
Grosvenor Stakes, Match with Dictator, Great Subscription Race (York), King's Purse (Lichfield).
Ardrossan (GB 1809)
Irvine Silver Cup, Ayr Gold Cup (twice), Irvine Gold Cup.

Crucifix (GB 1837: filly)
July, Chesterfield, Molecomb, Hopeful, Clearwell, Prendergast, Criterion, 2000 Guineas, 1000 Guineas and Oaks Stakes.
Asteroid (USA 1861)
Woodlawn Vase.
Barcaldine (Ireland/GB 1878)
Railway, National Produce and Beresford Stakes, Baldoyle Derby, 3 Queen's Plates (The Curragh), Westminster Cup, Orange Cup, Northumberland Plate.
Braque (Italy 1954)
Derby Italiano, Gran Premio d'Italia, Gran Premio di Milano, Premio Piazzale, St Leger Italiano.

11

Goldfinder (GB 1764)
Ascot Subscription, The Cup (Newmarket, twice).

10

Nereïde (Germany 1933: filly)
Zukunfts-Rennen, Kisasszony-Rennen, Preis der Diana, Deutsches Derby, Braunes Band von Deutschland.

9

Regulus (GB 1739)
King's Plates at Winchester, Salisbury, Nottingham, Canterbury, Lewes, Lincoln and Newmarket (2).
Grand Flaneur (Australia 1877)
AJC Derby, AJC Mares' Produce Stakes, VRC Derby, Melbourne Cup, VRC Mares' Produce Stakes, VRC Champion Stakes, VRC St Leger.
St Simon (GB 1881)
Epsom Gold Cup, Ascot Gold Cup, Newcastle Gold Cup, Goodwood Cup.
Patience (Austria-Hungary 1902: filly)
Austria-Preis, Österreichisches Derby, Deutsches Derby, Hungarian Oaks, Austrian Oaks.
Bahram (GB 1932)
National Breeders' Produce, Gimcrack, Middle Park, 2000 Guineas, Derby, St James's Palace and St Leger Stakes.
Combat (GB 1944)
Windsor Castle, Blue Riband Trial, Rous Memorial, Sandringham and Sussex Stakes.

8

Sweetbriar (GB 1769)
The Cup (Newmarket)
American Eclipse (USA 1814)
3 Jockey Club Purses (Union Course), Matches with Sir Charles and Henry.
Sensation (USA 1877)
Juvenile, July, Flash, Saratoga, August, Criterion, Nursery and Central Stakes.
Tiffin (GB 1926: filly)
National Breeders' Produce Stakes, Ham Produce Stakes, Convivial Plate, Cheveley Park Stakes, Fern Hill Stakes, July Cup, King George Stakes.
Caracalla (France 1942)
Prix Reiset, Grand Prix de Paris, Prix Royal-Oak, Prix Edgard Gillois, Ascot Gold Cup, Prix de l'Arc de Triomphe.
Rare Brick (USA 1983)
Land of 10,000 Lakes, Mountain Valley, Southwest and Rebel Stakes.

7

Woodpecker (USA 1828)
sire of Grey Eagle.
Rodolph (USA 1831)
Inter-state match.
Bay Middleton (GB 1833)
Riddlesworth, 2000 Guineas, Derby, Buckhurst and Grand Duke Michael Stakes.
Monarch (USA 1834)
Jockey Club Purse and Tattersall Whip (Charleston).
Salvator (France 1872)
Prix de l'Espérance, Prix Reiset, Prix du Jockey-Club, Grand Prix de Paris.
El Rio Rey (USA 1887)
Hyde Park Stakes, Eclipse Stakes, White Plains Handicap.
The Tetrarch (GB 1911)
Woodcote, Coventry, National Breeders' Produce, Champion Breeders' Foal and Champagne Stakes.

Mannamead (GB 1929)
Malton Plate, Clearwell Stakes, Doncaster Autumn Foal Plate, Chippenham Stakes, Rous Memorial Stakes.
Claude (Italy 1964)
Premio Emanuele Filiberto, Premio Mario Locatelli, Premio Antonio dall'Acqua.
Viani (Italy 1967)
Criterium Nazionale, Gran Criterium, Premio Alfonso Doria.
Itajara (Brazil 1983) Grande Primo Cruzeiro do Sul, Grande Premio Jockey Club Brasiliero.

6

Dismal (GB 1733)
Great Stakes (Newmarket), King's Plates at Ipswich, Guildford, Salisbury, Canterbury and Lincoln.
Quintessence (GB 1900: filly)
Ascot Biennial Stakes, Molecomb Stakes, 1000 Guineas, Park Hill Stakes, Newmarket Oaks.
Aldford (GB 1911)
Salisbury, Ascot Triennial, Stud Produce and Newbury Autumn Foal Stakes.
Hurry On (GB 1913)
September Stakes (St Leger), Newmarket St Leger, Jockey Club Cup.
Tolgus (GB 1923)
Imperial Produce Stakes, Lingfield Park Spring Stakes.
Payaso (Argentina 1929)
Gran Premio Jockey Club, Gran Premio Nacional, Gran Premio Carlos Pellegrini.
Albany Girl (GB 1935: filly)
Coombe July Stakes.
Windsor Slipper (Ireland 1939)
Waterford Testimonial, Railway and Beresford Stakes, Irish 2000 Guineas, Irish Derby, Irish St Leger.
Manantial (Argentina 1955)
Polla de Potrillos, Gran Premio Jockey Club, Gran Premio Nacional, Gran Premio Carlos Pellegrini.

5

Albert (GB 1827)
Audley End Stakes.
Norfolk (USA 1861)
Jersey Derby, 3 Matches with Lodi.
Frontin (France 1880)
Prix Reiset, Prix du Jockey-Club, Grand Prix de Paris.
Ajax (France 1901)
Prix Noailles, Prix Lupin, Prix du Jockey-Club, Grand Prix de Paris.
Landgraf (Germany 1914)
Henckel-Rennen, Union-Rennen, Deutsches Derby, Grosser Preis von Berlin.
Pazman (Austria 1916)
Austria-Preis, Wiener Derby.
Dice (USA 1925)
Keene Memorial, Juvenile, Hudson and Great American Stakes.
Cavaliere d'Arpino (Italy 1926)
Premio Ambrosiano, Omnium, Gran Premio di Milano.
Melody (Argentina 1947: filly)
Polla de Potrancas.
Paddy's Sister (Ireland 1957: filly)
Queen Mary, Gimcrack and Champagne Stakes.
Emerson (Brazil 1958)
Grande Premio Cruzeiro do Sul, Derby Paulista, Grande Premio Derby Sul-Americano.
Eileen's Choice (GB 1967: filly)
Acorn Stakes.
Star Shower (Australia 1976)
Maribyrnong Trial, Merson Cooper Stakes, Maribyrnong Plate, Blue Diamond Stakes.
Landaluce (USA 1980: filly)
Hollywood Lassie, Del Mar Debutante, Anoakia and Oak Leaf Stakes.
Precocious (GB 1981)
National, Norfolk, Molecomb and Gimcrack Stakes.
Kneller (GB 1985)
Ebor Handicap, Doncaster Cup, Jockey Club Cup.

4

Snap (GB 1750)
2 Matches with Marske.
Ball's Florizel (USA 1801)
Match with Peace Maker.

Tennessee Oscar (USA 1814)
2 Jockey Club Purses (Nashville).
Clairvaux (GB 1880)
Fern Hill Stakes, July Cup, Bunbury Stakes.
Magus (Austria-Hungary 1891)
Austria-Preis, Österreichisches Derby.
Saphir (Austria-Hungary 1894)
Austria-Preis, Jubiläums-Preis, Österreichisches Derby.
Morazzona (Italy 1939: filly)
Premio Laveno.
Ocarina (France 1947)
Grand Prix de Saint-Cloud.
Pharsalia (GB 1954: filly)
Queen Mary, Molecomb and Lowther Stakes.
Raise a Native (USA 1961)
Juvenile Stakes, Great American Stakes.
Drone (USA 1966)
grandsire of Dancing Brave.
Blood Royal (Ireland 1971)
Queen's Vase, Jockey Club Cup.
Madelia (France 1974: filly)
Poule d'Essai des Pouliches, Prix Saint-Alary, Prix de Diane.
Golden Fleece (Ireland 1979)
Ballymoss Stakes, Nijinsky Stakes, Derby.
Saratoga Six (USA 1982)
Hollywood Juvenile Championship, Balboa Stakes, Del Mar Futurity.

3

Lath (GB 1732)
Great Stakes (Newmarket), Match with Squirt.
Slamerkin (Pennsylvania 1769: filly)
City and Jockey Club Purses (Philadelphia).
Cobweb (GB 1821: filly)
1000 Guineas, Oaks.
Achmet (GB 1834)
Riddlesworth Stakes, 2000 Guineas.
Attila (USA 1871)
Travers Stakes.
Suspender (GB 1889)
Royal Hunt Cup.
Meddler (GB 1890)
Chesterfield Stakes, Dewhurst Plate.
Boniform (New Zealand 1904)
AJC Breeders' Plate, Great Northern Derby, Great Autumn Handicap.
Inchcape (USA 1918)
Tremont Stakes.
Prince Meteor (Ireland 1926)
Leopardstown Produce Stakes, Irish Breeders' Produce Stakes.
Early School (GB 1934)
Coventry Stakes, Malton Plate.
Rosewell (Ireland 1935)
Railway Stakes, Beresford Stakes, Irish Derby.
Pharis (France 1936)
Prix Noailles, Prix du Jockey-Club, Grand Prix de Paris.
Blue Train (GB 1944)
Swinley Forest, Sandown Park Trial and Newmarket Stakes.
Berberis (West Germany 1949: filly)
Hamburger Criterium, Rudolf Oetker-Rennen.
Sagitaria (Argentina 1951: filly)
Premio Coronel Pringles, Premio Cabildo.
Pronto (Argentina 1958)
Premio Miguel A Martinez de Hoz.
Whistling Wind (Ireland 1960)
Youngsters' Stakes, National Stakes (Sandown Park).
Hardicanute (Ireland 1962)
Champagne Stakes, Timeform Gold Cup, Ballymoss Stakes.

Left, above *Kneller (Paul Eddery) wins the 1988 Ebor Handicap at York – the third of 5 races for this unbeaten colt, who died of colic two months later. (Gerry Cranham)*

Left, below *Morston (Edward Hide) triumphs in the 1973 Derby on only his second racecourse appearance. He never ran again. (Gerry Cranham)*

Veiled Wonder (USA 1969)
Native Diver Stakes, Golden Gate Juvenile Dinner Stakes.
Sir Wimborne (Ireland 1973)
National Stakes (The Curragh), Royal Lodge Stakes.
Solar (Ireland 1976: filly)
Railway Stakes, Park Stakes.
Danzig (USA 1977)
sire of Chief's Crown, Danzig Connection, Green Desert, Polonia.
Judge Smells (USA 1983)
Juaneno Stakes, Hollywood Prevue Stakes.
Meadowlake (USA 1983)
Arlington-Washington Futurity.

2

Flying Childers (GB 1715)
Matches with Speedwell and Chanter.
Monkey (GB 1725)
King's Plate (York).
Shock (GB 1729)
October Stakes (Newmarket).
Selima (Maryland 1745: filly)
Inter-colonial race.
Sailor (GB 1817)
Derby.
Battledore (GB 1824)
Palatine Stakes, Manchester St Leger.
Ghuznee (GB 1838: filly)
Oaks, Coronation Stakes.
Sir Amyas (GB 1869)
July Stakes.
Thyestes (GB 1928)
National Breeders' Produce Stakes.
Tai-Yang (GB 1930)
Jockey Club Stakes, Chippenham Stakes.
Quisquillosa (Argentina 1941: filly)
Polla de Potrancas.
Burg-el-Arab (USA 1942)
Tremont Stakes.
Labrador (Argentina 1953)
Gran Premio Nacional.
Abdos (France 1959)
Grand Critérium.
Royal Indiscretion (Ireland 1960: filly)
Molecomb Stakes.
Naujwan (Ireland 1960: filly)
dam of Giacometti.
Calchaqui (France 1960)
Prix Noailles.
Groton (USA 1962)
grandsire of Summing.
Embroidery (Ireland 1969: filly)
Ascot 1000 Guineas Trial.
Morston (GB 1970)
Derby.
Le Melody (Ireland 1971: filly)
dam of Ardross.
Rukann (USA 1971: filly)
dam of Temperate Sil.
Lady Seymour (Ireland 1972: filly)
Phoenix Stakes.
Brahms (Ireland 1974)
Railway Stakes.
Fairy Bridge (Ireland 1975: filly)
Arnott Stakes.
Tarona (France 1975: filly)
Critérium des Pouliches.

1

Young Marske (GB 1771)
sire of Ruler.
Sister to Tuckahoe (USA 1814: filly)
dam of Boston.
Fillagree (GB 1815: filly)
dam of Cobweb, Charlotte West and Riddlesworth.
Ardrossan filly (GB 1817: filly)
dam of Beeswing.
Middleton (GB 1822)
Derby.
Amato (GB 1835)
Derby.

Chattanooga (GB 1862)
Criterion Stakes.
Hero (GB 1872)
Sweepstakes (Newmarket).
Plebeian (GB 1872)
Middle Park Plate.
Chouberski (France 1902)

Prix Reiset: sire of Brûleur.
Cherimoya (GB 1908: filly)
Oaks.
Puits d'Amour (France 1932)
Prix du Bois: sire of Rigolo.
Tourzima (France 1939: filly)
dam of Corejada.

Atan (USA 1961)
sire of Sharpen Up.
Balkan Knight (Ireland 1970)
sire of Bound To Honour and Suttle Knight.
Seneca (France 1973: filly)
dam of Sagace.

Oldest Horses

The greatest age at which any horse has won a race is 18, and of the 5 horses who share the record Wild Aster is the only one to win 3 times at that age.

Wild Aster, foaled in 1901, started his career in England and was then sent to France, where he dead-heated for a valuable steeplechase, the Grand Prix de la Ville de Nice, in 1909. The gelding returned to England and, at the age of 18, won 3 hurdle races within a week in March 1919. He dead-heated for the Selling Handicap Hurdle at Wolverhampton on 4 March; finished second in the Farm Selling Handicap Hurdle at Haydock Park on 8 March but was awarded the race because the jockey on the original winner had been warned off; and dead-heated for the Milverton Selling Handicap Hurdle at Warwick on 10 March, only to be awarded the race outright when the jockey on the other dead-heater dismounted in the wrong place.

Sonny Somers, foaled in 1962, was an English steeplechaser who gained his last 2 victories in 1980. He won the Star and Garter Handicap Chase at Southwell by 8 lengths on 14 February and the Westerham Handicap Chase at Lingfield Park by 5 lengths on 28 February.

On the Flat 2 stallions, 18-year-old Revenge and 14-year-old Tommy (the 1779 St Leger winner) took part in a bizarre match over 2 miles at Shrewsbury on 23 September 1790. Revenge beat his younger rival.

Marksman, foaled in 1808, was a high-class gelding who won the Wokingham Stakes at Ascot in 1814, the King's Plate at Lewes in 1817 and the Yeomen's Plate at Ashford, Kent on 4 September 1826. He lost the first heat of that race but won the next two, galloping a total of 7½ miles for his £50 prize.

Jorrocks, foaled in 1833, was the best horse to emerge in the early days of Australian racing. He gained the last of his 65 recorded wins in the Publican's Purse at Bathurst on 28 February 1851, though the only other runner threw his rider and galloped loose before the race.

The oldest horse to take part in a race is Creggmore Boy. Foaled in 1940, this veteran enjoyed his last victory in the Furness Selling Handicap Chase at Cartmel, Lancashire, England in 1957 and·5 years later, at the age of 22, ended his career by running fourth in the same race on 9 June 1962. He once finished second as a 21-year-old.

Record Times

It is one of the ironies of horse racing that while, through the history of the Thoroughbred, man's constant quest has been for the horse who can run fastest between two given points, records in terms of time have tended to be meaningless. Hand timing could never be thoroughly reliable, but even since electrical timing became commonplace, other factors have been apt to make time alone a poor and misleading guide to racing class. In all but a tiny minority of races, horses are ridden with the intention of beating other horses, not of beating the clock. As a consequence, many recognized top horses do not break time records, whereas many manifestly ordinary horses do.

The condition and contours of the track and wind direction commonly have as much to do with the setting of time records as the intrinsic merit of the record-breaker, and comparisons between time records set in various parts of the world have little significance. Inevitably, most of the world's fastest times attributed to British horses were set at Epsom and Brighton, courses which feature sharp descents, and while the American record-holders might seem more legitimate on account of the almost uniformly level tracks, it is American practice to clock races from a flying start and to return times to the nearest fifth of a second, as opposed to the one-hundredth of a second common in other countries.

Distance	Time	Name	Age	Weight (lb)	Course	Date
5 furlongs	53.6*	**Indigenous**	4	131	Epsom, England (g)	2 June 1960
	53.70	**Spark Chief**	4	110	Epsom, England (g)	30 Aug 1983
	55.2	**Chinook Pass**	3	113	Longacres, USA (d)	17 Sep 1982
6 furlongs	1:06.2*	**b g (unnamed) Blink–Broken Tendril**	2	123	Brighton, England (g)	6 Aug 1929
	1:06.8	**Zany Tactics**	6	126	Turf Paradise, USA (d)	8 Mar 1987
1 mile	1:31.1*	**Al-Torfanan**	5	115	Brighton, England (g)	19 June 1989
	1:32.2	**Dr Fager**	4	134	Arlington Park, USA (d)	24 Aug 1968
1¼ miles	1:57.4	**Double Discount**	4	113	Santa Anita, USA (g)	6 Oct 1977
	1:57.8	**Spectacular Bid**	4	126	Santa Anita, USA (d)	3 Feb 1980
1½ miles	2:22.8	**Hawkster**	3	121	Santa Anita, USA (g)	14 Oct 1989
	2:24.0	**Secretariat**	3	126	Belmont Park, USA (d)	9 June 1973
2 miles	3:16.75	**Il Tempo**	7	130	Trentham, New Zealand (g)	17 Jan 1970
2½ miles	4:14.6	**Miss Grillo**	6	118	Pimlico, USA (d)	12 Nov 1948

* Hand-timed. (g) *denotes grass course,* (d) *denotes dirt track.*

Breeding Records

Most national sires' championships

The record number of sires' championships won in one country is 16, achieved by the great American horse Lexington (foaled 1850). His stock dominated US racing to a remarkable degree virtually throughout the 1860s and 1870s, and having headed the list from 1861 to 1874 inclusive, he led again in 1876 and 1878.

The English-bred horse Buccaneer (foaled 1857) also compiled a formidable score. He topped the British table in 1868, by which time he had already been exported to Austria-Hungary. In due course he headed the Hungarian list 15 times and was 4 times top in Germany, giving him a total of 20 titles.

Champion sires on both sides of the Atlantic

The first horse to head the sires' lists on both sides of the Atlantic was 1830 Derby winner Priam. Champion in Britain in 1839 and 1840 (on money won), he topped the American tables (races won) for 1842, 1844, 1845 and 1846.

Nasrullah (foaled 1940) was another exported horse credited with the feat. His five championships (1955, 1956, 1959, 1960 and 1962) in North America were earned legitimately, but he gained his 1951 title in Great Britain and Ireland only because of the doubtful paternity of that season's leading winner, Supreme Court.

American-bred Lyphard (foaled 1969) was the champion sire in France in 1978 and 1979, and after repatriation he topped the North American table for 1986.

The only horse to win championships on both sides of the Atlantic without having himself changed loca-tions is Northern Dancer (foaled 1961). He was the 1971 leader in North America and he dominated 4 seasons in Great Britain and Ireland – 1970, 1977, 1983 and 1984.

Champion sire in Britain and France in the same season

Blandford (1919–35), who stood as a stallion in both Ireland and England, achieved the unique feat of heading the lists in both Britain and France in the year of his death.

Most winners sired in a career

Irish-bred Smokey Eyes (1947–73), whose own most notable victory came in the 1952 Stewards' Cup at Goodwood, sired the winners of 2,796 races in Australia between 1956 and 1980.

Most winners sired in a season

Star Shoot, an English-bred son of Triple Crown winner Isinglass, is credited as the horse whose stock won most races in a single season. Foaled in 1898 and exported to the USA as a 3-year-old, he became champion North American sire on five occasions, recording a score of 216 races won by 87 individual offspring in 1916.

Most mares covered in one stud season

Spread Eagle, the 1795 Derby winner, attracted huge demand for his services after his importation to Virginia in 1798. It is recorded that in 1801 he covered no fewer than 234 mares. He was subsequently transferred to Kentucky and died there in 1805.

In recent years it has become customary for the most popular Irish National Hunt stallions to cover large books of mares. In the 16 seasons between 1971 and 1986 Deep Run covered a total of 2,148 registered broodmares, including 231 in 1984 and 224 in 1986. He died in 1987, aged 21. The dual Ascot Gold Cup winner Le Moss covered 210 mares in 1986.

Oldest active stallions

The French-bred stallion Mystic (foaled 1954) covered a mare at Windfields Farm, Maryland in 1985, and the result was a filly named Last Mystic.

Diomed, the 1780 Derby winner, covered as a 30-year-old in Virginia and was due to cover again when he died at 31 in March 1808.

The most notable instance of a big-race winner sired by a horse at an advanced age concerns Tetotum, who won the Oaks of 1780. Her sire Matchem was 28 years old at the time of her conception. Opaline, the French-trained champion 2-year-old in England in 1960, was sired by Hyperion when he was 27 years old.

Most consistently productive broodmare

Queen Esther (foaled 1864), a daughter of St Leger winner Warlock, ran four times without success as a 2-year-old before being put to stud. She proceeded to produce a foal every year for 21 seasons (1868–88) before proving barren for the first time. She died in 1890 after giving birth to a dead filly, her 22nd foal in 23 years.

Oldest productive broodmare

Contract (foaled 1862), a mare by Stockwell who won 12 of her 63 races, had her first foal at the age of 7 and was sold to France for 200 gns when 9. In 1893, at the age of 31, she was safely delivered of a filly by Begonia at the Haras de la Bourdonnière.

Contract's record may have been matched by Flora, a mare by Regulus who produced a colt by Chillaby in 1780, when she was either 30 or 31 years old.

Perhaps the most productive of all broodmares was Betsy Ross (foaled 1939), an English-bred daughter of Derby winner Mahmoud. Exported to the USA, she ran once unplaced there before her retirement to stud, where she produced 23 foals, the last of them at the age of 30. She was covered again when 33 years old, but – not surprisingly – proved barren.

Another recent example of an old productive mare was Wayward Miss, a daughter of Brumeux. Foaled in 1936, she produced a filly by Pendragon in 1966. Her final mating was with Kolper in 1967, when the ages of horse and mare aggregated 55 years, but no produce resulted.

Best production/success record

The Australian-bred mare Charivari (foaled 1929), a daughter of Melbourne Cup winner Comedy King, bred 16 foals, all of whom won and 7 of whom won stakes races.

Another whose first 16 foals all won was the Irish-based Borealis mare Northern Beauty (foaled 1955), whose produce included stakes winners Northern Deamon and Piccadilly Lil. Her 17th foal was born totally blind.

In foal when winning big races

Pregnancy does not necessarily inhibit racing performance, and there are numerous instances of mares who won big races while carrying foals. The most notable include The Princess (1844 Oaks), Glass Doll (1907 Oaks) and La Flèche (1894 Ascot Gold Cup and Champion Stakes). Legerdemain slipped the foal she had been carrying on the day after her Cesarewitch triumph in 1849.

North American Record Auction Yearlings

For many years the yearling market in North America lagged far behind Europe's, and it was not until 1919 that the first $25,000 sale was registered. That deal concerned the Sunstar colt Sun Turret, whose buyer was John Ross. Four years later Gifford Cochran gave the same sum for each of five colts entered in the Saratoga Sales, but their sale constituted a package deal, the yearlings not being submitted to auction.

The market really 'took off' in 1925, when Hamilton Farm gave $50,000 for the Man o' War filly **War Feathers**. If she seemed a bad bargain on account of her racing record – one win and $1,350 in earnings – she later excelled as a broodmare, with four stakes winners among her foals, including War Plumage, who won two of America's top filly races, the Coaching Club American Oaks and the Alabama Stakes, in addition to the valuable Washington Park Handicap. The financier and philanthropist William Coe could well afford to throw away $70,000 on **Hustle On** in 1927, and that was how the deal turned out, because the Hurry On colt proved a total failure. **New Broom**, who took the record from him a year later, was another of the same sort, adding more discouragement for the idea of speculating on high-priced yearlings.

New Broom retained his record for 26 years, and when it eventually fell, in 1954, Sayajirao's world record went with it. From the time when **Nalur** was knocked down for $86,000 at Keeneland the world

North America's Record Auction Yearlings

Year	Horse	Buyer	$
1925	**War Feathers** (ch f Man o' War – Tuscan Red, by William Rufus)	Hamilton Farm	50,500
1927	**Hustle On** (b c Hurry On – Fatima, by Radium)	William Coe	70,000
1928	**New Broom** (ch c Whisk Broom – Payment, by All Gold)	Eastland Farms Syndicate	75,000
1954	**Nalur** (ch c Nasrullah – Lurline B., by Alibhai)	F J Adams Syndicate	86,000
1956	**Rise 'n Shine** (gr c Hyperion – Deodora, by Dante)	Mrs Liz Lunn	87,000
1961	**Swapson** (ch c Swaps – Obedient, by Mahmoud)	John Olin	130,000
1964	**One Bold Bid** (br c Bold Ruler – Forgetmenow, by Menow)	Mrs Velma Morrison	170,000
1966	**Bold Discovery** (br c Bold Ruler – La Dauphine, by Princequillo)	Frank McMahon	200,000
1967	**Majestic Prince** (ch c Raise a Native – Gay Hostess, by Royal Charger)	Frank McMahon	250,000
1968	**Exemplary** (b c Fleet Nasrullah – Sequence, by Count Fleet)	Mrs Ada Martin	280,000
1968	**Reine Enchanteur** (ch f Sea-Bird – Libra, by Hyperion)	Wendell Rosso	405,000
1970	**Crowned Prince** (ch c Raise a Native – Gay Hostess, by Royal Charger)	Frank McMahon	510,000
1973	**Wajima** (b c Bold Ruler – Iskra, by Le Haar)	East-West Stable	600,000
1974	**Kentucky Gold** (b c Raise a Native – Gold Digger, by Nashua)	Wallace Gilroy	625,000
1975	**Elegant Prince** (ch c Raise a Native – Gay Hostess, by Royal Charger)	Franklin Groves	715,000
1976	**Canadian Bound** (ch c Secretariat – Charming Alibi, by Honeys Alibi)	Theodore Burnett *et al*	1,500,000
1979	**Hoist the King** (br c Hoist the Flag – Royal Dowry, by Royal Charger)	Kazuo Nakamura	1,600,000
1980	**Lichine** (b c Lyphard – Stylish Genie, by Bagdad)	Stavros Niarchos	1,700,000
1981	**Ballydoyle** (br c Northern Dancer – South Ocean, by New Providence)	Robert Sangster *et al*	3,500,000
1982	**Empire Glory** (b c Nijinsky – Spearfish, by Fleet Nasrullah)	Robert Sangster *et al*	4,250,000
1983	**Foxboro** (b c Northern Dancer – Desert Vixen, by In Reality)	Robert Sangster *et al*	4,250,000
1983	**Snaafi Dancer** (b c Northern Dancer – My Bupers, by Bupers)	Sheikh Mohammed	10,200,000
1985	**Seattle Dancer** (b c Nijinsky – My Charmer, by Poker)	Robert Sangster *et al*	13,100,000

record has been an American preserve. Nalur did not wear his badge of honour with much distinction at the races, managing only two minor wins for earnings of $6,575. His successor, the English-bred Hyperion colt **Rise 'n Shine**, was not much better, registering only four modest wins from 41 starts over six seasons in training. He even went four years without a victory, but eventual total earnings of $17,515 allowed his optimistic owner the idea that he would own credibility as a sire. He proved a dismal failure in that rôle.

The first yearling to raise a six-figure bid was **Swapson**, bought by Humphrey Finney on behalf of John Olin for $130,000 at Keeneland in 1961. He won six minor races, earned $21,245 and was exported to Venezuela. **One Bold Bid** was an aptly-named individual, as Mrs Velma Morrison made only one offer for the Bold Ruler colt and got him for $170,000. The venture proved a disaster, as One Bold Bid never got to the races. At least the next record-holder, **Bold Discovery**, became a racehorse, but he was a bad one, making a nil return on Frank McMahon's $200,000 investment.

McMahon enjoyed much better fortune with **Majestic Prince**, a colt he bred in partnership with Leslie Combs of Spendthrift Farm. His bid of $250,000 at Keeneland secured the colt outright, and the son of Raise a Native proved himself an outstanding runner, collecting both the Kentucky Derby and the Preakness Stakes while still unbeaten. Retired after his first – and only – loss in the Belmont Stakes, Majestic Prince became a sire of some consequence. He owns a claim to recognition as the best bargain of all the North American record-holders.

Exemplary, who raised the record to $280,000, turned out to be a tough colt, packing 70 races into a six-season career, but he lacked quality and was never up to stakes class. Still, his record of 15 wins

and earnings of $39,651 dollars established him as a more gifted athlete than his successor, **Reine Enchanteur**, a $405,000 Sea-Bird filly whose half-brothers Ribocco and Ribero had both won Classics in Ireland and England. Reine Enchanteur never aspired to that calibre of competition, and her buyer, the previously obscure Wendell P Rosso, promptly became obscure again.

The first to break the half-million barrier was **Crowned Prince**, a brother to Majestic Prince still regarded by many sound judges as the perfect yearling specimen. As was the case with Majestic Prince, Frank McMahon bought out his partner at the Keeneland auction, and it seemed that history might be repeated when Crowned Prince was named England's champion 2-year-old of 1971. But the colt did not progress, developing a soft palate problem as a 3-year-old, and he was retired to a stud career of strictly limited importance. Crowned Prince had completed his first season at stud in Ireland by the time **Wajima** erased his record. The $600,000 bid for him by a syndicate of Japanese and Americans proved a sound investment, as he became the champion US 3-year-old and recovered almost 90 per cent of his purchase price at the races before being re-syndicated for a lucrative sum. However, he was markedly less conspicuous as a sire than his half-brother Naskra, a decidedly inferior runner.

Brothers to outstanding racehorses often prove more successful as sales yearlings than as runners, and that was the case with each of the next two record-setters. **Kentucky Gold**, the brother to leading sprinter (and subsequently outstanding sire) Mr Prospector, realized $625,000 in the ring, but earned only $5,950 at the track. **Elegant Prince**, the brother to Majestic Prince and Crowned Prince who lifted the record to $715,000 a year later, never even ran.

Seattle Dancer (a half-brother to Seattle Slew) who cost a record $13.1 million as a yearling. He was a high-class racehorse in Europe and is now at stud in America. (Gerry Cranham)

Both colts became cheap stallions of no account.

The first yearling bid into seven figures was **Canadian Bound**, an impeccably-bred colt by Triple Crown winner Secretariat out of the dam of the champion racemare Dahlia. A solitary second place in a minor event in France was all he had to show for an outlay of $1,500,000. **Hoist the King**, who raised the record by a further $100,000 in 1979, was another to try racing on both sides of the Atlantic, but he proved no better than Canadian Bound and, like him, never won a race. His Japanese owners eventually took him home for stud duty.

After three record-holders who could not register a victory between them, **Lichine** represented something of an improvement. His buyer was Stavros Niarchos, the first man to give record sums for yearlings in both America and Europe, and this $1,700,000 transaction brought him a racehorse of decidedly above-average merit – three wins in France, and on the fringe of Pattern-race form – and ultimately a stallion for his Haras de Fresnay-le-Buffard. He was a far better runner than the colt who demolished his record, **Ballydoyle**, who won only an indifferent maiden race at Naas and never promised to be worth $3,500,000.

Ballydoyle was the first of four record-breaking yearlings purchased by Robert Sangster and part-

ners, but none of them compiled a racing record to match those of others bought more 'cheaply' by the same highly-successful buying team. **Empire Glory**, a $4,250,000 yearling of 1982, won a weak Group III event in Ireland, the Royal Whip, and was beaten only a neck in a moderately-contested Irish St Leger, but he was never a top-class runner. **Foxboro**, who equalled his record a year later, proved to be a runner of no consequence at all.

Still, Foxboro was almost never in the limelight, because his reign as joint-holder of the record lasted little more than a day, virtually obliterated from the public consciousness by the staggering duel between Sangster and Sheikh Mohammed which took the price of **Snaafi Dancer** to the dizzy heights of $10,200,000. The third son of Northern Dancer to take the record, he sadly descended to the status of a figure of fun. Allegedly so slow on the gallops that the idea of racing him was embarrassing, he was finally shunted off to a small stud in Canada for a stallion career which started inauspiciously when he was able to get only two of his first-season mares in foal.

When the market had started to take a downward turn, and Snaafi Dancer's record seemed impregnable, along came **Seattle Dancer** to confound the experts. A half-brother to US Triple Crown winner Seattle Slew, and to the 2000 Guineas victor Lomond, he was the subject of fierce rivalry between European- and American-based bidders at Keeneland in 1985. The duel ended with Californian trainer D Wayne Lukas conceding defeat at $13,100,000, and

Seattle Dancer was despatched to Ireland to race for Robert Sangster and friends. In a brief career which endured only from 18 April to 28 June of his 3-year-old season, the Nijinsky colt ran five times and won two Group II races – the Leopardstown Derby Trial and the Gallinule Stakes. He also finished sixth in the Prix du Jockey-Club and second in the Grand Prix de Paris.

European Record Auction Yearlings

		Buyer	Guineas
1837	**Glenlivat** (ch c Rowton *or* Cetus – Camarine, by Juniper)	5th Duke of Richmond	1,010
1854	**Voivode** (ch c Surplice – Hybla, by The Provost)	James Merry	1,020
1855	**Lord of the Hills** (br c Touchstone – Fair Helen, by Pantaloon)	William Stirling Crawfurd	1,800
1866	**St Ronan** (ch c St Albans – Elspeth, by Irish Birdcatcher)	Henry Chaplin	2,000
1866	**Angus** (b c Newminster – Lady Elcho, by Sleight-of-Hand)	12th Duke of Hamilton	2,500
1876	**Maximilian** (b c Macaroni – Duchess, by St Albans)	1st Duke of Westminster	4,100
1890	**La Flèche** (br f St Simon – Quiver, by Toxophilite)	Baron Maurice de Hirsch	5,500
1891	**Childwick** (br c St Simon – Plaisanterie, by Wellingtonia)	John Blundell Maple	6,000
1900	**Cupbearer** (b c Orme – Kissing Cup, by Hampton)	2nd Duke of Westminster	9,100
1900	**Sceptre** (b f Persimmon – Ornament, by Bend Or)	Bob Sievier	10,000
1919	**Westward Ho** (br c Swynford – Blue Tit, by Wildfowler)	1st Baron Glanely	11,500
1920	**Blue Ensign** (ch c The Tetrarch – Blue Tit, by Wildfowler)	1st Baron Glanely	14,500
1936	**Colonel Payne** (b c Fairway – Golden Hair, by Golden Sun)	Miss Dorothy Paget	15,000
1945	**Sayajirao** (br c Nearco – Rosy Legend, by Dark Legend)	HH Maharaja of Baroda	28,000
1966	**Rodrigo** (b c Charlottesville – Rosmerta, by Nearula)	Tim Vigors & Co	31,000
1967	**Exalt** (ch c Exbury – San Luis Rey, by Hard Sauce)	Charles Engelhard	31,000
1967	**Démocratie** (b f Immortality – Review, by Panorama)	Mme Pierre Wertheimer	36,000
1968	**Entrepreneur** (b c Ribot – Montea, by Seaulieu)	William Harder and Herbert Allen	37,000
1969	**La Hague** (b f Immortality – Review, by Panorama)	Souren Vanian	51,000
1970	**Cambrienne** (br f Sicambre – Torbella, by Tornado)	John Mulcahy	65,000
1971	**Bigivor** (b c Sir Ivor – Clorinda, by Set Fair)	Lady Beaverbrook	81,000
1971	**Princely Review** (b c Native Prince – Review, by Panorama)	Sir Douglas Clague	117,000
1975	**Be My Guest** (ch c Northern Dancer – What a Treat, by Tudor Minstrel)	Mrs Diana Manning *et al*	127,000
1975	**Million** (ch c Mill Reef – Labibela, by Honeyway)	Lady Beaverbrook	202,000
1977	**Link** (b c Lyphard – Chain, by Herbager)	Mrs Diana Manning *et al*	250,000
1978	**Millième** (b f Mill Reef – Hardiemma, by Hardicanute)	Stavros Niarchos	250,000
1978	**Sand Hawk** (ch c Grundy – Parsimony, by Parthia)	Khalid bin Abdullah	264,000
1979	**Centurius** (ch c Great Nephew – Word from Lundy, by Worden)	Jim McCaughey	270,000
1979	**Ghadeer** (b c Lyphard – Swanilda, by Habitat)	Hamdan al Maktoum	625,000
1981	**South Atlantic** (b c Mill Reef – Arkadina, by Ribot)	Robert Sangster *et al*	640,000
1983	**Trojan Prince** (b c Troy – Princess Matilda, by Habitat)	Sheikh Mohammed	1,120,000
1983	**Convention** (b c General Assembly – Sarah Siddons, by Le Levanstell)	Khalid bin Abdullah	1,400,000
1983	**Hero Worship** (ch c Hello Gorgeous – Centre Piece, by Tompion)	Robert Sangster *et al*	1,550,000
1984	**Authaal** (b c Shergar – Galletto, by Nijinsky)	Sheikh Mohammed	2,588,000*

* Figure converted from 3,100,000 Irish guineas, to nearest 1,000 guineas.

Auction sales of yearlings came into vogue in England in the late 1820s, and in 1837 history was made by the first four-figure transaction. The purchase of **Glenlivat** for 1,010 gns by the Duke of Richmond at the sale of the late Sir Mark Wood's bloodstock in Hare Park, near Newmarket, caused a sensation at the time and set a world record which endured for 17 years. The longevity of the record was possibly connected with the fact that Glenlivat turned out a bad bargain. He won one match as a 3-year-old, but had been gelded by the time he recorded his only other 'success' (a dead-heat with a contemporary who conceded him 36 lb) and he died soon afterwards. The next record-holder, **Voivode**, proved to be a runner of no consequence, finishing unplaced in his only start after his purchase for 1,020 gns. His successor, the 1,800 gns buy **Lord of the Hills**, was one of many high-priced yearlings whose cost was influenced by a pedigree which had suddenly become fashionable. His brother, Lord of the Isles, had won the 2000 Guineas in the year of his sale, but the implied recommendation proved misleading. The younger brother won only one race – and that against a single opponent – before breaking down. He was sent as a stallion to Australia, where one of his sons, Glencoe, won the 1868 Melbourne Cup. The record changed hands twice within a few minutes at the sale of the Middle Park Stud's yearlings in Eltham in 1866, first when **St Ronan** was knocked down to Henry Chaplin for 2,000 gns, and again when the Duke of Hamilton bid 2,500 gns for **Angus**. Remarkably, the pair were to meet in a two-horse sweepstakes at Newmarket a year later, when St Ronan came out the better by half a length. He progressed to take third place in the 2000 Guineas and won a couple of other minor races, whereas Angus won only a modest juvenile event at Stamford in an unexciting career. After an interval of 10 years the record passed to **Maximilian**, a 4,100 gns purchase by the immensely wealthy young Duke of Westminster. He ran unplaced in his only start at two and did not run at all at three, but as a 4-year-old he won four handicaps, including the Liverpool Cup.

A landmark was reached in 1890 with the sale, for 5,500 gns, of a filly who was to prove a real bargain. **La Flèche**, sister to that season's Oaks and St Leger winner Memoir, was bought by Baron Maurice de Hirsch, who won a string of prestige races with her, among them the 1000 Guineas, the Oaks, the St Leger, the Cambridgeshire, the Ascot Gold Cup and the Champion Stakes. She was also an unlucky second in the Derby, and at stud she produced John o' Gaunt, runner-up in two Classics and sire of influential Swynford. **Childwick**, who took the record up to 6,000 gns in 1891, was not quite the bargain that La Flèche had been, but he did well, beating the brilliant Orme 'in the Limekiln Stakes and winning the Cambridgeshire by four lengths. He later became the sire of La Camargo, an outstanding filly in France.

The death of the 1st Duke of Westminster sparked the next market sensation, with two yearlings offered at his executors' sale on 4 July 1900 leaving the old record far behind. **Cupbearer**, who was never to win a race, was taken by the 2nd Duke of Westminster for 9,100 gns, and minutes later **Sceptre** became the first five-figure yearling when she was sold to Bob Sievier for 10,000 gns. The filly might have been considered cheap at twice the price, as she went on to establish herself as one of the greatest racemares of all time. She still ranks as the only outright winner of four Classic races, and had she been in more professional hands throughout her career, her achievements would have been even more impressive. Sceptre's reign as record-priced yearling lasted for 19 years, falling when Lord Glanely gave 11,500 gns for **Westward Ho**, a colt who was to notch the better of two victories in the Great Yorkshire Stakes. He was at least an appreciably better runner than his younger half-brother **Blue Ensign**, who advanced the record to 14,500 gns. That one yielded no return at all for Lord Glanely, in whose colours he ran inconspicuously on a single occasion. The first 15,000 gns yearling, **Colonel Payne**, fared only a little better. He won just a maiden and two minor races for Miss Dorothy Paget, fuelling the by now prevalent notion that high-priced unproven horses were for those with more money than sense.

That thought recurred in many minds when the fabulously wealthy Maharaja of Baroda laid out 28,000 gns for **Sayajirao** in 1945, but that brother to Derby hero Dante proved to be worth every penny. He ran third in the 2000 Guineas and the Derby, then won the Irish Derby and the St Leger, and as a 4-year-old he took the Hardwicke Stakes before embarking on a stud career most notable for producing a couple of high-class fillies in Gladness and Lynchris, and later for a pair of top-grade colts in Indiana and I Say. When Sayajirao died, at the age of 22, he still ranked as Europe's highest-priced auction yearling, but his record fell some six months later when **Rodrigo** fetched 31,000 gns. The group who bought him were unlucky; the colt never ran and was

sold, at a considerable loss, as a stallion prospect in Japan. Nevertheless, Rodrigo's eclipse of a record that had begun to seem impregnable proved a turning-point; after almost 130 years in which the record had changed hands only 14 times, there now came 14 more record-holders in the space of 13 years.

Rodrigo's purchase price was matched 12 months later when David McCall bought **Exalt** for Charles Engelhard. The colt was made ante-post favourite for the 1969 Derby after winning a Newmarket maiden event on his juvenile début, but he flopped on his two subsequent starts and was exported to Australia, where he became a stallion of little consequence.

Démocratie, only the third filly (after La Flèche and Sceptre) to take the record, proved well worth the 36,000 gns she cost Mme Pierre Wertheimer in 1967. She owed her price to the fact that she was a sister to that season's 1000 Guineas heroine Fleet, and she proved almost as good as that filly, notching her best win in the Prix de la Forêt. The next record-holder, **Entrepreneur**, did nothing like so well, winning only a modest 3-year-old handicap for his American purchasers. Having made a poor return on the 37,000 gns investment, he went to New Zealand as a stallion and proved no more conspicuous in that rôle. The record fell to fillies again in each of the next two years, with **La Hague** (sister to Fleet and Démocratie) making 51,000 gns in 1969 and **Cambrienne** fetching 65,000 gns in 1970. Each won only a single race, the former in France and the latter in Ireland, but Cambrienne at least succeeded as a broodmare, becoming the dam and grand-dam of important winners.

In 1971 the record changed hands twice within a matter of minutes, when two colts from Peter Fitz-Gerald's Mondellihy Stud (which had also sold Démocratie and La Hague) fetched 81,000 gns and 117,000 gns. Neither excelled on the racecourse, **Bigivor** running badly when he eventually reached the races as a 4-year-old, and **Princely Review**, the first European six-figure yearling, managing only a single victory in a Salisbury handicap at the same age. Princely Review, the third produce of the Panorama mare Review to hold the record, became a poor stallion in Australia. The first American-bred record-holder was **Be My Guest**, who registered two other landmarks by being the first to set his record at an Irish auction and by becoming the first record-holder to head the sires' list. Winner as a 3-year-old of three Pattern races – the Blue Riband Trial, Desmond Stakes and Waterford Crystal Mile – he returned little more than a fifth of his 127,000 gns purchase price, but he found instant success as a stallion and was the leading sire in Great Britain and Ireland for 1982. However, his yearling record lasted less than a month. That fell to **Million** at Newmarket, when Lady Beaverbrook (undeterred by the failure of Bigivor) outbid Ravi Tikkoo at 202,000 gns.

Million won a couple of modest races and was afterwards a sire of no distinction in New South Wales.

The first to the quarter-million mark was **Link**, bought by a partnership which included Mrs Diana Manning, Robert Sangster and Simon Fraser. He won his only race in Ireland, later scored four times in ordinary company in America and wound up as a stallion in Venezuela. The Epsom and Curragh Derby victories of Shirley Heights in 1978 were largely responsible for the record-equalling bid for his sister **Millième** by Stavros Niarchos. She showed promise when second on her début, but failed to progress and never won a race. No filly has held the record since Millième, who forfeited her share of the dubious distinction when **Sand Hawk** realized 264,000 gns less than a month afterwards. The first of five record-setters to have been purchased by Middle Eastern owners, he won nothing better than a modest seven-furlong handicap in the colours of Saudi Arabian Prince Khalid bin Abdullah. A year later the record advanced twice, first by a small step, then by a giant leap. Jim McCaughey outlasted Sir Freddie Laker at 270,000 gns for **Centurius**, a brother to dual Derby winner Grundy, and in due course enjoyed a measure of success with him, most notably in the Group III Blue Riband Trial at Epsom. As for **Ghadeer**, the first ever to increase the record by more than 100 per cent, he never promised to repay the 625,000 gns he cost Sheikh Hamdan al Maktoum, but he did win the Group III Premio Carlo Porta in Italy.

Ghadeer's record lasted for two years and could hardly be said to have been broken when **South Atlantic** was knocked down for 640,000 gns. Robert Sangster was both part-vendor and part-purchaser

Be My Guest, a record-priced European auction yearling and subsequently champion sire, cantering to the start of the 1977 Derby, in which he finished 11th. (All-Sport)

in that transaction, and exactly how much money changed hands was never disclosed. The Mill Reef colt won a weak Group II event in Ireland, the Blandford Stakes, before becoming a cheap stallion in America.

The market went mad on the first day of the 1983 Highflyer Sales in Newmarket, when the record changed hands three times in the space of three hours, with the million-guinea and 1½ million-guinea barriers being breached. The first seven-figure yearling was **Trojan Prince**, for whom Sheikh Mohammed outbid Stavros Niarchos at 1,120,000 gns. Soon afterwards an all-Arab battle ended in favour of Khalid bin Abdullah at 1,400,000 gns, with **Convention** as the prize. But before the evening was out he ranked only as number two, the record passing to **Hero Worship** at 1,550,000 gns when Robert Sangster and partners finally outstayed the representative of Sheikh Mohammed. All three 'millionaires' turned out to be poor racehorses. Trojan Prince won one small race at three and was gelded a year later; Convention failed to win at all, though he did place second on four occasions; and Hero Worship, gelded after his second disappointing effort in Ireland at two, had to descend to the weakest company before he could win in America.

The current record-holder, barring exceptional circumstances, seems destined to retain his crown longer than any since Sayajirao. The bidding went all the way to 3,100,000 Irish gns (roughly 2,588,000 gns) for **Authaal** at Kill in 1984, when the fact that he was the star yearling from Shergar's only crop was a strong selling point. Although there was never a chance that he would recover his purchase price at the races – no record holder since Sceptre has man-

aged that – Authaal did win one Group I race in Europe, the 1986 Irish St Leger, and when sent to Australia he won two more – the Queen Elizabeth Stakes at Randwick in April 1988 and the Underwood Stakes at Caulfield in September 1988.

Champion Sires in Great Britain and Ireland

Year	Name	Races won	£	Year	Name	Races won	£	Year	Name	Races won	£
1751	Blaze	13	973	1818	Walton	29	9,990	1885	Hermit	59	30,737
1752	Cade	17	1,170	1819	Soothsayor	18	6,700	1886	Hermit	54	22,017
1753	Cade	28	3,299	1820	Phantom	21	9,093	1887	Hampton	62	31,454
1754	Regulus	25	2,052	1821	Rubens	48	7,217	1888	Galopin	51	30,211
1755	Regulus	32	3,117	1822	Rubens	56	10,572	1889	Galopin	22	43,516
1756	Regulus	38	4,470	1823	Orville	22	9,978	1890	St Simon	27	32,804
1757	Regulus	39	4,127	1824	Phantom	35	11,435	1891	St Simon	25	26,890
1758	Cade	45	6,130	1825	Election	27	9,425	1892	St Simon	47	56,139
1759	Cade	53	5,120	1826	Whalebone	60	12,140	1893	St Simon	45	36,319
1760	Cade	42	3,762	1827	Whalebone	66	8,133	1894	St Simon	44	42,092
1761	Regulus	37	5,576	1828	Filho da Puta	78	8,395	1895	St Simon	35	30,469
1762	Blank	41	7,180	1829	Blacklock	62	8,380	1896	St Simon	38	59,740
1763	Regulus	40	9,423	1830	Emilius	46	15,762	1897	Kendal	31	28,845
1764	Blank	42	7,301	1831	Emilius	57	18,378	1898	Galopin	18	21,699
1765	Regulus	24	7,535	1832	Sultan	35	9,605	1899	Orme	29	46,643
1766	Regulus	15	5,267	1833	Sultan	47	10,348	1900	St Simon	27	58,625
1767	Snap	28	5,149	1834	Sultan	43	12,777	1901	St Simon	33	28,964
1768	Snap	41	8,078	1835	Sultan	46	10,993	1902	Persimmon	16	36,868
1769	Snap	35	9,389	1836	Sultan	53	20,580	1903	St Frusquin	36	26,526
1770	Blank	25	6,786	1837	Sultan	50	13,297	1904	Gallinule	28	30,925
1771	Snap	46	11,547	1838	Camel	24	8,215	1905	Gallinule	45	25,229
1772	Matchem	82	22,046	1839	Priam	33	8,228	1906	Persimmon	31	21,737
1773	Matchem	81	17,177	1840	Priam	37	9,986	1907	St Frusquin	45	25,355
1774	Matchem	79	19,512	1841	Taurus	37	9,413	1908	Persimmon	28	28,484
1775	Marske	59	16,054	1842	Touchstone	18	9,630	1909	Cyllene	39	35,550
1776	Marske	66	18,608	1843	Touchstone	37	19,544	1910	Cyllene	30	42,518
1777	Herod	56	14,129	1844	Bay Middleton	48	13,648	1911	Sundridge	31	33,284
1778	Herod	102	20,736	1845	Slane	35	11,445	1912	Persimmon	7	21,993
1779	Herod	95	18,962	1846	Venison	58	12,369	1913	Desmond	42	30,973
1780	Herod	95	16,319	1847	Venison	73	19,963	1914	Polymelus	34	29,607
1781	Herod	121	19,127	1848	Touchstone	39	21,475	1915	Polymelus	16	17,738
1782	Herod	99	16,737	1849	Bay Middleton	28	14,804	1916	Polymelus	15	16,031
1783	Herod	112	13,544	1850	Epirus	24	8,665	1917	Bayardo	15	12,337
1784	Herod	91	13,562	1851	Orlando	21	12,181	1918	Bayardo	8	15,650
1785	Highflyer	53	9,130	1852	Birdcatcher	75	17,149	1919	The Tetrarch	31	27,376
1786	Highflyer	86	12,298	1853	Melbourne	53	21,299	1920	Polymelus	43	40,447
1787	Highflyer	92	12,198	1854	Orlando	72	16,975	1921	Polymelus	47	34,307
1788	Highflyer	77	10,797	1855	Touchstone	55	20,147	1922	Lemberg	45	32,888
1789	Highflyer	91	14,479	1856	Birdcatcher	80	17,041	1923	Swynford	30	37,897
1790	Highflyer	109	15,982	1857	Melbourne	51	18,206	1924	Son-in-Law	34	32,008
1791	Highflyer	87	16,076	1858	Orlando	63	15,283	1925	Phalaris	34	41,471
1792	Highflyer	88	11,864	1859	Newminster	72	17,338	1926	Hurry On	26	59,109
1793	Highflyer	70	11,561	1860	Stockwell	51	18,201	1927	Buchan	38	45,918
1794	Highflyer	48	7,020	1861	Stockwell	89	24,029	1928	Phalaris	31	46,393
1795	Highflyer	61	6,292	1862	Stockwell	89	33,336	1929	Tetratema	35	53,025
1796	Highflyer	77	12,726	1863	Newminster	81	22,465	1930	Son-in-Law	49	44,588
1797	King Fergus	29	4,457	1864	Stockwell	86	28,708	1931	Pharos	27	43,922
1798	Highflyer	34	5,079	1865	Stockwell	88	33,302	1932	Gainsborough	34	34,789
1799	Sir Peter Teazle	37	6,067	1866	Stockwell	132	61,340	1933	Gainsborough	32	38,138
1800	Sir Peter Teazle	39	5,850	1867	Stockwell	113	42,521	1934	Blandford	58	75,707
1801	Sir Peter Teazle	43	5,411	1868	Buccaneer	68	33,713	1935	Blandford	23	57,538
1802	Sir Peter Teazle	41	6,890	1869	Thormanby	58	15,857	1936	Fairway	38	57,931
1803	Trumpator	46	6,331	1870	King Tom	45	20,376	1937	Solario	26	52,888
1804	Sir Peter Teazle	72	8,180	1871	King Tom	23	18,116	1938	Blandford	27	31,840
1805	Sir Peter Teazle	85	10,688	1872	Blair Athol	69	14,537	1939	Fairway	35	53,481
1806	Sir Peter Teazle	119	18,954	1873	Blair Athol	84	18,362	1940	Hyperion	25	13,407
1807	Sir Peter Teazle	85	12,519	1874	Adventurer	35	21,667	1941	Hyperion	38	25,837
1808	Sir Peter Teazle	95	14,815	1875	Blair Athol	67	19,704	1942	Hyperion	30	13,801
1809	Sir Peter Teazle	80	12,788	1876	Lord Clifden	52	19,288	1943	Fairway	31	12,133
1810	Waxy	47	8,478	1877	Blair Athol	62	28,830	1944	Fairway	32	15,704
1811	Sorceror	51	13,163	1878	Speculum	84	27,071	1945	Hyperion	60	39,727
1812	Sorceror	42	11,000	1879	Flageolet	10	18,657	1946	Hyperion	64	54,021
1813	Sorceror	42	13,546	1880	Hermit	66	30,907	1947	Nearco	42	45,087
1814	Selim	43	7,761	1881	Hermit	49	27,223	1948	Nearco	40	41,541
1815	Rubens	30	7,109	1882	Hermit	81	47,311	1949	Bois Roussel	42	57,161
1816	Walton	28	9,376	1883	Hermit	62	30,406	1950	Fair Trial	42	38,323
1817	Orville	41	6,439	1884	Hermit	75	29,418	1951	Nasrullah	40	47,055

Year		Races won	£	Year		Races won	£	Year		Races won	£
1952	Tehran	31	86,072	1965	Court Harwell	29	145,336	1978	Mill Reef	27	312,922
1953	Chanteur	30	57,296	1966	Charlottesville	19	109,817	1979	Petingo	21	471,574
1954	Hyperion	28	46,894	1967	Ribot	9	128,530	1980	Pitcairn	16	463,693
1955	Alycidon	34	54,954	1968	Ribot	11	119,355	1981	Great Nephew	23	559,999
1956	Court Martial	61	49,237	1969	Crepello	42	88,538	1982	Be My Guest	28	469,421
1957	Court Martial	47	58,307	1970	Northern Dancer	14	247,450	1983	Northern Dancer	21	442,206
1958	Mossborough	42	66,471	1971	Never Bend	9	133,160	1984	Northern Dancer	27	1,041,346
1959	Petition	44	75,955	1972	Queen's Hussar	23	185,337	1985	Kris	25	582,120
1960	Aureole	28	90,087	1973	Vaguely Noble	5	127,908	1986	Nijinsky	20	684,233
1961	Aureole	27	90,898	1974	Vaguely Noble	8	151,885	1987	Mill Reef	19	1,243,799
1962	Never Say Die	31	65,902	1975	Great Nephew	29	313,284	1988	Caerleon	46	895,320
1963	Ribot	11	121,290	1976	Wolver Hollow	37	210,765				
1964	Chamossaire	13	141,819	1977	Northern Dancer	13	380,982				

Champion Sires in North America

Year		Races won	$	Year		Races won	$	Year		Races won	$
1829			—	1888	Glenelg	134	130,746	1947	Bull Lea	128	1,259,718
-30	Sir Charles	38	—	1889	Rayon d'Or	101	175,877	1948	Bull Lea	147	1,344,027
1831	Sir Charles	19	—	1890	St Blaise	105	185,005	1949	Bull Lea	165	991,842
1832	Sir Charles	43	—	1891	Longfellow	143	189,334	1950	Heliopolis	167	852,292
1833	Sir Charles	23	—	1892	Iroquois	145	183,206	1951	Count Fleet	124	1,160,847
1834	Monsieur Tonson	28	—	1893	Himyar	138	249,502	1952	Bull Lea	136	1,630,655
1835	Bertrand	30	—	1894	Sir Modred	137	134,318	1953	Bull Lea	107	1,155,846
1836	Sir Charles	28	—	1895	Hanover	133	106,908	1954	Heliopolis	148	1,406,638
1837	Leviathan	38	—	1896	Hanover	157	86,853	1955	Nasrullah	69	1,433,660
1838	Leviathan	92	—	1897	Hanover	159	122,374	1956	Nasrullah	106	1,462,413
1839	Leviathan	48	—	1898	Hanover	124	118,590	1957	Princequillo	147	1,698,427
1840	Medoc	61	—	1899	Albert	64	95,975	1958	Princequillo	110	1,394,540
1841	Medoc	51	—	1900	Kingston	110	116,368	1959	Nasrullah	141	1,434,543
1842	Priam	53	—	1901	Sir Dixon	94	165,682	1960	Nasrullah	122	1,419,683
1843	Leviathan	26	—	1902	Hastings	63	113,865	1961	Ambiorix	148	936,976
1844	Priam	36	—	1903	Ben Strome	91	106,965	1962	Nasrullah	107	1,474,831
1845	Priam	23	—	1904	Meddler	55	222,555	1963	Bold Ruler	56	917,531
1846	Priam	16	—	1905	Hamburg	60	153,160	1964	Bold Ruler	88	1,457,156
1847	Glencoe	34	—	1906	Meddler	54	151,243	1965	Bold Ruler	90	1,091,924
1848	Leviathan/Trustee	19	—	1907	Commando	34	270,345	1966	Bold Ruler	107	2,306,523
1849	Glencoe	21	—	1908	Hastings	93	154,061	1967	Bold Ruler	135	2,249,272
1850	Glencoe	22	—	1909	Ben Brush	67	75,143	1968	Bold Ruler	99	1,988,427
1851	Boston	31	—	1910	Kingston	41	85,220	1969	Bold Ruler	90	1,357,144
1852	Boston	46	—	1911	Star Shoot	103	53,895	1970	Hail to Reason	82	1,400,839
1853	Boston	56	—	1912	Star Shoot	126	79,973	1971	Northern Dancer	93	1,288,580
1854	Glencoe	56	—	1913	Broomstick	114	76,009	1972	Round Table	98	1,199,933
1855	Glencoe	42	—	1914	Broomstick	90	99,043	1973	Bold Ruler	74	1,488,622
1856	Glencoe	45	—	1915	Broomstick	108	94,387	1974	TV Lark	121	1,242,000
1857	Glencoe	62	—	1916	Star Shoot	216	138,163	1975	What a Pleasure	101	2,011,878
1858	Glencoe	60	—	1917	Star Shoot	167	131,674	1976	What a Pleasure	108	1,622,159
1859	Albion	37	—	1918	Sweep	69	139,057	1977	Dr Fager	124	1,593,079
1860	Revenue	48	49,450	1919	Star Shoot	108	197,233	1978	Exclusive Native	106	1,969,867
1861	Lexington	27	22,425	1920	Fair Play	72	269,102	1979	Exclusive Native	104	2,872,605
1862	Lexington	14	9,700	1921	Celt	124	206,167	1980	Raja Baba	149	2,483,352
1863	Lexington	25	14,235	1922	McGee	125	222,491	1981	Nodouble	115	2,800,884
1864	Lexington	38	28,440	1923	The Finn	31	285,759	1982	His Majesty	86	2,675,823
1865	Lexington	87	58,750	1924	Fair Play	84	296,204	1983	Halo	86	2,773,637
1866	Lexington	112	92,725	1925	Sweep	185	237,564	1984	Seattle Slew	49	5,361,259
1867	Lexington	86	54,030	1926	Man o' War	49	408,137	1985	Buckaroo	50	4,145,272
1868	Lexington	92	68,340	1927	Fair Play	77	361,518	1986	Lyphard	49	4,051,985
1869	Lexington	81	56,375	1928	High Time	109	307,631	1987	Mr Prospector	104	5,877,385
1870	Lexington	82	129,360	1929	Chicle	88	289,123	1988	Mr Prospector	106	8,986,790
1871	Lexington	102	109,095	1930	Sir Gallahad	49	422,200				
1872	Lexington	82	71,915	1931	St Germans	47	315,585				
1873	Lexington	71	71,565	1932	Chatterton	93	210,040				
1874	Lexington	70	51,889	1933	Sir Gallahad	78	136,428				
1875	Leamington	32	64,518	1934	Sir Gallahad	92	180,165				
1876	Lexington	34	90,570	1935	Chance Play	88	191,465				
1877	Leamington	49	41,170	1936	Sickle	128	209,800				
1878	Lexington	36	50,198	1937	The Porter	104	292,262				
1879	Leamington	56	70,837	1938	Sickle	107	327,822				
1880	Bonnie Scotland	137	135,700	1939	Challenger	99	316,281				
1881	Leamington	67	139,219	1940	Sir Gallahad	102	305,610				
1882	Bonnie Scotland	169	103,475	1941	Blenheim	64	378,981				
1883	Billet	48	89,998	1942	Equipoise	82	437,141				
1884	Glenelg	108	69,862	1943	Bull Dog	172	372,706				
1885	Virgil	56	73,235	1944	Chance Play	150	431,100				
1886	Glenelg	136	113,638	1945	War Admiral	59	591,352				
1887	Glenelg	120	120,031	1946	Mahmoud	101	638,025				

* From 1829–30 to 1859 the championship was determined on the basis of races won, and no account was made of prize money earned.

Champion Sires in Australia

Year	Name	Races won	£	Year	Name	Races won	£	Year	Name	Races won	£
1883/84	St Albans	48	8,260	1916/17	Linacre	115	21,396	1953/54	Delville Wood	87	94,974
1884/85	St Albans	59	10,523	1917/18	Linacre	102	26,883	1954/55	Delville Wood	49	64,829
1885/86	Musket	75	16,503	1918/19	The Welkin	73	31,371	1955/56	Delville Wood	58	59,364
1886/87	Robinson Crusoe	25	8,387	1919/20	Comedy King	75	30,803	1956/57	Delville Wood	22	72,709
1887/88	Chester	27	12,605	1920/21	The Welkin	61	32,112	1957/58	Khorassan	26	54,437
1888/89	Musket	54	30,023	1921/22	The Welkin	88	40,374	1958/59	Star Kingdom	61	81,241
1889/90	Chester	28	17,872	1922/23	Comedy King	92	43,114	1959/60	Star Kingdom	79	77,515
1890/91	Musket	24	19,844	1923/24	Valais	29	28,379	1960/61	Star Kingdom	79	81,862
1891/92	Chester	30	13,391	1924/25	Valais	47	38,876	1961/62	Star Kingdom	85	74,521
1892/93	Chester	38	13,505	1925/26	Valais	58	57,368	1962/63	Wilkes	110	94,529
1893/94	Newminster	38	10,894	1926/27	Valais	62	43,455	1963/64	Wilkes	97	110,244
1894/95	Grand Flaneur	25	9,162	1927/28	Valais	69	36,166	1964/65	Star Kingdom	83	105,138
				1928/29	Magpie	96	44,231				$
1895/96	Trenton	53	13,126	1929/30	Night Raid	27	48,359	1965/66	Better Boy	85	176,220
1896/97	Newminster	30	9,181	1930/31	Night Raid	21	27,449	1966/67	Alcimedes	40	216,977
1897/98	Lochiel	97	15,222	1931/32	Limond	26	24,332	1967/68	Agricola	49	212,776
1898/99	Gozo	54	12,683	1932/33	Heroic	94	25,468	1968/69	Wilkes	124	312,148
1899/1900	Lochiel	110	16,137	1933/34	Heroic	103	32,851	1969/70	Alcimedes	71	254,520
1900/01	Lochiel	120	12,668	1934/35	Heroic	91	26,540	1970/71	Better Boy	123	285,236
1901/02	Trenton	19	11,843	1935/36	Heroic	105	26,703	1971/72	Better Boy	129	283,605
1902/03	Pilgrim's Progress	44	12,329	1936/37	Heroic	108	32,825	1972/73	Oncidium	64	363,775
1903/04	Grafton	107	15,154	1937/38	Heroic	141	53,213	1973/74	Matrice	107	365,011
1904/05	Lochiel	97	15,227	1938/39	Heroic	101	35,496	1974/75	Oncidium	75	756,981
1905/06	Lochiel	98	19,064	1939/40	Beau Père	71	31,295	1975/76	Showdown	116	472,266
1906/07	Grafton	164	22,831	1940/41	Beau Père	89	41,710	1976/77	Better Boy	74	563,195
1907/08	Grafton	195	20,443	1941/42	Beau Père	42	23,410	1977/78	Showdown	106	584,269
1908/09	Grafton	183	22,833	1942/43	Spearfelt	75	25,784	1978/79	Century	58	621,093
1909/10	Maltster	145	36,972	1943/44	Manitoba	48	31,039	1979/80	Bletchingly	58	876,575
1910/11	Maltster	145	27,629	1944/45	Manitoba	57	40,217	1980/81	Bletchingly	92	623,200
1911/12	Maltster	163	32,957	1945/46	Emborough	94	37,248	1981/82	Bletchingly	96	950,610
1912/13	Ayr Laddie	145	26,140	1946/47	The Buzzard	74	39,676	1982/83	Sir Tristram	83	1,982,315
1913/14	Maltster	167	31,592	1947/48	Midstream	62	52,407	1983/84	Vain	157	1,508,175
1914/15	Maltster	183	25,274	1948/49	Helios	74	71,297	1984/85	Sir Tristram	84	1,606,765
1915/16	Wallace	25	24,945	1949/50	The Buzzard	60	56,794	1985/86	Sir Tristram	99	1,959,465
				1950/51	Midstream	58	64,528	1986/87	Sir Tristram	118	3,999,555
				1951/52	Midstream	68	63,700	1987/88	Zamazaan	70	3,290,042
				1952/53	Delville Wood	59	59,090	1988/89	Sir Tristram	102	4,032,370

Champion Sires in New Zealand

Year	Name	Races won	£	Year	Name	Races won	£	Year	Name	Races won	£
1892/93	St Leger	—*	—	1924/25	Solferino	—	28,281	1957/58	Faux Tirage	53	34,908
1893/94	St George	—	—	1925/26	Absurd	—	27,606	1958/59	Fair's Fair	56	40,657
1894/95	St Leger	—	—	1926/27	Absurd	—	23,309	1959/60	Summertime	65	42,289
1895/96	St Leger	—	5,090	1927/28	Lucullus	—	17,489	1960/61	Summertime	63	40,549
1896/97	St Leger	—	6,981	1928/29	Paper Money	79	22,067	1961/62	Le Filou	45	40,086
1897/98	St Leger	—	8,283	1929/30	Chief Ruler	75	20,136	1962/63	Count Rendered	62	57,157
1898/99	Castor	—	6,928	1930/31	Limond	49	16,033	1963/64	Le Filou	42	43,139
1899/1900	St Leger	—	6,707	1931/32	Chief Ruler	88	14,098	1964/65	Summertime	58	47,251
1900/01	St Leger	—	9,999	1932/33	Hunting Song	93	9,646	1965/66	Le Filou	67	68,207
1901/02	St Leger	—	11,327	1933/34	Hunting Song	104	10,301	1966/67	Le Filou	59	59,447
1902/03	Stepniak	—	8,098	1934/35	Hunting Song	113	15,194				$
1903/04	Seaton Delaval	—	8,783	1935/36	Hunting Song	123	14,013	1967/68	Copenhagen	93	101,537
1904/05	Stepniak	—	8,785	1936/37	Hunting Song	111	16,054	1968/69	Pakistan	78	103,388
1905/06	Multiform	—	11,634	1937/38	Hunting Song	114	19,761	1969/70	Copenhagen	56	104,305
1906/07	Seaton Delaval	—	9,114	1938/39	Beau Père	51	17,950	1970/71	Pakistan	90	138,360
1907/08	Stepniak	—	10,411	1939/40	Beau Père	61	24,490	1971/72	Better Honey	71	146,105
1908/09	Soult	—	16,000	1940/41	Foxbridge	79	23,459	1972/73	Mellay	103	188,569
1909/10	Soult	—	16,044	1941/42	Foxbridge	61	21,003	1973/74	Pakistan	76	222,767
1910/11	Soult	—	18,483	1942/43	Foxbridge	37	21,225	1974/75	Copenhagen	88	180,787
1911/12	Soult	—	16,678	1943/44	Foxbridge	59	28,256	1975/76	Copenhagen	77	187,970
1912/13	Soult	—	20,685	1944/45	Foxbridge	75	40,874	1976/77	Mellay	133	266,198
1913/14	Martian	—	15,173	1945/46	Foxbridge	98	62,111	1977/78	Bandmaster	32	214,225
1914/15	Martian	—	22,848	1946/47	Foxbridge	121	80,620	1978/79	Gate Keeper	53	185,230
1915/16	Martian	—	17,750	1947/48	Foxbridge	114	76,382	1979/80	Alvaro	48	232,392
1916/17	Martian	—	18,586	1948/49	Foxbridge	85	55,350	1980/81	War Hawk	41	275,640
1917/18	Martian	—	13,980	1949/50	Foxbridge	100	65,829	1981/82	Noble Bijou	87	434,452
1918/19	Martian	—	22,951	1950/51	Foxbridge	60	51,695	1982/83	Noble Bijou	88	367,512
1919/20	Demosthenes	—	27,756	1951/52	Balloch	67	47,798	1983/84	Noble Bijou	80	362,740
1920/21	Martian	—	30,735	1952/53	Balloch	65	44,945	1984/85	Three Legs	43	410,800
1921/22	Absurd	—	36,498	1953/54	Ruthless	31	37,732	1985/86	Zamazaan	50	454,895
1922/23	Absurd	—	26,313	1954/55	Fair's Fair	58	48,030	1986/87	Sir Tristram	53	861,485
1923/24	Absurd	—	29,690	1955/56	Count Rendered	58	43,837	1987/88	Sound Reason	62	1,125,879
				1956/57	Ruthless	50	47,150	1988/89	Three Legs	44	1,095,730

* Figures unavailable.

Polls and Ratings

Virago, the greatest filly of the 19th century according to the
Sporting Times *poll of 1886, won Epsom's City and Suburban
and Great Metropolitan Handicaps on the same afternoon a
month before her 1000 Guineas triumph in 1854. (Popperfoto)*

English Poll

In May 1886 the leading English racing newspaper
The Sporting Times sent a circular to about 100 of
the most prominent figures on the Turf, including
owners, trainers, jockeys, journalists and officials,
asking each of them to name the 10 best horses of the
19th century. The most popular nominations (colts
unless otherwise specified), with the number of
voters who placed them in their top 10, were published on 17 July 1886.

1.	**Gladiateur** (1862)	65
2.	**West Australian** (1850)	63
3.	**Isonomy** (1875)	62
4.	**St Simon** (1881)	53
5.	**Blair Athol** (1861)	52
6.	**The Flying Dutchman** (1846)	49
7=	**Virago** (1851) filly	36
	St Gatien (1881)	36
9.	**Ormonde** (1883)	34
10.	**Robert the Devil** (1877)	31
11.	**Cremorne** (1869)	30
12=	**Foxhall** (1878)	27
	Plaisanterie (1882) filly	27
14.	**Stockwell** (1849)	24
15.	**Bay Middleton** (1833)	22
16.	**Barcaldine** (1878)	21
17.	**Thormanby** (1857)	16
18.	**Plenipotentiary** (1831)	15
19.	**Galopin** (1872)	14
20=	**Crucifix** (1837) filly	13
	Teddington (1848)	13
22=	**Touchstone** (1831)	12
	Blink Bonny (1854) filly	12
	Springfield (1873)	12
	Bend Or (1877)	12

26.	**Wheel of Fortune** (1876) filly	11
27=	**Priam** (1827)	9
	Fisherman (1853)	9
	Achievement (1864) filly	9
30=	**Velocipede** (1825)	8
	Voltigeur (1847)	8
	Blue Gown (1865)	8
33.	**Favonius** (1868)	7
34=	**Surplice** (1845)	6
	Hermit (1864)	6
	Sterling (1868)	6
37=	**Don John** (1835)	5
	Alice Hawthorn (1838) filly	5
	Macgregor (1867)	5
	Doncaster (1870)	5
	Kincsem (1874) filly	5
	Bendigo (1880)	5

Of these, champion fillies Plaisanterie (France)
and Kincsem (Hungary) were the only ones not
trained in England.

The poll was taken before Ormonde won the Derby
and there is little doubt that he would have come first
had it been conducted later that year. Despite the
bias towards recent champions St Simon, who had
been retired less than 12 months before, was decisively outvoted by 3 earlier champions.

The experts were also asked to name absolutely
the best horse they had ever seen. The most popular
nominations, with the number of votes they received,
were as follows:

1.	**Gladiateur** (1862)	11
2.	**Isonomy** (1875)	10
3.	**West Australian** (1850)	9

4. **St Simon** (1881)	8
5=**Virago** (1851) filly	6
Blair Athol (1861)	6

American Polls

In 1973 the American magazine *The Thoroughbred Record* asked its readers to list, in order of merit, the 10 greatest horses of all time. The result, published on 17 November 1973, was determined by awarding 10 points for each first-place vote down to one point for each tenth-place vote. Most voters ignored foreign horses and Ribot was the only one to reach the final top 10. These top-rated champions, with the number of points they received, were as follows:

1. **Man o' War** (1917)	1,487
2. **Citation** (1945)	1,021
3. **Secretariat** (1970)	923
4. **Kelso** (1957)	780
5. **Native Dancer** (1950)	520
6. **Count Fleet** (1940)	455
7. **Buckpasser** (1963)	357
8. **Ribot** (1952)	320
9. **Dr Fager** (1964)	259
10. **Tom Fool** (1949)	241

In December 1983 the American magazine *The Blood-Horse* published a list of the 41 Horses of the Year in the United States from 1936 to 1982 plus the best horses of 1933 (Equipoise), 1934 (Cavalcade) and 1935 (Discovery). From those 44 champions of the previous half-century, it asked its readers to name the best 10 in no particular order. The top 20 champions, with the percentage of voters who nominated them, were published on 23 June 1984.

1. **Secretariat** (1970)	89
2. **Kelso** (1957)	88
3. **Citation** (1945)	74
4. **Native Dancer** (1950)	70
5. **Forego** (1970)	67
6. **Seattle Slew** (1974)	58
7. **Affirmed** (1975)	55
8. **Spectacular Bid** (1976)	53
9. **Round Table** (1954)	53
10. **John Henry** (1975)	50
11. **Buckpasser** (1963)	46
12. **Swaps** (1952)	45
13. **Count Fleet** (1940)	30
14. **Nashua** (1952)	29
15. **Bold Ruler** (1954)	26
16. **War Admiral** (1934)	23
17. **Tom Fool** (1949)	19
18=**Equipoise** (1928)	16
Seabiscuit (1933)	16
Whirlaway (1938)	16

Among the racing journalists who took part in the poll, the most popular choices were Secretariat (100 per cent), Citation (97 per cent) and Kelso (83 per cent).

The American Racing Manual is America's most authoritative racing annual and among its features is a section on 'Great Horses of the 20th Century'. The 22 champions currently included are:

Sysonby (1902)	**Man o' War** (1917)
Colin (1905)	**Equipoise** (1928)
Exterminator (1915)	**Count Fleet** (1940)

Citation (1945)	**Dr Fager** (1964)
Tom Fool (1949)	**Secretariat** (1970)
Native Dancer (1950)	**Forego** (1970)
Nashua (1952)	**Ruffian** (1972) filly
Swaps (1952)	**Seattle Slew** (1974)
Kelso (1957)	**Affirmed** (1975)
Buck Passer (1963)	**John Henry** (1975)
Damascus (1964)	**Spectacular Bid** (1976)

Notable Thoroughbreds

In 1980 a huge, meticulously-researched book called *Notable New Zealand Thoroughbreds* was published by Alister Taylor in New Zealand. At the heart of it was a series of 54 chapters, each describing in detail the career of a great New Zealand champion selected by the authors on the basis of racecourse performance alone. Two companion volumes, *Notable Australian Thoroughbreds* and *Notable English and Irish Thoroughbreds*, were published in 1981 and 1984 respectively.

The 54 Notable **New Zealand** Thoroughbreds (colts unless otherwise specified) were:

Lurline (1869) filly	**Royal Chief** (1934)
Welcome Jack (1879)	**Defaulter** (1935)
Nelson (1880)	**Beaulivre** (1936)
Trenton (1881)	**Beau Vite** (1936)
Lochiel (1882)	**Kindergarten** (1937)
Carbine (1885)	**Sleepy Fox** (1939) gelding
Multiform (1894)	**Soneri** (1942) filly
Advance (1896)	**Beaumaris** (1946)
Cruciform (1898) filly	**Mainbrace** (1947)
Menschikoff (1898)	**Dalray** (1948)
Achilles (1899)	**Rising Fast** (1949) gelding
Gladsome (1900) filly	**Redcraze** (1950) gelding
Machine Gun (1900)	**Somerset Fair** (1951)
Bobrikoff (1904) gelding	**Great Sensation** (1952) gelding
Warstep (1910) filly	**Syntax** (1952)
Desert Gold (1912)	**Yahabeebe** (1953) filly
Sasanof (1913) gelding	**Cadiz** (1956) gelding
Gloaming (1915) gelding	**Even Stevens** (1957)
Amythas (1916) gelding	**Il Tempo** (1962) gelding
The Hawk (1918) gelding	**Daryl's Joy** (1966)
Rapine (1919) gelding	**Battle Heights** (1967) gelding
Ballymena (1920) gelding	**Show Gate** (1969) filly
Reremoana (1920) gelding	**Grey Way** (1970) gelding
Limerick (1923) gelding	**Good Lord** (1971) gelding
Nightmarch (1925)	**Balmerino** (1972)
Phar Lap (1926) gelding	**La Mer** (1973) filly
Cuddle (1929) filly	**Uncle Remus** (1974)

The 51 Notable **Australian** Thoroughbreds were:

Jorrocks (1833) gelding	**Bernborough** (1939)
The Barb (1863)	**Flight** (1940) filly
Chester (1874)	**Russia** (1940)
Grand Flaneur (1877)	**Shannon** (1941)
Malua (1879)	**Royal Gem** (1942)
Abercorn (1884)	**Comic Court** (1945)
Carbine (1885)	**Delta** (1946)
Wakeful (1896) filly	**Carioca** (1947)
Poseidon (1903)	**Hydrogen** (1948)
Poitrel (1914)	**Rising Fast** (1949) gelding
Eurythmic (1916)	**Sailor's Guide** (1952)
Heroic (1921)	**Todman** (1954)
Windbag (1921)	**Tulloch** (1954)
Amounis (1922) gelding	**Sky High** (1957)
Manfred (1922)	**Wenona Girl** (1957) filly
Phar Lap (1926) gelding	**Light Fingers** (1961) filly
Rogilla (1927) gelding	**Galilee** (1962) gelding
Chatham (1928)	**Tobin Bronze** (1962)
Peter Pan (1929)	**Rain Lover** (1964)
Hall Mark (1930)	**Vain** (1966)
Ajax (1934)	**Baguette** (1967)
High Caste (1936)	**Gunsynd** (1967)
Tranquil Star (1937) filly	**Leilani** (1970) filly

Maybe Mahal (1972) filly	**Manikato** (1975) gelding
Surround (1973) filly	**Kingston Town** (1976) gelding
Dulcify (1975) gelding	

Carbine, Phar Lap and Rising Fast appeared in both the New Zealand and the Australian volumes.

The 50 Notable **English and Irish** Thoroughbreds were:

Eclipse (1764)	**Ormonde** (1883)
Highflyer (1774)	**Orme** (1889)
Dungannon (1780)	**Isinglass** (1890)
Sir Peter Teazle (1784)	**Persimmon** (1893)
Hambletonian (1792)	**Flying Fox** (1896)
Eleanor (1798) filly	**Sceptre** (1899) filly
Velocipede (1825)	**Pretty Polly** (1901) filly
Priam (1827)	**Bayardo** (1906)
Plenipotentiary (1831)	**The Tetrarch** (1911)
Touchstone (1831)	**Hurry On** (1913)
Bay Middleton (1833)	**Gay Crusader** (1914)
Beeswing (1833) filly	**Fairway** (1925)
Crucifix (1837) filly	**Hyperion** (1930)
Alice Hawthorn (1838) filly	**Windsor Lad** (1931)
The Flying Dutchman (1846)	**Bahram** (1932)
Stockwell (1849)	**Sun Chariot** (1939) filly
West Australian (1850)	**Tudor Minstrel** (1944)
Virago (1851) filly	**Abernant** (1946)
Blink Bonny (1854) filly	**Pinza** (1950)
Blair Athol (1861)	**Petite Etoile** (1956) filly
Gladiateur (1862)	**Nijinsky** (1967)
Galopin (1872)	**Brigadier Gerard** (1968)
Isonomy (1875)	**Mill Reef** (1968)
Wheel of Fortune (1876) filly	**Alleged** (1974)
St Simon (1881)	**Shergar** (1978)

Timeform Ratings: Flat

The Timeform organization in Halifax, Yorkshire was founded by Phil Bull (1910–89) in 1947 and has a world-wide reputation based on its annual publication *Racehorses of 19—*. This book contains comments and ratings for each horse that has run on the Flat in Great Britain during the year, and for the best horses in Ireland and France. The ratings express racing merit in pounds, ranging from 130–145 for top-class horses down to 30–40 for selling platers. All horses with the same rating are deemed to be of equal merit regardless of age, sex or distance requirements. Timeform ratings are calculated on an unvarying scale so that champions of different eras can be compared, though the fact that the mean annual level of the ratings is kept constant means that they cannot measure any rise or fall in the absolute merit of the Thoroughbred.

In Timeform's universal handicap all ratings are expressed at weight-for-age, so only mature horses (i.e. aged 4 and above) are rated exactly as they have performed, the ratings of 2- and 3-year-olds being boosted by an immaturity allowance specified by Timeform's weight-for-age scale. For instance, in 1952 the 2-year-old Nearula and the 4-year-old Royal Serenade were both rated 132, yet Nearula's im-

maturity would have required him to receive 20 lb in order to compete on level terms over 6 furlongs at the end of the season. The weight-for-age scale is based on the average rate of physical development of Thoroughbreds, but many top-class 2- and 3-year-olds are mature for their age and their high Timeform ratings allow for scope for development which they did not possess. In terms of achievement the best horse rated by Timeform is Brigadier Gerard, whose rating of 144 was achieved as a 4-year-old, whereas the ratings of 3-year-olds Sea-Bird (145) and Tudor Minstrel (144) were notional.

Among the horses who seem flattered by their Timeform ratings are Windy City, Star of India and several other top 2-year-olds of the 1950s. In 1951 Windy City was one of 5 juvenile colts rated 132 or higher, and the following year 4 juvenile fillies were rated 129 or higher.

Until the early 1960s some of the best French-trained horses did not appear in Timeform's annuals, and even when they did their ratings were often based not on Timeform's own assessments but on their official French ratings. The most notable omission was 7-year-old Marsyas, who gave Souverain (rated 135) 3 kg (nearly 7 lb) and beat him by 3 lengths when winning the Prix du Cadran for the fourth consecutive time in 1947.

In the following lists of top Timeform ratings, horses are ranked according to their highest annual rating, together with the year in which they achieved it, their age, the country in which they were trained

Phil Bull, the Yorkshireman who produced the first Timeform *annual in 1947. Nowadays a full set can fetch thousands of pounds on the second-hand market. (Bob Thomas)*

and their most important wins that season. Many horses did not achieve their highest Timeform rating in the same year as their most famous victory, including English Classic winners My Babu, Black Tarquin, Zabara, Nearula, Cambremer, Ballymoss, Pall Mall, Alcide, Never Too Late, Sweet Solera, Aurelius, Santa Claus, Brigadier Gerard, Bustino, Flying Water, Teenoso, Pebbles and Commanche Run.

Top Timeform Ratings: Colts

145
Sea-Bird 1965 (3yr, France)
Prix Greffulhe, Prix Lupin, Derby, Grand Prix de Saint-Cloud, Prix de l'Arc de Triomphe.

144
Tudor Minstrel 1947 (3yr, GB)
Somerset, 2000 Guineas, St James's Palace and Knight's Royal Stakes.
Brigadier Gerard 1972 (4yr, GB)
Lockinge, Westbury, Prince of Wales's, Eclipse, King George VI and Queen Elizabeth, Queen Elizabeth II and Champion Stakes.

142
Abernant 1950 (4yr, GB)
Lubbock Sprint Stakes, July Cup, King George Stakes, Nunthorpe Stakes.
Windy City 1951 (2yr, Ireland)
Oulton Stakes, Phoenix Plate, Gimcrack Stakes, (2nd) Prix d'Arenberg.
Ribot 1956 (4yr, Italy)
Premio Giulio Venino, Premio Vittuone, Premio Garbagnate, Gran Premio di Milano, King George VI and Queen Elizabeth Stakes, Premio Piazzale, Prix de l'Arc de Triomphe.

French champion Sea-Bird (Pat Glennon) wins the 1965 Derby on the bridle from Meadow Court and I Say. Timeform rate him the best horse to have raced in Europe since World War II. (BBC Hulton Picture Library)

141
Mill Reef 1971 (3yr, GB)
Greenham, Derby, Eclipse and King George VI and Queen Elizabeth Stakes, Prix de l'Arc de Triomphe, (2nd) 2000 Guineas.
1972 (4yr, GB)
Prix Ganay, Coronation Cup.

140
Vaguely Noble 1968 (3yr, France)
Prix de Guiche, Prix du Lys, Prix de Chantilly, Prix de l'Arc de Triomphe.
Shergar 1981 (3yr, GB)
Classic Trial, Chester Vase, Derby, Irish Derby, King George VI and Queen Elizabeth Stakes.
Dancing Brave 1986 (3yr, GB)
Craven, 2000 Guineas, Eclipse, King George VI and Queen Elizabeth and Select Stakes, Prix de l'Arc de Triomphe, (2nd) Derby.

139
Pappa Fourway 1955 (3yr, GB)
Prince of Wales's Handicap, Stewards' Handicap, Festival Stakes, Gosforth Park Cup Handicap, July Cup, King's Stand, Diadem and Tetrarch Stakes.
Reference Point 1987 (3yr, GB)
Dante, Derby, King George VI and Queen Elizabeth, Great Voltigeur and St Leger Stakes.

138
Alycidon 1949 (4yr, GB)
Ormonde Stakes, Corporation Stakes, Ascot Gold Cup, Goodwood Cup, Doncaster Cup.
Exbury 1963 (4yr, France)
Prix Boïard, Prix Ganay, Coronation Cup, Grand Prix de Saint-Cloud, Prix de l'Arc de Triomphe.
Nijinsky 1970 (3yr, Ireland)
Gladness Stakes, 2000 Guineas, Derby, Irish Derby, King George VI and Queen Elizabeth Stakes, St Leger, (2nd) Prix de l'Arc de Triomphe.
Alleged 1978 (4yr, Ireland)
Royal Whip, Prix du Prince d'Orange, Prix de l'Arc de Triomphe.

137
Pinza 1953 (3yr, GB)
Newmarket Stakes, Derby, King George VI and Queen Elizabeth Stakes.
Never Say Die 1954 (3yr, GB)
Derby, St Leger.
Princely Gift 1955 (4yr, GB)
Waterbeach Handicap, Chichester Handicap, Hungerford Stakes, Portland Handicap.
Right Boy 1959 (5yr, GB)
Cork and Orrery Stakes, July Cup, King George Stakes, Nunthorpe Stakes, (2nd) Portland Handicap.
Molvedo 1961 (3yr, Italy)
Premio Estate, Grand Prix du Centenaire de Deauville, Prix de l'Arc de Triomphe, Gran Premio del Jockey Club.

Ragusa 1963 (3yr, Ireland)
Irish Derby, King George VI and Queen
    Elizabeth Stakes, Great Voltigeur
    Stakes, St Leger.
Reliance 1965 (3yr, France)
Prix des Marronniers, Prix Hocquart, Prix
    du Jockey-Club, Grand Prix de Paris,
    Prix Royal-Oak, (2nd) Prix de l'Arc de
    Triomphe.
Rheingold 1973 (4yr, GB)
John Porter Stakes, Prix Ganay,
    Hardwicke Stakes, Grand Prix de Saint-
    Cloud, Prix de l'Arc de Triomphe, (2nd)
    King George VI and Queen Elizabeth
    Stakes.
Apalachee 1973 (2yr, Ireland)
Lee Stakes, Moy Stakes, Observer Gold
    Cup.
Grundy 1975 (3yr, GB)
Irish 2000 Guineas, Derby, Irish Derby,
    King George VI and Queen Elizabeth
    Stakes, (2nd) 2000 Guineas.
Troy 1979 (3yr, GB)
Classic Trial, Predominate Stakes, Derby,
    Irish Derby, King George VI and Queen
    Elizabeth Stakes, Benson and Hedges
    Gold Cup.
Moorestyle 1980 (3yr, GB)
Free Handicap, Norwest Holst Trophy
    Handicap, July Cup, Vernons Sprint
    Cup, Prix de l'Abbaye de Longchamp,
    Challenge Stakes, Prix de la Forêt.

136
My Babu 1947 (2yr, GB)
Norfolk, Woodcote, New, Nell Gwyn and
    Champagne Stakes.
    1949 (4yr, GB)
Tottenham Welter Plate, Victoria Cup,
    Craven Plate.
Black Tarquin 1949 (4yr, GB)
Chippenham, Burwell and White Rose
    Stakes, (2nd) Ascot Gold Cup.

Tantième 1950 (3yr, France)
Prix de Sèvres, Poule d'Essai des
    Poulains, Prix Lupin, Queen Elizabeth
    Stakes, Prix de l'Arc de Triomphe, (2nd)
    Prix du Jockey-Club.
Hafiz 1956 (4yr, France)
Prix d'Automne, (2nd) Hardwicke Stakes,
    (2nd) Cambridgeshire.
Crepello 1957 (3yr, GB)
2000 Guineas, Derby.
Ballymoss 1958 (4yr, Ireland)
Coronation Cup, Eclipse Stakes, King
    George VI and Queen Elizabeth Stakes,
    Prix de l'Arc de Triomphe.
Alcide 1959 (4yr, GB)
Victor Wild, Winston Churchill and King
    George VI and Queen Elizabeth Stakes,
    (2nd) Ascot Gold Cup.
Herbager 1959 (3yr, France)
Prix Greffulhe, Prix Hocquart, Prix du
    Jockey-Club, Grand Prix de Saint-
    Cloud, Prix du Prince d'Orange.
Floribunda 1961 (3yr, Ireland)
King George Stakes, Nunthorpe Stakes,
    (2nd) King's Stand Stakes.
Relko 1963 (3yr, France)
Prix de Guiche, Poule d'Essai des
    Poulains, Derby, Prix Royal-Oak.
    1964 (4yr, France)
Prix Ganay, Coronation Cup, Grand Prix
    de Saint-Cloud.
Thatch 1973 (3yr, Ireland)
Vauxhall Trial Stakes, St James's Palace
    Stakes, July Cup, Sussex Stakes.
Bustino 1975 (4yr, GB)
Coronation Cup, (2nd) King George VI and
    Queen Elizabeth Stakes.
Northjet 1981 (4yr, France)
Prix du Muguet, Prix Jacques le Marois,
    Prix du Moulin de Longchamp.
El Gran Senor 1984 (3yr, Ireland)
Gladness Stakes, 2000 Guineas, Irish
    Derby, (2nd) Derby.

*Brigadier Gerard (Joe Mercer), probably
the greatest European miler of the post-
war era, romps away with the Queen
Elizabeth II Stakes at Ascot in
September 1972. (Gerry Cranham)*

Slip Anchor 1985 (3yr, GB)
Heathorn, Derby Trial and Derby Stakes,
    (2nd) Champion Stakes.
Bering 1986 (3yr, France)
Prix Noailles, Prix Hocquart, Prix du
    Jockey-Club, Prix Niel, (2nd) Prix de
    l'Arc de Triomphe.
Warning 1988 (3yr, England)
Bet With The Tote Trophy, Sussex Stakes,
    Queen Elizabeth II Stakes, (2nd) Prix
    Jacques le Marois.

135
Chanteur 1947 (5yr, France)
Prix Edmond Blanc, Prix des Sablons,
    Grand Prix du Tremblay, Winston
    Churchill Stakes, White Rose Stakes,
    Coronation Cup, (2nd) Ascot Gold Cup.
Souverain 1947 (4yr, France)
Prix Jean Prat, Ascot Gold Cup, Prix
    Kergorlay, (2nd) Prix du Cadran.
The Bug 1947 (4yr, GB)
Cork and Orrery Stakes.
Arbar 1948 (4yr, France)
Prix Jean Prat, Prix du Cadran, Ascot Gold
    Cup, (2nd) Goodwood Cup.
Tenerani 1948 (4yr, Italy)
Premio di Marzo, Premio Montava, Premio
    Gorla, Premio Olona, Omnium, Queen
    Elizabeth Stakes, Goodwood Cup.
Arctic Prince 1951 (3yr, GB)
Derby.
Sicambre 1951 (3yr, France)
Prix de Guiche, Prix Greffulhe, Prix
    Hocquart, Prix du Jockey-Club, Grand
    Prix de Paris.

Supreme Court 1951 (3yr, GB)
White Lodge Stakes, Chester Vase, King Edward VII Stakes, King George VI and Queen Elizabeth Festival of Britain Stakes.

Charlottesville 1960 (3yr, France)
Prix de Vivienne, Prix Lupin, Prix du Jockey-Club, Grand Prix de Paris, Prix du Prince d'Orange.

Right Royal 1961 (3yr, France)
Poule d'Essai des Poulains, Prix Lupin, Prix du Jockey-Club, King George VI and Queen Elizabeth Stakes, Prix Henri Foy, (2nd) Prix de l'Arc de Triomphe.

Match 1962 (4yr, France)
Prix Boïard, Grand Prix de Saint-Cloud, King George and Queen Elizabeth Stakes, Washington DC International.

Petingo 1967 (2yr, GB)
Felix Leach, Gimcrack and Middle Park Stakes.

Sir Ivor 1968 (3yr, Ireland)
2000 Guineas Trial, 2000 Guineas, Derby, Champion Stakes, Washington DC International, (2nd) Prix de l'Arc de Triomphe.

Sassafras 1970 (3yr, France)
Prix Androcles, Prix La Force, Prix du Jockey-Club, Prix Royal-Oak, Prix de l'Arc de Triomphe.

Youth 1976 (3yr, France)
Prix Greffulhe, Daru, Lupin, du Jockey-Club and Niel, Canadian International Championship, Washington DC International.

The Minstrel 1977 (3yr, Ireland)
Ascot 2000 Guineas Trial, Derby, Irish Derby, King George VI and Queen Elizabeth Stakes.

Kris 1979 (3yr, GB)
Greenham, Heron, St James's Palace, Sussex, Waterford Crystal Mile, Queen Elizabeth II and Challenge Stakes, (2nd) 2000 Guineas.

Le Moss 1980 (5yr, GB)
Ascot Gold Cup, Goodwood Cup, Doncaster Cup.

Known Fact 1980 (3yr, GB)
2000 Guineas, Waterford Crystal Mile, Kiveton Park Steel Stakes, Queen Elizabeth II Stakes.

Shareef Dancer 1983 (3yr, GB)
King Edward VII Stakes, Irish Derby.

Sagace 1984 (4yr, France)
Prix Foy, Prix de l'Arc de Triomphe.

Teenoso 1984 (4yr, GB)
Ormonde Stakes, Grand Prix de Saint-Cloud, King George VI and Queen Elizabeth Stakes.

Never So Bold 1985 (5yr, GB)
Temple Stakes, King's Stand Stakes, July Cup, William Hill Sprint Championship.

Petoski 1985 (3yr, GB)
Princess of Wales's Stakes, King George VI and Queen Elizabeth Stakes.

Shadeed 1985 (3yr, GB)
Craven, 2000 Guineas and Queen Elizabeth II Stakes.

Shahrastani 1986 (3yr, GB)
Classic Trial, Dante Stakes, Derby, Irish Derby.

Trempolino 1987 (3yr, France)
Prix de Courcelles, Prix Niel, Prix de l'Arc de Triomphe, (2nd) Prix du Jockey-Club, (2nd) Breeders' Cup Turf.

134p

Abdos 1961 (2yr, France)
Prix de Bry, Grand Critérium.

134

Scratch 1950 (3yr, France)
Prix de Guiche, Prix Greffulhe, Prix du Jockey-Club, St Leger.

Ki Ming 1951 (3yr, GB)
2000 Guineas, Diadem Stakes.

Tulyar 1952 (3yr, GB)
Henry VIII, Ormonde, Derby Trial, Derby, Eclipse, King George VI and Queen Elizabeth, and St Leger Stakes.

Skindles Hotel 1956 (2yr, Ireland)
New Stakes, Rous Stakes, Prix d'Arenberg.

Tanerko 1958 (5yr, France)
Prix Ganay, Prix d'Harcourt, Grand Prix de Saint-Cloud.

Sing Sing 1959 (2yr, GB)
Pampisford, Scarbrough, National Breeders' Produce, Prince of Wales's, Rous and Cornwallis Stakes.

Bleep-Bleep 1960 (4yr, GB)
Ely, Great Central and Rievaulx Handicaps, King George Stakes, Nunthorpe Stakes, (2nd) Portland Handicap.

Aurelius 1962 (4yr, GB)
Coombe, Hardwicke and Atalanta Stakes, (2nd) King George VI and Queen Elizabeth Stakes.

Arctic Storm 1962 (3yr, Ireland)
Finglas Stakes, Irish 2000 Guineas, Champion Stakes, (2nd) Irish Derby, (3rd) King George VI and Queen Elizabeth Stakes.

Hethersett 1962 (3yr, GB)
Brighton Derby Trial, Great Voltigeur Stakes, St Leger, (2nd) Champion Stakes.

Prince Royal 1964 (3yr, Italy/France)
Premio Alpino, Premio Morone, Premio Naviglio, Gran Premio di Milano, Premio Besana, Prix de l'Arc de Triomphe.

Danseur 1966 (3yr, France)
Prix des Gobelins, Prix d'Iéna, Prix du Lys, Grand Prix de Paris.

Busted 1967 (4yr, GB)
Coronation, Eclipse and King George VI and Queen Elizabeth Stakes, Prix Henri Foy.

Habitat 1969 (3yr, GB)
Lockinge Stakes, Prix Quincey, Wills Mile, Prix du Moulin de Longchamp.

My Swallow 1970 (2yr, GB)
Zetland Stakes, Woodcote Stakes, Prix du Bois, Prix Robert Papin, Prix Morny, Prix de la Salamandre, Grand Critérium.

Deep Diver 1971 (2yr, GB)
Brocklesby, Tattersalls Yorkshire and July Stakes, Prix d'Arenberg, Cornwallis Stakes, Prix du Petit Couvert.
1972 (3yr, GB)
Nunthorpe Stakes, Prix de l'Abbaye de Longchamp.

Sallust 1972 (3yr, GB)
Diomed Stakes, Prix de la Porte Maillot, Sussex Stakes, Goodwood Mile, Prix du Moulin de Longchamp.

Flirting Around 1975 (4yr, France)
Prix de Saint-Georges, King's Stand Stakes.

Bolkonski 1975 (3yr, GB)
2000 Guineas, St James's Palace Stakes, Sussex Stakes.

Crow 1976 (3yr, France)
Prix Northeast, Prix Eugène Adam, St Leger, (2nd) Prix de l'Arc de Triomphe.

Tromos 1978 (2yr, GB)
Clarence House Stakes, Dewhurst Stakes.

Storm Bird 1980 (2yr, Ireland)
Anglesey, National, Larkspur and Dewhurst Stakes.

Bikala 1981 (3yr, France)
Prix du Bel Air, Prix du Jockey-Club, (2nd) Prix de l'Arc de Triomphe.

Ardross 1982 (6yr, GB)
Jockey Club Stakes, Yorkshire Cup, Henry II Stakes, Ascot Gold Cup, Geoffrey Freer Stakes, Doncaster Cup, (2nd) Prix de l'Arc de Triomphe.

Assert 1982 (3yr, Ireland)
Gallinule Stakes, Prix du Jockey-Club, Irish Derby, Benson and Hedges Gold Cup, Joe McGrath Memorial Stakes, (2nd) King George VI and Queen Elizabeth Stakes.

Green Forest 1982 (3yr, France)
Prix du Moulin de Longchamp, (2nd) Prix Jacques le Marois.

Rainbow Quest 1985 (4yr, GB)
Clive Graham Stakes, Coronation Cup, Prix de l'Arc de Triomphe, (2nd) Eclipse Stakes, (3rd) King George VI and Queen Elizabeth Stakes.

Shardari 1986 (4yr, GB)
Princess of Wales's Stakes, Matchmaker International, (2nd) King George VI and Queen Elizabeth Stakes.

Mtoto 1987 (4yr, GB)
Brigadier Gerard, Prince of Wales's and Eclipse Stakes.
1988 (5yr, GB)
Prince of Wales's, Eclipse, King George VI and Queen Elizabeth and Select Stakes, (2nd) Prix de l'Arc de Triomphe.

Tony Bin 1988 (5yr, Italy)
Premio dell'Esercito, Premio Presidente della Repubblica, Gran Premio di Milano, Premio Federico Tesio, Prix de l'Arc de Triomphe, (3rd) King George VI and Queen Elizabeth Stakes.

133+

Prince Simon 1950 (3yr, GB)
Wood Ditton Stakes, Newmarket Stakes, (2nd) 2000 Guineas, (2nd) Derby.

Santa Claus 1963 (2yr, Ireland)
National Stakes.

133

My Love 1948 (3yr, France)
Prix Hocquart, Derby, Grand Prix de Paris.

Galcador 1950 (3yr, France)
Prix Daphnis, Derby, (2nd) Poule d'Essai des Poulains.

Palestine 1950 (3yr, GB)
Henry VIII, 2000 Guineas, Red Rose, St James's Palace and Sussex Stakes.

Big Dipper 1950 (2yr, GB)
Norfolk, Coventry, July, Champagne and Middle Park Stakes.

Violoncelle 1951 (5yr, France)
Prix d'Hedouville, Grand Prix de Saint-Cloud.

Auriban 1951 (2yr, France)
Prix de Chatou, Prix Robert Papin, Prix Morny, Houghton Stakes.

Dynamiter 1952 (4yr, France)
Hardwicke Stakes, Champion Stakes, (2nd) Rose of York Stakes, (3rd) Prix de l'Arc de Triomphe.

Nuccio 1952 (4yr, France)
Coronation Cup, Prix de l'Arc de Triomphe.

Zucchero 1952 (4yr, GB)
Princess of Wales's Stakes, Rose of York Stakes.

Oroso 1957 (4yr, France)
Prix Jean Prat, Prix de l'Arc de Triomphe.

Altipan 1957 (3yr, France)
Prix de l'Espérance, Grand Prix de Paris.
Amber 1957 (3yr, France)
Prix Greffulhe, Prix Daru, Prix du Jockey-Club, Prix de Chantilly.
Angers 1959 (2yr, France)
Grand Critérium.
St Paddy 1960 (3yr, GB)
Dante, Derby, Great Voltigeur and St Leger Stakes.
Prudent 1961 (2yr, France)
Prix Yacowlef, Prix Morny, Prix de la Salamandre, (2nd) Grand Critérium.
Soltikoff 1962 (3yr, France)
Prix Henry Delamarre, Prix de l'Arc de Triomphe, (disqualified) Prix Edgard de la Charme.
Tambourine 1962 (3yr, France)
Prix de Nointel, Prix de Neuilly, Irish Derby.
Val de Loir 1962 (3yr, France)
Prix Cid Campéador, Prix Noailles, Prix Hocquart, Prix du Jockey-Club, (3rd) Prix de l'Arc de Triomphe.
Twilight Alley 1963 (4yr, GB)
Ascot Gold Cup.
Le Mesnil 1963 (3yr, France)
Prix Greffulhe, Prix Hocquart, Prix de Chantilly, (2nd) Prix de l'Arc de Triomphe.
Linacre 1963 (3yr, Ireland)
Irish 2000 Guineas, Prix de la Porte Maillot, Whitehall Stakes, (2nd) Champion Stakes.
Showdown 1963 (2yr, GB)
Kirk and Kirk, Coventry, Gorleston and Middle Park Stakes.
Le Fabuleux 1964 (3yr, France)
Prix Noailles, Prix Lupin, Prix du Jockey-Club, Prix du Prince d'Orange.
Soleil 1965 (2yr, France)
Prix de la Reine Blanche, Prix Morny, Grand Critérium.
Young Emperor 1965 (2yr, Ireland)
Marble Hill, Coventry and Gimcrack Stakes.
Nelcius 1966 (3yr, France)
Prix Henri de la Mettrie, Prix du Jockey-Club, Prix de Chantilly.
Bold Lad 1966 (2yr, Ireland)
Youngsters', Coventry, Champagne and Middle Park Stakes.
Levmoss 1969 (4yr, Ireland)
Prix du Cadran, Ascot Gold Cup, Leinster Handicap, Prix de l'Arc de Triomphe.
Balidar 1970 (4yr, GB)
Bretby Handicap, Great Eastern Handicap, Prix du Gros-Chêne, Prix de Meautry, Prix de l'Abbaye de Longchamp, (3rd) King's Stand Stakes.
Amber Rama 1970 (3yr, France)
King's Stand Stakes, (2nd) Prix de Seine-et-Oise.
Huntercombe 1970 (3yr, GB)
July Cup, Nunthorpe Stakes, Prix de Seine-et-Oise, (2nd) King's Stand Stakes, (2nd) Prix de l'Abbaye de Longchamp.
Bonami 1970 (2yr, France)
(2nd) Grand Critérium.
Caro 1971 (4yr, France)
Prix d'Harcourt, Prix Ganay, Prix Dollar, (2nd) Eclipse Stakes, (4th) Prix de l'Arc de Triomphe.
Homeric 1972 (4yr, GB/France)
Prix Maurice de Nieuil, Prix Kergorlay, (2nd) Coronation Cup, (3rd) Prix de l'Arc de Triomphe.
Sandford Lad 1973 (3yr, GB)
Sheffield Handicap, King George Stakes, Nunthorpe Stakes, Prix de l'Abbaye de Longchamp.

Margouillat 1974 (4yr, France)
Prix Dollar, (2nd) Prix d'Ispahan, (3rd) Prix de l'Arc de Triomphe.
Mariacci 1974 (2yr, France)
Prix de Crèvecoeur, Prix des Chênes, Grand Critérium.
Star Appeal 1975 (5yr, West Germany)
Grosser Preis der Badischen Wirtschaft, Gran Premio di Milano, Eclipse Stakes, Prix de l'Arc de Triomphe.
Sagaro 1977 (6yr, France)
Ascot Gold Cup, (2nd) Prix du Cadran.
Balmerino 1977 (5yr, NZ/USA/GB)
Air New Zealand Stakes, Awapuni Gold Cup, Autumn Stakes, Ormond Memorial Gold Cup, Toluca Lake Purse, Valdoe Stakes, (disqualified) Gran Premio del Jockey Club, (2nd) Prix de l'Arc de Triomphe.
Buckskin 1978 (5yr, GB)
Prix du Cadran, Doncaster Cup, Jockey Club Cup.
Ile de Bourbon 1978 (3yr, GB)
King Edward VII, King George VI and Queen Elizabeth, and Geoffrey Freer Stakes.
1979 (4yr, GB)
Clive Graham Stakes, Coronation Cup.
Argument 1980 (3yr, France)
Prix Mary, Grand Prix Prince Rose, Washington DC International, (2nd) Prix de l'Arc de Triomphe.
To-Agori-Mou 1980 (2yr, GB)
Foxhall, Crawley and Solario Stakes, (2nd) Dewhurst Stakes.
1981 (3yr, GB)
2000 Guineas, St James's Palace Stakes, Waterford Crystal Mile, Queen Elizabeth II Stakes, (2nd) Irish 2000 Guineas, (2nd) Sussex Stakes, (2nd) Prix Jacques le Marois.
Kings Lake 1981 (3yr, Ireland)
Irish 2000 Guineas, Sussex Stakes, Joe McGrath Memorial Stakes, (2nd) St James's Palace Stakes, (3rd) Prix Jacques le Marois.
Vayrann 1981 (3yr, France)
Prix Ajax, Prix Jean de Chaudenay, Prix du Prince d'Orange, Champion Stakes.
Golden Fleece 1982 (3yr, Ireland)
Ballymoss Stakes, Nijinsky Stakes, Derby.
Pas de Seul 1982 (3yr, Ireland)
Hungerford Stakes, Prix de la Forêt.
Diesis 1982 (2yr, GB)
Middle Park Stakes, Dewhurst Stakes.
Darshaan 1984 (3yr, France)
Prix Greffulhe, Prix Hocquart, Prix du Jockey-Club.
Commanche Run 1985 (4yr, GB)
Brigadier Gerard Stakes, Benson and Hedges Gold Cup, Phoenix Champion Stakes.
Rousillon 1985 (4yr, GB)
Queen Anne Stakes, Sussex Stakes, Prix du Moulin de Longchamp.

133?
Trepan 1976 (4yr, France)
Prix de la Reine Marguerite, (disqualified) Prince of Wales's Stakes, (disqualified) Eclipse Stakes.

133d
Thunderhead 1952 (3yr, France)
Prix de Fontainebleau, 2000 Guineas, (2nd) Poule d'Essai des Poulains.

132
Tourment 1947 (3yr, France)
Prix de Sèvres, Poule d'Essai des Poulains, Prix Royal-Oak, (2nd) Prix du Jockey-Club, (2nd) Grand Prix de Paris.
Migoli 1947 (3yr, GB)
Craven, Royal Standard, King Edward VII, Eclipse and Champion Stakes, Aintree Derby, (2nd) Derby.
1948 (4yr, GB)
White Rose Stakes, Great Midland Breeders' Plate, Rose of York Stakes, Prix de l'Arc de Triomphe.
Sayajirao 1947 (3yr, GB)
Derby Trial, Irish Derby, Warren Stakes, St Leger.
1948 (4yr, GB)
Hardwicke Stakes, (2nd) Eclipse Stakes.
Luminary 1948 (2yr, GB)
Saxham, Boscawen and Clearwell Stakes.
Masked Light 1949 (2yr, GB)
Rous Stakes, Middle Park Stakes.
Vieux Manoir 1950 (3yr, France)
Prix Le Justicier, Prix Louqsor, Grand Prix de Paris, (2nd) St Leger.
Agitator 1951 (2yr, GB)
Selsey Stakes, Hopeful Stakes.
King's Bench 1951 (2yr, GB)
Somerville, Coventry and Middle Park Stakes.
Orgoglio 1951 (2yr, GB)
Lonsdale Foal, Exeter, Thirsk Juvenile Trial and Champagne Stakes, (2nd) Middle Park Stakes.
Royal Serenade 1951 (3yr, GB)
Jersey Stakes, Nunthorpe Stakes, (2nd) Diadem Stakes.
1952 (4yr, GB)
Cork and Orrery, King George and Nunthorpe Stakes.
Dragon Blanc 1952 (2yr, France)
Prix Thormanby, Grand Critérium.
Nearula 1952 (2yr, GB)
Middle Park Stakes.
The Pie King 1953 (2yr, Ireland)
Coventry, Richmond and Gimcrack Stakes.
Aureole 1954 (4yr, GB)
Victor Wild Stakes, Coronation Cup, Hardwicke Stakes, King George VI and Queen Elizabeth Stakes.
Le Petit Prince 1954 (3yr, France)
Prix Noélie, Prix du Jockey-Club.
Sica Boy 1954 (3yr, France)
Prix Lupin, Prix de Chantilly, Prix Royal-Oak, Prix de l'Arc de Triomphe.
Acropolis 1955 (3yr, GB)
Thirsk Classic Trial, Newmarket, Commonwealth and Voltigeur Stakes, (2nd) King George VI and Queen Elizabeth Stakes, (3rd) Derby.
Phil Drake 1955 (3yr, France)
Prix La Rochette, Derby, Grand Prix de Paris.
Vimy 1955 (3yr, France)
Prix Lagrange, Prix Noailles, King George VI and Queen Elizabeth Stakes, (2nd) Prix du Jockey-Club.
Hugh Lupus 1956 (4yr, GB)
Fryston, March, Hardwicke, Scarbrough and Champion Stakes.
Gilles de Retz 1956 (3yr, GB)
2000 Guineas.
Philius 1956 (3yr, France)
Prix Djebel, Prix du Jockey-Club.
Cambremer 1957 (4yr, France)
Prix du Cadran, (2nd) Ascot Gold Cup.
Pipe of Peace 1957 (3yr, GB)
Greenham Stakes, Gordon Stakes, (3rd) Derby.
Carnoustie 1958 (2yr, GB)
Windsor Castle Stakes, Rous Memorial Stakes, (2nd) Champagne Stakes.
Pall Mall 1959 (4yr, GB)

Lockinge Stakes, Midsummer Stakes, (2nd) Royal Hunt Cup.
Dan Cupid 1959 (3yr, France)
Prix de Saint-James, Prix Pourtalès, (2nd) Prix du Jockey-Club.
Parthia 1959 (3yr, GB)
White Rose, Dee, Derby Trial and Derby Stakes.
Saint Crespin 1959 (3yr, France)
Prix de Guiche, Eclipse Stakes, Prix de l'Arc de Triomphe.
Shantung 1959 (3yr, France)
Prix Edgard de la Charme, Prix La Rochette, (2nd) Grand Prix de Saint-Cloud, (3rd) Derby.
Sheshoon 1960 (4yr, France)
Prix de Barbeville, Ascot Gold Cup, Grand Prix de Saint-Cloud, Prix Gontaut-Biron, Grosser Preis von Baden.
Puissant Chef 1960 (3yr, France)
Prix La Force, Prix de Chantilly, Prix Royal-Oak, Prix de l'Arc de Triomphe.
Sound Track 1960 (3yr, Ireland)
Kingsway Handicap, King's Stand Stakes.
Pandofell 1961 (4yr, GB)
Queen's Prize, Yorkshire Cup, Ascot Gold Cup, Doncaster Cup.
Misti 1961 (3yr, France)
Prix Fourire, Prix de Troarn, Prix Henry Delamarre, (3rd) Prix de l'Arc de Triomphe.
1963 (5yr, France)
Prix Henri Foy, (2nd) Prix du Cadran, (3rd) Prix de l'Arc de Triomphe.
Sanctus 1963 (3yr, France)
Prix Badajoz, Prix Lagrange, Prix du Jockey-Club, Grand Prix de Paris.
Neptunus 1963 (2yr, France)
Prix de la Reine Blanche, Prix d'Aumale, Grand Critérium.
Grey Dawn 1964 (2yr, France)
Prix de Villiers, Prix Morny, Prix de la Salamandre, Grand Critérium.
Carlemont 1965 (3yr, Ireland)
Sussex Stakes.
Diatome 1966 (4yr, France)
Prix Boïard, Prix Ganay, (2nd) Grand Prix de Saint-Cloud.
Bon Mot 1966 (3yr, France)
Prix des Marronniers, La Bourse, Prix de l'Arc de Triomphe, (2nd) Prix du Jockey-Club.
Hauban 1966 (3yr, France)
Prix Greffulhe, Prix Hocquart, (2nd) Grand Prix de Paris.
Reform 1967 (3yr, GB)
St James, St James's Palace, Sussex, Queen Elizabeth II and Champion Stakes.
Karabas 1969 (4yr, GB)
City and Suburban, Turn of the Lands and Fetcham Handicaps, Scarbrough Stakes, La Coupe, Mitre Stakes, Prix du Conseil Municipal, Washington DC International.
Song 1969 (3yr, GB)
Abernant, Temple, King's Stand and Diadem Stakes.
Welsh Pageant 1971 (5yr, GB)
Lockinge Stakes, Hungerford Stakes, (3rd) Eclipse Stakes, (3rd) Champion Stakes.
Hard To Beat 1972 (3yr, France)
Prix de Fontainebleau, Prix Lupin, Prix du Jockey-Club, Prix Niel.
Lyphard 1972 (3yr, France)
Prix Lagrange, Prix Daru, Prix Jacques le Marois, Prix de la Forêt, (2nd) Prix du Moulin de Longchamp.
Green Dancer 1974 (2yr, France)
Prix de Tancarville, Observer Gold Cup.
Bay Express 1975 (4yr, GB)

Sceptre Stakes, Nunthorpe Stakes.
Roman Warrior 1975 (4yr, GB)
Gosforth Park Cup, Canada Dry Shield and Ayr Gold Cup Handicaps, Diadem Stakes, (2nd) Vernons Sprint Cup.
Bruni 1975 (3yr, GB)
Friends of the Variety Club Stakes, St Leger.
Gay Fandango 1975 (3yr, Ireland)
Jersey Stakes, Waterford Crystal Mile, (2nd) Queen Elizabeth II Stakes.
Lochnager 1976 (4yr, GB)
Temple Stakes, King's Stand Stakes, July Cup, William Hill Sprint Championship.
Vitigès 1976 (3yr, France/GB)
Prix Djebel, Champion Stakes, (2nd) 2000 Guineas.
Wollow 1976 (3yr, GB)
Greenham, 2000 Guineas, Eclipse and Sussex Stakes, Benson and Hedges Gold Cup.
Crystal Palace 1977 (3yr, France)
Prix de Courcelles, Prix du Jockey-Club, Prix Niel, (3rd) Prix de l'Arc de Triomphe.
Sirlad 1977 (3yr, Italy)
Premio Merano, Premio Emanuele Filiberto, Derby Italiano, Gran Premio di Milano.
Ela-Mana-Mou 1980 (4yr, GB)
Earl of Sefton, Prince of Wales's, Eclipse and King George VI and Queen Elizabeth Stakes, (3rd) Prix de l'Arc de Triomphe.
Sharpo 1981 (4yr, GB)
Prix de Saint-Georges, William Hill Sprint Championship, (2nd) Prix de l'Abbaye de Longchamp.
Wind and Wuthering 1981 (2yr, GB)
Kris Plate, Somerville Tattersall Stakes, Dewhurst Stakes.
Kalaglow 1982 (4yr, GB)
Earl of Sefton, Brigadier Gerard, Eclipse and King George VI and Queen Elizabeth Stakes.
Gorytus 1982 (2yr, GB)
Acomb Stakes, Champagne Stakes.
Caerleon 1983 (3yr, Ireland)
Prix du Jockey-Club, Benson and Hedges Gold Cup, (2nd) Irish Derby.
Sadler's Wells 1984 (3yr, Ireland)
Derrinstown Stud Derby Trial, Irish 2000 Guineas, Eclipse and Phoenix Champion Stakes, (2nd) Prix du Jockey-Club, (2nd) King George VI and Queen Elizabeth Stakes.
Huntingdale 1985 (2yr, GB)
Dewhurst Stakes.
Celestial Storm 1987 (4yr, GB)
Princess of Wales's Stakes, (2nd) King George VI and Queen Elizabeth Stakes.

131

Solar Slipper 1948 (3yr, GB)
Star King 1948 (2yr, GB)
Djeddah 1949 (4yr, France)
Abadan 1950 (3yr, GB)
Alizier 1950 (3yr, France)
Ocarina 1951 (4yr, France)
Hard Sauce 1951 (3yr, GB)
Stephen Paul 1951 (3yr, GB)
Mât de Cocagne 1952 (4yr, France)
Silnet 1953 (4yr, France)
Beau Prince 1954 (2yr, France)
Our Babu 1954 (2yr, GB)
Royal Palm 1955 (3yr, GB)
Verrières 1955 (2yr, France)
Zarathustra 1956 (5yr, GB)
Klairon 1956 (4yr, France)

Donald 1956 (3yr, GB)
Matador 1956 (3yr, GB)
Arcandy 1957 (4yr, GB)
Tissot 1957 (4yr, France)
Guard's Tie 1957 (3yr, France)
Scot 1957 (3yr, France)
Drum Beat 1958 (5yr, GB)
Hard Ridden 1958 (3yr, Ireland)
Welsh Abbot 1958 (3yr, GB)
Primera 1959 (5yr, GB)
Birum 1959 (3yr, France)
Le Loup Garou 1959 (3yr, France)
Midnight Sun 1959 (3yr, France)
Galivanter 1959 (3yr, GB)
1961 (3yr, GB)
Martial 1960 (3yr, Ireland)
High Hat 1961 (4yr, GB)
Silver Tor 1961 (3yr, Ireland)
Taine 1962 (5yr, France)
Armistice 1962 (3yr, France)
Déboulé 1963 (3yr, France)
Derring-Do 1963 (2yr, GB)
Baldric 1964 (3yr, France)
Double Jump 1964 (2yr, GB)
Sigebert 1966 (3yr, France)
Behistoun 1966 (3yr, France)
Sea Hawk 1966 (3yr, France)
Falcon 1966 (2yr, GB)
Royal Palace 1967 (3yr, GB)
1968 (4yr, GB)
Jimmy Reppin 1969 (4yr, GB)
Right Tack 1969 (3yr, GB)
Tudor Music 1969 (3yr, GB)
Gyr 1970 (3yr, France)
Hallez 1971 (4yr, France)
High Top 1971 (2yr, GB)
Riverman 1972 (3yr, France)
Roberto 1972 (3yr, Ireland)
1973 (4yr, Ireland)
Mississipian 1973 (2yr, France)
Caracolero 1974 (3yr, France)
Dankaro 1974 (3yr, France)
Nonoalco 1974 (3yr, France)
Ramirez 1975 (3yr, France)
Malacate 1976 (3yr, France)
Blushing Groom 1976 (2yr, France)
1977 (3yr, France)
Orange Bay 1977 (5yr, GB)
Gentilhombre 1977 (4yr, GB)
Relkino 1977 (4yr, GB)
Thatching 1979 (4yr, Ireland)
Irish River 1979 (3yr, France)
Nureyev 1980 (3yr, France)
Salieri 1983 (3yr, GB)
Salmon Leap 1983 (3yr, Ireland)
Chief Singer 1984 (3yr, GB)
Shernazar 1985 (4yr, GB)
Last Tycoon 1986 (3yr, France)
Thrill Show 1986 (3yr, France/USA)
Most Welcome 1987 (3yr, GB)
Village Star 1988 (5yr, France)
Boyatino 1988 (4yr, France)
Unfuwain 1988 (3yr, GB)

131?

Turco 1950 (2yr, GB)
Bellotto 1987 (3yr, GB)

130p

Try My Best 1977 (2yr, Ireland)

130

Pearl Diver 1947 (3yr, France)
The Cobbler 1947 (2yr, GB)
Petition 1948 (4yr, GB)
Ambiorix 1948 (2yr, France)
Fontenay 1948 (2yr, France)
Impeccable 1949 (5yr, GB)
Sterope 1949 (4yr, GB)
Nimbus 1949 (3yr, GB)

Krakatao 1950 (4yr, GB)
Bob Cherry 1951 (4yr, GB)
Pan 1951 (4yr, France)
Pardal 1951 (4yr, France)
Le Tyrol 1951 (3yr, France)
Talma 1951 (3yr, France)
Gay Time 1952 (3yr, GB)
Chamant 1953 (3yr, France)
Northern Light 1953 (3yr, France)
Premonition 1953 (3yr, GB)
Vamos 1954 (5yr, France)
Panaslipper 1955 (3yr, Ireland)
Rapace 1955 (3yr, France)
Chantelsey 1956 (3yr, GB)
Talgo 1956 (3yr, GB)
Wayne 1956 (2yr, France)
Tyrone 1956 (2yr, France)
　1957 (3yr, France)
Chief 1957 (4yr, France)
Gratitude 1957 (4yr, GB)
Hornbeam 1957 (4yr, GB)
Vigo 1957 (4yr, GB)
Al Mabsoot 1957 (3yr, France)
Argel 1957 (3yr, France)
Brioche 1957 (3yr, GB)
Court Harwell 1957 (3yr, GB)
Magic North 1957 (3yr, France)
Chris 1959 (3yr, GB)
Aggressor 1960 (5yr, GB)
Exar 1960 (4yr, GB)
Negresco 1960 (3yr, France)
Psidium 1961 (3yr, GB)
Escort 1961 (2yr, GB)
Miralgo 1961 (2yr, GB)
Snob 1961 (2yr, France)
　1962 (3yr, France)
French Plea 1962 (3yr, GB)
Crocket 1962 (2yr, GB)
Cirio 1963 (4yr, France)
Nyrcos 1963 (3yr, France)
Talahasse 1963 (2yr, GB)
Althrey Don 1964 (3yr, GB)
Timmy Lad 1964 (3yr, France)
Hardicanute 1964 (2yr, Ireland)
Provoke 1965 (3yr, GB)
Zeddaan 1967 (2yr, France)
So Blessed 1967 (2yr, GB)
　1968 (3yr, GB)
Be Friendly 1968 (4yr, GB)
Carmarthen 1968 (4yr, France)
Ribofilio 1968 (2yr, GB)
Yelapa 1968 (2yr, France)
Tower Walk 1969 (3yr, GB)
Breton 1969 (2yr, France)
Connaught 1970 (5yr, GB)
Lorenzaccio 1970 (5yr, GB)
Raffingora 1970 (5yr, GB)
Roll of Honour 1970 (3yr, France)
Faraway Son 1971 (4yr, France)

Ramsin 1971 (4yr, France)
Royalty 1971 (3yr, GB)
Sparkler 1971 (3yr, GB)
Simbir 1972 (2yr, France)
Targowice 1972 (2yr, France)
Parnell 1972 (4yr, GB)
　1973 (5yr, GB)
Giacometti 1974 (3yr, GB)
Saritamer 1974 (3yr, Ireland)
Val de l'Orne 1975 (3yr, France)
Manado 1975 (2yr, France)
Gravelines 1976 (4yr, France)
J O Tobin 1976 (2yr, GB)
Godswalk 1977 (3yr, Ireland)
Marinsky 1977 (3yr, Ireland)
North Stoke 1977 (3yr, GB)
Pharly 1977 (3yr, France)
Acamas 1978 (3yr, France)
Homing 1978 (3yr, GB)
Shirley Heights 1978 (3yr, GB)
Solinus 1978 (3yr, Ireland)
Double Form 1979 (4yr, GB)
Bellypha 1979 (3yr, France)
Dickens Hill 1979 (3yr, Ireland)
Le Marmot 1979 (3yr, France)
Tap on Wood 1979 (3yr, GB)
Henbit 1980 (3yr, GB)
Posse 1980 (3yr, GB)
Perrault 1981 (4yr, France)
Akarad 1981 (3yr, France)
Beldale Flutter 1981 (3yr, GB)
Cut Above 1981 (3yr, GB)
Diamond Shoal 1983 (4yr, GB)
Lovely Dancer 1983 (3yr, France)
Lear Fan 1983 (2yr, GB)
Seattle Song 1984 (3yr, France)
Law Society 1985 (3yr, Ireland)
Bakharoff 1985 (2yr, GB)
Sure Blade 1985 (2yr, GB)
Ajdal 1986 (2yr, GB)
　1987 (3yr, GB)
Ascot Knight 1987 (3yr, GB)
Half a Year 1987 (3yr, GB)
Kahyasi 1988 (3yr, GB)
Minster Son 1988 (3yr, GB)

130§
Edmundo 1956 (3yr, GB)

130?
Moonlight Express 1953 (2yr, Ireland)

130d
Melyno 1982 (3yr, France)

129+
Botticelli 1955 (4yr, Italy)
Tudor Melody 1958 (2yr, GB)
Venture 1959 (2yr, France)

The top Timeform ratings
achieved by colts in their
'second-best' seasons have been:

141
Brigadier Gerard (1971) (also rated 132 in 1970)

138
Abernant (1949) (also rated 133 in 1948)

137
Alleged (1977)

135
Tantième (1971)
Right Boy (1958)
Alcide (1958)
Floribunda (1960)

134
Black Tarquin (1948)
Sir Ivor (1967)
Grundy (1974)
Kris (1980)
Sagace (1985)

133
My Babu (1948)
Ribot (1955)
Right Royal (1960)
Santa Claus (1964)
Mill Reef (1970)

133§
Zucchero (1951)
Auriban (1952)

132
Arbar (1947)
Alycidon (1948)
Nuccio (1951)
Ballymoss (1957)
St Paddy (1961)
Val de Loir (1963)
Ragusa (1964)
Vaguely Noble (1967)
My Swallow (1971)
Moorestyle (1981)
Teenoso (1983)
Shardari (1985)
Reference Point (1986)

Top Timeform Ratings: Fillies

138
Star of India 1955 (2yr, GB)
Selsey, Prince of Wales's, Newmarket Foal, Prendergast and Moulton Stakes.

136
Texana 1957 (2yr, France)
Prix Cappiello, Jus d'Orange, de la Croix Saint-Jacques, de Meaux, de Colmar, Yong Lo, des Rêves d'Or, de la Vallée d'Auge, des Foals, d'Arenberg and de l'Abbaye de Longchamp.
Allez France 1974 (4yr, France)
Prix d'Harcourt, Ganay, d'Ispahan, Foy and de l'Arc de Triomphe.
Habibti 1983 (3yr, GB)
July Cup, William Hill Sprint Championship, Vernons Sprint Cup, Prix de l'Abbaye de Longchamp.

135
Coronation 1949 (3yr, France)
Poule d'Essai des Pouliches, Prix de l'Arc de Triomphe, (2nd) Oaks.
La Tendresse 1961 (2yr, Ireland)
Blackwater Plate, Emily Persse Cup, Seaton Delaval, Molecomb and Lowther Stakes.
Dahlia 1974 (4yr, France)
Grand Prix de Saint-Cloud, King George VI and Queen Elizabeth Stakes, Benson and Hedges Gold Cup, Man o' War Stakes, Canadian International Championship.

Pebbles 1985 (4yr, GB)
Trusthouse Forte Mile, Eclipse Stakes, Champion Stakes, Breeders' Cup Turf.

134
Zabara 1951 (2yr, GB)
Guernsey Stud Produce, Imperial Produce and Cheveley Park Stakes.
Petite Etoile 1959 (3yr, GB)
Free Handicap, 1000 Guineas, Oaks, Sussex Stakes, Yorkshire Oaks, Champion Stakes.
　1960 (4yr, GB)
Victor Wild Stakes, Coronation Cup, (2nd) King George VI and Queen Elizabeth Stakes.
All Along 1983 (4yr, France)

Cont. p. 94

Sir Gordon Richards

Sir Gordon Richards was the greatest jockey of his time. Among British riders only Fred Archer and Lester Piggott can be compared with him, and statistically Richards was the best. He won a record 4,870 races in Great Britain and a record 26 championships, and became the only jockey ever to be knighted. For more than 20 years until his retirement in 1954 he was the outstanding figure on the Turf, and his attractive personality and unbroken success made him a national hero.

Gordon Richards, one of a family of 12 children, was born on 5 May 1904 in the small Shropshire town of Oakengates, where his father worked in the coal mines. At the age of 15 he answered an advertisement for stable-lads placed in a local paper by Martin Hartigan, who trained at Foxhill, and later Ogbourne, in Wiltshire.

Nicknamed 'Moppy' because of his thick black hair, he had his first ride in October 1920 and his first win on Gay Lord at Leicester on 31 March 1921. Through ambition and hard work he mastered his craft and in 1925, his first season as a fully-fledged jockey, he became champion with 118 wins.

The following year Richards contracted tuberculosis and it seemed his career would be cut short, but he regained the title in 1927 and thereafter held it every year until his retirement except 1930, when Freddie Fox beat him by one, and 1941, when he broke a leg.

From 1925 to 1931 he was first jockey to Tommy Hogg, who trained for Lord Glanely, and in 1932 he began his 16-year partnership with Fred Darling. A ruthless perfectionist, Darling was the outstanding Classic trainer of his time and his Beckhampton stable was the

Sir Gordon Richards (S&G Press Agency)

most powerful in the land.

Richards soon benefited from his new retainer, for in 1933 his tally of 259 wins beat Fred Archer's British record of 246 which had stood since 1885; the runner-up in the jockeys' table had 72 wins. In October that year he won a world record 12 races in succession, 11 of them at Chepstow.

Although he excelled on all types of horses, from the brilliantly fast fillies Tiffin and Myrobella to champion stayers Singapore and Felicitation, Richards did not enjoy the same success as Archer and Piggott in the Classics and other big races. In 1942 he won 4 of the 5 Classics in the royal colours, on Big Game and fillies' Triple Crown heroine Sun Chariot, the best filly he ever rode, but the

Derby eluded him.

Big Game, like many of the best colts he rode, possessed exceptional speed but lacked stamina; others included Tudor Minstrel, who won the 2000 Guineas by a record margin of 8 lengths in 1947 but failed to stay in the Derby; Abernant, champion sprinter in 1949 and 1950; and Windy City, champion 2-year-old of 1951.

Richards was retained by Abernant's trainer Noel Murless after Fred Darling's retirement in 1947, the year in which he beat his own record by winning 269 races.

His last full season, 1953, was a fitting climax to a magnificent career. His unique place in the life of the nation was recognized by the award of a knighthood, and in the same week, at his 28th and final attempt, he won the Derby on Pinza, the best middle-distance colt he ever rode.

Gordon Richards's riding was unorthodox, since he had an upright style and rode with a long rein. He was quick at the starting-gate, and in a driving finish he would turn his body almost sideways, flourish his whip and apparently throw the reins at his mount; yet, guided by his powerful legs, horses ran straight and true for him.

His strength and determination often seemed to inspire his mounts to victory but he was also capable of finesse, as he showed on the brilliant but temperamental Sun Chariot. In his autobiography he asserted that the secret of his success was his will to win, by which he meant concentration on the job at all times.

He never had to waste, as his riding weight was less than 8 stone for most of his career, and he did not suffer the privations of Archer and Piggott. He took part in more races per season than any other jockey in Great Britain has ever done, though he seldom rode abroad. He would spend the winter in St Moritz and return in time to get fighting fit for the start of the new season.

It was Richards's qualities as a man, as much as his achievements in the saddle, which made people idolize him. His integrity and loyalty were beyond reproach and these, together with his warm, generous and modest nature, enabled him to command the respect and admiration of both the public and his fellow jockeys.

In July 1954 his riding career ended when a filly reared up and fell on him before a race at Sandown Park, breaking his pelvis, though he had already

decided to start training the following year. His new career was inevitably an anti-climax, though he did train Pipe of Peace, top-rated colt in the 1956 Free Handicap, and champion miler Reform, the best 3-year-old in Europe in 1967.

He gave up training in 1970 but continued for some years to act as racing manager to Sir Michael Sobell and Lady Beaverbrook. He died on 10 November 1986.

Sir Gordon Richards dominated the British Turf during the golden age of jockeyship. The records he set may stand for all time, and throughout his career he set a shining example both as a jockey and as a man. By his skill, consistency and longevity in the saddle, and his strength of character out of it, he brought more credit to his profession than any other jockey has ever done.

The highlight of a brilliant career: Sir Gordon wins the 1953 Derby on Pinza from the Queen's colt Aureole. (BBC Hulton Picture Library)

Prix de l'Arc de Triomphe, Rothmans International, Turf Classic, Washington DC International.

133

Apollonia 1955 (2yr, France)
Prix Yacowlef, Prix Morny, Grand Critérium.
Hula Dancer 1962 (2yr, France)
Prix Yacowlef, Prix de la Salamandre, Grand Critérium.
   1963 (3yr, France)
Prix Imprudence, 1000 Guineas, Prix Jacques le Marois, Prix du Moulin de Longchamp, Champion Stakes.
Noblesse 1963 (3yr, Ireland)
Musidora Stakes, Oaks.
Pistol Packer 1971 (3yr, France)
Prix Chloë, Prix Saint-Alary, Prix de Diane, Prix de la Nonette, Prix Vermeille, (2nd) Prix de l'Arc de Triomphe.
San San 1972 (3yr, France)
Prix des Tulipes, Prix de Psyché, Prix Vermeille, Prix de l'Arc de Triomphe.
Jacinth 1972 (2yr, GB)
George Lambton Stakes, Cheveley Park Stakes.
Lianga 1975 (4yr, France)
Prix de Samois, July Cup, Prix Jacques le Marois, Prix de l'Abbaye de Longchamp, Vernons Sprint Cup.
Rose Bowl 1975 (3yr, GB)
Nell Gwyn Stakes, Queen Elizabeth II Stakes, Champion Stakes.
Dunfermline 1977 (3yr, GB)
Pretty Polly Stakes, Oaks, St Leger.
Three Troikas 1979 (3yr, France)
Prix Vanteaux, Poule d'Essai des Pouliches, Prix Saint-Alary, Prix Vermeille, Prix de l'Arc de Triomphe, (2nd) Prix de Diane.
Marwell 1981 (3yr, GB)
Fred Darling, Gus Demmy Memorial and King's Stand Stakes, July Cup, Prix de l'Abbaye de Longchamp.
Triptych 1987 (5yr, France)
Prix Ganay, Coronation Cup, Matchmaker International, Phoenix Champion, Champion and Fuji Stakes, (3rd) Eclipse Stakes, (3rd) King George VI and Queen Elizabeth Stakes, (3rd) Prix de l'Arc de Triomphe.
Indian Skimmer 1988 (4yr, GB)
Phoenix Champion, Sun Chariot and Champion Stakes, (3rd) Breeders' Cup Turf.
Miesque 1988 (4yr, France)
Prix d'Ispahan, Prix Jacques le Marois, Breeders' Cup Mile, (2nd) Prix du Moulin de Longchamp.

132

Diableretta 1949 (2yr, GB)
Acorn Plate, Queen Mary, July, Cherry Hinton, Molecomb and Hopeful Stakes, (2nd) Cheveley Park Stakes.
   1950 (3yr, GB)
Katheryn Howard Stakes.
Rosalba 1958 (2yr, GB)
Convivial Stakes, Cornwallis Stakes, (2nd) Cheveley Park Stakes.
Matatina 1963 (3yr, GB)
Great St Wilfrid Handicap, Nunthorpe Stakes, (2nd) King's Stand Stakes, (2nd) July Cup.
Ivanjica 1975 (3yr, France)
Poule d'Essai des Pouliches, Prix de la Nonette, Prix Vermeille.
   1976 (4yr, France)

Prix du Prince d'Orange, Prix de l'Arc de Triomphe.
Flying Water 1977 (4yr, France)
Prix Maurice de Gheest, Prix Jacques le Marois, Champion Stakes.
Sigy 1978 (2yr, France)
Prix de la Rablais, Prix de la Vallée d'Auge, Prix d'Arenberg, Prix de l'Abbaye de Longchamp.
Gold River 1981 (4yr, France)
Prix Jean Prat, Prix du Cadran, Prix de l'Arc de Triomphe.

131

Careless Nora 1948 (3yr, GB)
Queen Elizabeth Handicap, Alington Sprint, Eager and Nunthorpe Stakes.
Corejada 1949 (2yr, France)
Findon, Lowther and Cheveley Park Stakes.
Constantia 1951 (2yr, GB)
Nimble Plate, National Breeders' Produce Stakes, Lowther Stakes.
Neemah 1952 (2yr, GB)
Virginia Water, Lyme Park and Royal Lodge Stakes.
Palariva 1956 (3yr, France)
Prix de Saint-Georges, King's Stand Stakes, King George Stakes, Prix du Gros-Chêne, Prix de Seine-et-Oise, Prix du Petit Couvert.
Sarcelle 1956 (2yr, GB)
Imperial Produce Stakes, Cheveley Park Stakes.
Refined 1957 (3yr, Ireland)
King George Stakes, Portland Handicap.
Gladness 1958 (5yr, Ireland)
Ascot Gold Cup, Goodwood Cup, Ebor Handicap, (2nd) Prix du Cadran.
Bella Paola 1958 (3yr, France)
Prix Imprudence, 1000 Guineas, Oaks, Prix Vermeille, Champion Stakes, (2nd) Prix du Jockey-Club.
Kathy Too 1960 (2yr, Ireland)
Blackwater Plate, Emily Persse Cup, Phoenix Stakes, Lowther Stakes.
Display 1961 (2yr, Ireland)
Marble Hill, National and Cheveley Park Stakes.
Gay Mairi 1962 (3yr, GB)
Nunthorpe Stakes.
Secret Step 1962 (3yr, GB)
Empire, Singleton and Vernons Gold Cup Handicaps.
Park Top 1969 (5yr, GB)
Prix de la Seine, Coronation Cup, Hardwicke Stakes, King George VI and Queen Elizabeth Stakes, Prix Foy, (2nd) Prix de l'Arc de Triomphe.
Cawston's Pride 1970 (2yr, GB)
St Anne's, Cucumber, George Lambton, Queen Mary, Star Fillies', Molecomb, Lowther and Cornwallis Stakes.
Comtesse de Loir 1974 (3yr, France)
Prix Saint-Alary, (2nd) Prix de Diane, (2nd) Prix Vermeille, (2nd) Prix de l'Arc de Triomphe.
Broadway Dancer 1974 (2yr, France)
Prix de Coye, Prix Morny, (2nd) Prix Robert Papin.
Nobiliary 1975 (3yr, France)
Prix de la Grotte, Prix Saint-Alary, Washington DC International, (2nd) Derby, (2nd) Prix Vermeille.
Pawneese 1976 (3yr, France)
Prix La Camargo, Pénélope and Cléopâtre, Oaks, Prix de Diane, King George VI and Queen Elizabeth Stakes.
Detroit 1980 (3yr, France)
Prix Timandra, Fille de l'Air, Chloë, de la

Nonette and de l'Arc de Triomphe.
April Run 1981 (3yr, France)
Prix Dushka, Cléopâtre, de Pomone and Vermeille, Turf Classic, (2nd) Washington DC International, (3rd) Prix de l'Arc de Triomphe.
Akiyda 1982 (3yr, France)
Prix des Tuileries, Prix de l'Arc de Triomphe, (2nd) Prix de Diane, (2nd) Prix Vermeille.
Time Charter 1982 (3yr, GB)
Masaka, Oaks, Sun Chariot and Champion Stakes.
Northern Trick 1984 (3yr, France)
Prix de Chaillot, Prix de Diane, Prix de la Nonette, Prix Vermeille, (2nd) Prix de l'Arc de Triomphe.
Oh So Sharp 1985 (3yr, GB)
Nell Gwyn Stakes, 1000 Guineas, Oaks, St Leger, (2nd) King George VI and Queen Elizabeth Stakes.

130

Lady Sophia 1952 (3yr, GB)
1000 Guineas Trial, Beaufort Handicap, Clayton Handicap, (2nd) Challenge Stakes.
Wilna 1952 (2yr, GB)
Quickly Plate, Erroll Stakes, Moulton Stakes.
Midget 1955 (2yr, France)
Cheveley Park Stakes, (3rd) Prix Morny.
Honeylight 1956 (3yr, GB)
Free Handicap, 1000 Guineas.
Be Careful 1958 (2yr, GB)
Selsey, Gimcrack and Champagne Stakes.
Lindsay 1958 (2yr, GB)
Pretty Polly Plate, Seaton Delaval, Duchy of Lancaster and Cheveley Park Stakes.
Never Too Late 1959 (2yr, France)
Prix de la Masselière, Prix de la Salamandre, (2nd) Grand Critérium.
Opaline 1960 (2yr, France)
Prix Yacowlef, Prix des Foals, Cheveley Park Stakes.
La Sega 1962 (3yr, France)
Prix de la Grotte, Poule d'Essai des Pouliches, Prix Saint-Alary, Prix de Diane, Prix d'Ispahan.
Cambrizzia 1971 (3yr, France)
Prix du Mont-Valérien, Prix Finlande, Prix de Minerve, (2nd) Prix de Diane, (2nd) Prix Vermeille, (3rd) Prix de l'Arc de Triomphe.
Rescousse 1972 (3yr, France)
Prix Pénélope, Prix de Diane, Prix de la Nonette, (2nd) Prix de l'Arc de Triomphe.
Hippodamia 1973 (2yr, France)
Prix d'Escoville, Critérium des Pouliches.
Paulista 1974 (3yr, France)
Prix de Minerve, Prix de Psyché, Prix de la Nonette, Prix Vermeille.
Be Tuneful 1975 (3yr, GB)
Glenlivet Handicap, William Hill Gold Trophy, Challenge Stakes.
Cloonlara 1976 (2yr, Ireland)
Hurry-On, Probationers' and Phoenix Stakes.
Producer 1979 (3yr, France)
Prix Egérie, de Royaumont, Chloë, de l'Opéra and de la Forêt, (2nd) Irish Oaks, (3rd) Prix de Diane.
Awaasif 1982 (3yr, GB)
Kama Stakes, Yorkshire Oaks, (3rd) Prix de l'Arc de Triomphe.
Luth Enchantée 1983 (3yr, France)
Prix des Dahlias, Prix d'Astarté, Prix Jacques le Marois, Prix du Moulin de

Longchamp, (3rd) Prix de l'Arc de
Triomphe.
Sun Princess 1983 (3yr, GB)
Oaks, Yorkshire Oaks, St Leger, (2nd) Prix
de l'Arc de Triomphe.
Cormorant Wood 1984 (4yr, GB)
Lockinge Stakes, Benson and Hedges
Gold Cup.
Milligram 1987 (3yr, GB)
Coronation Stakes, Waterford Crystal Mile,
Queen Elizabeth II Stakes, (2nd) 1000
Guineas, (2nd) Irish 1000 Guineas.

129

Pharaos 1951 (2yr, France)
Poule de 2 Ans, Prix du Bois, Prix de la
Forêt, (2nd) Gimcrack Stakes.
Bebe Grande 1952 (2yr, GB)
Scurry Plate, National Breeders' Produce
Stakes, New Ham Foal Stakes, Dickens
Plate, Gimcrack, Champagne and
Cheveley Park Stakes.
Tessa Gillian 1952 (2yr, GB)
Molecomb Stakes, Prince of Wales's
Stakes, Ladykirk Plate, Hopeful Stakes,
(2nd) Cheveley Park Stakes.
Cordova 1953 (2yr, France)
Prix de la Reine Blanche, Prix Robert
Papin, Prix Morny.
Kandy Sauce 1956 (3yr, GB)
Queen Anne, Atalanta, Old Rowley and
Limekiln Stakes, (2nd) Yorkshire Oaks.
Rose Royale 1957 (3yr, France)
1000 Guineas, Prix du Moulin de
Longchamp, Champion Stakes.
Toro 1957 (3yr, France)
Poule d'Essai des Pouliches, Coronation
Stakes, Prix du Casino.
Cantelo 1959 (3yr, GB)
Cheshire Oaks, Ribblesdale Stakes, St
Leger, (2nd) Oaks.
Marguerite Vernaut 1960 (3yr, Italy)
Premio Firenze, Premio Emanuele
Filiberto, Gran Premio d'Italia,
Champion Stakes.
Solitude 1960 (2yr, France)
Prix de Clairfeuille, Prix des Rêves d'Or,
Prix Morny.
Sweet Solera 1960 (2yr, GB)
Princess Stakes, Cherry Hinton Stakes.
Caerphilly 1961 (2yr, GB)
Chesterfield, Lavant and Nottinghamshire
Breeders' Yearling Stakes.
Monade 1962 (3yr, France)
Prix Imprudence, Prix Pénélope, Oaks,
Prix Vermeille, (2nd) Prix de l'Arc de
Triomphe.
La Bamba 1964 (3yr, France)
Prix Astronomie, Prix Jacques le Marois,
Prix de la Côte Normande, (3rd) Prix de
l'Arc de Triomphe.
Sovereign 1967 (2yr, GB)
Ann Boleyn, Queen Mary, National and
Lowther Stakes.
Flossy 1969 (3yr, France)
Prix Le Marois, Prix La Rochette,
Champion Stakes.
Highest Hopes 1970 (3yr, GB)
Ascot 1000 Guineas Trial, Fred Darling
Stakes, Prix Eugène Adam, Prix
Vermeille, (2nd) Prix de Diane.
Miss Dan 1970 (3yr, France)
Prix Fille de l'Air, (2nd) Prix Vermeille,
(2nd) Washington DC International,
(3rd) Prix de l'Arc de Triomphe.
First Bloom 1971 (2yr, France)
Prix de la Cascade, Prix Thomas Bryon.
Hurry Harriet 1973 (3yr, Ireland)
Pretty Polly Stakes, Champion Stakes,
(2nd) Prix Vermeille.

Dibidale 1974 (3yr, GB)
Cheshire Oaks, Irish Oaks, Yorkshire
Oaks.
Highclere 1974 (3yr, GB)
1000 Guineas, Prix de Diane, (2nd) King
George VI and Queen Elizabeth Stakes.
Cry of Truth 1974 (2yr, GB)
Wills Embassy Stakes Final, Lowther
Stakes, Champion 2-Y-O Trophy,
Cheveley Park Stakes.
Sanedtki 1978 (4yr, France)
Prix Edmond Blanc, Prix de Ris-Orangis,
Prix du Moulin de Longchamp, Prix de
la Forêt, (2nd) July Cup.
Trillion 1978 (4yr, France)
Prix Ganay, Dollar and Foy, (2nd) Prix de
l'Arc de Triomphe.
Swiss Maid 1978 (3yr, GB)
Twyford, Twickenham, Virginia, Sun
Chariot and Champion Stakes.
Harbour 1982 (3yr, France)
Prix Vanteaux, Prix Saint-Alary, Prix de
Diane.
Darara 1986 (3yr, France)
Prix Albarelle, Prix de Psyché, Prix
Vermeille.
Sonic Lady 1986 (3yr, GB)
Nell Gwyn, Irish 1000 Guineas,
Coronation, Child and Sussex Stakes,
Prix du Moulin de Longchamp.

128

Arbele 1951 (2yr, France)
Princess Elizabeth Stakes.
La Sorellina 1953 (3yr, France)
Prix Finlande, Prix de Diane, Prix de l'Arc
de Triomphe.
Crimson 1953 (2yr, GB)
Warwickshire Breeders' Foal Stakes,
Lowther Stakes, Princess Mary Nursery,
Malton Stakes.
Banassa 1954 (4yr, France)
Prix Boïard, Grand Prix de Saint-Cloud,
Prix du Prince d'Orange, (2nd) Prix de
l'Arc de Triomphe, (2nd) Washington
DC International.
Meld 1955 (3yr, GB)
1000 Guineas, Oaks, Coronation Stakes,
St Leger.
Sicarelle 1956 (3yr, France)
Prix Perdita, Prix des Lilas, Oaks.
Abelia 1958 (3yr, GB)
Alington Stakes, (3rd) King's Stand
Stakes.
Thyra Lee 1958 (2yr, GB)
Lichfield Nursery, Wantage Nursery,
Moulton Stakes.
Cynara 1960 (2yr, GB)
Sceptre, Queen Mary and Molecomb
Stakes, (2nd) Lowther Stakes.
Almiranta 1962 (3yr, GB)
Princess Elizabeth Stakes, Park Hill
Stakes, (2nd) Yorkshire Oaks.
Texanita 1963 (2yr, France)
Prix de la Croix Saint-Jacques, de
Martinvast, Yong Lo, de la Vallée
d'Auge, des Foals, d'Arenberg, de
l'Abbaye de Longchamp and du Petit
Couvert.
Aunt Edith 1965 (3yr, GB)
Nassau Stakes, Prix Vermeille.
Abergwaun 1972 (4yr, Ireland)
Gold Leaf Stakes, Greenlands Stakes, Prix
Maurice de Gheest, Challenge Stakes,
Vernons Sprint Cup, (2nd) King's Stand
Stakes.
Theia 1975 (2yr, France)
Prix de Lisieux, Prix du Calvados,
Critérium des Pouliches.
Riverqueen 1976 (3yr, France)
Prix de la Grotte, Poule d'Essai des

Pouliches, Prix Saint-Alary, Grand Prix
de Saint-Cloud, (2nd) Prix de Diane.
Stanerra 1983 (5yr, Ireland)
Brigadier Gerard, Prince of Wales's,
Hardwicke and Joe McGrath Memorial
Stakes, Japan Cup.
Committed 1984 (4yr, Ireland)
Cork and Orrery Stakes, Hardwicke Cup,
William Hill Sprint Championship, Prix
de l'Abbaye de Longchamp.
Lacovia 1986 (3yr, France)
Prix Saint-Alary, Prix de Diane.

127p

Collyria 1958 (2yr, GB)
(2nd) Imperial Produce Stakes.

127

La Mirambule 1952 (3yr, France)
Prix Guillaume le Conquérant, Prix de
Pomone, Prix Vermeille, Prix de Flore,
(2nd) 1000 Guineas, (2nd) Prix de
Diane, (2nd) Prix de l'Arc de Triomphe.
Fairy Flax 1953 (4yr, GB)
King's Stand Stakes, King George Stakes.
Gloria Nicky 1954 (2yr, GB)
Princess, Lambton and Cheveley Park
Stakes.
Cerisoles 1957 (3yr, France)
Prix Cléopâtre, Prix de Diane.
Mi Carina 1959 (3yr, France)
Prix de Royaumont, Prix Vermeille, (4th)
Prix de l'Arc de Triomphe.
Paddy's Sister 1959 (2yr, Ireland)
Blackwater Plate, Brooke, Queen Mary,
Gimcrack and Champagne Stakes.
Sly Pola 1959 (2yr, France)
Prix de la Reine Blanche, Prix Robert
Papin, Prix de l'Abbaye de Longchamp.
Lynchris 1960 (3yr, Ireland)
Irish Oaks, Yorkshire Oaks, Irish St Leger.
Favorita 1960 (2yr, GB)
Patcham, July, Nottinghamshire Breeders'
Yearling, Manchester Autumn Breeders'
and Cornwallis Stakes.
Crisper 1961 (3yr, GB)
Ely Handicap, Red Rose Stakes, Surrey
Handicap.
Wakamba 1961 (2yr, France)
Prix Frivola, Prix Robert Papin, (2nd) Prix
Morny, (2nd) Prix de la Salamandre.
Hidden Meaning 1962 (3yr, GB)
1000 Guineas Trial, Swinley Forest
Handicap, Cambridgeshire.
West Side Story 1962 (3yr, GB)
Nell Gwyn Stakes, Yorkshire Oaks, (2nd)
Oaks, (2nd) Park Hill Stakes.
The Creditor 1963 (3yr, GB)
Jersey, Invicta and Queen Elizabeth II
Stakes, (3rd) Champion Stakes.
Roselière 1968 (3yr, France)
Prix Pénélope, Prix de Diane, Prix
Vermeille, (4th) Prix de l'Arc de
Triomphe.
Humble Duty 1970 (3yr, GB)
1000 Guineas, Ebbisham, Coronation and
Sussex Stakes, Wills Mile.
Rose Dubarry 1971 (2yr, GB)
Raynes Park, Lowther and Norfolk Stakes.
Mysterious 1973 (3yr, GB)
Fred Darling Stakes, 1000 Guineas, Oaks,
Yorkshire Oaks, (2nd) Irish Oaks.
Calaba 1975 (5yr, GB)
Great Yorkshire Handicap, Cumberland
Lodge Stakes, Mitre Stakes.
Swingtime 1975 (3yr, Ireland)
Cork and Orrery Stakes, Diadem Stakes.
Madelia 1977 (3yr, France)
Prix Jus d'Orange, Poule d'Essai des
Pouliches, Prix Saint-Alary, Prix de
Diane.

Dunette 1979 (3yr, France)
Prix de Diane.
Bireme 1980 (3yr, GB)
Musidora Stakes, Oaks.
Cairn Rouge 1980 (3yr, Ireland)
Mulcahy, Irish 1000 Guineas, Coronation and Champion Stakes.
Mrs Penny 1980 (3yr, GB)
Prix de Diane, Prix Vermeille, (2nd) King George VI and Queen Elizabeth Stakes.
Shoot a Line 1980 (3yr, GB)
Cheshire Oaks, Ribblesdale Stakes, Irish Oaks, Yorkshire Oaks, Park Hill Stakes.
Blue Wind 1981 (3yr, Ireland)
Edenderry Stakes, Oaks, Irish Oaks.
Soba 1983 (4yr, GB)
King George Stakes, Scarbrough Stakes, (2nd) King's Stand Stakes, (2nd) July Cup, (2nd) Vernons Sprint Cup, (2nd) Prix de l'Abbaye de Longchamp.
Parioli 1984 (3yr, France)
Prix de Bonneval, Prix de Servanne, Prix de Cagny, Prix du Petit Couvert.
Proskona 1984 (3yr, France)
Prix Macdonald II, Kempton Park Stakes, Prix de Boulogne, Prix de Seine-et-Oise, Premio Umbria.
Kozana 1985 (3yr, France)
Prix de la Bascoe, Prix de Bagatelle, Prix de Sandringham, Prix de Malleret, (2nd) Prix du Moulin de Longchamp, (3rd) Prix de l'Arc de Triomphe.
Forest Flower 1986 (2yr, GB)
Volvo, Queen Mary, Cherry Hinton and Mill Reef Stakes, (disqualified) Cheveley Park Stakes.
1987 (3yr, GB)
Irish 1000 Guineas.

126
Masaka 1947 (2yr, GB)
Red Peak 1949 (2yr, GB)
The Accused 1950 (3yr, GB)
Djelfa 1950 (2yr, France)
Sanguine 1950 (2yr, France)
Esquilla 1951 (2yr, France)
Frieze 1952 (3yr, GB)
Happy Laughter 1953 (3yr, GB)
Rose Coral 1953 (3yr, GB)
Sixpence 1953 (2yr, Ireland)
Vamarie 1953 (2yr, France)
La Fresnes 1955 (2yr, GB)
Sarissa 1955 (2yr, Ireland)
Ephemeral 1956 (4yr, GB)
Kalitka 1957 (3yr, GB)
Liberal Lady 1957 (2yr, GB)
Rich and Rare 1957 (2yr, GB)
Almeria 1958 (4yr, GB)
Barbaresque 1959 (2yr, France)
Mesopotamia 1963 (2yr, Ireland)
Homeward Bound 1964 (3yr, GB)
Patti 1964 (3yr, Ireland)

Fall In Love 1964 (2yr, France)
Tadolina 1965 (3yr, Italy)
Casaque Grise 1967 (3yr, France)
Altesse Royale 1971 (3yr, GB)
Hill Circus 1971 (3yr, GB)
Regal Exception 1972 (3yr, France)
Stilvi 1972 (3yr, GB)
Realty 1975 (3yr, France)
Antrona 1975 (2yr, France)
Suvanee 1975 (2yr, France)
Kamicia 1977 (3yr, France)
Dancing Maid 1978 (3yr, France)
Kilijaro 1980 (4yr, France)
Little Bonny 1980 (3yr, Ireland)
Phydilla 1981 (3yr, France)
River Lady 1982 (3yr, France)
Walensee 1985 (3yr, France)
Midway Lady 1986 (3yr, GB)
Bint Pasha 1987 (3yr, GB)
Unite 1987 (3yr, GB)
Dimuendo 1988 (3yr, GB)

125p
Victoria Cross 1955 (2yr, GB)

125
Bagheera 1949 (3yr, France)
Double Rose 1949 (3yr, France)
Pambidian 1949 (3yr, France)
Belle of All 1950 (2yr, GB)
Dented Bell 1950 (2yr, GB)
Gamble In Gold 1950 (2yr, GB)
Pampa 1953 (4yr, Ireland)
Philante 1954 (3yr, France)
Cigalon 1956 (3yr, France)
Arbencia 1957 (3yr, France)
Favréale 1959 (3yr, France)
Queensberry 1959 (2yr, GB)
Sunny Cove 1960 (3yr, France)
Timandra 1960 (3yr, France)
High Bulk 1960 (2yr, France)
Kerrabee 1960 (2yr, GB)
Moskova 1960 (2yr, France)
Tchita 1960 (2yr, France)
Fair Astronomer 1963 (3yr, GB)
Crimea 1963 (2yr, GB)
Silver Cloud 1966 (2yr, France)
Pola Bella 1967 (2yr, France)
La Lagune 1968 (3yr, France)
Saraca 1968 (2yr, France)
Lucyrowe 1969 (3yr, GB)
Mange Tout 1969 (2yr, GB)
Paysanne 1972 (3yr, France)
Attica Meli 1972 (3yr, GB)
1973 (4yr, GB)
Melchbourne 1973 (2yr, GB)
Princesse Lee 1974 (2yr, France)
Cherry Hinton 1977 (2yr, GB)
Fair Salinia 1978 (3yr, GB)
Reine de Saba 1978 (3yr, France)
One in a Million 1979 (3yr, GB)
Aryenne 1980 (3yr, France)

Leandra 1981 (3yr, France)
Madam Gay 1981 (3yr, GB)
Chalon 1982 (3yr, GB)
Grease 1982 (3yr, France)
On the House 1982 (3yr, GB)
Ma Biche 1983 (3yr, France)
Silverdip 1983 (3yr, GB)
Katies 1984 (3yr, GB)
Free Guest 1985 (4yr, GB)
Fitnah 1985 (3yr, France)
Lypharita 1985 (3yr, France)
Vilikaia 1985 (3yr, France)
Gayane 1987 (3yr, GB)
Indian Rose 1988 (3yr, France)
Resless Kara 1988 (3yr, France)

125?
Corteira 1948 (3yr, France)

The top Timeform ratings achieved by fillies in their 'second-best' seasons have been:

132
Coronation (1950)
Apollonia (1956)
Dahlia (1973) (also rated 128 in 1975)
Allez France (1973, 1975) (also rated 126p in 1972)
Triptych (1986)
Indian Skimmer (1987)

131
Petite Etoile (1961)
Noblesse (1962)
Rose Bowl (1976)
Miesque (1987)

130
La Tendresse (1962)
Comtesse de Loir (1975)
April Run (1982)
Time Charter (1983)

129
Park Top (1970)
All Along (1982)

128
Zabara (1952)
Midget (1957)
Gladness (1959)
Never Too Late (1960)
Gay Mairi (1961)
Secret Step (1963)
Three Troikas (1980)

127
Texana (1958)
Sweet Solera (1961)
Awaasif (1983)

Top Timeform Ratings: Geldings

133
Admetus 1974 (4yr, France)
Prix de la Plaine Monceau, Grand Prix d'Evry, Prince of Wales's Stakes, Prix Maurice de Nieuil, Washington DC International, (disqualified) Grand Prix de Deauville.

131
Combined Operations 1948 (6yr, GB)
Diadem Stakes, (disqualified) Cavalier Stakes, (2nd) King George Stakes, (2nd) Challenge Stakes.
Durante 1955 (7yr, GB)
Rosebery, Falmouth, Arthur Loraine Memorial, Copeland and Liverpool

Autumn Cup Handicaps, (2nd) Coronation Stakes.

130
Morecambe 1958 (5yr, GB)
Grantley, Nottingham and Cesarewitch Handicaps.
Teleprompter 1985 (5yr, GB)
Pacemaker International Stakes, Arlington Million, (2nd) Lockinge Stakes, (2nd) Queen Elizabeth II Stakes.

128
Kistinie 1962 (3yr, France)
Grand Prix de Compiègne, Prix du Val des Fleurs, Prix de Chantilly, Prix du Prince

d'Orange, (2nd) Prix Kergorlay, (2nd) Prix du Conseil Municipal.
Trelawny 1964 (8yr, GB)
(2nd) Ascot Stakes, (2nd) Brown Jack Handicap.
Daring Boy 1973 (2yr, GB)
Windsor Castle, Home Ales and National Stakes, (2nd) Harry Rosebery Challenge Trophy.

127
Royal Gait 1988 (5yr, France)
Prix de Barbeville, Prix Vicomtesse Vigier, (disqualified) Ascot Gold Cup, (2nd) Prix du Cadran.

126+
Manati 1955 (3yr, GB)
Gordon Stakes.

126
High Stakes 1948 (6yr, GB)
Spelthorne, Martley, Chippenham, Victor Wild, St Oswald and Stewards' Stakes, Preston Plate, Lowther Stakes, Limekiln Stakes.
Summer Solstice 1954 (2yr, GB)
Caterham, Windsor Castle, Granville and Hopeful Stakes, (2nd) Gimcrack Stakes.
Apollo Nine 1971 (4yr, GB)
Bretby, Selhurst Park and Stewards' Cup Handicaps, (2nd) Diadem Stakes, (3rd) Vernons Sprint Cup.
Boldboy 1973 (3yr, GB)
Greenham Stakes, Prix de la Porte Maillot, Diadem Stakes, Challenge Stakes.
1976 (6yr, GB)
Abernant Stakes, Sanyo Stakes, (2nd) Waterford Crystal Mile.
1977 (7yr, GB)
Abernant, Duke of York, Sanyo and Challenge Stakes, Vernons Sprint Cup.

125
Noholme 1952 (5yr, GB)
Thursby, Palace, Kelston, East Grinstead, Newhaven and Blue Boy Handicaps.
Todman 1952 (5yr, GB)
Great Surrey, Exning Welter and Marine Handicaps, (3rd) King's Stand Stakes.
Operatic Society 1960 (4yr, GB)
Brighton Cup, Brighton August Handicap.
Shamrock Star 1960 (4yr, GB)
Ripon City, Champion Sprint, Gosforth Park Cup, Merseyside and Rails Bookmakers' Sprint Handicaps, (2nd) Diadem Stakes.
Catilina 1963 (6yr, France)
Prix de la Jonchère, Colonel Gillois, Orféo, La Sorellina and Messidor.
Apprentice 1965 (5yr, GB)
Yorkshire Cup, Goodwood Cup.
Montgomery 1971 (4yr, France)
Prix de Coulonges, Jacques Lafitte, de Saint-Georges and du Gros-Chêne, (2nd) Prix du Petit Couvert.
John Cherry 1976 (5yr, GB)
Chester Cup, Newbury Autumn Cup, Cesarewitch.
1977 (6yr, GB)
Queen Alexandra Stakes, Stonehill Handicap, Prix Gladiateur.
Bedtime 1984 (3yr, GB)
Racal-Vodafone Handicap, Land of Burns Stakes, Prix Gontaut-Biron, September Stakes, Cumberland Lodge Stakes, (2nd) Japan Cup.

124
Shaker 1954 (5yr, France)
Prix Simonian, Grand Handicap du Tremblay, Sunninghill Park Stakes, Grand Prix de la Ville de Vichy, (2nd) Cumberland Lodge Stakes.
Agreement 1958 (4yr, GB)
Doncaster Cup.
Mullin 1959 (4yr, GB)

Queenborough, Newhaven, Norwich and Autumn Handicaps.
Predominate 1959 (7yr, GB)
Goodwood Stakes, Rufford Abbey Handicap, (disqualified) Harewood Handicap.
1960 (8yr, GB)
Queen Alexandra Stakes, Goodwood Stakes, (2nd) Goodwood Cup.
Petty Officer 1974 (7yr, GB)
Timeform Gold Trophy, Jockey Club Cup, (2nd) Yorkshire Cup.

123
Strathspey 1950 (5yr, GB)
Goodwood Stakes, (2nd) Ascot Stakes.
1951 (6yr, GB)
Thurlow Handicap, George Lambton Cup, Queen Alexandra Stakes, Shakespeare Stakes, Brocas Handicap, (3rd) Doncaster Cup.
Idler 1957 (2yr, GB)
Taplow Plate, Bentinck Nursery, Prendergast Stakes.
Clichy 1958 (6yr, France)
Prix de Barbeville, (3rd) Goodwood Cup.
Thames Trader 1961 (5yr, GB)
Egmont, Bessborough and Charles Greenwood Handicaps, Danum Stakes, Purley Stakes.
Constans 1971 (6yr, GB)
Cicero Handicap, Cherkley Sprint Handicap, Prix Hampton, King George Stakes.
1972 (7yr, GB)
Prix de Saint-Georges.
Sea Pigeon 1980 (10yr, GB)
Bull and Bear Stakes, Vaux Breweries' Gold Tankard, Doonside Cup, (3rd) Cumberland Lodge Stakes.

122
Greek Justice 1947 (3yr, GB)
Red Rose, King's Stand and Fleet Stakes.
Karali 1957 (7yr, France)
Prix Prince Chevalier, Prix Fould, Prix de Bois Roussel.
Coup de Vent 1957 (2yr, GB)
Buckenham Stakes, Leyburn Stakes.
Ranchiquito 1958 (7yr, France)
Prix de Fitz-James, Rieussec, Rainbow, Jouvence and Gladiateur, (2nd) Goodwood Cup.
Induna 1959 (6yr, GB)
Claremont Handicap, Hwfa Williams Handicap, August Welter Stakes, Poulsen Stakes, Gordon Carter Handicap.
Farrney Fox 1960 (5yr, Ireland)
Irish Lincolnshire Handicap, Fingall Stakes, Triumph Herald Handicap, (2nd) Queen's Vase.
Paul Jones 1960 (5yr, GB)
Dean Swift, Eaton, Shefford and King Arthur Handicaps.
Sailor 1964 (5yr, France)
Prix Mousson, Prix Georges Baltazzi, Grand Prix du Centenaire des Courses de Deauville, (2nd) Prix Kergorlay.
1965 (6yr, France)
Prix Simonian, Prix La Sorellina, Grand

Prix de Deauville, (2nd) Grand Prix du Printemps, (2nd) Prix Kergorlay.
Grey of Falloden 1965 (6yr, GB)
Henry II Stakes, Queen Alexandra Stakes, (2nd) Northumberland Plate, (2nd) Prix Gladiateur, (3rd) Doncaster Cup.
Kamundu 1969 (7yr, GB)
Airey of Leeds Gold Cup, Royal Hunt Cup, Flatman Handicap, (3rd) Lincoln Handicap, (3rd) Cambridgeshire.
Great Bear 1969 (5yr, GB)
Thames Stakes, Duke of York Stakes, (2nd) July Cup, (3rd) Challenge Stakes.
Prominent 1971 (4yr, GB)
Devizes, Channel, Magnet Cup and PTS Laurels Handicaps, Prix Foy.
Knockroe 1972 (4yr, GB)
Jockey Club Stakes, Yorkshire Cup, Cumberland Lodge Stakes, St Simon Stakes.
1973 (5yr, GB)
Weetabix Wildlife Handicap, Operatic Society Challenge Cup, (2nd) John Porter Stakes.
Fool's Mate 1976 (5yr, GB)
Trundle Handicap, PTS Laurels Handicap, (2nd) Magnet Cup.
1977 (6yr, GB)
South Coast Stakes, Winter Hill Stakes, (2nd) Doonside Cup.
Crews Hill 1981 (5yr, GB)
Happy Valley, Stewards' Cup and Top Rank Club Handicaps, (2nd) Cork and Orrery Stakes, (2nd) Diadem Stakes.

The top Timeform ratings achieved by geldings in their 'second-best' seasons have been:

129
Combined Operations (1949) (also rated 125 in 1950 and 122 in 1951)
Admetus (1975)

128
Durante (1956, 1957)

127
Morecambe (1959)
Trelawny (1963)

126
Manati (1956)

125
Boldboy (1974) (also rated 124 in 1978 and 122 in 1975)

124
High Stakes (1947, 1949)
Noholme (1953) (also rated 123 in 1954)
Teleprompter (1986) (also rated 122 in 1984)

123
Todman (1951) (also rated 122 in 1953)
Agreement (1959)
Operatic Society (1959)
Catilina (1962)

Timeform's top-rated horses in each age and sex category have been:

2yr colt:	142	Windy City (1951)		**4yr colt:**	144	Brigadier Gerard (1972)
filly:	138	Star of India (1955)		**filly:**	136	Allez France (1974)
gelding:	128	Daring Boy (1973)		**gelding:**	133	Admetus (1974)
3yr colt:	145	Sea-Bird (1965)		**5yr horse:**	137	Right Boy (1959)
filly:	136	Habibti (1983)		**mare:**	133	Triptych (1987)
gelding:	128	Kistinie (1962)		**gelding:**	130	Morecambe (1958), Teleprompter (1985)

6yr	horse:	134	Ardross (1982)
	mare:	129	Park Top (1970)
	gelding:	131	Combined Operations (1948)
7yr	horse:	128	Osborne (1954)
	mare:	111	Granville Greta (1964)
	gelding:	131	Durante (1955)
8yr	horse:	121	Dignitary (1956)
	mare:	115	Granville Greta (1965)
	gelding:	128	Durante (1956), Trelawny (1964)
9yr		128	Durante (1957)
10yr		123	Sea Pigeon (1980)
11yr		106	Sugar Palm (1949)
12yr		101	Caught Out (1964)
13yr		98	Be Hopeful (1972)
14yr		93	Be Hopeful (1973)

The following symbols are sometimes attached to Timeform ratings:

p the horse is likely to make more than normal progress and to improve on his rating.

+ the horse may be rather better than his rating.

§ the horse may give his running on occasions, but cannot be relied upon to do so.

? the rating is based upon inadequate or unsatisfactory data.

d the horse appears to have deteriorated, and might no longer be capable of running to his rating.

The top-rated horses with these symbols have been:

134p Abdos (1961)

133+ Prince Simon (1950), Santa Claus (1963)

133§ Zucchero (1951), Auriban (1952)

133? Trepan (1976)

133d Thunderhead (1952)

The highest Timeform rating achieved by a horse who never won a race is 133, awarded to Bonami in 1970 after he had come third in a newcomers' event and second to My Swallow in the Grand Critérium. He broke a leg on his reappearance in 1971.

Lowest Timeform Ratings

There are 23 Group I races in Great Britain in 1990. Their lowest-rated winners have been:

2000 Guineas
120 **Rockavon (1961)**

1000 Guineas
113 **Night Off (1965)** (rated 124 in 1964)
114 **Imprudence (1947)**

Derby
123 **Blakeney (1969)** (rated 126 in 1970)
125 **Morston (1973)**
125 **Snow Knight (1974)** (US turf champion 1975)

Oaks
112 **Long Look (1965)**

St Leger
124 **Ridge Wood (1949)**
124 **Intermezzo (1969)** (rated 125 in 1970)
124 **Boucher (1972)**

King George VI and Queen Elizabeth Stakes
125 **Nasram (1964)**

Coronation Cup
122 **Quiet Fling (1976)** (rated 124 in 1975)
122 **Easter Sun (1982)**
122 **Be My Native (1983)**

St James's Palace Stakes
116 **Tudor Treasure (1961)** (rated 119 in 1963)
116 **Court Sentence (1962)**

Coronation Stakes
105 **Fortuity (1948)**
105 **Sutton Place (1978)**

Ascot Gold Cup
116 **Random Shot (1971)**

Eclipse Stakes
120 **Canisbay (1965)**

July Cup
112 **Palm Vista (1948)**

Sussex Stakes
115 **My Kingdom (1955)**
115 **Le Levanstell (1961)** (rated 122 in 1959)

International Stakes
127 **Shady Heights (1988)**

Yorkshire Oaks
103 **Feevagh (1954)**

York Sprint Championship (formerly Nunthorpe Stakes)
119 **Haveroid (1977)** (rated 122 in 1976)
120 **Como (1947)**
120 **My Beau (1954)**

Blakeney (Ernie Johnson) is led back in triumph after the 1969 Derby. On Timeform ratings he was the least distinguished post-war winner of England's premier Classic. (Syndication International)

Haydock (formerly Vernons) Sprint Cup
120 **Golden Orange (1970)**

Queen Elizabeth II Stakes
115 **Le Levanstell (1961)** (rated 122 in 1959)
115 **Trusted (1977)**

Cheveley Park Stakes
113 **Ash Blonde (1947)**
113 **Woodstream (1981)**

Middle Park Stakes
115 **Skymaster (1960)** (rated 126 in 1961)
118 **Tudenham (1972)**

Dewhurst Stakes
107 **Bounteous (1960)** (rated 125 in 1962)
111 **My Smokey (1954)** (rated 125 in 1956 and 1957)
111 **Dart Board (1966)** (rated 121 in 1967)
117 **Marsyad (1951)**
117 **Dacian (1955)** (rated 118 in 1956)

Champion Stakes
119 **Narrator (1954)** (rated 127 in 1955)
125 **Cormorant Wood (1983)** (rated 130 in 1984)
126 **Peter Flower (1950)** (rated 127 in 1951)

Racing Post Trophy (formerly Futurity Stakes)
119 **Dactylographer (1977)**

Lowest-rated winners of other races:

Prix de l'Arc de Triomphe
128 **La Sorellina (1953)**
129 **Topyo (1967)**

Irish Derby
119 **Hindostan (1949)**
119 **Thirteen of Diamonds (1952)** (rated 126 in 1953)

The lowest-rated horse to be placed in an English Classic has been Petite Gina, rated 90 after dead-heating for third place in the 1964 1000 Guineas.

The following stallions have sired horses with a best annual Timeform rating at least 20 lb higher than their own:

Rolfe (rated 77 in 1976) sired **Mighty Flutter** (rated 122? in 1984)
Moulin (rated 103 in 1978) sired **Village Star** (rated 131 in 1988)
Bewildered (102 in 1951) sired **Operatic Society** (125 in 1960)
Grit (95 in 1955) sired **Chalkey** (116 in 1962)
Maestoso (94 in 1964) sired **Welsh City** (115 in 1972)
Hard Tack (111 § in 1958) sired **Right Tack** (131 in 1969)
Queen's Hussar (124 in 1963) sired **Brigadier Gerard** (144 in 1972)

Timeform Ratings: Jumping

From 1975/76 the Timeform organization has given a rating to each jumper in Great Britain, and also to the best in Ireland, in its *Chasers & Hurdlers* annual. In the following lists of top ratings, jumpers are ranked according to their highest annual rating, together with the season in which they achieved it, their age, the country in which they were trained and their most important wins that season. All horses are geldings unless otherwise specified. The champions who were past their best when the first *Chasers & Hurdlers* annual was published include Lanzarote, Comedy of Errors, Bula, Tingle Creek and Pendil.

Since the early 1960s Timeform has published ratings for jumpers in its weekly 'black book'. They are not strictly comparable to the ratings in the *Chasers & Hurdlers* annual, but Arkle was rated 220 in early 1966 and later that year his stablemate Flyingbolt was assessed at 210 after winning the National Hunt Two Mile Champion Chase and the Irish Grand National.

Many jumpers did not achieve their highest Timeform rating in the same season as their most famous victory, including Cheltenham Gold Cup winners Burrough Hill Lad and Forgive'N Forget, and Queen Mother Champion Chase winner Drumgora.

Note that the symbols used in Timeform Flat ratings (see p. 98) can apply to the jump ratings, with one addition: ✕—not a good jumper.

Top Timeform Ratings: Hurdlers

182
Night Nurse 1976/77 (6yr, GB)
William Hill, John Skeaping, Champion, Templegate and Welsh Champion Hurdles.

180
Monksfield 1978/79 (7yr horse, Ireland)
A R Soudavar Memorial Trial, Champion, Colt Sigma and Welsh Champion Hurdles, (2nd) Royal Doulton Handicap Hurdle.

176
Birds Nest 1975/76 (6yr, GB)
Wolverhampton Champion Hurdle Trial, (2nd) Champion Hurdle.
1976/77 (7yr, GB)
Fighting Fifth Hurdle, Oteley Hurdle, Wolverhampton Champion Hurdle Trial, (2nd) Scottish Champion Hurdle.
Golden Cygnet 1977/78 (6yr, Ireland)
Redmonstown, Roundwood, Slaney, Fournoughts, Waterford Crystal Supreme Novices' and Fingal Hurdles.

175
Sea Pigeon 1976/77 (7yr, GB)
Culzean, Embassy and Allied Manufacturing Handicap Hurdles, Scottish Champion Hurdle, (4th) Champion Hurdle.
1977/78 (8yr, GB)
Oteley Hurdle, Scottish Champion Handicap Hurdle, (2nd) Champion Hurdle.
1978/79 (9yr, GB)
William Hill Hurdle, Fighting Fifth Hurdle, (2nd) Champion Hurdle, (2nd) Scottish Champion Handicap Hurdle.
1979/80 (10yr, GB)
Holsten Diat Pils, Champion and Welsh Champion Hurdles.
1980/81 (11yr, GB)
Holsten Diat Pils, Fighting Fifth and Champion Hurdles.
Gaye Brief 1982/83 (6yr, GB)
Cambridgeshire, Tom Masson Trophy, Fred Rimell, City Trial Handicap, Champion and Sun Templegate Hurdles.

174
Lanzarote 1976/77 (9yr, GB)
A Day At The Races Hurdle, (2nd) John Skeaping Hurdle.
Dramatist 1976/77 (6yr, GB)
Kirk and Kirk, Christmas and Kingwell Pattern Hurdles, (2nd) Welsh Champion Hurdle, (3rd) Champion Hurdle.
For Auction 1981/82 (6yr, Ireland)
Sweeps Handicap Hurdle, Champion Hurdle.

173
Dawn Run 1983/84 (6yr mare, Ireland)
A R Soudavar Memorial Trial, VAT Watkins, Christmas, Wessel Cable Champion, Champion and Sandeman Aintree Hurdles, Prix La Barka, Grande Course de Haies d'Auteuil.
See You Then 1985/86 (6yr, GB)
Oteley Hurdle, Champion Hurdle.
1986/87 (7yr, GB)
De Vere Hotels Hurdle, Champion Hurdle.

172

Bannow Rambler 1975/76 (7yr, Ireland)
Free Handicap Hurdle, (2nd) Scalp Hurdle.
Boreen Prince 1982/83 (6yr, Ireland)
October, Vulgan and Celbridge Handicap
Hurdles, (2nd) Champion Hurdle.
Browne's Gazette 1984/85 (7yr, GB)
Fighting Fifth, Bula, Christmas, Morebattle
and Welsh Champion Hurdles.
Prideaux Boy 1985/86 (8yr, GB)
Snow Hill, Lanzarote and Swinton
Insurance Brokers' Trophy Handicap
Hurdles, (4th) Champion Hurdle.
Flatterer 1986/87 (8yr, USA)
Colonial Cup Steeplechase, Iroquois
Steeplechase, (2nd) Champion Hurdle.
Beech Road 1988/89 (7yr, GB)
National Spirit Challenge Trophy,
Champion Hurdle, Sandeman Aintree
Hurdle.

171+

Daring Run 1980/81 (6yr, Ireland)
Kildare, Proudstown Handicap, Erin Foods
Champion and Sun Templegate
Hurdles, (3rd) Champion Hurdle.

171

Pollardstown 1980/81 (6yr, GB)
Berkshire Hurdle, Welsh Champion
Hurdle, (2nd) Erin Foods Champion
Hurdle, (2nd) Champion Hurdle, (2nd)
Sun Templegate Hurdle.
Barnbrook Again 1986/87 (6yr, GB)
Seven Barrows Handicap, Gerry Feilden
and Ladbroke Handicap Hurdles, (2nd)
Wessel Cable Champion Hurdle, (3rd)
Champion Hurdle.

170

Comedy of Errors 1975/76 (9yr, GB)
New Year's Day, National Spirit Challenge
Trophy Pattern and Templegate
Hurdles, (4th) Champion Hurdle.
Celtic Shot 1987/88 (6yr, GB)
Pirbright Handicap, Allinson Bread
Handicap, Mecca Bookmakers'
Handicap, New Year's Day and
Champion Hurdles.

169

Kybo 1978/79 (6yr, GB)
Kirk and Kirk, SGB Hire Shop and
Christmas Hurdles, (2nd) Colt Sigma
Hurdle, (3rd) Scottish Champion
Handicap Hurdle.
Ekbalco 1981/82 (6yr, GB)
Fighting Fifth Hurdle, Welsh Champion
Hurdle, (2nd) Schweppes Gold Trophy,
(3rd) Champion Hurdle.
Rustle 1988/89 (7yr, GB)
Waterford Crystal Stayers' Hurdle, (2nd)
Daily Telegraph Hurdle.

168

Flash Imp 1975/76 (7yr, GB)
Castle Cary, City Trial Handicap and
Wallands Hurdles, (2nd) Christmas
Hurdle, (3rd) Champion Hurdle.
Beacon Light 1976/77 (6yr, GB)
Berkshire Hurdle, (3rd) Welsh Champion
Hurdle.
Broadsword 1981/82 (5yr horse, GB)
Lansdown, Tote Treble and City Trial
Handicap Hurdles, (2nd) Champion
Hurdle, (3rd) Welsh Champion Hurdle.

167

Tree Tangle 1975/76 (7yr, GB)
Embassy Handicap Hurdle.
Master Monday 1976/77 (7yr, Ireland)
Wilderness Handicap, Sweeps Handicap
and Erin Foods Champion Hurdles.
Starfen 1980/81 (5yr, GB)
Haydock Park Champion Hurdle Trial,
(4th) Champion Hurdle.
Celtic Ryde 1981/82 (7yr, GB)
Holsten Diat Pils, Thorpe Satchville,
Mecca Bookmakers' Handicap and
New Year's Day Hurdles.
Very Promising 1983/84 (6yr, GB)
(2nd) Sandeman Aintree Hurdle, (3rd)
Champion Hurdle.

166

Super Nova 1975/76 (6yr mare, GB)
Ladbroke Leaders Handicap Hurdle.
Cima 1983/84 (6yr, GB)
(2nd) Champion Hurdle.
Celtic Chief 1987/88 (5yr, GB)
Flavel-Leisure, Tom Masson Trophy, Gerry
Feilden, Lee Cooper and Sandeman
Aintree Hurdles, (3rd) Champion Hurdle.
Classical Charm 1987/88 (5yr, Ireland)
Carrickmines Hurdle, Wessel Cable
Champion Hurdle, (2nd) Champion
Hurdle.

166?

River Ceiriog 1986/87 (6yr, GB)
(3rd) Gerry Feilden Hurdle, (3rd) New
Year's Day Hurdle.

165

Royal Vulcan 1982/83 (5yr horse, GB)
Newbury Autumn, Lansdown, Kennel
Gate, Gerry Feilden, Wessel Industries
Champion, Welsh Champion and
Scottish Champion Handicap Hurdles.
Nohalmdun 1985/86 (5yr, GB)
British Beef Company Hurdle, Brian
Ingamells Charles Street Club Hurdle,
(3rd) Champion Hurdle. **1986/87** (6yr, GB)
HSS Hire Shops Hurdle, Christmas
Hurdle, Haydock Park Champion
Hurdle Trial.
Galmoy 1986/87 (8yr, Ireland)
Waterford Crystal Stayers' Hurdle.
Deep Idol 1986/87 (7yr, Ireland)
Carling Lager, Ali and Mohamad Soudavar
Memorial Trial and Wessel Cable
Champion Hurdles, (4th) Champion
Hurdle.
Stepaside Lord 1986/87 (5yr, Ireland/
GB)
Junction, Brown Lad Handicap and City
Trial Handicap Hurdles, (5th) Champion
Hurdle.

165§

Connaught Ranger 1979/80 (6yr, GB)
Kirk and Kirk Hurdle, (2nd) Berkshire
Hurdle, (2nd) Bula Hurdle.
1980/81 (7yr, GB)
Long Town Hurdle, Kirk and Kirk Hurdle,
(3rd) Sweeps Handicap Hurdle.

164

Derring Rose 1980/81 (6yr horse, GB)
Long Walk, Rendlesham and Waterford
Crystal Stayers' Hurdles.
Heighlin 1981/82 (6yr, GB)
Berkshire Hurdle, Oteley Hurdle.
Floyd 1986/87 (7yr, GB)
Snow Hill Handicap Hurdle, Bula Hurdle.
Cloughtaney 1987/88 (7yr, Ireland)
Sean P Graham Memorial Hurdle, Bishops
Cleeve Hurdle.
Kingsmill 1988/89 (6yr, Ireland)
Limerick Racing Club Handicap Hurdle,
Wessel Cable Champion Hurdle.

163

Sunyboy 1975/76 (6yr horse, GB)
Fernbank Hurdle, (3rd) Christmas Hurdle.
Bonalma 1985/86 (6yr, Ireland)
Black and White Whisky Handicap Hurdle,
Sweeps Handicap Hurdle.
Aonoch 1986/87 (8yr, GB)
Clairefontaine, Teroson, Mecca
Bookmakers' Handicap, Premier Long-
Distance, Rendlesham and Sandeman
Aintree Hurdles, (2nd) Waterford Crystal
Stayers' Hurdle.
Kribensis 1988/89 (5yr, GB)
Flavel-Leisure, Gerry Feilden and
Christmas Hurdles.

162

Straight Row 1976/77 (7yr, Ireland)
Decent Fellow 1978/79 (6yr horse, GB)
Venture To Cognac 1978/79 (6yr, GB)
Passage Creeper 1984/85 (8yr, Ireland)
Bajan Sunshine 1984/85 (6yr, GB)
Crimson Embers 1985/86 (11yr, GB)
Kesslin 1985/86 (6yr, GB)
Mole Board 1988/89 (7yr, GB)
Vagador 1988/89 (6yr, GB)

161p

Swingit Gunner 1987/88 (7yr, GB)

161

Supreme Halo 1975/76 (6yr, GB)
Richdee 1980/81 (5yr, GB)
Buck House 1983/84 (6yr, Ireland)
Herbert United 1985/86 (7yr, Ireland)
First Bout 1985/86 (5yr, GB)
Past Glories 1987/88 (5yr horse, GB)

161?

High Knowl 1987/88 (5yr horse, GB)

160

Grand Canyon 1976/77 (7yr, GB)
Fish Quiz 1976/77 (6yr, Ireland)
Town Ship 1976/77 (6yr, GB)
Slaney Idol 1980/81 (6yr, Ireland)
Gay George 1982/83 (7yr horse, GB)
Fane Ranger 1982/83 (6yr, Ireland)
Sula Bula 1982/83 (5yr horse, GB)
Fredcoteri 1983/84 (8yr, Ireland)
Corporal Clinger 1985/86 (7yr, GB)
Out of the Gloom 1988/89 (8yr, GB)
Vicario di Bray 1988/89 (6yr, GB)

The top Timeform ratings
achieved by hurdlers in their
'second-best' seasons have been:

178

Night Nurse (1975/76) (also rated 170 in
1977/78)

177

Monksfield (1977/78) (also rated 176 in
1976/77 and 169 in 1979/80)

171

Birds Nest (1978/79) (also rated 168§
in 1977/78 and 1979/80, and 166§ in
1980/81)
Daring Run (1981/82)

169

Lanzarote (1975/76)

168

For Auction (1982/83)
Dawn Run (1982/83)

167+

Gaye Brief (1983/84) (also rated 167 in
1985/86 and 165§ in 1984/85)

Top Timeform Ratings: Steeplechasers

184
Burrough Hill Lad 1984/85 (9yr, GB)
Silver Buck Handicap, Hennessy Cognac Gold Cup Handicap, Charlie Hall Memorial Wetherby Pattern, King George VI and Gainsborough Handicap Chases.

182
Captain Christy 1975/76 (9yr, Ireland)
Punchestown Chase, King George VI Chase.
Desert Orchid 1988/89 (10yr, GB)
Terry Biddlecombe Challenge Trophy, Tingle Creek Handicap, King George VI, Victor Chandler Handicap and Gainsborough Handicap Chases, Cheltenham Gold Cup.

179
Badsworth Boy 1982/83 (8yr, GB)
White Hart Chase, Year's End and Bidford Handicap Chases, Queen Mother Champion Chase.

177
Bregawn 1982/83 (9yr, GB)
Palace Hotel Torquay Chase, Rehearsal Chase, Hennessy Cognac Gold Cup, Newent Handicap Chase, Cheltenham Gold Cup.

176
Little Owl 1980/81 (7yr, GB)
David M Adams Developments, Peter Marsh Handicap, Tote Double and Timeform Chases, Cheltenham Gold Cup.

175
Brown Lad 1975/76 (10yr, Ireland)
Silk Cut, Thyestes, National Trial and Irish Grand National Handicap Chases, (2nd) Cheltenham Gold Cup.
Night Nurse 1980/81 (10yr, GB)
Red Alligator Handicap Chase, (2nd) Freshfields Holidays Handicap Chase, (2nd) Cheltenham Gold Cup.
Silver Buck 1981/82 (10yr, GB)
Terry Biddlecombe Challenge Trophy, Edward Hanmer Memorial Handicap Chase, Cox Moore Sweaters Handicap Chase, Cheltenham Gold Cup.
Wayward Lad 1983/84 (9yr, GB)
Charlie Hall Memorial Wetherby, Peterborough, King George VI and Pennine Chases.

174
Bula 1975/76 (11yr, GB)
Sundew, Gainsborough and Fairlawne Chases, (2nd) King George VI Chase, (3rd) SGB Handicap Chase.
Pearlyman 1987/88 (9yr, GB)
John Seyfried Mickleton Handicap, Castleford Handicap and Queen Mother Champion Chases.

173
Captain John 1982/83 (9yr, GB)
Arpal Conquest, SGB and Kelso Handicap Chases, (2nd) Hennessy Cognac Gold Cup, (2nd) Cheltenham Gold Cup.

172
Brown Chamberlin 1983/84 (9yr, GB)
Terry Biddlecombe Challenge Trophy, Courage Cup Qualifier, Hennessy Cognac Gold Cup, Compton Chase, (2nd) King George VI Chase, (2nd) Cheltenham Gold Cup.

171
Anaglogs Daughter 1980/81 (8yr mare, Ireland)
Buchanan Whisky Gold Cup, PZ Mower Chase, Foxrock Cup, (2nd) King George VI Chase, (2nd) Queen Mother Champion Chase.
Charter Party 1987/88 (10yr, GB)
Gainsborough Handicap Chase, Cheltenham Gold Cup.
Nupsala 1987/88 (9yr, France)
King George VI Chase, (2nd) Grand Steeple-Chase de Paris.

170
Ten Up 1975/76 (9yr, Ireland)
Bunker Hill Chase, (2nd) Newlands Handicap Chase.
Rathgorman 1981/82 (10yr, GB)
Associated Tyre Specialists Handicap, Rufford Handicap, Garforth Handicap, Lowesmoor and Edwards, Bigwood and Bewlay Handicap Chases, Queen Mother Champion Chase.
1982/83 (11yr, GB)
John Seyfried Mickleton Handicap Chase, Fairford Handicap Chase.
The Mighty Mac 1983/84 (9yr, GB)
Legsby, Glynwed International, Emmerdale Farm, Harrogate and SGB Handicap Chases, Cathcart Chase, (3rd) King George VI Chase.
Combs Ditch 1985/86 (10yr, GB)
Still Fork Trucks Gold Cup, John Bull Chase, Peter Marsh Handicap Chase, (2nd) King George VI Chase.
Playschool 1987/88 (10yr, GB)
Hennessy Cognac Gold Cup, Welsh National, Vincent O'Brien Irish Gold Cup.
Kildimo 1987/88 (8yr, GB)
Allied Dunbar Handicap Chase, Jim Ford Challenge Cup, (2nd) Chivas Regal Cup, (2nd) Whitbread Gold Cup.

169p
Carvill's Hill 1988/89 (7yr, Ireland)
Joe Norris Renault Novices' Chase, Red Mills Trial Chase, Vincent O'Brien Irish Gold Cup, Power Gold Cup, Tattersalls Gold Cup.

169
Spartan Missile 1980/81 (9yr, GB)
Corinthian Hunters' Chase, Duke of Gloucester Memorial Trophy, (disqualified) Wilfred Johnstone Hunters' Chase, (2nd) Grand National, (4th) Cheltenham Gold Cup.
Sunset Cristo 1981/82 (8yr, GB)
(2nd) Edward Hanmer Memorial Handicap Chase, (3rd) Cheltenham Gold Cup.
Fifty Dollars More 1982/83 (8yr, GB)
Mackeson Gold Cup, Pond and Anthony Mildmay, Peter Cazalet Memorial Handicap Chases, Timeform Chase, (2nd) King George VI Chase.
1983/84 (9yr, GB)
Kennedy Construction Gold Cup, Wincanton Challenge Cup.
Forgive'N Forget 1985/86 (9yr, GB)
Edward Hanmer Memorial Handicap Chase, (3rd) Cheltenham Gold Cup.
1986/87 (10yr, GB)
Charlie Hall Memorial Wetherby Pattern, Edward Hanmer Memorial Handicap and Tommy Whittle Chases, Vincent O'Brien Irish Gold Cup.

1987/88 (11yr, GB)
(2nd) Vincent O'Brien Irish Gold Cup.
Yahoo 1988/89 (8yr, GB)
Martell Cup, (2nd) Cheltenham Gold Cup.

168
Diamond Edge 1979/80 (9yr, GB)
John Bull Chase, Freshfields Holidays Handicap Chase, Jim Ford Challenge Cup.
1980/81 (10yr, GB)
Terry Biddlecombe Challenge Trophy, McEwans Lager Handicap Chase, Whitbread Gold Cup, (3rd) King George VI Chase.
1981/82 (11yr, GB)
Hennessy Cognac Gold Cup, (4th) Cheltenham Gold Cup.
Run and Skip 1985/86 (8yr, GB)
Bic Razor, Food Brokers Armour, Welsh National and Anthony Mildmay, Peter Cazalet Memorial Handicap Chases, (2nd) Hennessy Cognac Gold Cup, (4th) Cheltenham Gold Cup.
Very Promising 1986/87 (9yr, GB)
Mackeson Gold Cup, Black and White Whisky Champion Chase, (2nd) Vincent O'Brien Irish Gold Cup, (2nd) Queen Mother Champion Chase.
Barnbrook Again 1988/89 (8yr, GB)
Haldon Gold Challenge Cup, Arlington Premier Chase Qualifier, Arlington Premier Chase Final, Queen Mother Champion Chase.

168?
Beau Ranger 1988/89 (11yr, GB)
Edward Hanmer Memorial Handicap Chase, Hardanger Properties Chase, (2nd) AF Budge Gold Cup, (3rd) Queen Mother Champion Chase.

167
Lough Inagh 1975/76 (9yr, Ireland)
Webster Cup Handicap Chase, (3rd) Thyestes Handicap Chase.
Jack of Trumps 1979/80 (7yr, Ireland)
Hermitage Handicap Chase, Punchestown Chase, (2nd) King George VI Chase.
1980/81 (8yr, Ireland)
(2nd) Kilternan Handicap Chase, (3rd) Foxrock Cup.
Drumgora 1981/82 (10yr, Ireland)
Goffs Handicap Chase, (3rd) Queen Mother Champion Chase.
Dawn Run 1985/86 (8yr mare, Ireland)
Punchestown Chase, Sean P Graham Chase, Cheltenham Gold Cup, Match with Buck House.
Cavvies Clown 1987/88 (8yr, GB)
SGB Handicap Chase, (disqualified) Mandarin Handicap Chase, (disqualified) John Bull Chase, (disqualified) Charterhouse Mercantile Chase, (2nd) Cheltenham Gold Cup.

166p
The Thinker 1986/87 (9yr, GB)
Rowland Meyrick Handicap Chase, Peter Marsh Handicap Chase, Cheltenham Gold Cup.

166
Tingle Creek 1975/76 (10yr, GB)
Harrison Construction Chase, Hesketh Challenge Cup, Castleford Handicap Chase, Express Chase, Alex Fetherstonhaugh Challenge Cup,

Sherburn and Colwick Hall Handicap
Chases.
Gay Spartan 1978/79 (8yr, GB)
King George VI Chase, Jim Ford
Challenge Cup.
Royal Bond 1981/82 (9yr, Ireland)
Colt Car Diamond Handicap Chase,
Harold Clarke Leopardstown Handicap
Chase.

165
Artifice 1982/83 (12yr, GB)
Metropole Cup, Sandown Pattern,
Frogmore, Park Hampers and
Washington Singer Memorial Challenge
Cup Handicap Chases, (2nd) Mackeson
Gold Cup, (2nd) Queen Mother
Champion Chase.
Righthand Man 1984/85 (8yr, GB)
Coombe Hill, St Helens, Welsh National
and Hamilton Memorial Handicap
Chases, (2nd) Cheltenham Gold Cup,
(2nd) Scottish National.
Buck House 1985/86 (8yr, Ireland)
Fortria Handicap, PZ Mower, Queen
Mother Champion and National Hunt
Championship Chases.
Ten Plus 1988/89 (9yr, GB)
Silver Buck Handicap, Rehearsal
Handicap, Mandarin Handicap and
Compton Chases.

164+
Bobsline 1984/85 (9yr, Ireland)
Maddenstown Handicap Chase,
Punchestown Chase, Foxrock Cup.

164
Midnight Court 1977/78 (7yr, GB)
Embassy Premier Chase Qualifier, Baxter
Gate, Kirk and Kirk Handicap, SGB
Handicap and Geoffrey Gilbey
Memorial Handicap Chases, Aynsley
China Cup, Cheltenham Gold Cup.
News King 1981/82 (8yr, GB)
Dunkirk, Manicou, Tingle Creek, New
Year, Game Spirit and Gold Label
Handicap Chases.
Drumlargan 1983/84 (10yr, Ireland)
National Trial Handicap Chase, (3rd)
Cheltenham Gold Cup.
Half Free 1985/86 (10yr, GB)
Mackeson Gold Cup, Cathcart Chase.
 1986/87 (11yr, GB)
Terry Biddlecombe Challenge Trophy,
Cathcart Chase, (2nd) Mackeson Gold
Cup.
Stearsby 1986/87 (8yr, GB)
Welsh National, Anthony Mildmay, Peter
Cazalet Memorial Handicap Chase.
Royal Stag 1988/89 (7yr, GB)
Ferry Boat, Merrill Lynch, Elmbridge and
Mole Handicap Chases, (2nd) Queen
Mother Champion Chase.

163
Bannow Rambler 1976/77 (8yr, Ireland)
Sweet Dreams, Thyestes Handicap and
Harold Clarke Leopardstown Handicap
Chases.
I'm a Driver 1979/80 (9yr, GB)
Sandown Pattern, Darlington and Mansion
House Handicap Chases.
Bright Highway 1980/81 (7yr, Ireland)
Alice Maythorn Handicap Chase,
Mackeson Gold Cup, Hennessy
Cognac Gold Cup.
Observe 1983/84 (8yr, GB)
Rehearsal, Mandarin Handicap and
Sidbury Handicap Chases.
Earls Brig 1984/85 (10yr, GB)
John Eustace Smith Trophy, Mercedes-
Benz and Greenall Whitley Breweries
Handicap Chases, (disqualified) Ripon
Handicap Chase, (2nd) Whitbread Gold
Label Cup, (3rd) Cheltenham Gold Cup.
Simon Legree 1986/87 (10yr, GB)
Bigmore Handicap Chase, (2nd) National
Hunt Handicap Chase, (2nd) Whitbread
Gold Label Cup.
Pegwell Bay 1988/89 (8yr, GB)
Glynwed International, Mackeson Gold
Cup and AF Budge Gold Cup Handicap
Chases, (2nd) Gainsborough Handicap
Chase.

163§
Royal Judgement 1982/83 (10yr, GB)
Ewell Handicap Chase, Graham-Reeves
Chase, (3rd) Whitbread Gold Cup.

162
Colebridge 1975/76 (12yr, Ireland)
Cybrandian 1986/87 (9yr, GB)
Townley Stone 1986/87 (8yr, GB)
Midnight Count 1987/88 (8yr, GB)

162§
Little Bay 1983/84 (9yr, GB)
 1984/85 (10yr, GB)

161
Stopped 1980/81 (9yr, GB)
Corbière 1984/85 (10yr, GB)
By The Way 1984/85 (7yr, GB)
 1986/87 (9yr, GB)
Galway Blaze 1985/86 (10yr, GB)
Maori Venture 1986/87 (11yr, GB)
Weather the Storm 1987/88 (8yr,
Ireland)
Delius 1988/89 (11yr, GB)

161x
Flashy Boy 1975/76 (8yr, Ireland)

160p
Noddy's Ryde 1983/84 (7yr, GB)

The top Timeform ratings
achieved by steeplechasers in
their 'second-best' seasons have
been:

183
Burrough Hill Lad (1985/86) (also rated
175 in 1983/84)

177
Badsworth Boy (1983/84)
Desert Orchid (1986/87, 1987/88)

174
Silver Buck (1980/81) (also rated 171 in
1979/80 and 1982/83)
Bregawn (1981/82)

173
Night Nurse (1981/82)

172
Wayward Lad (1982/83) (also rated 171
in 1985/86, 169 in 1986/87 and 168 in
1984/85)

171
Pearlyman (1986/87)

168
Anaglogs Daughter (1981/82)

166
The Mighty Mac (1984/85)
Forgive 'N Forget (1984/85)

166?
Gay Spartan (1979/80)

165
Drumgora (1980/81)

The following jumpers have
achieved an annual Timeform
rating of at least 160 over both
hurdles and fences:

Night Nurse: 182 hurdles (1976/77), 175
fences (1980/81)
Dawn Run: 173 hurdles (1983/84), 167
fences (1985/86)
Bannow Rambler: 172 hurdles (1975/
76), 163 fences (1976/77)
Barnbrook Again: 171 hurdles (1986/
87), 168 fences (1988/89)
Very Promising: 167 hurdles (1983/84),
168 fences (1986/87)
Buck House: 161 hurdles (1983/84), 165
fences (1985/86)

The highest-rated Grand National winner since 1975
has been Maori Venture (rated 161 in 1986/87),
though Corbière was also rated 161 in 1984/85, two
seasons after his triumph at Liverpool.

The lowest-rated winners of England's three most
important jumping races have been:

Champion Hurdle
166p **See You Then (1984/85)**
 (rated 173 in 1985/86 and
 1986/87)
170 **Celtic Shot (1987/88)**

Cheltenham Gold Cup
150 **Master Smudge (1979/80)**

Grand National
124 **Rubstic (1978/79)**
 (rated 140 in 1979/80)
138 **Lucius (1977/78)**
 (rated 139 in 1979/80)

3. HUMAN ACHIEVEMENTS

Owners

Most wins in a lifetime

Marion H Van Berg owned the winners of a record 4,775 races in North America between 1937 and 1971. Van Berg (1895–1971), by original profession a live-stock dealer from Columbus, Nebraska, concentrated on quantity rather than quality and most of his wins came in claiming races in the Midwest. He placed his horses so shrewdly that he was North America's champion owner 14 times in races won (1952, 55, 56, 60–70) and 4 times in money earned (1965, 68, 69, 70). In his peak year, 1969, the horses carrying his gold-and-purple silks won 393 races, a world record at the time.

'Mr Van' trained 1,475 of his winners himself but gradually handed over such duties to his son Jack, who was the first man in racing history to train 5,000 winners (see below). Amid the rapid turn-over of cheap claimers Van Berg's barn did house a few stakes-winners, notably Estacion, a mare whom he trained to win the Arlington Matron Handicap at Arlington Park in 1958, and Rose's Gem, a prolific winner in the late 1950s.

When Marion Van Berg died on 3 May 1971 his horses had recorded a total of 4,775 wins, 3,964 seconds and 3,341 thirds from 24,697 starts.

Marion Van Berg's career record

	Wins	$		Wins	$
1937	2	1,260	1957	111	303,225
1938	8	4,018	1958	131	375,217
1939	10	6,780	1959	148	458,096
1940	20	11,535	1960	221*	642,607
1941	19	15,010	1961	192*	556,732
1942	15	11,167	1962	205*	597,625
1943	18	19,025	1963	201*	670,367
1944	22	33,635	1964	258*	822,305
1945	30	44,860	1965	270*	895,246*
1946	42	79,475	1966	279*	867,108
1947	51	110,210	1967	268*	1,001,568
1948	75	162,780	1968	339*	1,105,388*
1949	118	256,992	1969	393*	1,453,679*
1950	102	182,264	1970	391*	1,347,289*
1951	116	223,810	1971	84	320,774
1952	140*	311,560			
1953	134	347,210	Total	4,775	14,257,739
1954	117	354,397			
1955	127*	348,580	** denotes champion in North*		
1956	118*	315,945	*America*		

Most wins in a year: world record

Dan R Lasater owned the winners of a record 494 races in North America in 1974. Lasater (born 1943), who made a fortune in the restaurant franchise business and retired at the age of 28, owned his first winner in 1971 and was North America's champion

owner 4 times in races won (1974–77) and 4 times in money earned (1973–76).

In 1974 Lasater employed 13 trainers, and the 380 horses carrying his red-and-white silks recorded 494 wins, 336 seconds and 272 thirds from 2,109 starts, earning $3,022,960. The best of them were Hot N Nasty (Hollywood Lassie and Arlington-Washington Lassie Stakes), Honky Star (Monmouth Oaks and Cotillion Handicap) and Royal Glint (Sun Beau Handicap). The previous record was 393 wins by Marion Van Berg in 1969.

Lasater, who won the Eclipse Award as outstanding owner in 1974, 1975 and 1976, sold nearly all his horses in 1983.

Most wins in a year: British record

Sheikh Mohammed owned the winners of 130 races on the flat in Great Britain in 1989, beating his own record of 126 wins set in 1987. Sheikh Mohammed bin Rashid al Maktoum, one of four racehorse-owning sons of the ruler of Dubai, is the defence minister of that oil-rich Arab emirate, and his first winner was Hatta at Brighton on 20 June 1977. In 1989 he was champion owner in money won in Great Britain for the fifth consecutive year, with earnings of £2,097,405. The 130 races in Great Britain won by his horses included 17 Pattern races:

Musical Bliss: 1,000 Guineas
Old Vic: Classic Trial, Chester Vase
Shaadi: Craven Stakes, St James's Palace Stakes
Golden Opinion: Coronation Stakes
Alydaress: Ribblesdale Stakes
Ensconse: Nell Gwyn Stakes
Scenic: William Hill Classic
Warrshan: Gordon Stakes
Sadeem: Henry II Stakes, Ascot Gold Cup
Indian Skimmer: Gordon Richards Stakes
Reprimand: Earl of Sefton Stakes, Trusthouse Forte Mile
Dancing Dissident: Temple Stakes
Moon Cactus: Prestige Stakes

Breeders

Most wins in a lifetime Kentucky-based John Edward Madden (1856–1929) is generally acknowledged as the breeder whose produce won most races. Reliable authorities credit him as breeder of the winners of more than 10,000 races, but as official statistics were not kept during most of his career on the Turf the exact number cannot be determined.

Most wins in a year Eddie Taylor (1901–89) owner of Windfields Farms in Ontario, Canada, and Maryland, USA, bred the winners of 442 races in North America in 1978.

The British record for wins in a year is 52, achieved by Lionel Holliday in 1954.

Trainers

Most wins in a career

Jack Van Berg has won more races than any other trainer in racing history, with a career total of 5,266 at the start of 1989. He scored his 5,000th win with Art's Chandelle at Arlington Park, Chicago, on 15 July 1987.

Jack Charles Van Berg was born in Columbus, Nebraska, on 7 June 1936 and started in racing as an assistant in the stable owned by his father Marion Van Berg (see above), the world's most prolific winning owner. He became a trainer in his own right in 1955 and his first stakes-winner was Dagazha in the George Brandeis Memorial Handicap at Ak-Sar-Ben, Nebraska, on 25 June 1955. From the mid-1960s he was in charge of the largest division of his father's vast string of horses, concentrating on claiming races in the Midwest, and continued his mass-production of winners after his father's death in 1971.

Van Berg has gradually improved the quality of his stable, and his handling of Preakness Stakes winner Gate Dancer brought him an Eclipse Award as Best Trainer of 1984. He won the Kentucky Derby and Preakness Stakes with Alysheba in 1987, and the world's richest race, the Breeders' Cup Classic, with the same colt in 1988, when he was Horse of the Year. Van Berg has 150 horses in training at five tracks across America and travels constantly, spending $100,000 a year on airline tickets and car rentals.

He has been North America's champion trainer 9 times in races won (1968, 69, 70, 72, 74, 76, 83, 84, 86) and once in money earned (1976). In 1981 he passed the previous record for the most wins in a career by a trainer, 3,596 by Hirsch Jacobs.

Jack Van Berg's biggest wins include:

Kentucky Derby: Alysheba (1987).
Preakness Stakes: Gate Dancer (1984), Alysheba (1987).
Breeders' Cup Classic: Alysheba (1988)
Apple Blossom Handicap: Summertime Promise (1976).
Arkansas Derby: Bold Ego (1981).
Charles H Strub Stakes: Alysheba (1988)
Cornhusker Handicap: Gate Dancer (1985).
Count Fleet Handicap: Dave's Friend (1983–84).
Fantasy Stakes: Brindy Brindy (1983).
Hawthorne Gold Cup Handicap: Almost Grown (1976).
Hollywood Turf Cup: Vilzak (1987).
Meadowlands Cup Handicap: Alysheba (1988)
New Orleans Handicap: Herat (1986).
Oaklawn Handicap: Bold Style (1983).
Philip H Iselin Handicap: Alysheba (1988)
Roseben Handicap: Dave's Friend (1980).
San Bernardino Handicap: Alysheba (1988)
Santa Anita Handicap: Alysheba (1988)
Santa Maria Handicap: Targa (1982).
Secretariat Stakes: Joachim (1976).
Super Derby Invitational: Gate Dancer (1984), Alysheba (1987).
Woodward Handicap: Alysheba (1988)

Most wins in a year: world record

Jack Van Berg trained the winners of a record 496 races in 1976. The world's most prolific winning

Jack Van Berg's career record

	wins	$
1955–56	6	17,735
1957	10	28,695
1958	16	62,641
1959	16	66,655
1960	27	95,150
1961	16	74,733
1962	19	78,122
1963	21	105,414
1964	124	335,623
1965	146	394,410
1966	116	343,163
1967	187	619,039
1968	256*	776,330
1969	239*	952,207
1970	282*	974,818
1971	190	838,793
1972	286*	1,381,067
1973	281	1,401,492
1974	329*	1,567,418
1975	206	991,690
1976	496*	2,976,196*
1977	110	904,936
1978	78	1,168,133
1979	67	1,136,402
1980	48	790,447
1981	90	1,163,022
1982	230	2,521,603
1983	258*	3,212,318
1984	250*	4,163,118
1985	235	4,626,821
1986	266*	5,536,478
1987	215	6,009,882
1988	150	6,820,396
Total	5,266	52,134,947

* denotes champion in North America

Jack Van Berg, the Nebraskan who has set new standards in the mass-production of winners. (All-Sport)

Alysheba (left), America's Horse of the Year in 1988, is the best horse Jack Van Berg has ever trained. (All-Sport)

trainer was represented mostly by cheap claiming horses but his winners also included Joachim (Omaha Gold Cup, President's Cup and Secretariat Stakes), Almost Grown (Hawthorne Gold Cup Handicap) and Summertime Promise (Apple Blossom, Indian Maid and Yo Tambien Handicaps). Van Berg's horses recorded 496 wins, 374 seconds and 293 thirds from 2,362 starts, earning $2,976,196 to give him his only financial championship. The previous record was 352 wins by Dick Dutrow in 1975.

Martin Pipe, who set new standards for British trainers when sending out the winners of 208 races in the 1988/89 jump season. (Gerry Cranham)

Most wins in a year: British record

Martin Pipe trained the winners of a record 208 races over jumps in Great Britain in the 1988/89 season (1 July 1988–30 June 1989).

Martin Charles Pipe (born Wellington, Somerset, 29 May 1945) trains at Pond Farm House, Nicholashayne, Devonshire, and gained the first win of his career with Hit Parade at Taunton on 9 May 1975. In 1988/89 he had 133 runners who started a total of 566 times for 208 wins, 78 seconds, 44 thirds and 44 fourths, earning £683,654 and giving him his first British jump trainers' financial championship. Of his wins, 150 were over hurdles and 58 over fences, and he saddled 2 winners at Cheltenham's National Hunt meeting – Sondrio and Sayfar's Lad. He broke his own 1987/88 record of 129 wins in a jump season when Delkusha won at Fontwell Park on 6 February 1989, and broke Henry Cecil's 1987 record of 180 wins in a British season (see below) when High Bid won at Uttoxeter on 22 April 1989. Pipe also reached the following milestones:

50 wins: 29 October 1988, Afford at Ascot
100 wins: 29 December 1988, Delkusha at Taunton
150 wins: 1 March 1989, Beau Ranger at Worcester
200 wins: 19 May 1989, Anti Matter at Stratford-on-Avon

Pipe trained 87 individual winners, of whom the most prolific were Celcius (9 wins), My Cup Of Tea (8), Pertemps Network (8), Sayfar's Lad (7), Liadett (6), Au Bon (5) and Pharoah's Laen (5). His most important winners were:

Beau Ranger: Edward Hanmer Memorial Handicap Chase
Strands of Gold: Hennessy Cognac Gold Cup
Bonanza Boy: Welsh National, Racing Post Handicap Chase
Sabin du Loir: Ascot Hurdle, Thunder and Lightning Novices' Chase
Corporal Clinger: Mecca Bookmakers' Handicap Hurdle
Out of the Gloom: Premier Long-Distance Hurdle
Chatam: City Trial Handicap Hurdle
Travel Mystery: Imperial Cup
Pertemps Network: Philip Cornes Saddle of Gold Hurdle Final
Sondrio: Waterford Crystal Supreme Novices' Hurdle
Sayfar's Lad: Sun Alliance Novices' Hurdle
Enemy Action: Finale Junior Hurdle
Liadett: Victor Ludorum Hurdle

Martin Pipe shared 158 of his 208 wins with Peter Scudamore, who set a record for the number of wins in a season by a jump jockey (see below). During the 1988/89 jump season Pipe also trained the winners of 4 races on the Flat, notably Travel Mystery in the 1989 Sagaro Stakes (Group 3) at Ascot.

Most wins in a year: British Flat record

Henry Cecil trained the winners of a British record 180 Flat races in 1987.

Henry Richard Amherst Cecil (born near Aberdeen, 11 January 1943) gained his first training success with Celestial Cloud at Ripon on 17 May 1969. In 1987 he had the largest string in Great Britain, 209 horses in two Newmarket yards, Warren Place and Sefton Lodge. His 132 runners started a total of 446 times for 180 wins, 86 seconds, 47 thirds and 32 fourths with winnings of £1,882,359 – giving him his seventh British trainers' financial championship.

Cecil saddled 7 winners at Royal Ascot – Midyan, Arden, Primitive Rising, Paean, Queen Midas, Space Cruiser and Orban – and he broke John Day junior's 1867 record of 146 wins when Madam Cyn won at Yarmouth on 15 September 1987. Cecil also reached the following milestones:

50 wins: 9 June 1987, Gatchina at Goodwood
100 wins: 23 July 1987, Dafinah at Catterick Bridge
150 wins: 15 September 1987, Kristal Rock at Yarmouth

Cecil trained 89 individual winners, of whom the most prolific were Belle Poitrine, McCubbin, Proud Crest, Reference Point and Sanquirico with 5 wins each. The 180 races in Great Britain won by Cecil's horses included 24 Pattern races:

Reference Point: Dante, Derby, King George VI and Queen Elizabeth, Great Voltigeur and St Leger Stakes.
Rakaposhi King: John Porter Stakes, Ormonde Stakes.
Martha Stevens: Nell Gwyn Stakes.
Legal Bid: Derby Trial.
Indian Skimmer: Musidora Stakes.
Verd-Antique: Yorkshire Cup.
Midyan: Jersey Stakes.
Paean: Ascot Gold Cup.
Queen Midas: Ribblesdale Stakes.
Orban: Hardwicke Stakes.

Diminuendo: Cherry Hinton Stakes, Hoover Fillies' Mile.
Sanquirico: July, Solario and Royal Lodge Stakes.
Bluebook: Princess Margaret Stakes.
Nom de Plume: Nassau Stakes.
Reprimand: Gimcrack Stakes.
Intimate Guest: May Hill Stakes.

Henry Cecil shared 116 of his 180 wins with stable jockey Steve Cauthen. He also won 3 races abroad in 1987, with Indian Skimmer (Prix Saint-Alary and Prix de Diane) and Orban (Premio Roma).

Most wins in a day

The most races won by a trainer in one day is 12 by Michael Dickinson on 27 December 1982. He had 21 runners in 20 races at 6 different courses within a period of 3 hours.

Michael William Dickinson (born Gisburn, Yorkshire, 3 February 1950) trained at Poplar House, Dunkeswick, near Harewood, West Yorkshire. He saddled Wayward Lad and Silver Buck, first and third in the King George VI Chase at Kempton Park, and his other winners were Marnik and Thornacre at Huntingdon; W Six Times and Fearless Imp at Market Rasen; Londolozi and B Jaski at Sedgefield; Delius and Happy Voyage at Wetherby; and Brunton Park, Prominent Artist and Slieve Bracken at Wolverhampton. These 12 winning rides (8 in steeplechases, 4 in hurdle races) were shared among 8 jockeys.

Dickinson's 9 losers included 5 seconds, 2 thirds and one fourth; only one horse failed to contribute to his afternoon's haul of £48,930. Fifteen of his runners, including 9 of his winners, started favourite. The Welder, the hottest favourite of all and the one which the 32-year-old trainer most expected to succeed, lost by a short head at Wetherby.

The world record for Flat-race wins in a day is 10, achieved by Colin Hayes in Australia on 23 January 1982. He scored a treble at Caulfield, Melbourne, with Mysterious Ways, McCabe and Glaisdale, and collected 7 wins on the 8-race card at Victoria Park, Adelaide, with Open Menu, High Drifter, War Chest, Ronleigh Bisque, Frivolous Lass, Black Mandate and Supertrack.

Trained first 5 in championship race

Michael Dickinson's 5 runners in the Cheltenham Gold Cup at Cheltenham on 17 March 1983 filled the first 5 places in a field of 11:

1st **Bregawn** (ridden by Graham Bradley)
2nd **Captain John** (David Goulding)
3rd **Wayward Lad** (Jonjo O'Neill)
4th **Silver Buck** (Robert Earnshaw)
5th **Ashley House** (Mr Dermot Browne)

The most notable comparable performance on the Flat was that of James Croft of Middleham, Yorkshire, whose 4 runners (Theodore, Violet, Professor and Corinthian) filled the first 4 places in a field of 23 for the St Leger at Doncaster on 16 September 1822.

Most English Classic wins

John Scott (1794–1871) trained the winners of a record 40 English Classic races between 1827 and 1863 at his Whitewall stable, Malton, Yorkshire. His most famous horses were Touchstone and West Australian, who in 1853 became the first Triple Crown winner, but Scott said the best horse he ever trained was Velocipede, whose leg problems prevented him finishing closer than third in the 1828 St Leger.

2000 Guineas (7): Meteor (1842), Cotherstone (1843), Nunnykirk (1849), West Australian (1853), Fazzoletto (1856), The Wizard (1860), The Marquis (1862).
1000 Guineas (4): Canezou (1848), Impérieuse (1857), Sagitta (1860), Hurricane (1862).
Derby (5): Mündig (1835), Attila (1842), Cotherstone (1843), Daniel O'Rourke (1852), West Australian (1853).
Oaks (8): Cyprian (1836), Industry (1838), Ghuznee (1841), The Princess (1844), Iris (1851), Songstress (1852), Marchioness (1855), Queen Bertha (1863).
St Leger (16): Matilda (1827), The Colonel (1828), Rowton (1829), Margrave (1832), Touchstone (1834), Don John (1838), Charles the Twelfth (1839), Launcelot (1840), Satirist (1841), The Baron (1845), Newminster (1851), West Australian (1853), Warlock (1856), Impérieuse (1857), Gamester (1859), The Marquis (1862).

Jockeys

Most wins in a career

Bill Shoemaker has won more races than any other jockey in racing history, with a career total of 8,789 at the start of 1989. Billie Lee Shoemaker, born near Fabens, Texas, on 19 August 1931, had his first ride on Waxahachie, fifth at Golden Gate Fields on 19 March 1949, and his first win on his third mount, Shafter, at the same track on 20 April 1949. Since then his career has been one of almost uninterrupted success:

• North America's champion jockey a record 5 times in races won (1950, 53, 54, 58, 59) including a then-record 485 wins in 1953.
• North America's champion jockey a record 10

times in money earned (1951, 53, 54, 58–64).
- winner of 3 Eclipse Awards – Jockey (1981), Special (1976), Merit (1981).
- regular rider of 9 Horses of the Year – Swaps (1955), Round Table (1958), Sword Dancer (1959), Damascus (1967), Ack Ack (1971), Forego (1976), Spectacular Bid (1980), John Henry (1981), Ferdinand (1987).
- winner of 4 Kentucky Derbys, 2 Preakness Stakes, 5 Belmont Stakes.
- winner of the first $1 million race, the 1981 Arlington Million, on John Henry.
- first jockey to reach $100 million in career earnings, on Lord at War in the Santa Anita Handicap on 3 March 1985.
- won the world's richest race, the Breeders' Cup Classic, on Ferdinand in 1987.
- 3,000th win: Eternal Pere, Santa Anita, 31 January 1958.
- 4,000th win: Guaranteeya, Hollywood Park, 19 May 1961.
- 5,000th win: Slapstick, Aqueduct, 22 October 1964.
- 6,000th win: Shining Count, Del Mar, 8 August 1970.
- world record 6,033rd win: Dares J, Del Mar, 7 September 1970.
- 7,000th win: Royal Derby, Santa Anita, 14 March 1976.
- 8,000th win: War Allied, Hollywood Park, 27 May 1981.
- 1,000th win in stakes race: Peace, Premiere Handicap, Hollywood Park, 30 April 1989.

Bill Shoemaker's career record

	Wins	2nd	3rd	Mounts	$
1949	219	195	147	1,089	458,010
1950	388*	266	230	1,640	844,040
1951	257	197	161	1,161	1,329,890*
1952	315	224	174	1,322	1,049,304
1953	485*	302	210	1,683	1,784,187*
1954	380*	221	142	1,251	1,876,760*
1955	307	178	138	1,149	1,846,884
1956	328	187	165	1,229	2,113,335
1957	295	183	134	1,191	2,544,782
1958	300*	185	137	1,133	2,961,693*
1959	347*	230	159	1,285	2,843,133*
1960	274	196	158	1,227	2,123,961*
1961	304	186	175	1,256	2,690,819*
1962	311	156	128	1,126	2,916,844*
1963	271	193	137	1,203	2,526,925*
1964	246	147	133	1,056	2,649,553*
1965	247	161	120	1,069	2,228,977
1966	221	158	107	1,037	2,671,198
1967	244	146	113	1,044	3,052,108
1968	19	14	11	104	175,950
1969	97	63	58	454	1,047,949
1970	219	133	106	952	2,063,194
1971	195	136	104	881	2,931,590
1972	172	137	111	869	2,519,384
1973	139	95	73	639	2,016,874
1974	160	126	108	922	2,558,862
1975	215	142	124	957	3,514,213
1976	200	154	146	1,035	3,815,645
1977	172	149	142	975	3,633,091
1978	271	194	156	1,245	5,231,390
1979	168	141	118	983	4,480,825
1980	159	140	132	1,052	5,188,883
1981	156	117	99	878	6,122,481
1982	113	110	88	717	4,691,342
1983	125	96	96	779	4,277,930
1984	108	102	96	831	4,324,667
1985	80	91	83	721	4,487,095
1986	114	97	79	708	7,029,211
1987	100	88	79	630	7,169,434
1988	68	59	77	581	3,995,573
Total	8,789	6,095	4,954	40,064	121,787,986

* denotes champion in North America

Bill Shoemaker's biggest wins include:

Kentucky Derby: Swaps (1955), Tomy Lee (1959), Lucky Debonair (1965), Ferdinand (1986).
Preakness Stakes: Candy Spots (1963), Damascus (1967).
Belmont Stakes: Gallant Man (1957), Sword Dancer (1959), Jaipur (1962), Damascus (1967), Avatar (1975).
Breeders' Cup Classic: Ferdinand (1987).
Acorn Stakes: Cicada (1962), Marking Time (1966).
Alabama Stakes: Primonetta (1961), Natashka (1966), Gamely (1967).
American Derby: Swaps (1955), Round Table (1957), Candy Spots (1963), Tom Rolfe (1965), Damascus (1967).
Arlington Classic: Candy Spots (1963), Tom Rolfe (1965).
Arlington Million: John Henry (1981).

Bill Shoemaker wins the 1979 Marlboro Cup at Belmont Park on Spectacular Bid. The world's most successful jockey says the grey is the best horse he has ever ridden, though many observers would nominate Forego. (Popperfoto)

Arlington-Washington Futurity: Candy Spots (1962), Sadair (1964), Diplomat Way (1966), Vitriolic (1967).
Beldame Stakes: Thelma Burger (1951), Pucker Up (1957), Cicada (1962), Love Sign (1981).
Blue Grass Stakes: Tomy Lee (1959), Tompion (1960), Lucky Debonair (1965), Abe's Hope (1966), Arts and Letters (1969), Linkage (1982).
Californian Stakes: Social Climber (1957), Cougar (1971–72), Spectacular Bid (1980), The Wonder (1983).
Champagne Stakes: Armageddon (1951), Jewel's Reward (1957).
Champions Invitational Handicap: Dulcia (1975), King Pellinore (1976).
Charles H Strub Stakes (formerly Santa Anita Maturity): Great Circle (1951), Prove It (1961), Gun Bow (1964), Bold Bidder (1966), Unconscious (1972), Stardust Mel (1975), Spectacular Bid (1980).
Cowdin Stakes: Dr Fager (1966).
Flamingo Stakes: Northern Dancer (1964), Buckpasser (1966).
Florida Derby: Correlation (1954), Candy Spots (1963), Northern Dancer (1964).
Frizette Stakes: Cicada (1961), Queen Empress (1964).
Futurity Stakes: Intentionally (1958), Never Bend (1962), Captain's Gig (1967).
Gardenia Stakes: Bowl of Flowers (1960), Cicada (1961), Queen Empress (1964).
Garden State Stakes: Crimson Satan (1961), Crewman (1962).
Gulfstream Park Handicap: Round Table (1958), Gun Bow (1964).
Hollywood Derby: Grantor (1951), Swaps (1955), Round Table (1957), Bagdad (1959), Agitate (1974), Crystal Water (1976), Racing Is Fun (1982), Thrill Show (1986).
Hollywood Futurity: Temperate Sil (1986).
Hollywood Gold Cup Handicap: Swaps (1956), Round Table (1957), Gallant Man (1958), Ack Ack (1971), Kennedy Road (1973), Tree of Knowledge (1974), Exceller (1978), Ferdinand (1987).
Hollywood Invitational Handicap: Fiddle Isle (1970), Cougar (1971), Dahlia (1976), Exceller (1978).
Hollywood Turf Cup: Alphabatim (1986).
Jersey Derby: Candy Spots (1963).
Jockey Club Gold Cup: Gallant Man (1957), Damascus (1967), Exceller (1978), John Henry (1981).
Kentucky Oaks: Cicada (1962), Blue Norther (1964), Blush With Pride (1982).
Man o' War Stakes: Galaxy Libra (1981).
Marlboro Cup Handicap: Forego (1976), Spectacular Bid (1979).
Meadowlands Cup Handicap: Spectacular Bid (1979).
Metropolitan Handicap: Gallant Man (1958), Sword Dancer (1959), Forego (1977).
Mother Goose Stakes: Cicada (1962).
Norfolk Stakes: MacArthur Park (1972), Groshawk (1972), Habitony (1976), Balzac (1977).
Oak Tree Invitational Stakes: Cougar (1971–72), Top Command (1975), King Pellinore (1976), Crystal Water (1977), Exceller (1978), John Henry (1981–82).
San Juan Capistrano Handicap: Don't Alibi (1961), Olden Times (1962), Fiddle Isle (1970), Cougar (1971), Exceller (1978).
Santa Anita Derby: Terrang (1956), Silky Sullivan (1958), Tompion (1960), Candy Spots (1963), Lucky Debonair (1965), Terlago (1970), Habitony (1977), Temperate Sil (1987).
Santa Anita Handicap: Rejected (1954), Poona (1955), Round Table (1958), Prove It (1961), Lucky Debonair (1966), Pretense (1967), Ack Ack (1971), Stardust Mel (1975), Spectacular Bid (1980), John Henry (1982), Lord At War (1985).
Santa Margarita Handicap: Special Touch (1951), Bed o' Roses (1952), Cerise Reine (1954), Straight Deal (1966), Turkish Trousers (1972), Sanedtki (1979).
Spinster Stakes: Primonetta (1962).
Sunset Handicap: Swaps (1956), Gallant Man (1958), Prove It (1962), Colorado King (1964), Hill Clown (1967), Cougar (1973), Greco (1974), Barclay Joy (1975), Today'n Tomorrow (1977), Exceller (1978), Inkerman (1980), Galaxy Libra (1981), Swink (1987).
Swaps Stakes: Agitate (1974), J O Tobin (1977), Temperate Sil (1987).
Travers Stakes: Gallant Man (1957), Jaipur (1962), Damascus (1967).

United Nations Handicap: Round Table (1957–59), Clem (1958).
Woodward Stakes: Clem (1958), Damascus (1967), Forego (1976–77), Spectacular Bid (1980).
Yellow Ribbon Stakes: Amazer (1978), Sangue (1983), Estrapade (1985).

Among the big races Shoemaker has never won are the Coaching Club American Oaks, Suburban Handicap, Turf Classic and Washington DC International, and the Breeders' Cup Turf, Mile, Distaff, Sprint, Juvenile and Juvenile Fillies' Stakes. Shoemaker's biggest win abroad came in the 1984 Bessborough Handicap at Royal Ascot on Sikorsky. He was also second in the 1978 Derby on Hawaiian Sound.

Before Shoemaker, the world's most prolific winning jockey was John Longden, who recorded his 6,032nd and last win on George Royal in the San Juan Capistrano Invitational Handicap at Santa Anita on 12 March 1966. Longden was born at Wakefield, Yorkshire on 15 February 1907 and remains the most successful of all English-born jockeys. He replaced Sir Gordon Richards as the world's most prolific winning jockey when scoring his 4,871st win on Arrogate at Del Mar on 3 September 1956.

Most wins in a career: British record

Sir Gordon Richards (1904–86) rode the winners of a British record 4,870 races between 1921 and 1954. Richards, born at Oakengates, Shropshire, on 5 May 1904, had his first ride on Clockwork, unplaced at

Gordon Richards wins on Sez You at Windsor in October 1945, the 18th of his 26 championship seasons. (Popperfoto)

Lingfield Park on 16 October 1920, and his first win on his third mount, Gay Lord at Leicester on 31 March 1921. His last winner was Princely Gift at Sandown Park on 9 July 1954 and his last mount Landau, third in the Eclipse Stakes at the same venue the next day. He was due to ride Abergeldie in the following race but was thrown before the start. In his 34-year career Richards achieved the following landmarks:

- Great Britain's champion jockey a record 26 times.
- won a record 269 races in 1947.
- scored 23 centuries and 12 double-centuries.
- became the only jockey to be knighted.
- won the Derby at his 28th and final attempt, on Pinza in 1953.
- won the fillies' Triple Crown on Sun Chariot in 1942.
- won the 2000 Guineas by a record margin of 8 lengths on Tudor Minstrel in 1947.
- rode 12 consecutive winners in 1933.

- became the oldest champion jockey, aged 49 in 1953.

Sir Gordon Richards's biggest wins included:

2000 Guineas: Pasch (1938), Big Game (1942), Tudor Minstrel (1947).
1000 Guineas: Sun Chariot (1942), Queenpot (1948), Belle of All (1951).
Derby: Pinza (1953).
Oaks: Rose of England (1930), Sun Chariot (1942).
St Leger: Singapore (1930), Chulmleigh (1937), Turkhan (1940), Sun Chariot (1942), Tehran (1944).
King George VI and Queen Elizabeth Stakes: Pinza (1953).
Ascot Gold Cup: Felicitation (1934), Owen Tudor (1942), Ujiji (1943), Umiddad (1944), Aquino (1952).
Challenge Stakes: Myrobella (1933), Closeburn (1947), The Cobbler (1948), Hard Sauce (1951), Agitator (1952).
Champagne Stakes: Myrobella (1932), Abernant (1948), Palestine (1949).
Champion Stakes: Cameronian (1932), Châtelaine (1933), Big Game (1942), Nasrullah (1943), Migoli (1947).
Cheveley Park Stakes: Tiffin (1928), Keystone (1940), Lady Sybil (1942), Neolight (1945), Pambidian (1948), Belle of All (1950), Zabara (1951), Bebe Grande (1952), Sixpence (1953).
Coronation Cup: His Grace (1937), Scottish Union (1939).

Sir Gordon Richards's career record

	Wins	2nd	3rd	Mounts
1920	–	–	–	1
1921	5	1	4	47
1922	5	7	3	72
1923	49	40	37	324
1924	61	70	63	517
1925	118*	101	91	730
1926	5	11	6	53
1927	164*	118	96	771
1928	148*	151	92	863
1929	135*	102	97	777
1930	128	105	100	832
1931	145*	122	108	899
1932	190*	151	118	945
1933	259*	163	113	975
1934	212*	175	114	965
1935	210*	143	132	942
1936	177*	159	109	1,000
1937	214*	141	116	987
1938	206*	136	135	971
1939	155*	111	75	726
1940	68*	53	45	344
1941	22	12	10	84
1942	67*	51	39	311
1943	65*	45	34	281
1944	88*	51	45	333
1945	104*	70	57	406
1946	212*	139	123	725
1947	269*	169	110	835
1948	224*	149	96	808
1949	261*	143	83	779
1950	201*	165	107	868
1951	227*	128	120	835
1952	231*	137	98	806
1953	191*	131	96	728
1954	54	50	37	275
Total	4,870	3,500	2,709	21,815

* denotes champion jockey

The newly-knighted Gordon Richards being led in on Pinza after winning the 1953 Derby, the highlight of his uniquely successful career. (Popperfoto)

Coronation Stakes: Solar Flower (1938), Neolight (1946), Belle of All (1951).
Coventry Stakes: Manitoba (1932), Medieval Knight (1933), Hairan (1934), Nasrullah (1942), Khaled (1945), Tudor Minstrel (1946), The Cobbler (1947), Palestine (1949), King's Bench (1951).
Dewhurst Stakes: Sultan Mahomed (1936), Fettes (1940), Effervescence (1943), Migoli (1946), Royal Forest (1948), Pinza (1952).
Doncaster Cup: Singapore (1931), Foxhunter (1932), Colorado Kid (1933), Buckleigh (1936), Haulfryn (1937), Aquino (1952).
Eclipse Stakes: Pasch (1938).
Falmouth Stakes: Tumbrel (1937), Goblet (1948).
Gimcrack Stakes: Black Watch (1927), The Black Abbot (1928), Tant Mieux (1939), Palestine (1949), Windy City (1951), The Pie King (1953).
Goodwood Cup: Brulette (1932), Loosestrife (1934).
Hardwicke Stakes: J R Smith (1935).
Jockey Club Cup: Brumeux (1930), Brulette (1932), Felicitation (1934), Foxglove (1938), Shahpoor (1943), Vic Day (1948–49).
Jockey Club Stakes: Tai-Yang (1933), Buckhound (1953).
July Cup: Myrobella (1933), Abernant (1949–50), Hard Sauce (1951), Devon Vintage (1953).
July Stakes: Hilla (1934), Rivaz (1945), Masaka (1947), Diableretta (1949), Tamerlane (1954).
King Edward VII Stakes: Field Day (1946), Migoli (1947), Rashleigh (1954).
King's Stand Stakes: Lemnarchus (1932), Sweet Polly (1936), Greek Justice (1947), Abernant (1949).
Knight's Royal Stakes: Tudor Minstrel (1947).
Middle Park Stakes: Medieval Knight (1933), Scottish Union (1937), Khaled (1945), The Cobbler (1947), Abernant (1948), Royal Challenger (1953).
Nassau Stakes: Solfatara (1933), Coppelia (1935), Barrowby Gem (1936), Goblet (1948), Jet Plane (1949), Sea Parrot (1951).
National Breeders' Produce Stakes: Tiffin (1928), Myrobella (1932), Colombo (1933), Tudor Minstrel (1946), The Cobbler (1947), Abernant (1948).
Newmarket Stakes: Cash Book (1937), Blue Train (1947), Faux Tirage (1949), Pinza (1953), Elopement (1954).
Nunthorpe Stakes: Portobello (1939), Abernant (1949–50), Royal Serenade (1952).
Oxfordshire Stakes: Ridge Wood (1949), Le Sage (1951).
Park Hill Stakes: Glorious Devon (1930), Typhonic (1933), Mitrailleuse (1947).
Princess of Wales's Stakes: Raymond (1933), Fairbairn (1935), Pound Foolish (1938).
Queen Anne Stakes (formerly Trial Stakes): Sunderland (1925), Sundry (1927), Coldstream (1931), Fair Trial (1935), Pambidian (1949), Southborne (1952).
Richmond Stakes: Palestine (1949), Artane (1952), The Pie King (1953).
Royal Lodge Stakes: Tabriz (1949), Infatuation (1953).
St James's Palace Stakes: Khaled (1946), Tudor Minstrel (1947), Faux Tirage (1949), King's Bench (1952).
Sussex Stakes: Marconigram (1928), Corpach (1936), Pascal (1937), Radiotherapy (1946), Combat (1947), Krakatao (1949), Le Sage (1951), Agitator (1952).
Yorkshire Oaks: Gioconda (1927), Glorious Devon (1930), Will o' the Wisp (1932), Trigo Verde (1935), Sculpture (1937), Sea Parrot (1951), Kerkeb (1953).
Ascot Stakes: Duke of Buckingham (1927).
Cambridgeshire: Fun Fair (1944), Jupiter (1953).
Cesarewitch: Hunters Moon (1940).
Chester Cup: Dick Turpin (1933), Winnebar (1939).
City and Suburban Handicap: Lucky Tor (1930), Montrose (1935), Impeccable (1949).
Ebor Handicap: Chapeau (1925), Cat o' Nine Tails (1932), Penny Royal (1936), Foxglove (1938).
Free Handicap: Cama (1946), Sun Festival (1954).
Great Jubilee Handicap: Abbot's Speed (1928), Fil d'Or (1949).
Great Metropolitan Handicap: Brisl (1925).
Lincolnshire Handicap: Quartier Maître (1940), Dramatic (1950).
Manchester Cup: Poor Man (1929).
Manchester November Handicap: Glorious Devon (1930), Pappageno (1938).
Northumberland Plate: Friseur (1954).
Portland Handicap: Stephen Paul (1952).
Royal Hunt Cup: Grand Salute (1931).
Stewards' Cup: Navigator (1928), Firozepore (1937), Closeburn (1947).
Victoria Cup: Fonab (1933).
Wokingham Stakes: Grandmaster (1930), The Cobbler (1949).

Lester Piggott rode the winners of 4,349 races in Great Britain between 1948 and 1985 but his global tally exceeds that of Richards, who rarely rode abroad. Piggott won 352 races in France and 176 in Ireland, and his career total probably exceeded 5,200.

Most wins in a career: record over jumps

Peter Scudamore scored his record-breaking 1,139th win over jumps in Great Britain when Arden won at Ascot on 18 November 1989. Peter Michael Scudamore (born Hereford, 13 June 1958), son of Grand National-winning jockey Michael Scudamore, started his riding career as an amateur. He was fourth on his first mount over jumps, Jack de Lilo at Chepstow on 19 April 1976, gained his first win on Rolyat at Devon & Exeter on 31 August 1978, turned professional in November 1979 and won his first jump hockeys' championship when he tied with John Francome in 1981/82. Scudamore rode for David Nicholson from 1978 to 1986, and for Fred Winter from 1986 to 1988, but most of his wins in recent years have been for Martin Pipe. He scored his 1,000th win on Avionne at Newton Abbot on 14 February 1989, and Arden's victory took him past John Francome's career record of 1,138 wins between 1970 and 1985. His best mounts have been champion steeplechasers Burrough Hill Lad and Pearlyman, and champion hurdler Celtic Shot.

Peter Scudamore's career record

	Wins	2nd	3rd	Mounts
1978/79	9	8	8	81
1979/80	34	23	19	193
1980/81	91	75	71	570
1981/82	120*	83	79	623
1982/83	93	89	70	694
1983/84	98	88	75	644
1984/85	50	65	70	508
1985/86	91*	61	52	537
1986/87	124*	86	66	578
1987/88	132*	93	60	558
1988/89	221*	112	55	663
1989/90 (to 18 Nov)	76	34	14	174
Totals	1,139	817	639	5,823

* denotes champion jump jockey

Peter Scudamore's biggest wins include:

Champion Hurdle: Celtic Shot (1988).
Queen Mother Champion Chase: Pearlyman (1987).
Anthony Mildmay, Peter Cazalet Memorial Handicap Chase: Run And Skip (1986).
Ascot Hurdle: Sabin du Loir (1987, 88).
Captain Morgan's Aintree Handicap Chase: Artifice (1983).
Cathcart Chase: Half Free (1987).
Cheltenham Grand Annual Handicap Chase: Pukka Major (1989).
Christmas Hurdle: Nohalmdun (1988).
Edward Hanmer Memorial Handicap Chase: Beau Ranger (1987, 88).
Gainsborough Handicap Chase: Burrough Hill Lad (1986).
Geoffrey Gilbey Memorial Handicap Chase: Kathies Lad (1983).
Gerry Feilden Hurdle: Celtic Chief (1987).

Golden Miller Handicap Chase: Charter Party (1985), Ten of Spades (1988).
H & T Walker Goddess Handicap Chase: Very Promising (1985).
Hennessy Cognac Gold Cup: Strands of Gold (1988).
HSS Hire Shops Hurdle: Nohalmdun (1986).
Imperial Cup: Travel Mystery (1989).
Keith Prowse Long-Distance Hurdle: Gaye Chance (1982), Bajan Sunshine (1985), Gaye Brief (1986), Mrs Muck (1987).
Long Walk Hurdle: Out of the Gloom (1985).
Mackeson Gold Cup: Pegwell Bay (1988).
Mecca Bookmakers' Handicap Hurdle: Celtic Shot (1987).
National Hunt Handicap Chase: Charter Party (1986).
Panama Cigar Hurdle Final: Passing Parade (1981), Gaye Brief (1982).
Racing Post Handicap Chase (formerly Tote Pattern Handicap Chase): Sugarally (1981), Bonanza Boy (1989).
Sandeman Aintree Hurdle: Bajan Sunshine (1985).
Scottish Champion Hurdle: Royal Vulcan (1983), Rushmoor (1984).
Scottish National: Little Polveir (1987).
Sean Graham Hurdle: Broadsword (1981).
Tia Maria Handicap Hurdle (now Swinton Insurance Trophy): Bajan Sunshine (1984).
Triumph Hurdle: Solar Cloud (1986),
Welsh Champion Hurdle: Celtic Shot (1989).
Welsh National: Run And Skip (1985), Bonanza Boy (1988).

Scudamore's biggest win abroad has been in the Temple Gwathmey Chase at Belmont Park, New York, on Jimmy Lorenzo in 1989.

Most wins in a year: world record

Chris McCarron rode the winners of a record 546 races in North America in 1974. McCarron, born at Dorchester, Massachusetts, on 27 March 1955, finished last on the first mount of his career on 24 January 1974 and did not ride his first winner until his tenth mount, Erezev at Bowie, Maryland on 9 February. Soon making up for lost time, he exploited his apprentice allowance in New England and his win on Ohmylove at Laurel on 16 December that year enabled him to break the previous record of 515 wins, set by Canadian Sandy Hawley in 1973. McCarron ended the season with 546 wins, 392 seconds and 297 thirds from 2,199 mounts, earning $2,646,227.

McCarron has been North America's champion jockey in races won 3 times (1974, 75, 80) and in money earned 3 times (1980, 81, 84). He has won Eclipse Awards as Apprentice (1974) and Jockey (1980). In mid-November 1989 Kent Desormeaux was set to break McCarron's record, having ridden the winners of 530 races in North America since the start of the year.

Most wins in a year: British record

Gordon Richards rode the winners of a British record 269 races in 1947.

Richards, in his 20th championship season, rode in 835 races for 269 wins, 169 seconds and 110 thirds. Second in the jockeys' table was Doug Smith with 173 wins. Richards was stable jockey to Fred Darling and partnered that trainer's Tudor Minstrel to a rec-

ord 8-length victory in the 2000 Guineas. The brilliant colt failed to stay in the Derby but was one of Richards's 7 winners at Royal Ascot, the others being The Cobbler, Combat, Migoli, Oros, Nebuchadnezzar and Greek Justice. The champion broke his own 1933 record of 259 wins when Twenty Twenty won at Leicester on 10 November 1947, and he also reached the following milestones:

50 wins: 19 May 1947, Overcast at Worcester
100 wins: 26 June 1947, Devon Market at Bath
150 wins: 5 August 1947, Khoma at Chepstow
200 wins: 16 September 1947, Mistress Gwyn at Leicester
250 wins: 31 October 1947, Ramponneau at Newmarket

Richards's most important winners of 1947 were:

Tudor Minstrel: 2000 Guineas, St James's Palace Stakes, Knight's Royal Stakes
Combat: Blue Riband Trial, Rous Memorial Stakes, Sussex Stakes
Blue Train: Sandown Park Trial, Newmarket Stakes
National Spirit: Cosmopolitan Cup
The Cobbler: Coventry, National Breeders' Produce and Middle Park Stakes
Migoli: King Edward VII Stakes, Champion Stakes, Aintree Derby
Greek Justice: King's Stand Stakes
Masaka: July Stakes
Closeburn: Stewards' Cup, Challenge Stakes
Careless Nora: Princess Mary Nursery
Mitrailleuse: Park Hill Stakes
Queenpot: Prendergast Stakes
High Stakes: Lowther Stakes, Limekiln Stakes

Most wins in a jump season

Peter Scudamore rode the winners of a record 221 races over jumps in Great Britain in the 1988/89 season (1 July 1988–30 June 1989).

He was in his fifth championship season when he rode 285 horses in 663 races for 221 wins, 112 seconds, 55 thirds and 61 fourths, earning £810,796; he also suffered 23 falls. Second in the jockeys' table was Mark Dwyer with 92 wins. Of Scudamore's wins, 127 were over hurdles and 94 over fences. He broke Jonjo O'Neill's 1977/78 record of 149 wins in a jump season when Anti Matter won at Warwick on 7 February 1989, scored his 1,000th career win over jumps in Great Britain on Avionne at Newton Abbot on 14 February 1989, and rode one winner, Pukka Major, at Cheltenham's National Hunt meeting. Scudamore also reached the following milestones:

50 wins: 27 October 1988, Pharoah's Laen at Wincanton
100 wins: 20 December 1988, Sayfar's Lad at Ludlow
150 wins: 7 February 1989, Anti Matter at Warwick
200 wins: 27 April 1989, Gay Moore at Towcester

Scudamore rode 111 individual winners, of whom the most prolific were My Cup Of Tea (8 wins), Celcius (6), Pertemps Network (6), Sayfar's Lad (6) and Liadett (5) – all trained by Martin Pipe. His most important winners were:

Pegwell Bay: Mackeson Gold Cup
Beau Ranger: Edward Hanmer Memorial Handicap Chase
Strands of Gold: Hennessy Cognac Gold Cup
Bonanza Boy: Welsh National, Racing Post Handicap Chase
Pukka Major: Cheltenham Grand Annual Handicap Chase
Phoenix Gold: Nottinghamshire Novices' Chase

Chris McCarron, who did not ride a winner until February 1974 but had notched a world record 546 by the end of the year. (All-Sport)

Peter Scudamore, the champion jump jockey who won a record 221 races in the 1988/89 season. (Gerry Cranham)

Laffit Pincay, the Panamanian who is financially the most successful jockey in racing history. (Sporting Pictures)

Sabin du Loir: Ascot Hurdle, Thunder and Lightning Novices' Chase
Celtic Shot: Welsh Champion Hurdle
Out of the Gloom: Premier Long-Distance Hurdle
Travel Mystery: Imperial Cup
Pertemps Network: Philip Cornes Saddle of Gold Hurdle Final
Enemy Action: Finale Junior Hurdle

Peter Scudamore shared 158 of his 221 wins with Martin Pipe, who set a record for the number of wins by a trainer in a British season (see above), and he also shared 28 wins with trainer Charlie Brooks. In addition he won the Temple Gwathmey Chase at Belmont Park, New York, on champion American steeplechaser Jimmy Lorenzo in June 1989.

Most wins in a day

The only jockey to ride 9 winners in one day is Chris Antley at Aqueduct, New York, and The Meadowlands, New Jersey, on 31 October 1987. Chris Wiley Antley (born Fort Lauderdale, Florida, 6 January 1966) rode 4 winners at Aqueduct in the afternoon and 5 at The Meadowlands in the evening. Antley had been North America's champion jockey in races won in 1985.

The highest number of wins recorded on a single programme is 8. The feat was first achieved by apprentice Hubert Jones (out of 13 mounts) at Caliente, California, on 11 June 1944, and later matched by Oscar Barattuci (8 consecutive mounts) at Independencia, Rosario City, Argentina, on 15 December 1957, Dave Gall (10 mounts) at Cahokia Downs, Illinois, on 18 October 1978, Chris Loseth (10 mounts) at Exhibition Park, British Columbia, on 9 April 1984, Robert Williams (10 mounts) at Lincoln, Nebraska, on 29 September 1984, and Pat Day (9 mounts) at Arlington International, Illinois, on 13 September 1989.

Jorge Tejeira rode at both Keystone (Pennsylvania) and Atlantic City (New Jersey) on 16 June 1976, winning with 8 out of a total of 12 mounts.

The only jockeys to ride 7 winners from 7 mounts on a single programme have been Albert Whittaker (at Huntley, New Zealand, on 19 February 1910), W. Thomas (at Townsville, Australia, on 29 July 1929), Geoff Prowse (at Elwick, Tasmania on 22 January 1972) and Richard DePass (at Florida Downs, USA, on 15 March 1980).

In Britain there have been only two instances of a jockey 'going through the card' on a 6-race programme. The feat of Gordon Richards, at Chepstow on 4 October 1933, was emulated by Alec Russell, at Bogside, on 19 July 1957.

George Fordham won with 6 of his 7 mounts on an 8-race card at Stockbridge on 18 June 1867. He also dead-heated for first place on his other mount, but was beaten in the run-off.

Fred Archer twice won on all 6 of his mounts on 7-race cards, at Newmarket on 19 April 1877 and at Lewes on 5 August 1882.

Joe Mercer had 6 wins from 10 rides on 14 July 1965, scoring 4 times from 5 attempts at Yarmouth in the afternoon and twice more at the Doncaster evening fixture.

Pat Eddery had 6 wins from 12 rides on 30 June 1986, scoring 3 times from 6 attempts at both Nottingham in the afternoon and Windsor in the evening.

The world record over jumps (and for an amateur rider) is held by Charlie Cunningham, who won with 6 of his 7 mounts on an 8-race card at Rugby on 29 March 1881.

Most money earned in a career

Laffit Pincay has won more prize money than any other jockey in racing history, with his mounts having earned a total of $136,751,245 at the start of 1989. A jockey in North America receives about 7½% of his mounts' earnings, after deduction of his agent's share.

Laffit Pincay junior (born Panama City, 29 December 1946) gained his first win on Huelen at the Presidente Remon racetrack, Panama City, on 19 May 1964 and rode for two years in his native country before going to the United States and winning on his first mount there, Teacher's Art at Arlington Park on 1 July 1966. Since then he has been champion jockey in North America once in races won (1971) and 7 times in money earned (1970–74, 79, 85), and has won 5 Eclipse Awards (1971, 73, 74, 79, 85). In 1985 he replaced Bill Shoemaker as the leading career earner among jockeys, and in the same year he took second place behind Shoemaker in the number of career wins.

Lester Piggott forces Commanche Run (far side) home in front of Baynoun in the 1984 St Leger – the record-breaking 28th Classic victory for the great jockey. (All-Sport).

Laffit Pincay's Career Record

	Wins	2nd	3rd	Mounts	$
1964–66	539	366	297	1,926	978,948
1967	231	181	166	1,240	1,933,618
1968	266	191	185	1,283	2,303,837
1969	162	133	112	899	1,671,118
1970	269	208	187	1,328	2,626,526*
1971	380*	288	214	1,627	3,784,377*
1972	289	215	205	1,388	3,225,827*
1973	350	254	209	1,444	4,093,492*
1974	341	227	180	1,278	4,251,060*
1975	268	224	185	1,211	3,459,906
1976	386	263	173	1,435	4,377,661
1977	295	247	200	1,329	4,385,951
1978	287	253	205	1,428	4,132,993
1979	420	302	261	1,708	8,183,535*
1980	291	225	223	1,426	6,512,611
1981	302	286	229	1,514	7,918,189
1982	302	240	221	1,478	9,076,024
1983	299	246	192	1,421	8,813,457
1984	299	235	192	1,407	10,909,948
1985	289	246	183	1,409	13,415,049*
1986	252	209	160	1,318	10,169,078
1987	314	272	199	1,467	11,952,663
1988	198	159	145	1,102	8,575,377
Total	7,029	5,470	4,523	32,066	136,751,245

* denotes champion in North America

Laffit Pincay's biggest wins include:

Kentucky Derby: Swale (1984).
Belmont Stakes: Conquistador Cielo (1982), Caveat (1983), Swale (1984).
Breeders' Cup Classic: Skywalker (1986).
Breeders' Cup Juvenile: Tasso (1985), Capote (1986), Is It True (1988).
Acorn Stakes: Cathy Honey (1970), Heavenly Cause (1981).
American Derby: Fast Hilarious (1969), Bold Reason (1971).
Arlington Million: Perrault (1982).
Arlington-Washington Futurity: Well Decorated (1980).
Beldame Stakes: Gamely (1968–69), Susan's Girl (1972), Desert Vixen (1974).
Blue Grass Stakes: Judger (1974).
Brooklyn Handicap: Dewan (1970).
Californian Stakes: Ancient Title (1975), Crystal Water (1977), Affirmed (1979), Erins Isle (1982), Greinton (1985).
Charles H Strub Stakes: Drin (1967), Snow Sporting (1970), Ancient Title (1974), Affirmed (1979).
Cowdin Stakes: Iron Ruler (1967).
Demoiselle Stakes: Chris Evert (1973), Free Journey (1975), Genuine Risk (1979).
Florida Derby: Judger (1974), Swale (1984).
Frizette Stakes: Molly Ballantine (1974), Heavenly Cause (1980), Family Style (1985).
Futurity Stakes: Spectacular Love (1984).
Hollywood Derby: Bold Reason (1971).
Hollywood Futurity: Tejano (1987).
Hollywood Gold Cup Handicap: Pleasure Seeker (1970), Ancient Title (1975), Crystal Water (1977), Affirmed (1979), Perrault (1982), Greinton (1985), Super Diamond (1986).
Hollywood Invitational Handicap: Life Cycle (1973), John Henry (1981), Exploded (1982), Erins Isle (1983).
Hollywood Starlet Stakes: Althea (1983).
Jersey Derby: Spend a Buck (1985).
Jockey Club Gold Cup: Affirmed (1979), Creme Fraiche (1987).
Kentucky Oaks: Heavenly Cause (1981).
Meadowlands Cup Handicap: Creme Fraiche (1987).
Metropolitan Handicap: Czaravich (1980).
Norfolk Stakes: Capote (1986).
Oak Leaf Stakes: Landaluce (1982), Folk Art (1984).
Oak Tree Invitational Stakes: Tallahto (1974), John Henry (1980).
Rothmans International Stakes: Majesty's Prince (1984).
Ruffian Handicap: It's In the Air (1979), Heartlight No. One (1983).
San Juan Capistrano Handicap: Practicante (1972), Erins Isle (1983), Load the Cannons (1984), Rosedale (1987).
Santa Anita Derby: Alley Fighter (1968), Solar Salute (1972), Sham (1973), An Act (1976), Affirmed (1978), Muttering (1982), Skywalker (1985).
Santa Anita Handicap: Cougar (1973), Crystal Water (1977), Affirmed (1979), John Henry (1981), Greinton (1986).
Santa Margarita Handicap: Miss Moona (1967), Manta (1971), Susan's Girl (1973), Princess Karenda (1981), Ack's Secret (1982), Bayakoa (1989).
Spinster Stakes: Numbered Account (1972), Susan's Girl (1975), Dontstop Themusic (1985).
Sunset Handicap: Fort Marcy (1968), One For All (1970).
Super Derby: Island Whirl (1981), Sunny's Halo (1983), Gate Dancer (1984).
Swaps Stakes: Valdez (1979), Noble Nashua (1981).
Travers Stakes: Bold Reason (1971), Carr de Naskra (1984).
Washington DC International: Le Glorieux (1987).
Woodward Stakes: Affirmed (1979).
Yellow Ribbon Stakes: Country Queen (1979).

Among the big races Pincay has never won are the Preakness Stakes, Coaching Club American Oaks, Suburban Handicap and Turf Classic, and the Breeders' Cup Turf, Mile, Distaff, Sprint and Juvenile Fillies' Stakes.

Most English Classic wins

Lester Keith Piggott (born Wantage, Berkshire, on 5 November 1935) rode the winners of a record 29 English Classic races between 1954 and 1985. His 28th victory, on Commanche Run in the 1984 St Leger, erased the longest-standing record in sport, the 157-year-old record of Classic winners established by Frank Buckle.

Lester Piggott's Classic Mounts

	2000 Guineas	1000 Guineas	Derby	Oaks	St Leger
1951	Manhattan (unpl)	Judith Paris (unpl)	Zucchero (13th)	—	—
1952	Gay Time (13th)	Enrapt (unpl)	Gay Time (2nd)	Triangle (unpl)	—
1953	Windsor Star (last)	—	Prince Charlemagne (15th)	—	—
1954	—	Big Berry (2nd)	**Never Say Die (won 33/1)**	Brilliant Green (8th)	—
1955	Time To Reason (last)	Blue Robe (5th)	Windsor Sun (13th)	Brave Venture (5th)	Nucleus (2nd)
1956	Final Court (unpl)	—	Affiliation Order (unpl)	Garden State (13th)	Court Command (10th)
1957	**Crepello (won 7/2)**	Sijui (unpl)	**Crepello (won 6/4 Fav)**	**Carrozza (won 100/8)**	Arctic Explorer (9th)
1958	Pinched (last)	Persian Wheel (4th)	Boccaccio (unpl)	Persian Wheel (8th)	—
1959	Carnoustie (3rd)	Collyria (7th)	Carnoustie (6th)	**Petite Etoile (won 11/2)**	Pindari (3rd)
1960	St Paddy (6th)	Plump (7th)	**St Paddy (won 7/1)**	Io (4th)	**St Paddy (won 4/6 Fav)**
1961	Pinturischio (4th)	Cynara (8th)	—	Vitality Plus (last)	**Aurelius (won 9/2)**
1962	Aznip (unpl)	—	—	—	—
1963	Moon Shot (8th)	—	Corpora (5th)	—	—
1964	Casabianca (unpl)	Zingaline (11th)	Sweet Moss (10th)	All Saved (5th)	I Titan (4th)
1965	Biomydrin (18th)	Miba (6th)	Meadow Court (2nd)	Miba (6th)	Meadow Court (2nd)
1966	Young Emperor (4th)	Soft Angels (5th)	Right Noble (9th)	**Valoris (won 11/10 Fav)**	David Jack (3rd)
1967	Starry Halo (unpl)	Royal Saint (9th)	Ribocco (2nd)	Pink Gem (10th)	**Ribocco (won 7/2 Jt-Fav)**
1968	**Sir Ivor (won 11/8 Fav)**	Lalibela (11th)	**Sir Ivor (won 4/5 Fav)**	Rimark (7th)	**Ribero (won 100/30)**
1969	Ribofilio (last)	Hecuba (2nd)	Ribofilio (5th)	Myastrid (3rd)	Ribofilio (2nd)
1970	**Nijinsky (won 4/7 Fav)**	**Humble Duty (won 3/1 Jt-Fav)**	**Nijinsky (won 11/8 Fav)**	Prime Abord (7th)	**Nijinsky (won 2/7 Fav)**
1971	Minsky (4th)	Super Honey (2nd)	The Parson (6th)	Maina (2nd)	**Athens Wood (won 5/2)**
1972	Grey Mirage (8th)	Princess Bonita (4th)	**Roberto (won 3/1 Fav)**	Arkadina (3rd)	**Boucher (won 3/1)**
1973	Thatch (4th)	Miss Petard (6th)	Cavo Doro (2nd)	Where You Lead (2nd)	Cavo Doro (10th)
1974	Apalachee (3rd)	Helmsdale (8th)	Arthurian (12th)	Escorial (13th)	Giacometti (2nd)
1975	Mark Anthony (6th)	Rose Bowl (4th)	Bruni (14th)	**Juliette Marny (won 12/1)**	King Pellinore (2nd)
1976	Loh (14th)	Cappuccilli (unpl)	**Empery (won 10/1)**	Sarania (6th)	General Ironside (7th)
1977	The Minstrel (3rd)	Cloonlara (4th)	**The Minstrel (won 5/1)**	—	Alleged (2nd)
1978	Try My Best (last)	Cherry Hinton (4th)	Inkerman (21st)	—	Arapahos (10th)
1979	Jeroboam (9th)	—	Milford (10th)	Godetia (9th)	—
1980	Night Alert (3rd)	Millingdale Lillie (4th)	Monteverdi (14th)	Forlene (last)	—
1981	Kind of Hush (13th)	**Fairy Footsteps (won 6/4 Fav)**	Shotgun (4th)	**Blue Wind (won 3/1 Jt-Fav)**	Bustomi (3rd)
1982	Rare Gift (21st)	Play It Safe (4th)	—	Tants (9th)	Jalmood (6th)
1983	Diesis (8th)	Myra's Best (unpl)	**Teenoso (won 9/2 Fav)**	Cormorant Wood (6th)	Carlingford Castle (3rd)
1984	Keen (5th)	Miss Beaulieu (7th)	Alphabatim (5th)	**Circus Plume (won 4/1)**	**Commanche Run (won 7/4 Fav)**
1985	**Shadeed (won 4/5 Fav)**	Bella Colora (3rd)	Theatrical (7th)	Dance Machine (last)	Lanfranco (3rd)

Piggott's Classic Summary

	Won	2nd	3rd	4th	Mounts
2000	4	–	4	4	34
1000	2	3	1	7	30
Derby	9	4	–	1	32
Oaks	6	2	2	1	29
St Leger	8	6	5	1	26
Totals	29	15	12	14	151

Piggott gains his 29th and final Classic success on Shadeed (far side) in the 1985 2000 Guineas. (Gerry Cranham)

Steve Cauthen, who has been champion jockey and ridden a Triple Crown winner (Affirmed, Oh So Sharp) on both sides of the Atlantic. (All-Sport)

Most consecutive wins

There have been two authenticated instances of jockeys riding 12 consecutive winners. The first was by Gordon Richards, who won on his last mount at Nottingham on 3 October 1933, all 6 at Chepstow on 4 October and the first 5 at Chepstow on 5 October. The feat was matched in Southern Rhodesia (now Zimbabwe) in June and July 1958 by Pieter Phillipus Stroebel.

Obituary notices of George Herring (killed in a race fall at Hull on 27 July 1796) credited him with having achieved 19 consecutive wins, but details were lacking and the feat cannot be verified.

The record winning sequence by a jump jockey is 10 by Johnny Gilbert (8–30 September 1959) and Phil Tuck (23 August–3 September 1986).

Champion in two countries

The only jockey to have won championships in both North America and Britain is Steve Cauthen. He headed the American list in 1977 and topped the British table in 1984, 1985 and 1987.

Tommy Burns, North American champion in 1898 and 1899, was the leader in Germany in 1907.

Charlie Maidment was champion in Ireland in 1866 and 1867, and shared the championship in Britain in both 1870 and 1871. Steve Donoghue led the Irish list in 1908 and was champion in Britain from 1914 to 1923, jointly on the last occasion. Pat Eddery, champion in Britain from 1974 to 1977 and in 1986, 1988 and 1989, topped the Irish table in 1982.

Scobie Breasley was champion 3 times in the state of Victoria (1943/44, 1944/45, 1945/46) and 4 times in Great Britain (1957, 1961, 1962, 1963).

World's oldest jockey

This was Harry Beasley (1852–1939), an Irishman who started his career in his teens. He rode Come Away to win the Grand National in 1891 and, at the age of 83, partnered his own filly Mollie to be unplaced in the Corinthian Plate, a Flat race for amateur riders at Baldoyle, Co Dublin on 10 June 1935.

Oldest jockey to record his first win

This was Victor Morley Lawson, who was 67 when partnering his own gelding Ocean King to victory in a division of the Corinthian Amateur Riders' Maiden Stakes at Warwick, England on 16 October 1973.

The identity of the world's youngest jockey is a matter for debate, though claims have been made on behalf of Frank Wootton. He was born in Australia in December 1893 and was not yet ten years old when riding winners in South Africa in 1903. His family then moved to England, where he became the youngest-ever champion jockey at the age of 15 in 1909.

The most notable victory by a disabled jockey

This was achieved by amateur Frank Wise, who wore an artificial leg when winning the 1929 Irish Grand National. Mr Wise had suffered war injuries, losing a leg and the tops of 3 fingers on his right hand, but he rode the favourite Alike (a mare whom he also owned and trained) to win Ireland's premier steeplechase at Fairyhouse on 1 April 1929. The partnership had finished fourth in the same race the previous year.

Gerald Foljambe rode 2 steeplechase winners at the Melton Hunt meeting, Leicestershire on 2 April 1925 despite having had a leg amputated just below the knee.

4. BIG-RACE RESULTS

English Classics

2000 Guineas

At Newmarket, Suffolk. For 3-year-olds. 1 mile.

		Owner	Trainer	Jockey	Ran	S.P.
1809	**Wizard**, ch c by Sorceror	C Wilson	T Perren	W Clift	8	4/5F
1810	**Hephestion**, b c by Alexander	Lord Grosvenor	R Robson	F Buckle	9	5/1
1811	**Trophonius**, bl c by Sorceror	R Andrew	R D Boyce	S Barnard	11	5/2F
1812	**Cwrw**, br c by Dick Andrews	Lord Darlington		S Chifney, jr	7	7/1
1813	**Smolensko**, bl c by Sorceror	Sir C Bunbury	Crouch	H Miller	12	7/4F
1814	**Olive**, b c by Sir Oliver	C Wyndham	R D Boyce	W Arnull	14	5/1
1815	**Tigris**, ch c by Quiz	Lord Rous	R D Boyce	W Arnull	10	7/4F
1816	**Nectar**, b c by Walton	Lord G H Cavendish	R D Boyce	W Arnull	12	5/2F
1817	**Manfred**, b c by Election	S Stonehewer	R Stephenson	W Wheatley	8	4/1
1818	**Interpreter**, b c by Soothsayer	Lord Foley	R Prince	W Clift	9	7/4F
1819	**Antar**, b c by Haphazard	Sir J Shelley	J Edwards	E Edwards	6	4/1
1820	**Pindarrie**, b c by Phantom	Duke of Grafton	R Robson	F Buckle	5	1/1F
1821	**Reginald**, b c by Haphazard	Duke of Grafton	R Robson	F Buckle	4	11/10F
1822	**Pastille**, b f by Rubens	Duke of Grafton	R Robson	F Buckle	3	4/6F
1823	**Nicolo**, ch c by Selim	J Rogers	J Rogers	W Wheatley	7	5/1
1824	**Schahriar**, b c by Shuttle Pope	J Haffenden		W Wheatley	7	10/1
1825	**Enamel**, ch c by Phantom	Lord Exeter	C Marson	J Robinson	6	7/4F
1826	**Dervise**, b c by Merlin	Duke of Grafton	R Robson	J B Day	7	7/2
1827	**Turcoman**, br b by Selim	Duke of Grafton	R Robson	F Buckle	5	5/1
1828	**Cadland**, br c by Andrew	Duke of Rutland	R D Boyce	J Robinson	5	5/2
1829	**Patron**, ch c by Partisan	Lord Exeter	C Marson	F Boyce	2	1/8F
1830	**Augustus**, ch c by Sultan	Lord Exeter	C Marson	P Conolly	2	4/7F
1831	**Riddlesworth**, ch c by Emilius	Lord Jersey	J Edwards	J Robinson	6	1/5F
1832	**Archibald**, b c by Paulowitz	J Peel		A Pavis	7	2/1F
1833	**Clearwell**, gr c by Jerry	Lord Orford		J Robinson	6	5/4F
1834	**Glencoe**, ch c by Sultan	Lord Jersey	J Edwards	J Robinson	7	6/1
1835	**Ibrahim**, br c by Sultan	Lord Jersey	J Edwards	J Robinson	4	1/7F
1836	**Bay Middleton**, b c by Sultan	Lord Jersey	J Edwards	J Robinson	6	4/6F
1837	**Achmet**, b c by Sultan	Lord Jersey	J Edwards	E Edwards	9	4/6F
1838	**Grey Momus**, gr c by Comus	Lord G Bentinck	J B Day	J B Day	6	4/1
1839	**The Corsair**, bl c by Sir Hercules	Lord Lichfield	J Doe	W Wakefield	3	10/1
1840	**Crucifix**, b f by Priam	Lord G Bentinck	J B Day	J B Day	6	8/11F
1841	**Ralph**, ch c by Doctor Syntax	Lord Albemarle	W Edwards	J B Day	8	5/2F
1842	**Meteor**, ch c by Velocipede	J Bowes	J Scott	W Scott	8	6/4F
1843	**Cotherstone**, b c by Touchstone	J Bowes	J Scott	W Scott	3	1/3F
1844	**The Ugly Buck**, b c by Venison	J B Day	J B Day	J Day, jr	7	2/7F
1845	**Idas**, b c by Liverpool	Lord Stradbroke	R Boyce, jr	E Flatman	5	5/6F
1846	**Sir Tatton Sykes**, b c by Melbourne	W Scott	W Oates	W Scott	6	5/1
1847	**Conyngham**, b c by Slane	Sir R Pigot	J Day, jr	J Robinson	10	4/1
1848	**Flatcatcher**, b c by Touchstone	B Green	H Stebbing	J Robinson	5	4/1
1849	**Nunnykirk**, bl c by Touchstone	A Nichol	J Scott	F Butler	8	5/6F
1850	**Pitsford**, ch c by Epirus	H Hill	J Day, jr	A Day	5	5/2
1851	**Hernandez**, br c by Pantaloon	Lord Enfield	J Kent, jr	E Flatman	10	5/1
1852	**Stockwell**, ch c by The Baron	Lord Exeter	W Harlock	J Norman	9	10/1
1853	**West Australian**, b c by Melbourne	J Bowes	J Scott	F Butler	7	4/6F
1854	**The Hermit**, br c by Bay Middleton	J Gully	J Day, jr	A Day	9	12/1
1855	**Lord of the Isles**, b c by Touchstone	J Merry	W Day	T Aldcroft	9	5/2
1856	**Fazzoletto**, b c by Orlando	Lord Derby	J Scott	E Flatman	10	5/1
1857	**Vedette**, br c by Voltigeur	Lord Zetland	G Abdale	J Osborne	12	5/2F
1858	**Fitzroland**, ch c by Orlando	Sir J Hawley	G Manning	J Wells	14	100/6
1859	**Promised Land**, b c by Jericho	W Day	W Day	A Day	9	1/1F
1860	**The Wizard**, b c by West Australian	A Nichol	J Scott	T Ashmall	15	20/1
1861	**Diophantus**, ch c by Orlando	Lord Stamford	Jos Dawson	A Edwards	16	25/1
1862	**The Marquis**, b c by Stockwell	S Hawke	J Scott	T Ashmall	17	5/1CF
1863	**Macaroni**, b c by Sweetmeat	R C Naylor	J Godding	T Chaloner	9	10/1
1864	**General Peel**, b c by Young Melbourne	Lord Glasgow	T Dawson	T Aldcroft	13	7/2
1865	**Gladiateur**, b c by Monarque	Comte F de Lagrange	T Jennings	H Grimshaw	18	7/1
1866	**Lord Lyon**, b c by Stockwell	R Sutton	J Dover	R Thomas	15	4/7F
1867	**Vauban**, br c by Muscovite	Duke of Beaufort	J Day, jr	G Fordham	18	5/2F
1868 {	**Moslem**, b c by The Knight of St Patrick	W S Crawfurd	A Taylor	T Chaloner	14	100/7
{	**Formosa**, ch f by Buccaneer	W Graham	H Woolcott	G Fordham		3/1
1869	**Pretender**, b c by Adventurer	J Johnstone	T Dawson	J Osborne	19	3/1F
1870	**Macgregor**, b c by Macaroni	J Merry	J Waugh	J Daley	10	100/30
1871	**Bothwell**, br c by Stockwell	J Johnstone	T Dawson	J Osborne	13	11/2
1872	**Prince Charlie**, ch c by Blair Athol	Jos Dawson	Jos Dawson	J Osborne	14	2/1F

Year	Horse	Owner	Trainer	Jockey	Ran	S.P.
1873	**Gang Forward**, ch c by Stockwell	W S Crawfurd	A Taylor	T Chaloner	10	8/1
1874	**Atlantic**, ch c by Thormanby	Lord Falmouth	M Dawson	F Archer	12	10/1
1875	**Camballo**, b c by Cambuscan	H F C Vyner	M Dawson	J Osborne	13	7/2F
1876	**Petrarch**, b c by Lord Clifden	Lord Dupplin	John Dawson	H Luke	14	20/1
1877	**Chamant**, b c by Mortemer	Comte F de Lagrange	T Jennings	J Goater	11	2/1JF
1878	**Pilgrimage**, ch f by The Earl *or* The Palmer	Lord Lonsdale	J Cannon	T Cannon	10	2/1F
1879	**Charibert**, ch c by Thormanby	Lord Falmouth	M Dawson	F Archer	15	25/1
1880	**Petronel**, bl c by Musket	Duke of Beaufort	J Cannon	G Fordham	17	20/1
1881	**Peregrine**, br c by Pero Gomez	Duke of Westminster	R Peck	F Webb	14	15/2
1882	**Shotover**, ch f by Hermit	Duke of Westminster	J Porter	T Cannon	18	10/1
1883	**Galliard**, br c by Galopin	Lord Falmouth	M Dawson	F Archer	15	9/2
1884	**Scot-Free**, br c by Macgregor	J Foy	T Chaloner	W Platt	10	3/1F
1885	**Paradox**, b c by Sterling	W B Cloete	J Porter	F Archer	7	1/3F
1886	**Ormonde**, b c by Bend Or	Duke of Westminster	J Porter	G Barrett	6	7/2
1887	**Enterprise**, ch c by Sterling	D Baird	J Ryan	T Cannon	8	2/1F
1888	**Ayrshire**, b c by Hampton	Duke of Portland	G Dawson	J Osborne	6	8/1
1889	**Enthusiast**, ch c by Sterling	D Baird	J Ryan	T Cannon	9	25/1
1890	**Surefoot**, b c by Wisdom	A W Merry	C Jousiffe	J Liddiard	9	5/4F
1891	**Common**, br c by Isonomy	Lord Alington	J Porter	G Barrett	9	9/1
1892	**Bona Vista**, ch c by Bend Or	C D Rose	W A Jarvis	W T Robinson	14	10/1
1893	**Isinglass**, b c by Isonomy	H McCalmont	J Jewitt	T Loates	10	4/5F
1894	**Ladas**, b c by Hampton	Lord Rosebery	M Dawson	J Watts	8	5/6F
1895	**Kirkconnel**, b c by Royal Hampton	Sir J Blundell Maple	Jos Day	J Watts	8	10/1
1896	**St Frusquin**, br c by St Simon	Leo de Rothschild	A Hayhoe	T Loates	7	12/100F
1897	**Galtee More**, b c by Kendal	J Gubbins	S Darling	C Wood	8	5/4F
1898	**Disraeli**, b c by Galopin	W Johnstone	John Dawson	S Loates	14	100/8
1899	**Flying Fox**, b c by Orme	Duke of Westminster	J Porter	M Cannon	8	5/6F
1900	**Diamond Jubilee**, b c by St Simon	HRH Prince of Wales	R Marsh	H Jones	10	11/4
1901	**Handicapper**, br c by Matchmaker	Sir E Cassel	F W Day	W Halsey	17	33/1
1902	**Sceptre**, b f by Persimmon	R S Sievier	R S Sievier	H Randall	14	4/1JF
1903	**Rock Sand**, br c by Sainfoin	Sir J Miller	G Blackwell	J H Martin	11	6/4F
1904	**St Amant**, b c by St Frusquin	Leo de Rothschild	A Hayhoe	K Cannon	14	11/4F
1905	**Vedas**, br c by Florizel	W F de Wend-Fenton	W T Robinson	H Jones	13	11/2
1906	**Gorgos**, br c by Ladas	A James	R Marsh	H Jones	12	20/1
1907	**Slieve Gallion**, bl c by Gallinule	J H Greer	S Darling	W Higgs	10	4/11F
1908	**Norman**, b c by Octagon	A Belmont, jr	J Watson	O Madden	17	25/1
1909	**Minoru**, br c by Cyllene	HM the King	R Marsh	H Jones	11	4/1
1910	**Neil Gow**, ch c by Marco	Lord Rosebery	P Peck	D Maher	13	2/1F
1911	**Sunstar**, br c by Sundridge	J B Joel	C Morton	G Stern	14	5/1
1912	**Sweeper**, ch c by Broomstick	H B Duryea	H S Persse	D Maher	14	6/1
1913	**Louvois**, b c by Isinglass	W Raphael	D Waugh	J Reiff	15	25/1
1914	**Kennymore**, b c by John o' Gaunt	Sir J Thursby	A Taylor, jr	G Stern	18	2/1F
1915	**Pommern**, b c by Polymelus	S B Joel	C Peck	S Donoghue	16	2/1F
1916	**Clarissimus**, ch c by Radium	Lord Falmouth	W Waugh	J Clark	17	100/7
1917	**Gay Crusader**, b c by Bayardo	A W Cox	A Taylor, jr	S Donoghue	14	9/4F
1918	**Gainsborough**, b c by Bayardo	Lady James Douglas	A Taylor, jr	J Childs	13	4/1
1919	**The Panther**, br c by Tracery	Sir A Black	G Manser	R Cooper	12	10/1
1920	**Tetratema**, gr c by The Tetrarch	D McCalmont	H S Persse	B Carslake	17	2/1F
1921	**Craig an Eran**, b c by Sunstar	Lord Astor	A Taylor, jr	J Brennan	26	100/6
1922	**St Louis**, b c by Louvois	Lord Queenborough	P P Gilpin	G Archibald	22	6/1
1923	**Ellangowan**, b c by Lemberg	Lord Rosebery	J Jarvis	E C Elliott	18	7/1
1924	**Diophon**, ch c by Grand Parade	HH Aga Khan	R C Dawson	G Hulme	20	11/2
1925	**Manna**, b c by Phalaris	H E Morriss	F Darling	S Donoghue	13	100/8
1926	**Colorado**, br c by Phalaris	Lord Derby	G Lambton	T Weston	19	100/8
1927	**Adam's Apple**, b c by Pommern	C W S Whitburn	H Cottrill	J Leach	23	20/1
1928	**Flamingo**, b c by Flamboyant	Sir L Philipps	J Jarvis	E C Elliott	17	5/1
1929	**Mr Jinks**, gr c by Tetratema	D McCalmont	H S Persse	H Beasley	22	5/2F
1930	**Diolite**, b c by Diophon	Sir H Hirst	F Templeman	F Fox	28	10/1
1931	**Cameronian**, b c by Pharos	J A Dewar	F Darling	J Childs	24	100/8
1932	**Orwell**, b c by Gainsborough	W M G Singer	J Lawson	R A Jones	11	1/1F
1933	**Rodosto**, ch c by Epinard	Princesse de Faucigny-Lucinge	H Count	R Brethès	27	9/1
1934	**Colombo**, b c by Manna	Lord Glanely	T Hogg	W R Johnstone	12	2/7F
1935	**Bahram**, b c by Blandford	HH Aga Khan	Frank Butters	F Fox	16	7/2
1936	**Pay Up**, br c by Fairway	Lord Astor	J Lawson	R Dick	19	11/2
1937	**Le Ksar**, b c by Ksar	E de Saint-Alary	F Carter	C H Semblat	18	20/1
1938	**Pasch**, b c by Blandford	H E Morriss	F Darling	G Richards	18	5/2F
1939	**Blue Peter**, ch c by Fairway	Lord Rosebery	J Jarvis	E Smith	25	5/1JF
1940	**Djebel**, b c by Tourbillon	M Boussac	A Swann	E C Elliott	21	9/4F
1941	**Lambert Simnel**, b c by Fair Trial	Duke of Westminster	F Templeman	E C Elliott	19	10/1
1942	**Big Game**, b c by Bahram	HM the King	F Darling	G Richards	14	8/11F
1943	**Kingsway**, b c by Fairway	A E Saunders	J Lawson	S Wragg	19	18/1

Cont. p. 122

Laffit Pincay

Laffit Pincay has won more prize-money than any other jockey in racing history. The Panamanian-born rider has, despite a severe weight problem, been at the top of his profession in America for a quarter of a century and his mounts earned more than $145 million up to the start of 1990.

Laffit Pincay junior was born in Panama City on 29 December 1946. His father was a successful jockey and 15-year-old Laffit junior followed him into racing, originally as a groom and hotwalker. He gained his first win on Huelen at the Presidente Remon racetrack on 19 May 1964, and notched 446 victories in his native land before, at the age of 19, being brought to the United States by owner-breeder Fred Hooper, who had already imported budding champions Braulio Baeza and Jorge Velasquez from Panama.

Pincay won on his very first mount in his new country, Teacher's Art at Arlington Park, Chicago, on 1 July 1966, and was soon in the front rank of jockeys, achieving his first championship in 1970.

Most of the best horses he rode early in his career were fillies, and he won the Beldame Stakes on champions Gamely (1968–69), Susan's Girl (1972) and Desert Vixen (1974). He also partnered prolific California stakes-winners Ancient Title and Crystal Water, and by 1979, when he gained his sixth financial title of the decade, Pincay had established his pre-eminence among American jockeys.

In that year he replaced Steve Cauthen on Triple Crown hero Affirmed, the greatest horse he has ridden. Together Pincay and Affirmed won seven consecutive races including the Charles H Strub Stakes, Santa Anita

Right *Laffit Pincay on the best horse he has ever ridden, Affirmed, winning the 1979 Woodward Stakes. (Gerry Cranham)*

Handicap, Californian Stakes, Hollywood Gold Cup, Woodward Stakes and Jockey Club Gold Cup, beating Spectacular Bid in the last-named event to clinch Horse of the Year honours.

For a period in 1980–81 Pincay was the regular rider of turf champion John Henry, winning the Oak Tree Invitational Stakes and the Santa Anita, San Luis Rey and Hollywood Invitational Handicaps, but it was not until 1982 that he recorded his first Classic success, with a spectacular 14-length triumph in the Belmont Stakes on Horse of the Year Conquistador Cielo.

He also rode turf champion Perrault to victory in the Santa Anita Handicap, Hollywood Gold Cup and Arlington Million, which was then the world's richest race. But perhaps his most memorable mount of 1982 was the unbeaten Landaluce, whom he partnered

in all her five races. The brilliant champion two-year-old filly had an average winning margin of nearly 10 lengths but died soon after her last victory.

In 1983 Pincay landed the Belmont Stakes on Caveat and the following year, at his tenth attempt, won the Kentucky Derby on the ill-fated Swale, on whom he also picked up his third consecutive Belmont.

Personal tragedy struck him when his wife Linda, who was suffering from cancer, shot herself in January 1985, but his competitiveness drove him back to the saddle a fortnight later and he enjoyed the most successful season of his career. He passed Bill Shoemaker's earnings to become the most financially successful jockey the

sport has ever known, and also moved into second place behind Shoemaker in the number of career wins. He won the Jersey Derby on Horse of the Year Spend a Buck, whose purse (including bonuses) of $2.6 million was the largest ever collected in one race; he won his first Breeders' Cup race, the Juvenile, on Tasso; and was again champion jockey and recipient of the Eclipse Award.

In 1986 Pincay won the world's richest race, the Breeders' Cup Classic, on Skywalker, as well as the Breeders' Cup Juvenile on Capote, and in 1988 he scored his 7,000th career win and gained his fourth Breeders' Cup victory, on Is It True in the Juvenile.

Pincay, who has long been based in California, was champion jockey in North America seven times in money earned between 1970 and 1985, putting him second only to Bill Shoemaker (10) in his number of financial championships, and was also champion in races won in 1971. He has carried off five Eclipse Awards – more than any other jockey since American racing's highest awards were inaugurated in 1971 – was the 1970 recipient of the George Woolf Memorial Award, and was elected to the Hall of Fame in the National Museum of Racing at Saratoga in 1975.

His main attribute as a jockey is his great strength, and he often gives the impression of holding his mounts together and lifting them home. In contrast to Shoemaker, with his light touch, the muscular Pincay is sometimes accused of being too hard on his mounts, but he has the versatility to ride any kind of race.

His main problem throughout his career has been his weight. At one stage depression caused by constant dieting led him to consider retirement but in the late 1970s, with the help of a nutritionist, he went on a natural foods diet which enables him to ride at a steady 8st 5lb. The self-discipline required to keep his body far below its natural weight indicates his burning will to win. His mounts earned more than $145 million up to the start of 1990 and since, after deduction of his agent's share, he received about 7½% of that, the incentive for him to keep riding is powerful.

Laffit Pincay, who plans to train when he eventually retires, is perhaps the best of the many Hispanic riders who have been prominent in American racing in the last 30 years. Now well into his 40s, he is as sharp and dedicated as ever, and is still regarded by many as the top jockey currently riding in America.

		Owner	Trainer	Jockey	Ran	S.P.
1944	**Garden Path**, br f by Fairway	Lord Derby	W Earl	H Wragg	26	5/1F
1945	**Court Martial**, ch c by Fair Trial	Lord Astor	J Lawson	C Richards	20	13/2
1946	**Happy Knight**, b c by Colombo	Sir W Cooke	H Jelliss	T Weston	13	28/1
1947	**Tudor Minstrel**, br c by Owen Tudor	J A Dewar	F Darling	G Richards	15	8/11F
1948	**My Babu**, b c by Djebel	HH Maharaja of Baroda	F Armstrong	C Smirke	18	2/1F
1949	**Nimbus**, b c by Nearco	Mrs M Glenister	G Colling	E C Elliott	13	10/1
1950	**Palestine**, gr c by Fair Trial	HH Aga Khan	M Marsh	C Smirke	19	4/1
1951	**Ki Ming**, br c by Ballyogan	Ley On	M Beary	A Breasley	27	100/8
1952	**Thunderhead**, ch c by Merry Boy	E Constant	E Pollet	R Poincelet	26	100/7
1953	**Nearula**, b c by Nasrullah	W Humble	C F Elsey	E Britt	16	2/1F
1954	**Darius**, b c by Dante	Sir P Loraine	H Wragg	E Mercer	19	8/1
1955	**Our Babu**, b c by My Babu	D Robinson	G Brooke	D Smith	23	13/2
1956	**Gilles de Retz**, b c by Royal Charger	A G Samuel	Mrs G T Johnson Houghton	F Barlow	19	50/1
1957	**Crepello**, ch c by Donatello	Sir V Sassoon	C F N Murless	L Piggott	14	7/2
1958	**Pall Mall**, b c by Palestine	HM the Queen	C Boyd-Rochfort	D Smith	14	20/1
1959	**Taboun**, b c by Tabriz	Prince Aly Khan	A Head	G Moore	13	5/2F
1960	**Martial**, ch c by Hill Gail	R N Webster	P J Prendergast	R Hutchinson	17	18/1
1961	**Rockavon**, b c by Rockefella	T C Yuill	G Boyd	N Stirk	22	66/1
1962	**Privy Councillor**, ch c by Counsel	G Glover	T Waugh	W Rickaby	19	100/6
1963	**Only for Life**, b c by Chanteur	Miss M Sheriffe	A J Tree	J Lindley	21	33/1
1964	**Baldric**, b c by Round Table	Mrs H E Jackson	E Fellows	W Pyers	27	20/1
1965	**Niksar**, ch c by Le Haar	W Harvey	W Nightingall	D Keith	22	100/8
1966	**Kashmir**, br c by Tudor Melody	P Butler	C W Bartholomew	J Lindley	25	7/1
1967	**Royal Palace**, b c by Ballymoss	H J Joel	C F N Murless	G Moore	18	100/30JF
1968	**Sir Ivor**, b c by Sir Gaylord	R R Guest	M V O'Brien	L Piggott	10	11/8F
1969	**Right Tack**, b c by Hard Tack	J R Brown	J R Sutcliffe	G Lewis	13	15/2
1970	**Nijinsky**, b c by Northern Dancer	C W Engelhard	M V O'Brien	L Piggott	14	4/7F
1971	**Brigadier Gerard**, b c by Queen's Hussar	Mrs J L Hislop	W R Hern	J Mercer	6	11/2
1972	**High Top**, b c by Derring-Do	Sir J Thorn	B van Cutsem	W Carson	12	85/40F
1973	**Mon Fils**, br c by Sheshoon	Mrs B M L Davis	R Hannon	F Durr	18	50/1
1974	**Nonoalco**, b c by Nearctic	Mme M F Berger	F Boutin	Y Saint-Martin	12	19/2
1975	**Bolkonski**, ch c by Balidar	C d'Alessio	H Cecil	G Dettori	24	33/1
1976	**Wollow**, b c by Wolver Hollow	C d'Alessio	H Cecil	G Dettori	17	1/1F
1977	**Nebbiolo**, ch c by Yellow God	N Schibbye	K Prendergast	G Curran	18	20/1
1978	**Roland Gardens**, b c by Derring-Do	J Hayter	D Sasse	F Durr	19	28/1
1979	**Tap on Wood**, ch c by Sallust	A D Shead	B W Hills	S Cauthen	20	20/1
1980	**Known Fact**, b c by In Reality	K Abdullah	A J Tree	W Carson	14	14/1
1981	**To-Agori-Mou**, br c by Tudor Music	Mrs A Muinos	G Harwood	G Starkey	19	5/2F
1982	**Zino**, b c by Welsh Pageant	G A Oldham	F Boutin	F Head	26	8/1
1983	**Lomond**, b c by Northern Dancer	R E Sangster	M V O'Brien	P Eddery	16	9/1
1984	**El Gran Senor**, b c by Northern Dancer	R E Sangster	M V O'Brien	P Eddery	9	15/8F
1985	**Shadeed**, b c by Nijinsky	Maktoum al Maktoum	M Stoute	L Piggott	14	4/5F
1986	**Dancing Brave**, b c by Lyphard	K Abdullah	G Harwood	G Starkey	15	15/8F
1987	**Don't Forget Me**, b c by Ahonoora	J Horgan	R Hannon	W Carson	14	9/1
1988	**Doyoun**, b c by Mill Reef	HH Aga Khan	M Stoute	W R Swinburn	9	4/5F
1989	**Nashwan**, ch c by Blushing Groom	Hamdan al Maktoum	W R Hern	W Carson	14	3/1F

1000 Guineas

At Newmarket, Suffolk. For 3-year-old fillies. 1 mile.

		Owner	Trainer	Jockey	Ran	S.P.
1814	**Charlotte**, b f by Orville	C Wilson	T Perren	W Clift	5	11/5F
1815	unnamed, br f by Selim	Lord Foley	R Prince	W Clift	4	3/1
1816	**Rhoda**, b f by Asparagus	Duke of Rutland	R D Boyce	S Barnard	6	3/1
1817	**Neva**, b f by Cervantes	G Watson	R D Boyce	W Arnull	10	7/4F
1818	**Corinne**, br f by Waxy	J Udney	R Robson	F Buckle	8	7/1
1819	**Catgut**, br f by Comus *or* Juniper	Duke of Grafton	R Robson		7	20/1
1820	**Rowena**, ch f by Haphazard	Duke of Grafton	R Robson	F Buckle	6	7/4F
1821	**Zeal**, b f by Partisan	Duke of Grafton	R Robson	F Buckle	6	4/6F
1822	**Whizgig**, ch f by Rubens	Duke of Grafton	R Robson	F Buckle	4	2/5F
1823	**Zinc**, br f by Woful	Duke of Grafton	R Robson	F Buckle	5	4/6F
1824	**Cobweb**, b f by Phantom	Lord Jersey	J Edwards	J Robinson	4	5/2
1825	**Tontine**, ch f by Election	Duke of Grafton	R Robson		1	—
1826	**Problem**, ch f by Merlin	Duke of Grafton	R Robson	J B Day	5	5/1
1827	**Arab**, br f by Woful	Duke of Grafton	R Robson	F Buckle	7	8/1
1828	**Zoë**, b f by Orville	A Molony	R Pettit	J Robinson	7	6/5F
1829	**Young Mouse**, b f by Godolphin	Lord G H Cavendish	R D Boyce	W Arnull	4	—
1830	**Charlotte West**, ch f by Tramp	Lord Jersey	J Edwards	J Robinson	7	5/1
1831	**Galantine**, b f by Reveller	Sir M Wood	H Scott	P Conolly	8	10/1
1832	**Galata**, br f by Sultan	Lord Exeter	C Marson	W Arnull	4	1/2F
1833	**Tarantella**, ch f by Tramp	T H Cookes	John Robinson	E Wright	10	2/1F
1834	**May-day**, ch f by Lamplighter	Lord Berners	J Doe	J B Day	7	6/1
1835	**Preserve**, ch f by Emilius	C Greville	R Prince, jr	E Flatman	3	1/3F

		Owner	Trainer	Jockey	Ran	S.P.
1836	**Destiny**, ch f by Sultan	T Houldsworth		J B Day	7	6/4F
1837	**Chapeau d'Espagne**, b f by Doctor Syntax	Lord G Bentinck	J B Day	J B Day	5	2/5F
1838	**Barcarolle**, b f by Emilius	Lord Albemarle	W Edwards	E Edwards	6	4/1
1839	**Cara**, b f by Belshazzar	R Watt	C Marson	G Edwards	5	7/4
1840	**Crucifix**, b f by Priam	Lord G Bentinck	J B Day	J B Day	4	1/10F
1841	**Potentia**, ch f by Plenipotentiary	S Batson	G Payne	J Robinson	5	6/4JF
1842	**Firebrand**, ch f by Lamplighter	Lord G Bentinck	J Kent, jr	S Rogers	7	6/1
1843	**Extempore**, b f by Emilius	T Thornhill	R Pettit	S Chifney, jr	9	7/1
1844	**Sorella**, ch f by The Saddler	G Osbaldeston	W Butler, jr	J Robinson	9	10/1
1845	**Pic-nic**, b f by Glaucus	Duke of Richmond	J Kent, jr	W Abdale	8	5/2
1846	**Mendicant**, br f by Touchstone	J Gully	J B Day	S Day	7	1/1F
1847	**Clementina**, b f by Venison	G Payne	M Dilly	E Flatman	5	5/2
1848	**Canezou**, br f by Melbourne	Lord Stanley	J Scott	F Butler	9	5/1
1849	**The Flea**, b f by Coronation	F Clarke	J Day, jr	A Day	10	—
1850	**Lady Orford**, ch f by Slane	Lord Orford	W Beresford	F Butler	5	5/6F
1851	**Aphrodité**, br f by Bay Middleton	Sir J Hawley	A Taylor	J Marson	6	5/6F
1852	**Kate**, b f by Auckland	J Sargent	J Woolcott	A Day	6	4/1
1853	**Mentmore Lass**, b f by Melbourne	Baron M de Rothschild	W King	J Charlton	11	12/1
1854	**Virago**, ch f by Pyrrhus the First	H Padwick	J B Day	J Wells	3	1/3F
1855	**Habena**, ch f by Irish Birdcatcher	Duke of Bedford	W Butler, jr	S Rogers	11	1/1F
1856	**Manganese**, ch f by Irish Birdcatcher	J W King	J Osborne, sr	J Osborne	5	2/1
1857	**Impérieuse**, b f by Orlando	J Scott	J Scott	E Flatman	8	100/8
1858	**Governess**, ch f by Chatham	G W K Gratwicke	T Eskrett	T Ashmall	9	6/1
1859	**Mayonaise**, b f by Teddington	W S Crawfurd	T Taylor	G Fordham	4	9/2
1860	**Sagitta**, b f by Longbow	Lord Derby	J Scott	T Aldcroft	13	5/2F
1861	**Nemesis**, b f by Newminster	G Hilton	W Harlock	G Fordham	9	10/1
1862	**Hurricane**, b f by Wild Dayrell	Lord Falmouth	J Scott	T Ashmall	11	11/2
1863	**Lady Augusta**, ch f by Stockwell	Lord Stamford	Jos Dawson	A Edwards	10	3/1F
1864	**Tomato**, b f by King Tom	Baron M de Rothschild	J Hayhoe	J Wells	15	10/1
1865	**Siberia**, br f by Muscovite	Duke of Beaufort	J Day, jr	G Fordham	11	3/1F
1866	**Repulse**, b f by Stockwell	Lord Hastings	J Day, jr	T Cannon	9	1/2F
1867	**Achievement**, br f by Stockwell	M Pearson	J Dover	H Custance	7	1/8F
1868	**Formosa**, ch f by Buccaneer	W Graham	H Woolcott	G Fordham	8	10/11F
1869	**Scottish Queen**, ch f by Blair Athol	Duke of Beaufort	J Day, jr	G Fordham	9	100/8
1870	**Hester**, b f by Thormanby	Jos Dawson	Jos Dawson	J Grimshaw	10	6/4F
1871	**Hannah**, b f by King Tom	Baron M de Rothschild	J Hayhoe	C Maidment	7	2/1F
1872	**Reine**, b f by Monarque	C J Lefèvre	T Jennings	H Parry	11	20/1
1873	**Cecilia**, b f by Blair Athol	Lord Falmouth	M Dawson	J Morris	14	100/3
1874	**Apology**, ch f by Adventurer	J W King	W Osborne	J Osborne	9	5/2F
1875	**Spinaway**, b f by Macaroni	Lord Falmouth	M Dawson	F Archer	6	10/1
1876	**Camélia**, ch f by Macaroni	Comte F de Lagrange	T Cunnington	T Glover	13	4/1
1877	**Belphoebe**, b f by Toxophilite	Lord Hartington	G Bloss	H Jeffery	19	100/6
1878	**Pilgrimage**, ch f by The Earl *or* The Palmer	Lord Lonsdale	J Cannon	T Cannon	9	4/5F
1879	**Wheel of Fortune**, b f by Adventurer	Lord Falmouth	M Dawson	F Archer	8	40/75F
1880	**Elizabeth**, b f by Statesman	T E Walker	Jos Dawson	C Wood	10	9/2
1881	**Thebais**, ch f by Hermit	W S Crawfurd	A Taylor	G Fordham	13	5/6F
1882	**St Marguerite**, ch f by Hermit	W S Crawfurd	R Sherrard	C Wood	6	10/1
1883	**Hauteur**, br f by Rosicrucian	C J Lefèvre	T Jennings, jr	G Fordham	9	9/4F
1884	**Busybody**, b f by Petrarch	G A Baird	M Dawson	T Cannon	6	85/40F
1885	**Farewell**, ch f by Doncaster	Duke of Westminster	J Porter	G Barrett	16	20/1
1886	**Miss Jummy**, br f by Petrarch	Duke of Hamilton	R Marsh	J Watts	10	3/1
1887	**Rêve d'Or**, ch f by Hampton	Duke of Beaufort	A Taylor	C Wood	12	1/1F
1888	**Briarroot**, b f by Springfield	D Baird	J Ryan	W Warne	14	100/9
1889	**Minthe**, b f by Camballo	R C Vyner	M Dawson	J Woodburn	14	4/1
1890	**Semolina**, b f by St Simon	Duke of Portland	G Dawson	J Watts	10	1/2F
1891	**Mimi**, b f by Barcaldine	N Fenwick	M Dawson	F Rickaby	12	7/1
1892	**La Flèche**, b f by St Simon	Baron M de Hirsch	J Porter	G Barrett	7	1/2F
1893	**Siffleuse**, ch f b Saraband	Sir J Blundell Maple	Jos Day	T Loates	11	33/1
1894	**Amiable**, b f by St Simon	Duke of Portland	G Dawson	W Bradford	13	100/8
1895	**Galeottia**, b f by Galopin	A W Cox	J Ryan	F C Pratt	15	100/8
1896	**Thaïs**, br f by St Serf	HRH Prince of Wales	R Marsh	J Watts	19	5/1
1897	**Chélandry**, ch f by Goldfinch	Lord Rosebery	W Walters, jr	J Watts	9	9/4
1898	**Nun Nicer**, br f by Common	Sir J Blundell Maple	W Waugh	S Loates	15	11/2JF
1899	**Sibola**, b f by The Sailor Prince	Lord W Beresford	J Huggins	J T Sloan	14	13/8F
1900	**Winifreda**, b f by St Simon	L Brassey	T Jennings, jr	S Loates	10	11/2
1901	**Aïda**, b f by Galopin	Sir J Miller	G Blackwell	D Maher	15	13/8F
1902	**Sceptre**, b f by Persimmon	R S Sievier	R S Sievier	H Randall	15	1/2F
1903	**Quintessence**, b f by St Frusquin	Lord Falmouth	J Chandler	H Randall	12	4/1
1904	**Pretty Polly**, ch f by Gallinule	E Loder	P P Gilpin	W Lane	7	1/4F
1905	**Cherry Lass**, b f by Isinglass	W Hall Walker	W T Robinson	G McCall	19	5/4F
1906	**Flair**, br f by St Frusquin	Sir D Cooper	P P Gilpin	B Dillon	12	11/10F
1907	**Witch Elm**, b f by Orme	W Hall Walker	W T Robinson	B Lynham	17	4/1F
1908	**Rhodora**, br f by St Frusquin	R Croker	J Allen	L Lyne	19	100/8
1909	**Electra**, b f by Eager	L Neumann	P P Gilpin	B Dillon	10	9/1

		Owner	Trainer	Jockey	Ran	S.P.
1910	**Winkipop**, b f by William the Third	W Astor	W Waugh	B Lynham	13	5/2F
1911	**Atmah**, b f by Galeazzo	J A de Rothschild	F C Pratt	F Fox	16	7/1
1912	**Tagalie**, gr f by Cyllene	W Raphael	D Waugh	L Hewitt	13	20/1
1913	**Jest**, ch f by Sundridge	J B Joel	C Morton	F Rickaby, jr	22	9/1
1914	**Princess Dorrie**, br f by Your Majesty	J B Joel	C Morton	W Huxley	13	100/9
1915	**Vaucluse**, b f by Dark Ronald	Lord Rosebery	F Hartigan	F Rickaby, jr	15	5/2F
1916	**Canyon**, b f by Chaucer	Lord Derby	G Lambton	F Rickaby, jr	10	9/2
1917	**Diadem**, ch f by Orby	Lord D'Abernon	G Lambton	F Rickaby, jr	14	6/4F
1918	**Ferry**, b f by Swynford	Lord Derby	G Lambton	B Carslake	8	50/1
1919	**Roseway**, br f by Stornoway	Sir E Hulton	F Hartigan	A Whalley	15	2/1F
1920	**Cinna**, b f by Polymelus	Sir R W B Jardine	R T Waugh	Wm Griggs	21	4/1
1921	**Bettina**, br f by Swynford	W Raphael	P Linton	G Bellhouse	24	33/1
1922	**Silver Urn**, ch f by Juggernaut	B W Parr	H S Persse	B Carslake	20	10/1
1923	**Tranquil**, b f by Swynford	Lord Derby	G Lambton	E Gardner	16	5/2F
1924	**Plack**, ch f by Hurry On	Lord Rosebery	J Jarvis	E C Elliott	16	8/1
1925	**Saucy Sue**, br f by Swynford	Lord Astor	A Taylor, jr	F Bullock	11	1/4F
1926	**Pillion**, b f by Chaucer	A de Rothschild	J Watson	R Perryman	29	25/1
1927	**Cresta Run**, b f by Hurry On	G Loder	P P Gilpin	A Balding	28	10/1
1928	**Scuttle**, b f by Captain Cuttle	HM the King	W R Jarvis	J Childs	14	15/8F
1929	**Taj Mah**, gr f by Lemberg	S Guthmann	J Torterolo	W Sibbritt	19	33/1
1930	**Fair Isle**, br f by Phalaris	Lord Derby	Frank Butters	T Weston	19	7/4F
1931	**Four Course**, b f by Tetratema	Lord Ellesmere	F Darling	E C Elliott	20	100/9
1932	**Kandy**, b f by Alcantara	E de Saint-Alary	F Carter	E C Elliott	19	33/1
1933	**Brown Betty**, br f by Friar Marcus	W Woodward	C Boyd-Rochfort	J Childs	22	8/1
1934	**Campanula**, b f by Blandford	Sir G Bullough	J Jarvis	H Wragg	10	2/5F
1935	**Mesa**, b f by Kircubbin	P Wertheimer	A Swann	W R Johnstone	22	8/1
1936	**Tide-way**, br f by Fairway	Lord Derby	C Leader	R Perryman	22	100/30
1937	**Exhibitionnist**, b f by Solario	Sir V Sassoon	J Lawson	S Donoghue	20	10/1
1938	**Rockfel**, br f by Felstead	Sir H Cunliffe-Owen	O Bell	S Wragg	20	8/1
1939	**Galatea**, br f by Dark Legend	R S Clark	J Lawson	R A Jones	18	6/1
1940	**Godiva**, b f by Hyperion	E Harmsworth	W R Jarvis	D Marks	11	10/1
1941	**Dancing Time**, b f by Colombo	Lord Glanely	J Lawson	R Perryman	13	100/8
1942	**Sun Chariot**, b f by Hyperion	HM the King	F Darling	G Richards	18	1/1F
1943	**Herringbone**, b f by King Salmon	Lord Derby .	W Earl	H Wragg	12	15/2
1944	**Picture Play**, b f by Donatello	H J Joel	J E Watts	E C Elliott	11	15/2
1945	**Sun Stream**, ch f by Hyperion	Lord Derby	W Earl	H Wragg	14	5/2F
1946	**Hypericum**, b f by Hyperion	HM the King	C Boyd-Rochfort	D Smith	13	100/6
1947	**Imprudence**, br f by Canot	Mme P Corbière	J Lieux	W R Johnstone	20	4/1F
1948	**Queenpot**, br f by Big Game	Sir P Loraine	C F N Murless	G Richards	22	6/1
1949	**Musidora**, b f by Nasrullah	N P Donaldson	C F Elsey	E Britt	18	100/8
1950	**Camarée**, gr f by Maurepas	J Ternynck	A Lieux	W R Johnstone	17	10/1
1951	**Belle of All**, b f by Nasrullah	H S Tufton	N Bertie	G Richards	18	4/1F
1952	**Zabara**, ch f by Persian Gulf	Sir M McAlpine	V Smyth	K Gethin	20	7/1
1953	**Happy Laughter**, ch f by Royal Charger	H D H Wills	J Jarvis	E Mercer	14	10/1
1954	**Festoon**, ch f by Fair Trial	J A Dewar	N Cannon	A Breasley	12	9/2
1955	**Meld**, b f by Alycidon	Lady Z Wernher	C Boyd-Rochfort	W H Carr	12	11/4F
1956	**Honeylight**, b f by Honeyway	Sir V Sassoon	C F Elsey	E Britt	19	100/6
1957	**Rose Royale**, b f by Prince Bio	HH Aga Khan	A Head	C Smirke	20	6/1
1958	**Bella Paola**, br f by Ticino	F Dupré	F Mathet	S Boullenger	11	8/11F
1959	**Petite Etoile**, gr f by Petition	Prince Aly Khan	C F N Murless	D Smith	14	8/1
1960	**Never Too Late**, ch f by Never Say Die	Mrs H E Jackson	E Pollet	R Poincelet	14	8/11F
1961	**Sweet Solera**, ch f by Solonaway	Mrs S M Castello	R Day	W Rickaby	14	4/1JF
1962	**Abermaid**, gr f by Abernant	R More O'Ferrall	H Wragg	W Williamson	14	100/6
1963	**Hula Dancer**, gr f by Native Dancer	Mrs P A B Widener	E Pollet	R Poincelet	12	1/2F
1964	**Pourparler**, b f by Hugh Lupus	Beatrice, Lady Granard	P J Prendergast	G Bougoure	18	11/2
1965	**Night Off**, b f by Narrator	L B Holliday	W Wharton	W Williamson	16	9/2F
1966	**Glad Rags**, ch f by High Hat	Mrs J P Mills	M V O'Brien	P Cook	21	100/6
1967	**Fleet**, b f by Immortality	R C Boucher	C F N Murless	G Moore	16	11/2
1968	**Caergwrle**, ch f by Crepello	Mrs C F N Murless	C F N Murless	A Barclay	19	4/1F
1969	**Full Dress**, b f by Shantung	R B Moller	H Wragg	R Hutchinson	13	7/1
1970	**Humble Duty**, gr f by Sovereign Path	Jean, Lady Ashcombe	P Walwyn	L Piggott	12	3/1JF
1971	**Altesse Royale**, ch f by Saint Crespin	F R Hue-Williams	C F N Murless	Y Saint-Martin	10	25/1
1972	**Waterloo**, ch f by Bold Lad	Mrs R Stanley	J W Watts	E Hide	18	8/1
1973	**Mysterious**, ch f by Crepello	G A Pope, jr	C F N Murless	G Lewis	14	11/1
1974	**Highclere**, b f by Queen's Hussar	HM the Queen	W R Hern	J Mercer	15	12/1
1975	**Nocturnal Spree**, gr f by Supreme Sovereign	Mrs D D O'Kelly	H V S Murless	J Roe	16	14/1
1976	**Flying Water**, ch f by Habitat	D Wildenstein	A Penna	Y Saint-Martin	25	2/1F
1977	**Mrs McArdy**, b f by Tribal Chief	Mrs E Kettlewell	M W Easterby	E Hide	18	16/1
1978	**Enstone Spark**, b f by Sparkler	R A N Bonnycastle	B W Hills	E Johnson	16	35/1
1979	**One in a Million**, b f by Rarity	Helena Springfield Ltd	H Cecil	J Mercer	17	1/1F
1980	**Quick as Lightning**, b f by Buckpasser	O M Phipps	J Dunlop	B Rouse	23	12/1
1981	**Fairy Footsteps**, b f by Mill Reef	H J Joel	H Cecil	L Piggott	14	6/4F
1982	**On the House**, b f Be My Guest	Sir P Oppenheimer	H Wragg	J Reid	15	33/1
1983	**Ma Biche**, br f by Key to the Kingdom	Maktoum al Maktoum	Mme C Head	F Head	18	5/2F

		Owner	Trainer	Jockey	Ran	S.P.
1984	**Pebbles**, ch f by Sharpen Up	M D Lemos	C Brittain	P Robinson	15	8/1
1985	**Oh So Sharp**, ch f by Kris	Sheikh Mohammed	H Cecil	S Cauthen	17	2/1F
1986	**Midway Lady**, b f by Alleged	H H Ranier	B Hanbury	R Cochrane	15	10/1
1987	**Miesque**, b f by Nureyev	S S Niarchos	F Boutin	F Head	14	15/8F
1988	**Ravinella**, b f by Mr Prospector	Ecurie Aland	Mme C Head	G W Moore	12	4/5F
1989	**Musical Bliss**, b f by The Minstrel	Sheikh Mohammed	M Stoute	W R Swinburn	7	7/2

Derby

At Epsom, Surrey. For 3-year-olds. 1 mile 4 furlongs.

		Owner	Trainer	Jockey	Ran	S.P.
1780	**Diomed**, ch c by Florizel	Sir C Bunbury	R Teasdale	S Arnull	9	6/4F
1781	**Young Eclipse**, b c by Eclipse	D O'Kelly		C Hindley	15	10/1
1782	**Assassin**, b c by Sweetbriar	Lord Egremont	F Neale	S Arnull	13	5/1
1783	**Saltram**, br c by Eclipse	J Parker	F Neale	C Hindley	6	5/2JF
1784	**Serjeant**, b c by Eclipse	D O'Kelly		J Arnull	11	3/1F
1785	**Aimwell**, b c by Mark Anthony	Lord Clermont	J Pratt	C Hindley	10	7/1
1786	**Noble**, b c by Highflyer	T Panton	F Neale	J White	15	30/1
1787	**Sir Peter Teazle**, br c by Highflyer	Lord Derby	Saunders	S Arnull	7	2/1
1788	**Sir Thomas**, ch c by Pontac	HRH Prince of Wales	F Neale	W South	11	5/6F
1789	**Skyscraper**, b c by Highflyer	Duke of Bedford	M Stephenson	S Chifney	11	4/7F
1790	**Rhadamanthus**, b c by Justice	Lord Grosvenor	J Pratt	J Arnull	10	5/4F
1791	**Eager**, b c by Florizel	Duke of Bedford	M Stephenson	M Stephenson	9	5/2
1792	**John Bull**, ch c by Fortitude	Lord Grosvenor	J Pratt	F Buckle	7	4/6F
1793	**Waxy**, b c by Potoooooooo	Sir F Poole	R Robson	W Clift	13	12/1
1794	**Daedalus**, b c by Justice	Lord Grosvenor	J Pratt	F Buckle	4	6/1
1795	**Spread Eagle**, b c by Volunteer	Sir F Standish	R Prince	A Wheatley	11	3/1
1796	**Didelot**, b c by Trumpator	Sir F Standish	R Prince	J Arnull	11	—
1797	unnamed, br c by Fidget	Duke of Bedford	M Stephenson	J Singleton, jr	7	10/1
1798	**Sir Harry**, br c by Sir Peter Teazle	J Cookson	F Neale	S Arnull	10	7/4F
1799	**Archduke**, br c by Sir Peter Teazle	Sir F Standish	R Prince	J Arnull	11	12/1
1800	**Champion**, b c by Potoooooooo	C Wilson	T Perren	W Clift	13	7/4F
1801	**Eleanor**, b f by Whiskey	Sir C Bunbury	J Frost	J Saunders	11	5/4F
1802	**Tyrant**, b c by Potoooooooo	Duke of Grafton	R Robson	F Buckle	9	7/1
1803	**Ditto**, b c by Sir Peter Teazle	Sir H Williamson	J Lonsdale	W Clift	6	7/2
1804	**Hannibal**, b c by Driver	Lord Egremont	F Neale	W Arnull	8	3/1
1805	**Cardinal Beaufort**, b c by Gohanna	Lord Egremont	R D Boyce	D Fitzpatrick	15	20/1
1806	**Paris**, br c by Sir Peter Teazle	Lord Foley	R Prince	J Shepherd	12	5/1
1807	**Election**, ch c by Gohanna	Lord Egremont	R D Boyce	J Arnull	13	3/1F
1808	**Pan**, ch c by St George	Sir H Williamson	J Lonsdale	F Collinson	10	25/1
1809	**Pope**, b c by Waxy	Duke of Grafton	R Robson	T Goodisson	10	20/1
1810	**Whalebone**, br c by Waxy	Duke of Grafton	R Robson	W Clift	11	2/1F
1811	**Phantom**, b c by Walton	Sir J Shelley	J Edwards	F Buckle	16	5/1
1812	**Octavius**, br c by Orville	R Ladbroke	R D Boyce	W Arnull	14	7/1
1813	**Smolensko**, bl c by Sorceror	Sir C Bunbury	Crouch	T Goodisson	12	1/1F
1814	**Blücher**, b c by Waxy	Lord Stawell	R D Boyce	W Arnull	14	5/2F
1815	**Whisker**, b c by Waxy	Duke of Grafton	R Robson	T Goodisson	13	8/1
1816	**Prince Leopold**, b c by Hedley	HRH Duke of York	W Butler	W Wheatley	11	20/1
1817	**Azor**, ch c by Selim	J Payne	R Robson	J Robinson	13	50/1
1818	**Sam**, ch c by Scud	T Thornhill	T Perren	S Chifney, jr	16	7/2
1819	**Tiresias**, br c by Soothsayer	Duke of Portland	R Prince	W Clift	16	5/2F
1820	**Sailor**, ch c by Scud	T Thornhill	W Chifney	S Chifney, jr	15	4/1
1821	**Gustavus**, gr c by Election	J Hunter	Crouch	S Day	13	2/1F
1822	**Moses**, b c by Seymour *or* Whalebone	HRH Duke of York	W Butler	T Goodisson	12	6/1
1823	**Emilius**, b c by Orville	J Udney	R Robson	F Buckle	11	11/8F
1824	**Cedric**, ch c by Phantom	Sir J Shelley	J Edwards	J Robinson	17	9/2
1825	**Middleton**, ch c by Phantom	Lord Jersey	J Edwards	J Robinson	18	7/4F
1826	**Lap-dog**, b c by Whalebone	Lord Egremont	R Stephenson	G Dockeray	19	50/1
1827	**Mameluke**, b c by Partisan	Lord Jersey	J Edwards	J Robinson	23	9/1
1828	**Cadland**, br c by Andrew	Duke of Rutland	R D Boyce	J Robinson	15	4/1
1829	**Frederick**, b c by Little John	G W K Gratwicke	J Forth	J Forth	17	40/1
1830	**Priam**, b c by Emilius	W Chifney	W Chifney	S Day	23	4/1F
1831	**Spaniel**, b c by Whalebone	Lord Lowther	J Rogers	W Wheatley	23	50/1
1832	**St Giles**, ch c by Tramp	R Ridsdale	J Webb	W Scott	22	3/1F
1833	**Dangerous**, ch c by Tramp	I Sadler	I Sadler	J Chapple	25	30/1
1834	**Plenipotentiary**, ch c by Emilius	S Batson	G Payne	P Conolly	22	9/4F
1835	**Mündig**, ch c by Catton	J Bowes	J Scott	W Scott	14	6/1
1836	**Bay Middleton**, b c by Sultan	Lord Jersey	J Edwards	J Robinson	21	7/4F
1837	**Phosphorus**, b c by Lamplighter	Lord Berners	J Doe	G Edwards	17	40/1
1838	**Amato**, br c by Velocipede	Sir G Heathcote	R Sherwood	J Chapple	23	30/1
1839	**Bloomsbury**, b c by Mulatto	W Ridsdale	W Ridsdale	S Templeman	21	25/1
1840	**Little Wonder**, b c by Muley	D Robertson	J Forth	W Macdonald	17	50/1
1841	**Coronation**, b c by Sir Hercules	A T Rawlinson	Painter	P Conolly	29	5/2F
1842	**Attila**, b c by Colwick	G Anson	J Scott	W Scott	24	5/1

Cont. p. 128

Peter Scudamore

The champion jump jockey off duty at Royal Ascot.

Statistically, Peter Scudamore is the most dominant jockey that jump racing has ever known. His 221 wins in 1988/89 easily beat the record for one season by a jump jockey and, through his determination and hard work, he has set new standards in the sport.

Peter Michael Scudamore, born in Hereford on 13 June 1958, was bred for the job. His father, Michael Scudamore, was a jockey who had won the Cheltenham Gold Cup on Linwell the previous year and was to win the Grand National on Oxo in 1959. Scudamore junior attended a minor Catholic public school but from an early age his sole ambition was to follow his father into the racing world.

He grew up in a training stable and, starting as an amateur, had his first ride on the Flat in 1975 and his first over jumps in 1976. On leaving school he worked for an estate agent for a year, but he also furthered his racing education with trainers Willie

Stephenson at Royston, Dennis Holmberg in Norway, Jim Bolger in Ireland and David Nicholson at Condicote, Gloucestershire.

His first winner under Rules was Rolyat over hurdles at Devon & Exeter on 31 August 1978 and he turned professional in November 1979, soon becoming stable jockey to David Nicholson.

The physical risks of jump racing – his father had been forced to retire when blinded in one eye – became apparent when his first three seasons as a professional were all curtailed by injury. He broke a leg in February 1980, was challenging John Francome for the championship when fracturing his skull in May 1981, and would have been clear champion the following season but for breaking an arm. On that occasion Francome sportingly stopped riding when he had equalled his rival's total of 120 wins, allowing him to share the title.

Nevertheless, until Francome's retirement in 1985 Scudamore rode in the shadow of that great jockey, and when he gained his first outright title in 1985/86 he seemed to have become champion by default.

The first top-class horse Scudamore rode was Broadsword, champion juvenile hurdler in 1980/81 and runner-up in the 1982 Champion Hurdle, but he had to wait until 1986 for his first win at Cheltenham's National Hunt meeting.

The best horse he has ridden is Burrough Hill Lad when that great stayer gained his last success, in the 1986 Gainsborough Handicap Chase at Sandown Park. Pearlyman in the 1987 Queen Mother Champion Chase at Cheltenham and Jimmy Lorenzo in the 1989 Temple Gwathmey Chase at Belmont Park are other champions on

whom he has won big races, but he was more regularly associated with Celtic Shot, the 1988 Champion Hurdle winner.

Celtic Shot was trained at Lambourn by Fred Winter, to whom Scudamore became stable jockey in the summer of 1986. Winter suffered a serious accident in 1987 and handed over to his assistant Charlie Brooks the following year, but by then Scudamore had forged a link with Devonshire trainer Martin Pipe, who was steadily becoming, numerically, the most successful trainer of jumpers in racing history.

Pipe's mass-production of winners led to the sequence of records broken by both trainer and jockey in 1988/89. Scudamore won on exactly one-third of his mounts that season and his unprecedented run of success attracted plenty of public attention for both himself and the sport. It became commonplace to see him lead from the start on one of Pipe's horses in order to exploit his judgment of pace and his mount's superior fitness.

Helped also by a mild winter with very few meetings cancelled, and by lack of serious injury, Scudamore ended the season with 221 wins, leaving Jonjo O'Neill's previous record of 149 well behind. He would have been champion even if he had ridden exclusively over hurdles or over fences.

He failed to win any of the championship events at the 1989 National Hunt meeting at Cheltenham – he could have ridden Pipe's two winners but chose the wrong horse both times – but picked up valuable handicaps on Pegwell Bay (Mackeson Gold Cup), Strands of Gold (Hennessy Cognac Gold Cup), Bonanza Boy (Welsh National) and Travel Mystery

(Imperial Cup) as well as the Welsh Champion Hurdle on Celtic Shot.

Martin Pipe alone provided 158 of Scudamore's 221 wins and it might be said that any competent jockey would have broken the record with the help of such a uniquely prolific source of winners. Yet Scudamore is himself responsible for a large measure of Pipe's success; he schools the horses himself and is full of confidence which communicates itself to his mounts.

Scudamore's main attribute is his determination to cultivate efficiency and professionalism. He is hardly ever seen out of position in a race and there is currently no jump jockey better in a finish. Early in his career his eagerness led to fines for excessive use of the whip but, through severe self-criticism, he has learned to temper zeal with discretion.

He once wrote: 'I have tried diligently to cut out my mistakes and I believe that each season I have eliminated a little more margin for error.' He also admits that he is intensely ambitious and that he wants 'to achieve in jumping the same prolonged domination that Piggott managed on the flat . . . the urge to seek out success, the dread of failure, remains as powerful a motivator as it ever was.'

Like most jockeys, he is on a permanent diet and, at a pinch, can still ride at the minimum of 10 stone.

'Scu' often seems serious and intense in his outlook, in contrast to John Francome with his irreverent wit and engaging personality, but he is modest, approachable and articulate, and is a fine ambassador for the sport.

He earns good money but only a fraction of the sums that the top Flat jockeys can command. A

Peter Scudamore after scoring his record-breaking 150th win of the 1988/89 jump season on Anti Matter at Warwick. (Sporting Pictures)

bad fall could end his career at any time, and even if he escapes serious injury in a notoriously hazardous profession, retirement beckons within five years.

Peter Scudamore, for all his success, is still hungry for winners. He is not necessarily the most gifted jump jockey riding today, yet his single-minded application, energy and unquenchable will to win have made him a statistical marvel.

	Owner	Trainer	Jockey	Ran	S.P.
1843 **Cotherstone**, b c by Touchstone	J Bowes	J Scott	W Scott	23	13/8F
1844 **Orlando**, b c by Touchstone	J Peel	W Cooper	E Flatman	29	20/1
1845 **The Merry Monarch**, b c by Slane	G W K Gratwicke	J Forth	F Bell	31	15/1
1846 **Pyrrhus the First**, ch c by Epirus	J Gully	J B Day	S Day	27	8/1
1847 **Cossack**, ch c by Hetman Platoff	T H Pedley	J Day, jr	S Templeman	32	5/1
1848 **Surplice**, b c by Touchstone	Lord Clifden	J Kent, jr	S Templeman	17	1/1F
1849 **The Flying Dutchman**, br c by Bay Middleton	Lord Eglinton	J Fobert	C Marlow	26	2/1JF
1850 **Voltigeur**, br c by Voltaire	Lord Zetland	R Hill	J Marson	24	16/1
1851 **Teddington**, ch c by Orlando	Sir J Hawley	A Taylor	J Marson	33	3/1F
1852 **Daniel O'Rourke**, ch c by Irish Birdcatcher	J Bowes	J Scott	F Butler	27	25/1
1853 **West Australian**, b c by Melbourne	J Bowes	J Scott	F Butler	28	6/4F
1854 **Andover**, b c by Bay Middleton	J Gully	J Day, jr	A Day	27	7/2
1855 **Wild Dayrell**, br c by Ion	F L Popham	J Rickaby	Robt Sherwood	12	1/1F
1856 **Ellington**, br c by The Flying Dutchman	O V Harcourt	T Dawson	T Aldcroft	24	20/1
1857 **Blink Bonny**, b f by Melbourne	W I'Anson	W I'Anson	J Charlton	30	20/1
1858 **Beadsman**, br c by Weatherbit	Sir J Hawley	G Manning	J Wells	23	10/1
1859 **Musjid**, br c by Newminster	Sir J Hawley	G Manning	J Wells	30	9/4F
1860 **Thormanby**, ch c by Melbourne *or* Windhound	J Merry	M Dawson	H Custance	30	4/1
1861 **Kettledrum**, ch c by Rataplan	C Towneley	G Oates	R Bullock	18	16/1
1862 **Caractacus**, c by Kingston	C Snewing	R Smith	J Parsons	34	40/1
1863 **Macaroni**, b c by Sweetmeat	R C Naylor	J Godding	T Chaloner	31	10/1
1864 **Blair Athol**, ch c by Stockwell	W I'Anson	W I'Anson	J Snowden	30	14/1
1865 **Gladiateur**, b c by Monarque	Comte F de Lagrange	T Jennings	H Grimshaw	29	5/2F
1866 **Lord Lyon**, b c by Stockwell	R Sutton	J Dover	H Custance	26	5/6F
1867 **Hermit**, ch c by Newminster	H Chaplin	G Bloss	J Daley	30	1,000/15
1868 **Blue Gown**, b c by Beadsman	Sir J Hawley	J Porter	J Wells	18	7/2
1869 **Pretender**, b c by Adventurer	J Johnstone	T Dawson	J Osborne	22	11/8F
1870 **Kingcraft**, b c by King Tom	Lord Falmouth	M Dawson	T French	15	20/1
1871 **Favonius**, ch c by Parmesan	Baron M de Rothschild	J Hayhoe	T French	17	9/1
1872 **Cremorne**, b c by Parmesan	H Savile	W Gilbert	C Maidment	23	3/1
1873 **Doncaster**, ch c by Stockwell	J Merry	R Peck	F Webb	12	45/1
1874 **George Frederick**, ch c by Marsyas	W S Cartwright	T Leader	H Custance	20	9/1
1875 **Galopin**, b c by Vedette	Prince Batthyany	John Dawson	J Morris	18	2/1F
1876 **Kisber**, b c by Buccaneer	A Baltazzi	J Hayhoe	C Maidment	15	4/1
1877 **Silvio**, b c by Blair Athol	Lord Falmouth	M Dawson	F Archer	17	100/9
1878 **Sefton**, b c by Speculum	W S Crawfurd	A Taylor	H Constable	22	100/12
1879 **Sir Bevys**, br c by Favonius	Baron L N de Rothschild	J Hayhoe	G Fordham	23	20/1
1880 **Bend Or**, ch c by Doncaster	Duke of Westminster	R Peck	F Archer	19	2/1F
1881 **Iroquois**, br c by Leamington	P Lorillard	J Pincus	F Archer	15	11/2
1882 **Shotover**, ch f by Hermit	Duke of Westminster	J Porter	T Cannon	14	11/2
1883 **St Blaise**, ch c by Hermit	Sir F Johnstone	J Porter	C Wood	11	5/1
1884 { **St Gatien**, b c by Rotherhill *or* The Rover	J Hammond	Robt Sherwood	C Wood	15	100/8
{ **Harvester**, br c by Sterling	Sir J Willoughby	J Jewitt	S Loates		100/7
1885 **Melton**, b c by Master Kildare	Lord Hastings	M Dawson	F Archer	12	75/40F
1886 **Ormonde**, b c by Bend Or	Duke of Westminster	J Porter	F Archer	9	4/9F
1887 **Merry Hampton**, b c by Hampton	G A Baird	M Gurry	J Watts	11	100/9
1888 **Ayrshire**, b c by Hampton	Duke of Portland	G Dawson	F Barrett	9	5/6F
1889 **Donovan**, b c by Galopin	Duke of Portland	G Dawson	T Loates	13	8/11F
1890 **Sainfoin**, ch c by Springfield	Sir J Miller	J Porter	J Watts	8	100/15
1891 **Common**, br c by Isonomy	Sir F Johnstone	J Porter	G Barrett	11	10/11F
1892 **Sir Hugo**, ch c by Wisdom	Lord Bradford	T Wadlow	F Allsopp	13	40/1
1893 **Isinglass**, b c by Isonomy	H McCalmont	J Jewitt	T Loates	11	4/9F
1894 **Ladas**, b c by Hampton	Lord Rosebery	M Dawson	J Watts	7	2/9F
1895 **Sir Visto**, b c by Barcaldine	Lord Rosebery	M Dawson	S Loates	15	9/1
1896 **Persimmon**, b c by St Simon	HRH Prince of Wales	R Marsh	J Watts	11	5/1
1897 **Galtee More**, b c by Kendal	J Gubbins	S Darling	C Wood	11	1/4F
1898 **Jeddah**, ch c by Janissary	J W Larnach	R Marsh	O Madden	18	100/1
1899 **Flying Fox**, b c by Orme	Duke of Westminster	J Porter	M Cannon	12	2/5F
1900 **Diamond Jubilee**, b c by St Simon	HRH Prince of Wales	R Marsh	H Jones	14	6/4F
1901 **Volodyovski**, b c by Florizel	W C Whitney	J Huggins	L Reiff	25	5/2F
1902 **Ard Patrick**, br c by St Florian	J Gubbins	S Darling	J H Martin	18	100/14
1903 **Rock Sand**, br c by Sainfoin	Sir J Miller	G Blackwell	D Maher	7	4/6F
1904 **St Amant**, b c by St Frusquin	Leo de Rothschild	A Hayhoe	K Cannon	8	5/1
1905 **Cicero**, ch c by Cyllene	Lord Rosebery	P Peck	D Maher	9	4/11F
1906 **Spearmint**, b c by Carbine	E Loder	P P Gilpin	D Maher	22	6/1
1907 **Orby**, ch c by Orme	R Croker	F F MacCabe	J Reiff	9	100/9
1908 **Signorinetta**, b f by Chaleureux	O Ginistrelli	O Ginistrelli	W Bullock	18	100/1
1909 **Minoru**, b c by Cyllene	HM the King	R Marsh	H Jones	15	7/2
1910 **Lemberg**, b c by Cyllene	A W Cox	A Taylor, jr	B Dillon	15	7/4F
1911 **Sunstar**, br c by Sundridge	J B Joel	C Morton	G Stern	26	13/8F
1912 **Tagalie**, gr f by Cyllene	W Raphael	D Waugh	J Reiff	20	100/8
1913 **Aboyeur**, b c by Desmond	A P Cunliffe	T Lewis	E Piper	15	100/1
1914 **Durbar**, b c by Rabelais	H B Duryea	T Murphy	M MacGee	30	20/1
1915 **Pommern**, b c by Polymelus	S B Joel	C Peck	S Donoghue	17	10/11F

		Owner	Trainer	Jockey	Ran	S.P.
1916	**Fifinella**, ch f by Polymelus	E Hulton	R C Dawson	J Childs	10	11/2
1917	**Gay Crusader**, b c by Bayardo	A W Cox	A Taylor, jr	S Donoghue	12	7/4F
1918	**Gainsborough**, b c by Bayardo	Lady James Douglas	A Taylor, jr	J Childs	13	8/13F
1919	**Grand Parade**, bl c by Orby	Lord Glanely	F B Barling	F Templeman	13	33/1
1920	**Spion Kop**, b c by Spearmint	G Loder	P P Gilpin	F O'Neill	19	100/6
1921	**Humorist**, ch c by Polymelus	J B Joel	C Morton	S Donoghue	23	6/1
1922	**Captain Cuttle**, ch c by Hurry On	Lord Woolavington	F Darling	S Donoghue	30	10/1
1923	**Papyrus**, br c by Tracery	B Irish	B Jarvis	S Donoghue	19	100/15
1924	**Sansovino**, b c by Swynford	Lord Derby	G Lambton	T Weston	27	9/2F
1925	**Manna**, b c by Phalaris	H E Morriss	F Darling	S Donoghue	27	9/1
1926	**Coronach**, ch c by Hurry On	Lord Woolavington	F Darling	J Childs	19	11/2
1927	**Call Boy**, ch c by Hurry On	F Curzon	J E Watts	E C Elliott	23	4/1F
1928	**Felstead**, b c by Spion Kop	Sir H Cunliffe-Owen	O Bell	H Wragg	19	33/1
1929	**Trigo**, b c by Blandford	W Barnett	R C Dawson	J Marshall	26	33/1
1930	**Blenheim**, br c by Blandford	HH Aga Khan	R C Dawson	H Wragg	17	18/1
1931	**Cameronian**, b c by Pharos	J A Dewar	F Darling	F Fox	25	7/2F
1932	**April the Fifth**, br c by Craig an Eran	T Walls	T Walls	F Lane	21	100/6
1933	**Hyperion**, ch c by Gainsborough	Lord Derby	G Lambton	T Weston	24	6/1F
1934	**Windsor Lad**, b c by Blandford	HH Maharaja of Rajpipla	M Marsh	C Smirke	19	15/2
1935	**Bahram**, b c by Blandford	HH Aga Khan	Frank Butters	F Fox	16	5/4F
1936	**Mahmoud**, gr c by Blenheim	HH Aga Khan	Frank Butters	C Smirke	22	100/8
1937	**Mid-day Sun**, b c by Solario	Mrs G B Miller	Fred Butters	M Beary	21	100/7
1938	**Bois Roussel**, br c by Vatout	P Beatty	F Darling	E C Elliott	22	20/1
1939	**Blue Peter**, ch c by Fairway	Lord Rosebery	J Jarvis	E Smith	27	7/2F
1940	**Pont l'Evêque**, b c by Barneveldt	F Darling	F Darling	S Wragg	16	10/1
1941	**Owen Tudor**, br c by Hyperion	Mrs R Macdonald-Buchanan	F Darling	W Nevett	20	25/1
1942	**Watling Street**, b c by Fairway	Lord Derby	W Earl	H Wragg	13	6/1
1943	**Straight Deal**, br c by Solario	Miss D Paget	W Nightingall	T Carey	23	100/6
1944	**Ocean Swell**, b c by Blue Peter	Lord Rosebery	J Jarvis	W Nevett	20	28/1
1945	**Dante**, br c by Nearco	Sir E Ohlson	M J Peacock	W Nevett	27	100/30F
1946	**Airborne**, gr c by Precipitation	J E Ferguson	R Perryman	T Lowrey	17	50/1
1947	**Pearl Diver**, b c by Vatellor	Baron G de Waldner	P Carter	G Bridgland	15	40/1
1948	**My Love**, b c by Vatellor	HH Aga Khan	R Carver	W R Johnstone	32	100/9
1949	**Nimbus**, b c by Nearco	Mrs M Glenister	G Colling	E C Elliott	32	7/1
1950	**Galcador**, ch c by Djebel	M Boussac	C H Semblat	W R Johnstone	25	100/9
1951	**Arctic Prince**, br c by Prince Chevalier	J McGrath	W Stephenson	C Spares	33	28/1
1952	**Tulyar**, br c by Tehran	HH Aga Khan	M Marsh	C Smirke	33	11/2F
1953	**Pinza**, b c by Chanteur	Sir V Sassoon	N Bertie	Sir G Richards	27	5/1JF
1954	**Never Say Die**, ch c by Nasrullah	R S Clark	J Lawson	L Piggott	22	33/1
1955	**Phil Drake**, br c by Admiral Drake	Mme L Volterra	F Mathet	F Palmer	23	100/8
1956	**Lavandin**, b c by Verso	P Wertheimer	A Head	W R Johnstone	27	7/1F
1957	**Crepello**, ch c by Donatello	Sir V Sassoon	C F N Murless	L Piggott	22	6/4F
1958	**Hard Ridden**, b c by Hard Sauce	Sir V Sassoon	J M Rogers	C Smirke	20	18/1
1959	**Parthia**, b c by Persian Gulf	Sir H de Trafford	C Boyd-Rochfort	W H Carr	20	10/1
1960	**St Paddy**, b c by Aureole	Sir V Sassoon	C F N Murless	L Piggott	17	7/1
1961	**Psidium**, ch c by Pardal	Mme A Plesch	H Wragg	R Poincelet	28	66/1
1962	**Larkspur**, ch c by Never Say Die	R R Guest	M V O'Brien	N Sellwood	26	22/1
1963	**Relko**, b c by Tanerko	F Dupré	F Mathet	Y Saint-Martin	26	5/1F
1964	**Santa Claus**, b c by Chamossaire	J Ismay	J M Rogers	A Breasley	17	15/8F
1965	**Sea-Bird**, ch c by Dan Cupid	J Ternynck	E Pollet	T P Glennon	22	7/4F
1966	**Charlottown**, b c by Charlottesville	Lady Z Wernher	G Smyth	A Breasley	25	5/1
1967	**Royal Palace**, b c by Ballymoss	H J Joel	C F N Murless	G Moore	22	7/4F
1968	**Sir Ivor**, b c by Sir Gaylord	R R Guest	M V O'Brien	L Piggott	13	4/5F
1969	**Blakeney**, b c by Hethersett	A M Budgett	A M Budgett	E Johnson	26	15/2
1970	**Nijinsky**, b c by Northern Dancer	C W Engelhard	M V O'Brien	L Piggott	11	11/8F
1971	**Mill Reef**, b c by Never Bend	P Mellon	I Balding	G Lewis	21	100/30F
1972	**Roberto**, b c by Hail to Reason	J W Galbreath	M V O'Brien	L Piggott	22	3/1F
1973	**Morston**, ch c by Ragusa	A M Budgett	A M Budgett	E Hide	25	25/1
1974	**Snow Knight**, ch c by Firestreak	Mrs N F Phillips	P Nelson	B Taylor	18	50/1
1975	**Grundy**, ch c by Great Nephew	C Vittadini	P Walwyn	P Eddery	18	5/1
1976	**Empery**, b c by Vaguely Noble	N B Hunt	M Zilber	L Piggott	23	10/1
1977	**The Minstrel**, ch c by Northern Dancer	R E Sangster	M V O'Brien	L Piggott	22	5/1
1978	**Shirley Heights**, b c by Mill Reef	Lord Halifax	J Dunlop	G Starkey	25	8/1
1979	**Troy**, b c by Petingo	Sir M Sobell	W R Hern	W Carson	23	6/1
1980	**Henbit**, b c by Hawaii	Mme A Plesch	W R Hern	W Carson	24	7/1
1981	**Shergar**, b c by Great Nephew	HH Aga Khan	M Stoute	W R Swinburn	18	10/11F
1982	**Golden Fleece**, b c by Nijinsky	R E Sangster	M V O'Brien	P Eddery	18	3/1F
1983	**Teenoso**, b c by Youth	E B Moller	G Wragg	L Piggott	21	9/2F
1984	**Secreto**, b c by Northern Dancer	L Miglietti	D V O'Brien	C Roche	17	14/1
1985	**Slip Anchor**, b c by Shirley Heights	Lord Howard de Walden	H Cecil	S Cauthen	14	9/4F
1986	**Shahrastani**, ch c by Nijinsky	HH Aga Khan	M Stoute	W R Swinburn	17	11/2
1987	**Reference Point**, b c by Mill Reef	L Freedman	H Cecil	S Cauthen	19	6/4F
1988	**Kahyasi**, b c by Ile de Bourbon	HH Aga Khan	L Cumani	R Cochrane	14	11/1
1989	**Nashwan**, ch c by Blushing Groom	Hamdan al Maktoum	W R Hern	W Carson	12	5/4F

Oaks

At Epsom, Surrey. For 3-year-old fillies. 1 mile 4 furlongs.

Year	Horse	Owner	Trainer	Jockey	Ran	S.P.
1779	**Bridget**, b f by Herod	Lord Derby	Saunders	R Goodisson	12	5/2F
1780	**Tetotum**, b f by Matchem	T Douglas			11	6/4JF
1781	**Faith**, b f by Herod	Lord Grosvenor	J Pratt		6	4/1
1782	**Ceres**, b f by Sweet William	Lord Grosvenor	J Pratt	S Chifney	12	4/7F
1783	**Maid of the Oaks**, ch f by Herod	Lord Grosvenor	J Pratt	S Chifney	10	4/1F
1784	**Stella**, b f by Plunder	P Burlton		C Hindley	10	20/1
1785	**Trifle**, br f by Justice	Lord Clermont	J Pratt	J Bird	8	5/1
1786	**Yellow Filly**, ch f by Tandem	Sir F Standish	R Prince	J Edwards	13	5/2F
1787	**Annette**, b f by Eclipse	R Vernon	J Watson	D Fitzpatrick	8	4/6F
1788	**Nightshade**, b f by Potoooooooo	Lord Egremont	F Neale	D Fitzpatrick	7	1/2F
1789	**Tag**, b f by Trentham	Lord Egremont	F Neale	S Chifney	7	5/2JF
1790	**Hippolyta**, ch f by Mercury	Duke of Bedford	M Stephenson	S Chifney	12	6/1
1791	**Portia**, ch f by Volunteer	Duke of Bedford	M Stephenson	J Singleton, jr	9	5/2
1792	**Volante**, b f by Highflyer	Lord Clermont	J Pratt	C Hindley	11	4/1
1793	**Caelia**, br f by Volunteer	Duke of Bedford	M Stephenson	J Singleton, jr	10	4/1
1794	**Hermione**, br f by Sir Peter Teazle	Lord Derby	Saunders	S Arnull	8	5/2
1795	**Platina**, ch f by Mercury	Lord Egremont	F Neale	D Fitzpatrick	11	3/1
1796	**Parisot**, br f by Sir Peter Teazle	Sir F Standish	R Prince	J Arnull	13	7/2
1797	**Niké**, b f by Alexander	Lord Grosvenor	J Pratt	F Buckle	5	15/8F
1798	**Bellissima**, b f by Phoenomenon	J H Durand	R Prince	F Buckle	7	6/4F
1799	**Bellina**, ch f by Rockingham	Lord Grosvenor	J Pratt	F Buckle	4	5/2
1800	**Ephemera**, ch f by Woodpecker	Lord Egremont	F Neale	D Fitzpatrick	8	9/4F
1801	**Eleanor**, b f by Whiskey	Sir C Bunbury	J Frost	J Saunders	6	4/7F
1802	**Scotia**, gr f by Delpini	J Wastell	R Robson	F Buckle	6	6/4F
1803	**Theophania**, b f by Delpini	Sir T Gascoigne	S King	F Buckle	7	5/2
1804	**Pelisse**, br f by Whiskey	Duke of Grafton	R Robson	W Clift	8	4/5F
1805	**Meteora**, b f by Meteor	Lord Grosvenor	R Robson	F Buckle	8	7/2
1806	**Bronze**, br f by Buzzard	B Craven	R D Boyce	W Edwards	12	10/1
1807	**Briseïs**, b f by Beningbrough	T Grosvenor	R Robson	S Chifney, jr	13	15/1
1808	**Morel**, ch f by Sorcerer	Duke of Grafton	R Robson	W Clift	10	3/1F
1809	**Maid of Orleans**, b f by Sorceror	J Leveson Gower	R Robson	J Moss	11	100/6
1810	**Oriana**, b f by Beningbrough	Sir W Gerard	W Peirse	W Peirse	11	4/1
1811	**Sorcery**, b f by Sorceror	Duke of Rutland	R D Boyce	S Chifney, jr	12	3/1F
1812	**Manuella**, b f by Dick Andrews	W N W Hewett	W Peirse	W Peirse	12	20/1
1813	**Music**, b f by Waxy	Duke of Grafton	R Robson	T Goodisson	9	5/2F
1814	**Medora**, ch f by Selim	Duke of Rutland	R D Boyce	S Barnard	9	10/1
1815	**Minuet**, b f by Waxy	Duke of Grafton	R Robson	T Goodisson	12	3/1JF
1816	**Landscape**, b f by Rubens	J Leveson Gower		S Chifney, jr	11	2/1F
1817	**Neva**, b f by Cervantes	G Watson	R D Boyce	F Buckle	11	1/1F
1818	**Corinne**, br f by Waxy	J Udney	R Robson	F Buckle	10	5/2
1819	**Shoveler**, b f by Scud	T Thornhill	W Chifney	S Chifney, jr	10	2/1
1820	**Caroline**, b f by Whalebone	Lord Egremont	R Stephenson	H Edwards	13	8/1
1821	**Augusta**, b f by Woful	Lord Exeter	R Prince, jr	J Robinson	7	20/11F
1822	**Pastille**, b f by Rubens	Duke of Grafton	R Robson	H Edwards	10	7/2
1823	**Zinc**, br f by Woful	Duke of Grafton	R Robson	F Buckle	10	1/1F
1824	**Cobweb**, b f by Phantom	Lord Jersey	J Edwards	J Robinson	13	8/11F
1825	**Wings**, ch f by The Flyer	T Grosvenor	R Robson	S Chifney, jr	10	13/1
1826	**Lilias**, b f by Interpreter	J Forth	J Forth	T Lye	15	15/1
1827	**Gulnare**, b f by Smolensko	Duke of Richmond	J Kent	F Boyce	19	14/1
1828	**Turquoise**, br f by Selim	Duke of Grafton	R Stephenson	J B Day	14	25/1
1829	**Green Mantle**, b f by Sultan	Lord Exeter	C Marson	G Dockeray	14	5/2
1830	**Variation**, b f by Bustard	S Stonehewer	R Pettit	G Edwards	18	28/1
1831	**Oxygen**, b f by Emilius	Duke of Grafton	R Stephenson	J B Day	21	12/1
1832	**Galata**, br f by Sultan	Lord Exeter	C Marson	P Conolly	19	9/4
1833	**Vespa**, br f by Muley	Sir M Wood	H Scott	J Chapple	19	50/1
1834	**Pussy**, br f by Pollio	T Cosby	W Day	J B Day	15	20/1
1835	**Queen of Trumps**, br f by Velocipede	E L M Mostyn	J Blenkhorn	T Lye	10	8/1
1836	**Cyprian**, b f by Partisan	J Scott	J Scott	W Scott	12	9/4F
1837	**Miss Letty**, b f by Priam	T Orde-Powlett	I Blades	J Holmes	13	7/1
1838	**Industry**, br f by Priam	Lord Chesterfield	J Scott	W Scott	16	9/2
1839	**Deception**, b f by Defence	F Craven	W Treen	J B Day	13	8/13F
1840	**Crucifix**, b f by Priam	Lord G Bentinck	J B Day	J B Day	15	1/3F
1841	**Ghuznee**, b f by Pantaloon	Lord Westminster	J Scott	W Scott	22	7/4F
1842	**Our Nell**, ch f by Bran	G Dawson	T Dawson	T Lye	16	8/1
1843	**Poison**, ch f by Plenipotentiary	G S Ford	R Fisher	F Butler	23	30/1
1844	**The Princess**, ch f by Slane	G Anson	J Scott	F Butler	25	5/1
1845	**Refraction**, br f by Glaucus	Duke of Richmond	J Kent, jr	H Bell	21	25/1

		Owner	Trainer	Jockey	Ran	S.P.
1846	**Mendicant**, br f by Touchstone	J Gully	J B Day	S Day	24	9/4F
1847	**Miami**, b f by Venison	Sir J Hawley	W Beresford	S Templeman	23	9/1
1848	**Cymba**, br f by Melbourne	H Hill	J Day, jr	S Templeman	26	7/1
1849	**Lady Evelyn**, br f by Don John	Lord Chesterfield	T Taylor	F Butler	15	3/1JF
1850	**Rhedycina**, b f by Wintonian	G Hobson	W Goodwin	F Butler	15	6/1
1851	**Iris**, ch f by Ithuriel	Lord Stanley	J Scott	F Butler	15	4/1
1852	**Songstress**, b f by Irish Birdcatcher	J Scott	J Scott	F Butler	14	2/1F
1853	**Catherine Hayes**, br f by Lanercost	J Don Wauchope	M Dawson	C Marlow	17	5/4F
1854	**Mincemeat**, b f by Sweetmeat	W Cookson	W Goodwin	J Charlton	15	10/1
1855	**Marchioness**, b f by Melbourne	W H Rudston Read	J Scott	S Templeman	11	12/1
1856	**Mincepie**, ch f by Sweetmeat	H Hill	J Day, jr	A Day	10	5/2F
1857	**Blink Bonny**, b f by Melbourne	W I'Anson	W I'Anson	J Charlton	13	4/5F
1858	**Governess**, ch f by Chatham	G W K Gratwicke	T Eskrett	T Ashmall	13	4/1
1859	**Summerside**, br f by West Australian	Lord Londesborough	T Taylor	G Fordham	15	4/1
1860	**Butterfly**, ch f by Turnus	R Eastwood	G Oates	J Snowden	13	10/1
1861	**Brown Duchess**, br f by The Flying Dutchman	J Saxon	J Saxon	L Snowden	17	100/7
1862	**Feu de Joie**, ch f by Longbow	R C Naylor	J Godding	T Chaloner	19	20/1
1863	**Queen Bertha**, b f by Kingston	Lord Falmouth	J Scott	T Aldcroft	20	40/1
1864	**Fille de l'Air**, ch f by Foig a Ballagh	Comte F de Lagrange	T Jennings	A Edwards	19	6/4F
1865	**Regalia**, ch f by Stockwell	W Graham	W Harlock	J Norman	18	20/1
1866	**Tormentor**, b f by King Tom	B Ellam	C Blanton	J Mann	17	5/1
1867	**Hippia**, b f by King Tom	Baron M de Rothschild	J Hayhoe	J Daley	8	11/1
1868	**Formosa**, ch f by Buccaneer	W Graham	H Woolcott	G Fordham	9	8/11F
1869	**Brigantine**, b f by Buccaneer	Sir F Johnstone	W Day	T Cannon	15	7/2
1870	**Gamos**, ch f by Saunterer	W Graham	H Woolcott	G Fordham	7	100/8
1871	**Hannah**, b f by King Tom	Baron M de Rothschild	J Hayhoe	C Maidment	9	6/5F
1872	**Reine**, b f by Monarque	C J Lefèvre	T Jennings	G Fordham	17	3/1
1873	**Marie Stuart**, ch f by Scottish Chief	J Merry	R Peck	T Cannon	18	2/1F
1874	**Apology**, ch f by Adventurer	J W King	W Osborne	J Osborne	11	5/2
1875	**Spinaway**, b f by Macaroni	Lord Falmouth	M Dawson	F Archer	7	5/4F
1876	**Enguerrande**, b f by Vermout	A Lupin	C Wetherall	Hudson	14	4/1
1876	**Camélia**, ch f by Macaroni	Comte F de Lagrange	T Cunnington	T Glover	14	5/4F
1877	**Placida**, br f by Lord Lyon	J Fiennes	J Marsh	H Jeffery	9	2/1F
1878	**Jannette**, b f by Lord Clifden	Lord Falmouth	M Dawson	F Archer	8	65/40
1879	**Wheel of Fortune**, b f by Adventurer	Lord Falmouth	M Dawson	F Archer	8	1/3F
1880	**Jenny Howlet**, ch f by The Palmer	C Perkins	W I'Anson, jr	J Snowden	13	33/1
1881	**Thebais**, ch f by Hermit	W S Crawfurd	A Taylor	G Fordham	12	4/6F
1882	**Geheimniss**, br f by Rosicrucian	Lord Stamford	J Porter	T Cannon	5	4/6F
1883	**Bonny Jean**, b f by Macaroni	Lord Rosebery	J Cannon	J Watts	14	5/1
1884	**Busybody**, b f by Petrarch	G A Baird	T Cannon	T Cannon	9	100/105F
1885	**Lonely**, b f by Hermit	Lord Cadogan	W Gilbert, jr	F Archer	10	85/40F
1886	**Miss Jummy**, b f by Petrarch	Duke of Hamilton	R Marsh	J Watts	12	1/1F
1887	**Rêve d'Or**, ch f by Hampton	Duke of Beaufort	A Taylor	C Wood	9	8/11F
1888	**Seabreeze**, ch f by Isonomy	Lord Calthorpe	J Jewitt	W T Robinson	6	7/4
1889	**L'Abbesse de Jouarre**, bl f by Trappist	Lord R Churchill	Robt Sherwood	J Woodburn	12	20/1
1890	**Memoir**, br f by St Simon	Duke of Portland	G Dawson	J Watts	7	100/30
1891	**Mimi**, b f by Barcaldine	N Fenwick	M Dawson	F Rickaby	6	4/7F
1892	**La Flèche**, br f by St Simon	Baron M de Hirsch	J Porter	G Barrett	7	8/11F
1893	**Mrs Butterwick**, b f by St Simon	Duke of Portland	G Dawson	J Watts	17	100/7
1894	**Amiable**, b f by St Simon	Duke of Portland	G Dawson	W Bradford	11	7/1
1895	**La Sagesse**, b f by Wisdom	Sir J Miller	M Gurry	S Loates	15	5/1
1896	**Canterbury Pilgrim**, ch f by Tristan	Lord Derby	G Lambton	F Rickaby	11	100/8
1897	**Limasol**, ch f by Poulet	Lord Hindlip	T Jennings, jr	W Bradford	8	100/8
1898	**Airs and Graces**, br f by Ayrshire	W T Jones	F W Day	W Bradford	13	100/8
1899	**Musa**, b f by Martagon	D Baird	H Enoch	O Madden	12	20/1
1900	**La Roche**, b f by St Simon	Duke of Portland	J Porter	M Cannon	14	5/1
1901	**Cap and Bells**, b f by Domino	F P Keene	S Darling	M Henry	21	9/4F
1902	**Sceptre**, b f by Persimmon	R S Sievier	R S Sievier	H Randall	14	5/2F
1903	**Our Lassie**, b f by Ayrshire	J B Joel	C Morton	M Cannon	10	6/1
1904	**Pretty Polly**, ch f by Gallinule	E Loder	P P Gilpin	W Lane	4	8/100F
1905	**Cherry Lass**, b f by Isinglass	W Hall Walker	W T Robinson	H Jones	12	4/5F
1906	**Keystone**, b f by Persimmon	Lord Derby	G Lambton	D Maher	12	5/2F
1907	**Glass Doll**, b f by Isinglass	J B Joel	C Morton	H Randall	14	25/1
1908	**Signorinetta**, b f by Chaleureux	O Ginistrelli	O Ginistrelli	W Bullock	13	3/1
1909	**Perola**, ch f by Persimmon	W Cooper	G S Davies	F Wootton	14	5/1
1910	**Rosedrop**, ch f by St Frusquin	Sir W Bass	A Taylor, jr	C Trigg	11	7/1
1911	**Cherimoya**, br f by Cherry Tree	W B Cloete	C Marsh	F Winter	21	25/1
1912	**Mirska**, b f by St Frusquin	J Prat	T Jennings, jr	J Childs	14	33/1
1913	**Jest**, ch f by Sundridge	J B Joel	C Morton	F Rickaby, jr	12	8/1
1914	**Princess Dorrie**, br f by Your Majesty	J B Joel	C Morton	W Huxley	21	11/4F
1915	**Snow Marten**, b f by Martagon	L Neumann	P P Gilpin	Wal Griggs	11	20/1
1916	**Fifinella**, ch f by Polymelus	E Hulton	R C Dawson	J Childs	7	8/13F
1917	**Sunny Jane**, ch f by Sunstar	W Astor	A Taylor, jr	O Madden	11	4/1
1918	**My Dear**, b f by Beppo	A W Cox	A Taylor, jr	S Donoghue	15	3/1F

Year	Horse	Owner	Trainer	Jockey	Ran	S.P.
1919	**Bayuda**, b f by Bayardo	Lady James Douglas	A Taylor, jr	J Childs	10	100/7
1920	**Charlebelle**, bl f by Charles O'Malley	A P Cunliffe	H Braime	A Whalley	17	7/2
1921	**Love in Idleness**, br f by Bachelor's Double	Jos Watson	A Taylor, jr	J Childs	22	5/1F
1922	**Pogrom**, b f by Lemberg	Lord Astor	A Taylor, jr	E Gardner	11	5/4F
1923	**Brownhylda**, b f by Stedfast	Vicomte de Fontarce	R C Dawson	V Smyth	12	10/1
1924	**Straitlace**, br f by Son-in-Law	Sir E Hulton	D Waugh	F O'Neill	12	100/30
1925	**Saucy Sue**, br f by Swynford	Lord Astor	A Taylor, jr	F Bullock	12	30/100F
1926	**Short Story**, b f by Buchan	Lord Astor	A Taylor, jr	R A Jones	16	5/1
1927	**Beam**, b f by Galloper Light	Lord Durham	Frank Butters	T Weston	16	4/1
1928	**Toboggan**, b f by Hurry On	Lord Derby	Frank Butters	T Weston	13	100/15
1929	**Pennycomequick**, br f by Hurry On	Lord Astor	J Lawson	H Jelliss	13	11/10F
1930	**Rose of England**, br f by Teddy	Lord Glanely	T Hogg	G Richards	15	7/1
1931	**Brulette**, b f by Brûleur	C W Birkin	F Carter	E C Elliott	15	7/2JF
1932	**Udaipur**, br f by Blandford	HH Aga Khan	Frank Butters	M Beary	12	10/1
1933	**Châtelaine**, b f by Phalaris	E Thornton-Smith	F Templeman	S Wragg	14	25/1
1934	**Light Brocade**, br f by Galloper Light	Lord Durham	Frank Butters	B Carslake	8	7/4F
1935	**Quashed**, br f by Obliterate	Lord Stanley	C Leader	H Jelliss	17	33/1
1936	**Lovely Rosa**, b f by Tolgus	Sir A Bailey	H Cottrill	T Weston	17	33/1
1937	**Exhibitionnist**, b f by Solario	Sir V Sassoon	J Lawson	S Donoghue	13	3/1F
1938	**Rockfel**, br f by Felstead	Sir H Cunliffe-Owen	O Bell	H Wragg	14	3/1F
1939	**Galatea**, br f by Dark Legend	R S Clark	J Lawson	R A Jones	21	10/11F
1940	**Godiva**, b f by Hyperion	E Harmsworth	W R Jarvis	D Marks	14	7/4F
1941	**Commotion**, b f by Mieuxcé	J A Dewar	F Darling	H Wragg	12	8/1
1942	**Sun Chariot**, b f by Hyperion	HM the King	F Darling	G Richards	12	1/4F
1943	**Why Hurry**, ch f by Precipitation	J V Rank	N Cannon	E C Elliott	13	7/1
1944	**Hycilla**, ch f by Hyperion	W Woodward	C Boyd-Rochfort.	G Bridgland	16	8/1
1945	**Sun Stream**, ch f by Hyperion	Lord Derby	W Earl	H Wragg	16	6/4F
1946	**Steady Aim**, b f by Felstead	Sir A Butt	Frank Butters	H Wragg	10	7/1
1947	**Imprudence**, br f by Canot	Mme P Corbière	J Lieux	W R Johnstone	11	7/4F
1948	**Masaka**, b f by Nearco	HH Aga Khan	Frank Butters	W Nevett	25	7/1
1949	**Musidora**, b f by Nasrullah	N P Donaldson	C F Elsey	E Britt	17	4/1F
1950	**Asmena**, ch f by Goya	M Boussac	C H Semblat	W R Johnstone	19	5/1
1951	**Neasham Belle**, b f by Nearco	L B Holliday	G Brooke	S Clayton	16	33/1
1952	**Frieze**, b f by Phideas	A M Keith	C F Elsey	E Britt	19	100/1
1953	**Ambiguity**, b f by Big Game	Lord Astor	R J Colling	J Mercer	21	18/1
1954	**Sun Cap**, gr f by Sunny Boy	Mme R Forget	Reg Carver	W R Johnstone	21	100/8
1955	**Meld**, b f by Alycidon	Lady Z Wernher	C Boyd-Rochfort	W H Carr	13	7/4F
1956	**Sicarelle**, b f by Sicambre	Mme L Volterra	F Mathet	F Palmer	14	3/1F
1957	**Carrozza**, br f by Dante	HM the Queen	C F N Murless	L Piggott	11	100/8
1958	**Bella Paola**, br f by Ticino	F Dupré	F Mathet	M Garcia	17	6/4F
1959	**Petite Etoile**, gr f by Petition	Prince Aly Khan	C F N Murless	L Piggott	11	11/2
1960	**Never Too Late**, ch f by Never Say Die	Mrs H E Jackson	E Pollet	R Poincelet	10	6/5F
1961	**Sweet Solera**, ch f by Solonaway	Mrs S M Castello	R Day	W Rickaby	12	11/4F
1962	**Monade**, br f by Klairon	G P Goulandris	J Lieux	Y Saint-Martin	18	7/1
1963	**Noblesse**, ch f by Mossborough	Mrs J M Olin	P J Prendergast	G Bougoure	9	4/11F
1964	**Homeward Bound**, ch f by Alycidon	Sir F Robinson	J Oxley	G Starkey	18	100/7
1965	**Long Look**, b f by Ribot	J Cox Brady	M V O'Brien	J Purtell	18	100/7
1966	**Valoris**, br f by Tiziano	C Clore	M V O'Brien	L Piggott	13	11/10F
1967	**Pia**, br f by Darius	Gräfin M Batthyany	C W C Elsey	E Hide	12	100/7
1968	**La Lagune**, b f by Val de Loir	H Berlin	F Boutin	G Thiboeuf	14	11/8F
1969	**Sleeping Partner**, gr f by Parthia	Lord Rosebery	D Smith	J Gorton	15	100/6
1970	**Lupe**, b f by Primera	Mrs S Joel	C F N Murless	A Barclay	16	100/30F
1971	**Altesse Royale**, ch f by Saint Crespin	F R Hue-Williams	C F N Murless	G Lewis	11	6/4F
1972	**Ginevra**, b f by Shantung	C A B St George	H R Price	A Murray	17	8/1
1973	**Mysterious**, ch f by Crepello	G A Pope, jr	C F N Murless	G Lewis	10	13/8F
1974	**Polygamy**, b f by Reform	L Freedman	P Walwyn	P Eddery	15	3/1F
1975	**Juliette Marny**, b f by Blakeney	J I Morrison	A J Tree	L Piggott	12	12/1
1976	**Pawneese**, b f by Carvin	D Wildenstein	A Penna	Y Saint-Martin	14	6/5F
1977	**Dunfermline**, b f by Royal Palace	HM the Queen	W R Hern	W Carson	13	6/1
1978	**Fair Salinia**, b f by Petingo	S Hanson	M Stoute	G Starkey	15	8/1
1979	**Scintillate**, b f by Sparkler	J I Morrison	A J Tree	P Eddery	14	20/1
1980	**Bireme**, ch f by Grundy	R D Hollingsworth	W R Hern	W Carson	11	9/2
1981	**Blue Wind**, ch f by Lord Gayle	Mrs B R Firestone	D K Weld	L Piggott	12	3/1JF
1982	**Time Charter**, b f by Saritamer	R Barnett	H Candy	W Newnes	13	12/1
1983	**Sun Princess**, b f by English Prince	Sir M Sobell	W R Hern	W Carson	15	6/1
1984	**Circus Plume**, b f by High Top	Sir R McAlpine	J Dunlop	L Piggott	16	4/1
1985	**Oh So Sharp**, ch f by Kris	Sheikh Mohammed	H Cecil	S Cauthen	12	6/4F
1986	**Midway Lady**, b f by Alleged	HH Ranier	B Hanbury	R Cochrane	15	15/8F
1987	**Unite**, ch f by Kris	Sheikh Mohammed	M Stoute	W R Swinburn	11	11/1
1988	**Diminuendo**, ch f by Diesis	Sheikh Mohammed	H Cecil	S Cauthen	11	7/4F
1989	**Aliysa**, b f by Darshaan	HH Aga Khan	M Stoute	W R Swinburn	9	11/10F

St Leger

At Doncaster, Yorkshire. For 3-year-olds. 1 mile 6 furlongs 127 yards.

Year	Horse	Owner	Trainer	Jockey	Ran	S.P.
1776	**Allabaculia**, br f by Sampson	Lord Rockingham	C Scaife	J Singleton	5	1/2F
1777	**Bourbon**, b c by Le Sang	W Sotheron		J Cade	10	3/1
1778	**Hollandaise**, gr f by Matchem	Sir T Gascoigne	J Rose	G Herring	8	5/2
1779	**Tommy**, ch c by Wildair	T Stapleton	J Rose	G Lowry	10	1/1F
1780	**Ruler**, b c by Young Marske	W Bethell		J Mangle	7	5/2
1781	**Serina**, b f by Goldfinder	W Radcliffe	J Lowther	R Foster	9	—
1782	**Imperatrix**, ch f by Alfred	H Goodricke	G Searle	G Searle	5	—
1783	**Phoenomenon**, ch c by Herod	Sir J L Kaye	I Cape	A Hall	4	4/5F
1784	**Omphale**, b f by Highflyer	J Coates	M Mason	J Kirton	7	—
1785	**Cowslip**, b f by Highflyer	R J Hill	G Searle	G Searle	4	F
1786	**Paragon**, b c by Paymaster	Lord A Hamilton	J Mangle	J Mangle	8	20/1
1787	**Spadille**, b c by Highflyer	Lord A Hamilton	J Mangle	J Mangle	6	2/1
1788	**Young Flora**, b f by Highflyer	Lord A Hamilton	J Mangle	J Mangle	5	2/1
1789	**Pewett**, b f by Tandem	Lord Fitzwilliam	C Scaife	W Wilson	6	F
1790	**Ambidexter**, b c by Phoenomenon	H Goodricke	G Searle	G Searle	8	5/1
1791	**Young Traveller**, ch c by King Fergus	J Hutchinson	J Hutchinson	J Jackson	8	3/1
1792	**Tartar**, ch c by Florizel	Lord A Hamilton	J Mangle	J Mangle	11	25/1
1793	**Ninety-three**, b c by Florizel	J Clifton		W Peirse	8	15/1
1794	**Beningbrough**, b c by King Fergus	J Hutchinson	J Hutchinson	J Jackson	8	2/1
1795	**Hambletonian**, b c by King Fergus	Sir C Turner	J Hutchinson	R D Boyce	5	4/6F
1796	**Ambrosio**, b c by Sir Peter Teazle	J Cookson		J Jackson	7	4/5F
1797	**Lounger**, b c by Drone	H Goodricke	G Searle	J Shepherd	8	—
1798	**Symmetry**, gr c by Delpini	Sir T Gascoigne	S King	J Jackson	10	4/1
1799	**Cockfighter**, br c by Overton	Sir H T Vane	T Fields	T Fields	7	4/6F
1800	**Champion**, b c by Potoooooooo	C Wilson	T Perren	F Buckle	10	2/1JF
1801	**Quiz**, ch c by Buzzard	H Goodricke	G Searle	J Shepherd	8	7/1
1802	**Orville**, b c by Beningbrough	Lord Fitzwilliam	C Scaife	J Singleton, jr	5	5/1
1803	**Remembrancer**, b c by Pipator	Lord Strathmore	J Smith	B Smith	8	5/2F
1804	**Sancho**, b c by Don Quixote	H F Mellish	B Atkinson	F Buckle	11	2/1F
1805	**Staveley**, b c by Shuttle	H F Mellish	B Atkinson	J Jackson	10	6/1
1806	**Fyldener**, b c by Sir Peter Teazle	J Clifton		T Carr	15	7/4F
1807	**Paulina**, b f by Sir Peter Teazle	Lord Fitzwilliam	C Scaife	W Clift	16	8/1
1808	**Petronius**, b c by Sir Peter Teazle	Duke of Hamilton	W Theakston	B Smith	12	20/1
1809	**Ashton**, b c by Walnut	Duke of Hamilton	W Theakston	B Smith	14	15/8F
1810	**Octavian**, ch c by Stripling	Duke of Leeds		W Clift	8	12/1
1811	**Soothsayer**, ch c by Sorceror	R O Gascoigne	T Sykes	B Smith	24	6/1
1812	**Otterington**, b c by Golumpus	Rob	W Hesseltine	R Johnson	24	100/1
1813	**Altisidora**, ch f by Dick Andrews	R Watt	T Sykes	J Jackson	17	5/2F
1814	**William**, b c by Governor	Duke of Hamilton	W Theakston	J Shepherd	12	7/1
1815	**Filho da Puta**, br c by Haphazard	Sir W Maxwell	J Croft	J Jackson	15	1/1F
1816	**The Duchess**, b f by Cardinal York	Sir B R Graham	J Croft	B Smith	13	12/1
1817	**Ebor**, b c by Orville	H Peirse	J Lonsdale	R Johnson	18	20/1
1818	**Reveller**, b c by Comus	H Peirse	J Lonsdale	R Johnson	21	4/1
1819	**Antonio**, b c by Octavian	J Ferguson	J Lonsdale	T Nicholson	19	33/1
1820	**St Patrick**, ch c by Walton	Sir E Smith	J Lonsdale	R Johnson	27	7/1
1821	**Jack Spigot**, br c by Marmion *or* Ardrossan	T Orde-Powlett	I Blades	W Scott	13	6/1
1822	**Theodore**, b c by Woful	E Petre	J Croft	J Jackson	23	200/1
1823	**Barefoot**, ch c by Tramp	R Watt	R Shepherd	T Goodisson	12	4/1
1824	**Jerry**, bl c by Smolensko	R O Gascoigne	J Croft	B Smith	23	9/1
1825	**Memnon**, b c by Whisker	R Watt	R Shepherd	W Scott	30	3/1F
1826	**Tarrare**, b c by Catton	Lord Scarbrough	S King	G Nelson	27	20/1
1827	**Matilda**, b f by Comus	E Petre	J Scott	J Robinson	26	10/1
1828	**The Colonel**, ch c by Whisker	E Petre	J Scott	W Scott	19	3/1F
1829	**Rowton**, ch c by Oiseau	E Petre	J Scott	W Scott	19	7/2F
1830	**Birmingham**, br c by Filho da Puta	J Beardsworth	T Flintoff	P Conolly	28	15/1
1831	**Chorister**, b c by Lottery	Lord Cleveland	J Smith	J B Day	24	20/1
1832	**Margrave**, ch c by Muley	J Gully	J Scott	J Robinson	17	8/1
1833	**Rockingham**, b c by Humphrey Clinker	R Watt	R Shepherd	S Darling	20	7/1
1834	**Touchstone**, br c by Camel	Lord Westminster	J Scott	G Calloway	11	40/1
1835	**Queen of Trumps**, br f by Velocipede	E L M Mostyn		J Blenkhorn	11	8/11F
1836	**Elis**, ch c by Langar	Lord G Bentinck	J Doe	J B Day	14	7/2
1837	**Mango**, br c by Emilius	C Greville	M Dilly	S Day, jr	13	13/2
1838	**Don John**, b c by Tramp *or* Waverley	Lord Chesterfield	J Scott	W Scott	7	13/8F
1839	**Charles the Twelfth**, br c by Voltaire	Yarburgh	J Scott	W Scott	14	4/6F
1840	**Launcelot**, br c by Camel	Lord Westminster	J Scott	W Scott	11	7/4F
1841	**Satirist**, br c by Pantaloon	Lord Westminster	J Scott	W Scott	11	6/1
1842	**Blue Bonnet**, b f by Touchstone	Lord Eglinton	T Dawson	T Lye	17	8/1
1843	**Nutwith**, b c by Tomboy	S Wrather	R Johnson	J Marson	9	100/6
1844	**Foig a Ballagh**, br c by Sir Hercules	E J Irwin	J Forth	H Bell	9	7/2
1845	**The Baron**, ch c by Irish Birdcatcher	G Watts	J Scott	F Butler	15	10/1

Cont. p. 136

Henry Cecil

Henry Cecil is by far the most successful British trainer of the 1980s. After 20 years as a licence-holder he has attained such a consistently high level of achievement that no other trainer can compare with him in both quality and quantity of winners, and in 1987 his tally of 180 wins in Great Britain smashed a record which had stood for 120 years.

Henry Richard Amherst Cecil was born near Aberdeen, Scotland, on 11 January 1943, just before his identical twin David. His father, who had been killed in action 2 weeks before, was a brother of Lord Amherst of Hackney and a descendant of William Cecil, Lord Burghley, the great Elizabethan statesman. In 1944 his mother married Cecil Boyd-Rochfort (later Sir Cecil) so he became the stepson of one of the most distinguished trainers in the land.

On leaving public school he worked on stud-farms in Europe and America, and attended agricultural college, before becoming Boyd-Rochfort's assistant at Freemason Lodge, Newmarket, in November 1964. The royal trainer had sent out the winners of 13 Classics but the stable was in decline when Cecil took over at the end of 1968.

He recorded his first win with Celestial Cloud in an amateur riders' event at Ripon on 17 May 1969 and finished the season eighth in the trainers' table thanks mainly to the victories of Wolver Hollow in the Eclipse Stakes and Approval in the Observer Gold Cup.

Cecil has always trained at Newmarket, but after that first season he moved to Marriott Stables and in December 1976 to Warren Place. The latter had been vacated by his father-in-law Noel Murless (later Sir Noel),

trainer of the winners of 19 Classics.

The first Classic winner, and the first champion, trained by Cecil was Bolkonski, who landed the 2000 Guineas, St James's Palace Stakes and Sussex Stakes in 1975. The following year Wollow's victories in the 2000 Guineas, Eclipse Stakes and Sussex Stakes helped Cecil towards his first trainers' title, and his third champion miler was the remarkably consistent Kris, who won 14 of his 16 races including the 1979 St James's Palace, Sussex and Queen Elizabeth II Stakes.

Between 1978 and 1982 he trained 3 champion stayers in Buckskin, Le Moss and Ardross. Le Moss beat Buckskin and Ardross into second place in the Ascot Gold Cup in 1979 and 1980 respectively, and in those years became the only horse ever to win the stayers' triple crown twice. Ardross, who won the Gold Cup in 1981 and 1982, possessed exceptional pace for a stayer and was beaten by only a head in the Prix de l'Arc de Triomphe at the end of his 1982 Horse of the Year campaign.

In 1985 Cecil won 4 of the 5 Classics including the Derby and Oaks each for the first time; Slip Anchor scored a spectacular 7-length Derby triumph and Oh So Sharp became the first fillies' triple crown winner since Meld in 1955. During the year one of his leading owners, Daniel Wildenstein, took all his horses back to France, but Cecil's score of 132 still set a 20th-century record for the number of races won by a trainer in a British season.

In 1987 he set an all-time record by winning 180 races, the previous best being 146 by John Day junior in 1867. The record-breakers were headed by Horse of the Year Reference Point, who

made all the running in the Derby, King George VI and Queen Elizabeth Stakes and St Leger, and Indian Skimmer, who gave the stable a rare foreign victory by taking the Prix de Diane. *En route* to his seventh championship, Cecil had 7 winners at Royal Ascot, notably 15-length Gold Cup hero Paean, and altogether he won 24 of the 99 British Pattern races run that year.

Henry Cecil was born with a silver spoon in his mouth but no one could have made more of the opportunities given to him. His youth was marked by heavy drinking, wild behaviour and wrecked cars, but he has left his playboy image well behind. Even now his casual air suggests that he is less interested in his horses than in his rose garden, his stylish clothes, his Gucci shoes and his latest Mercedes, but that masks a fierce desire to be the best in his profession.

Cecil is the first to acknowledge the contribution of his team at Warren Place, notably his wife Julie and head lad Paddy Rudkin, but only a master trainer can win so many Classics and Pattern races year after year. His hard work, dedication, enthusiasm and shrewd assessment of the ability and potential of all his 200-plus horses are phenomenal.

Patience has always been among his main virtues, and though he has handled champion 2-year-olds Wollow (1975), Diesis (1982), Reference Point (1986) and High Estate (1988), it is with Classic 3-year-olds and mature stayers that he has particularly excelled. As a person he is always modest, amiable and approachable, and can often be seen chatting to lorry-drivers and passers-by on Newmarket Heath.

Greville Starkey rode most of his early winners, and his

*Henry Cecil.
(Gerry Cranham)*

subsequent retained riders Joe Mercer (1977–80), Lester Piggott (1981–84) and American Steve Cauthen (from 1985) have all taken the jockeys' title with the help of the strongest stable in the country.

Henry Cecil's owners include Sheikh Mohammed, Lord Howard de Walden, Louis Freedman, Jim Joel, Charles St George and Stavros Niarchos, and they regularly send him the choicest yearlings from the world's studs and sales-rings. His skill at developing them into Classic material has enabled him to succeed Fred Darling and Noel Murless as the foremost trainer of his time. He still has driving ambition and, with perhaps more than half his career still in front of him, seems destined to break many more records.

		Owner	Trainer	Jockey	Ran	S.P.
1846	**Sir Tatton Sykes**, b c by Melbourne	W Scott	W Oates	W Scott	12	3/1JF
1847	**Van Tromp**, br c by Lanercost	Lord Eglinton	J Fobert	J Marson	8	4/1
1848	**Surplice**, b c by Touchstone	Lord Clifden	R Stephenson, jr	E Flatman	9	9/4
1849	**The Flying Dutchman**, br c by Bay Middleton	Lord Eglinton	J Fobert	C Marlow	10	4/9F
1850	**Voltigeur**, br c by Voltaire	Lord Zetland	R Hill	J Marson	8	8/13
1851	**Newminster**, b c by Touchstone	A Nichol	J Scott	S Templeman	18	12/1
1852	**Stockwell**, ch c by The Baron	Lord Exeter	W Harlock	J Norman	6	7/4F
1853	**West Australian**, b c by Melbourne	J Bowes	J Scott	F Butler	10	6/4F
1854	**Knight of St George**, b c by Irish Birdcatcher	J B Morris	H Stebbing	R Basham	18	11/1
1855	**Saucebox**, b c by St Lawrence	T Parr	T Parr	J Wells	12	40/1
1856	**Warlock**, b c by Irish Birdcatcher	A Nichol	J Scott	E Flatman	9	12/1
1857	**Impérieuse**, b f by Orlando	J Scott	J Scott	E Flatman	11	100/6
1858	**Sunbeam**, b f by Chanticleer	J Merry	J Prince	L Snowden	18	15/1
1859	**Gamester**, br c by Cossack	Sir C Monck	J Scott	T Aldcroft	11	20/1
1860	**St Albans**, ch c by Stockwell	Lord Ailesbury	A Taylor	L Snowden	15	8/1
1861	**Caller Ou**, br f by Stockwell	W I'Anson	W I'Anson	T Chaloner	18	1,000/15
1862	**The Marquis**, b c by Stockwell	S Hawke	J Scott	T Chaloner	15	100/30
1863	**Lord Clifden**, b c by Newminster	Lord St Vincent	E Parr	J Osborne	19	100/30F
1864	**Blair Athol**, ch c by Stockwell	W I'Anson	W I'Anson	J Snowden	10	2/1F
1865	**Gladiateur**, b c by Monarque	Comte F de Lagrange	T Jennings	H Grimshaw	14	8/13F
1866	**Lord Lyon**, b c by Stockwell	R Sutton	J Dover	H Custance	11	4/7F
1867	**Achievement**, br f by Stockwell	M Pearson	J Dover	T Chaloner	12	75/40
1868	**Formosa**, ch f by Buccaneer	W Graham	H Woolcott	T Chaloner	12	100/30JF
1869	**Pero Gomez**, br c by Beadsman	Sir J Hawley	J Porter	J Wells	11	3/1
1870	**Hawthornden**, b c by Lord Clifden	T V Morgan	Jos Dawson	J Grimshaw	19	1,000/35
1871	**Hannah**, b f by King Tom	Baron M de Rothschild	J Hayhoe	C Maidment	10	9/4F
1872	**Wenlock**, b c by Lord Clifden	Lord Wilton	T Wadlow	C Maidment	17	8/1
1873	**Marie Stuart**, ch f by Scottish Chief	J Merry	R Peck	T Osborne	8	9/4
1874	**Apology**, ch f by Adventurer	J W King	W Osborne	J Osborne	13	4/1F
1875	**Craig Millar**, ch c by Blair Athol	W S Crawfurd	A Taylor	T Chaloner	13	7/1
1876	**Petrarch**, b c by Lord Clifden	Lord Dupplin	John Dawson	J Goater	9	5/1
1877	**Silvio**, b c by Blair Athol	Lord Falmouth	M Dawson	F Archer	14	65/40F
1878	**Jannette**, b f by Lord Clifden	Lord Falmouth	M Dawson	F Archer	14	5/2F
1879	**Rayon d'Or**, ch c by Flageolet	Comte F de Lagrange	T Jennings	J Goater	17	3/1JF
1880	**Robert the Devil**, b c by Bertram	C Brewer	C Blanton	T Cannon	12	4/1
1881	**Iroquois**, br c by Leamington	P Lorillard	J Pincus	F Archer	15	2/1F
1882	**Dutch Oven**, br f by Dutch Skater	Lord Falmouth	M Dawson	F Archer	14	40/1
1883	**Ossian**, b c by Salvator	Duke of Hamilton	R Marsh	J Watts	9	9/1
1884	**The Lambkin**, b c by Camballo	R C Vyner	M Dawson	J Watts	13	9/1
1885	**Melton**, b c by Master Kildare	Lord Hastings	M Dawson	F Archer	10	40/95F
1886	**Ormonde**, b c by Bend Or	Duke of Westminster	J Porter	F Archer	7	1/7F
1887	**Kilwarlin**, br c by Arbitrator	Lord Rodney	J Jewitt	W T Robinson	9	4/1JF
1888	**Seabreeze**, ch f by Isonomy	Lord Calthorpe	J Jewitt	W T Robinson	16	5/2
1889	**Donovan**, b c by Galopin	Duke of Portland	G Dawson	F Barrett	12	8/13F
1890	**Memoir**, br f by St Simon	Duke of Portland	G Dawson	J Watts	15	10/1
1891	**Common**, br c by Isonomy	Sir F Johnstone	J Porter	G Barrett	9	4/5F
1892	**La Flèche**, br f by St Simon	Baron M de Hirsch	J Porter	J Watts	11	7/2
1893	**Isinglass**, b c by Isonomy	H McCalmont	J Jewitt	T Loates	7	40/75F
1894	**Throstle**, b f by Petrarch	Lord Alington	J Porter	M Cannon	8	50/1
1895	**Sir Visto**, b c by Barcaldine	Lord Rosebery	M Dawson	S Loates	11	9/4F
1896	**Persimmon**, b c by St Simon	HRH Prince of Wales	R Marsh	J Watts	7	2/11F
1897	**Galtee More**, b c by Kendal	J Gubbins	S Darling	C Wood	5	1/10F
1898	**Wildfowler**, ch c by Gallinule	J H Greer	S Darling	C Wood	12	10/1
1899	**Flying Fox**, b c by Orme	Duke of Westminster	J Porter	M Cannon	6	2/7F
1900	**Diamond Jubilee**, b c by St Simon	HRH Prince of Wales	R Marsh	H Jones	11	2/7F
1901	**Doricles**, br c by Florizel	Leo de Rothschild	A Hayhoe	K Cannon	13	40/1
1902	**Sceptre**, b f by Persimmon	R S Sievier	R S Sievier	F W Hardy	12	100/30F
1903	**Rock Sand**, br c by Sainfoin	Sir J Miller	G Blackwell	D Maher	5	2/5F
1904	**Pretty Polly**, ch f by Gallinule	E Loder	P P Gilpin	W Lane	6	2/5F
1905	**Challacombe**, b c by St Serf	W M G Singer	A Taylor, jr	O Madden	8	100/6
1906	**Troutbeck**, b c by Ladas	Duke of Westminster	W Waugh	G Stern	12	5/1
1907	**Wool Winder**, b c by Martagon	E W Baird	H Enoch	W Halsey	12	11/10F
1908	**Your Majesty**, b c by Persimmon	J B Joel	C Morton	Wal Griggs	10	11/8F
1909	**Bayardo**, b c by Bay Ronald	A W Cox	A Taylor, jr	D Maher	7	10/11F
1910	**Swynford**, br c by John o' Gaunt	Lord Derby	G Lambton	F Wootton	11	9/2
1911	**Prince Palatine**, b c by Persimmon	T Pilkington	H Beardsley	F O'Neill	8	100/30
1912	**Tracery**, br c by Rock Sand	A Belmont, jr	J Watson	G Bellhouse	14	8/1
1913	**Night Hawk**, b c by Gallinule	W Hall Walker	W T Robinson	E Wheatley	12	50/1
1914	**Black Jester**, br c by Polymelus	J B Joel	C Morton	Wal Griggs	18	10/1
1915	**Pommern**, b c by Polymelus	S B Joel	C Peck	S Donoghue	7	1/3F
1916	**Hurry On**, ch c by Marcovil	J Buchanan	F Darling	C Childs	5	11/10F
1917	**Gay Crusader**, b c by Bayardo	A W Cox	A Taylor, jr	S Donoghue	3	2/11F
1918	**Gainsborough**, b c by Bayardo	Lady James Douglas	A Taylor, jr	J Childs	5	4/11F

Year	Winner	Owner	Trainer	Jockey	Ran	S.P.
1919	**Keysoe**, br f by Swynford	Lord Derby	G Lambton	B Carslake	10	100/8
1920	**Caligula**, gr c by The Tetrarch	M Goculdas	H Leader	A Smith	14	100/6
1921	**Polemarch**, ch c by The Tetrarch	Lord Londonderry	T Green	J Childs	9	50/1
1922	**Royal Lancer**, b c by Spearmint	Lord Lonsdale	A D Sadler, jr	R A Jones	24	33/1
1923	**Tranquil**, b f by Swynford	Lord Derby	C Morton	T Weston	13	100/9
1924	**Salmon-Trout**, b c by The Tetrarch	HH Aga Khan	R C Dawson	B Carslake	17	6/1
1925	**Solario**, b c by Gainsborough	Sir J Rutherford	R Day	J Childs	15	7/2JF
1926	**Coronach**, ch c by Hurry On	Lord Woolavington	F Darling	J Childs	12	8/15F
1927	**Book Law**, b f by Buchan	Lord Astor	A Taylor, jr	H Jelliss	16	7/4F
1928	**Fairway**, b c by Phalaris	Lord Derby	Frank Butters	T Weston	13	7/4F
1929	**Trigo**, b c by Blandford	W Barnett	R C Dawson	M Beary	14	5/1
1930	**Singapore**, b c by Gainsborough	Lord Glanely	T Hogg	G Richards	13	4/1JF
1931	**Sandwich**, b c by Sansovino	Lord Rosebery	J Jarvis	H Wragg	10	9/1
1932	**Firdaussi**, ch c by Pharos	HH Aga Khan	Frank Butters	F Fox	19	20/1
1933	**Hyperion**, ch c by Gainsborough	Lord Derby	G Lambton	T Weston	14	6/4F
1934	**Windsor Lad**, b c by Blandford	M H Benson	M Marsh	C Smirke	10	4/9F
1935	**Bahram**, b c by Blandford	HH Aga Khan	Frank Butters	C Smirke	8	4/11F
1936	**Boswell**, br c by Bosworth	W Woodward	C Boyd-Rochfort	P Beasley	13	20/1
1937	**Chulmleigh**, b c by Singapore	Lord Glanely	T Hogg	G Richards	15	18/1
1938	**Scottish Union**, b c by Cameronian	J V Rank	N Cannon	B Carslake	9	7/1
1939	**no race**					
1940	**Turkhan**, b c by Bahram	HH Aga Khan	Frank Butters	G Richards	6	4/1
1941	**Sun Castle**, b c by Hyperion	Lord Portal	C Boyd-Rochfort	G Bridgland	16	10/1
1942	**Sun Chariot**, b f by Hyperion	HM the King	F Darling	G Richards	8	9/4
1943	**Herringbone**, b f by King Salmon	Lord Derby	W Earl	H Wragg	12	100/6
1944	**Tehran**, b c by Bois Roussel	HH Aga Khan	Frank Butters	G Richards	17	9/2
1945	**Chamossaire**, ch c by Precipitation	S Joel	R Perryman	T Lowrey	10	11/2
1946	**Airborne**, gr c by Precipitation	J E Ferguson	R Perryman	T Lowrey	11	3/1F
1947	**Sayajirao**, br c by Nearco	HH Maharaja of Baroda	F Armstrong	E Britt	11	9/2
1948	**Black Tarquin**, br c by Rhodes Scholar	W Woodward	C Boyd-Rochfort	E Britt	14	15/2
1949	**Ridge Wood**, br c by Bois Roussel	G R H Smith	C F N Murless	M Beary	16	100/7
1950	**Scratch**, ch c by Pharis	M Boussac	C H Semblat	W R Johnstone	15	9/2
1951	**Talma**, ch c by Pharis	M Boussac	C H Semblat	W R Johnstone	18	7/1
1952	**Tulyar**, br c by Tehran	HH Aga Khan	M Marsh	C Smirke	12	10/11F
1953	**Premonition**, b c by Precipitation	W P Wyatt	C Boyd-Rochfort	E Smith	11	10/1
1954	**Never Say Die**, ch c by Nasrullah	R S Clark	J Lawson	C Smirke	16	100/30F
1955	**Meld**, b f by Alycidon	Lady Z Wernher	C Boyd-Rochfort	W H Carr	8	10/11F
1956	**Cambremer**, ch c by Chamossaire	R B Strassburger	G Bridgland	F Palmer	13	8/1
1957	**Ballymoss**, ch c by Mossborough	J McShain	M V O'Brien	T P Burns	16	8/1
1958	**Alcide**, b c by Alycidon	Sir H de Trafford	C Boyd-Rochfort	W H Carr	8	4/9F
1959	**Cantelo**, b f by Chanteur	W Hill	C F Elsey	E Hide	11	100/7
1960	**St Paddy**, b c by Aureole	Sir V Sassoon	C F N Murless	L Piggott	9	4/6F
1961	**Aurelius**, b c by Aureole	Mrs V Lilley	C F N Murless	L Piggott	13	9/2
1962	**Hethersett**, b c by Hugh Lupus	L B Holliday	W R Hern	W H Carr	15	100/8
1963	**Ragusa**, b c by Ribot	J R Mullion	P J Prendergast	G Bougoure	7	2/5F
1964	**Indiana**, b c by Sayajirao	C W Engelhard	J F Watts	J Lindley	15	100/7
1965	**Provoke**, b c by Aureole	J J Astor	W R Hern	J Mercer	11	28/1
1966	**Sodium**, b c by Psidium	R J Sigtia	G Todd	F Durr	9	7/1
1967	**Ribocco**, b c by Ribot	C W Engelhard	R F Johnson Houghton	L Piggott	9	7/2JF
1968	**Ribero**, b c by Ribot	C W Engelhard	R F Johnson Houghton	L Piggott	8	100/30
1969	**Intermezzo**, b c by Hornbeam	G A Oldham	H Wragg	R Hutchinson	11	7/1
1970	**Nijinsky**, b c by Northern Dancer	C W Engelhard	M V O'Brien	L Piggott	9	2/7F
1971	**Athens Wood**, b c by Celtic Ash	Mrs J Rogerson	H Thomson Jones	L Piggott	8	5/2
1972	**Boucher**, ch c by Ribot	O Phipps	M V O'Brien	L Piggott	7	3/1
1973	**Peleid**, b c by Derring-Do	W E Behrens	C W C Elsey	F Durr	13	28/1
1974	**Bustino**, b c by Busted	Lady Beaverbrook	W R Hern	J Mercer	10	11/10F
1975	**Bruni**, gr c by Sea Hawk	C A B St George	H R Price	A Murray	12	9/1
1976	**Crow**, ch c by Exbury	D Wildenstein	A Penna	Y Saint-Martin	15	6/1CF
1977	**Dunfermline**, b f by Royal Palace	HM the Queen	W R Hern	W Carson	13	10/1
1978	**Julio Mariner**, b c by Blakeney	M D Lemos	C Brittain	E Hide	14	28/1
1979	**Son of Love**, ch c by Jefferson	A Rolland	R Collet	A Lequeux	17	20/1
1980	**Light Cavalry**, b c by Brigadier Gerard	H J Joel	H Cecil	J Mercer	7	3/1
1981	**Cut Above**, b c by High Top	Sir J J Astor	W R Hern	J Mercer	7	28/1
1982	**Touching Wood**, b c by Roberto	Maktoum al Maktoum	H Thomson Jones	P Cook	15	7/1
1983	**Sun Princess**, b f by English Prince	Sir M Sobell	W R Hern	W Carson	10	11/8F
1984	**Commanche Run**, b c by Run the Gantlet	I W Allen	L Cumani	L Piggott	11	7/4F
1985	**Oh So Sharp**, ch f by Kris	Sheikh Mohammed	H Cecil	S Cauthen	6	8/11F
1986	**Moon Madness**, b c by Vitigès	Lavinia, Duchess of Norfolk	J Dunlop	P Eddery	8	9/2
1987	**Reference Point**, b c by Mill Reef	L Freedman	H Cecil	S Cauthen	7	4/11F
1988	**Minster Son**, ch c by Niniski	Dowager Lady Beaverbrook	N Graham	W Carson	6	15/2
1989	**Michelozzo**, b c by Northern Baby	C A B St George	H Cecil	S Cauthen	8	6/4F

Classic summary

Most successful owners

		2000	1000	Derby	Oaks	St Leger	Total
4th Duke of Grafton	1813–1831	5	8	1	6	0	20
17th Earl of Derby	1910–1945	2	7	3	2	6	20
HH Aga Khan III	1924–1957	3	1	5	2	6	17
6th Viscount Falmouth	1862–1883	3	4	2	4	3	16
5th Earl of Jersey	1824–1837	5	2	3	1	0	11
1st Duke of Westminster	1880–1899	4	1	4	0	2	11
6th Duke of Portland	1888–1900	1	2	2	4	2	11
Jack Joel	1903–1921	1	2	2	4	2	11
5th Earl of Rosebery	1883–1924	3	3	3	1	1	11
2nd Viscount Astor	1910–1945	3	2	0	5	1	11
3rd Earl of Egremont	1782–1826	0	0	5	5	0	10
2nd Marquess of Exeter	1821–1852	4	1	0	3	1	9
Sir Victor Sassoon	1937–1960	1	2	4	1	1	9
1st Earl Grosvenor	1781–1799	0	0	3	5	0	8
John Bowes	1835–1853	3	0	4	0	1	8
Sir Joseph Hawley	1847–1869	1	1	4	1	1	8
Comte Frédéric de Lagrange	1864–1879	2	1	1	2	2	8
William Stirling Crawfurd	1859–1882	2	3	1	1	1	8
HM King Edward VII	1896–1909	2	1	3	0	2	8

Most successful breeders

		2000	1000	Derby	Oaks	St Leger	Total
4th Duke of Grafton	1815–1831	5	8	1	5	0	19
6th Viscount Falmouth	1863–1884	3	4	3	6	3	19
17th Earl of Derby	1916–1945	2	7	3	2	5	19
HH Aga Khan III	1929–1959	3	3	3	3	4	16
3rd Earl of Egremont	1788–1831	0	0	6	6	0	12
5th Earl of Jersey	1824–1847	5	3	2	2	0	12
1st Duke of Westminster	1880–1902	3	2	3	1	3	12
5th Earl of Rosebery	1883–1924	4	3	3	1	1	12
2nd Viscount Astor	1910–1953	3	2	0	6	1	12
James Cookson	1854–1880	2	2	1	5	1	11
HM Queen Victoria	1857–1892	2	3	1	2	3	11
Jack Joel	1903–1921	1	2	2	4	2	11
1st Earl Grosvenor	1781–1805	0	0	3	6	0	9
6th Duke of Portland	1888–1900	1	2	2	3	1	9
National Stud	1919–1957	2	1	0	2	3	8

N.B. HH Aga Khan III's total includes 6 winners bred in partnership with his son, Prince Aly Khan. The total for the 2nd Viscount Astor includes one bred in the name of his Cliveden Stud and one bred in partnership with his sons.

Most successful trainers

		2000	1000	Derby	Oaks	St Leger	Total
John Scott	1827–1863	7	4	5	8	16	40
Robert Robson	1793–1827	6	9	7	12	0	34
Mat Dawson	1853–1895	5	6	6	5	6	28
John Porter	1868–1900	5	2	7	3	6	23
Alec Taylor, jr	1905–1927	4	1	3	8	5	21
Fred Darling	1916–1947	5	2	7	2	3	19
Noel Murless	1948–1973	2	6	3	5	3	19
Dixon Boyce	1805–1829	5	3	5	4	0	17
Vincent O'Brien	1957–1984	4	1	6	2	3	16
Frank Butters	1927–1948	1	1	2	6	5	15
Dick Hern	1962–1989	2	1	3	3	6	15
James Edwards	1811–1837	6	2	5	1	0	14
Richard Marsh	1883–1909	3	2	4	1	3	13
Cecil Boyd-Rochfort	1933–1959	1	3	1	2	6	13
Henry Cecil	1975–1989	2	3	2	2	4	13
John Day, jr	1847–1869	4	4	2	2	0	12
Charles Morton	1903–1923	1	2	2	4	3	12
George Lambton	1896–1933	1	4	2	2	3	12
Joe Lawson	1929–1954	4	3	1	3	1	12
John Pratt	1781–1799	0	0	4	7	0	11
Alec Taylor, sr	1851–1887	2	3	2	2	2	11
Frank Neale	1782–1804	0	0	6	4	0	10
Richard Prince	1786–1819	1	1	5	3	0	10
John Barham Day	1837–1854	3	4	1	2	0	10
George Dawson	1888–1894	1	2	2	3	2	10

Hyperion, the 1933 Derby and St Leger winner who became one of the most influential stallions of the 20th century. (BBC Hulton Picture Library)

		2000	1000	Derby	Oaks	St Leger	Total
Peter Purcell Gilpin	1904–1927	1	4	2	2	1	10
Jack Jarvis	1923–1953	3	3	2	0	1	9
Joe Hayhoe	1864–1879	0	2	3	2	1	8
Tom Jennings, sr	1864–1879	2	1	1	2	2	8
Dick Dawson	1916–1930	1	0	3	2	2	8
Michael Stoute	1978–1989	2	1	2	3	0	8

Most successful jockeys

		2000	1000	Derby	Oaks	St Leger	Total
Lester Piggott	1954–1985	4	2	9	6	8	29
Frank Buckle	1792–1827	5	6	5	9	2	27
Jem Robinson	1817–1848	9	5	6	2	2	24
Fred Archer	1874–1886	4	2	5	4	6	21
Bill Scott	1821–1846	3	0	4	3	9	19
Jack Watts	1883–1897	2	4	4	4	5	19
John Barham Day	1826–1841	4	5	0	5	2	16
George Fordham	1859–1883	3	7	1	5	0	16
Joe Childs	1912–1933	2	2	3	4	4	15
Frank Butler	1843–1853	2	2	2	6	2	14
Steve Donoghue	1915–1937	3	1	6	2	2	14
Charlie Elliott	1923–1949	5	4	3	2	0	14
Gordon Richards	1930–1953	3	3	1	2	5	14
Bill Clift	1793–1819	2	2	5	2	2	13
Tom Cannon	1866–1889	4	3	1	4	1	13
Harry Wragg	1928–1946	1	3	3	4	2	13
Willie Carson	1972–1989	4	0	3	3	3	13
John Osborne	1856–1888	6	2	1	1	2	12
Rae Johnstone	1934–1956	1	3	3	3	2	12
Tommy Weston	1923–1956	2	1	2	3	3	11
Charlie Smirke	1934–1958	2	1	4	0	4	11
Nat Flatman	1835–1857	3	3	1	0	3	10
Tom Chaloner	1861–1875	3	0	1	1	5	10
Charlie Wood	1880–1898	1	3	3	1	2	10
Bill Arnull	1804–1832	3	3	3	0	0	9
Sam Chifney, jr	1807–1843	1	1	2	5	0	9
Danny Maher	1901–1912	2	1	3	1	2	9
Steve Cauthen	1979–1989	1	1	2	2	3	9
John Jackson	1791–1822	0	0	0	0	8	8
John Wells	1854–1869	1	2	3	0	2	8
Herbert Jones	1900–1909	4	0	2	1	1	8
Joe Mercer	1953–1981	1	2	0	1	4	8

Most successful sires

		2000	1000	Derby	Oaks	St Leger	Total
Stockwell	1860–1873	4	3	3	1	6	17
St Simon	1890–1900	2	4	2	5	4	17
Touchstone	1842–1855	4	1	3	1	3	12
Melbourne	1846–1857	2	2	2	3	2	11
Blandford	1929–1938	2	1	4	1	3	11
Hyperion	1940–1946	0	4	1	4	2	11
Sir Peter Teazle	1794–1808	0	0	4	2	4	10
Sultan	1829–1837	5	2	1	2	0	10
Highflyer	1784–1789	0	0	3	1	4	8
Sorceror	1808–1813	3	0	1	3	1	8
Waxy	1809–1818	0	1	4	3	0	8
Emilius	1830–1843	1	3	2	1	1	8
Isonomy	1888–1893	2	0	2	1	3	8
Persimmon	1902–1911	1	1	0	3	3	8
Polymelus	1914–1921	1	1	3	1	2	8
Swynford	1918–1925	0	4	1	1	2	8
Hurry On	1922–1929	0	2	3	2	1	8

MULTIPLE CLASSIC-WINNING HORSES

2000 Guineas, 1000 Guineas, Oaks, St Leger

Formosa (1868, dead-heat in 2000 Guineas), Sceptre (1902)

2000 Guineas, Derby, St Leger

West Australian (1853), Gladiateur (1865), Lord Lyon (1866), Ormonde (1886), Common (1891), Isinglass (1893), Galtee More (1897), Flying Fox (1899), Diamond Jubilee (1900), Rock Sand (1903), Pommern (1915), Gay Crusader (1917), Gainsborough (1918), Bahram (1935), Nijinsky (1970)

1000 Guineas, Oaks, St Leger

Hannah (1871), Apology (1874), La Flèche (1892), Pretty Polly (1904), Sun Chariot (1942), Meld (1955), Oh So Sharp (1985)

2000 Guineas, 1000 Guineas, Oaks

Crucifix (1840)

2000 Guineas, 1000 Guineas

Pilgrimage (1878)

2000 Guineas, Derby

Smolensko (1813), Cadland (1828), Bay Middleton (1836), Cotherstone (1843), Macaroni (1863), Pretender (1869), Shotover (1882), Ayrshire (1888), Ladas (1894), St Amant (1904), Minoru (1909), Sunstar (1911), Manna (1925), Cameronian (1931), Blue Peter (1939), Nimbus (1949), Crepello (1957), Royal Palace (1967), Sir Ivor (1968), Nashwan (1989)

2000 Guineas, Oaks

Pastille (1822)

2000 Guineas, St Leger

Sir Tatton Sykes (1846), Stockwell (1852), The Marquis (1862), Petrarch (1876)

1000 Guineas, Derby

Tagalie (1912)

1000 Guineas, Oaks

Neva (1817), Corinne (1818), Zinc (1823), Cobweb (1824), Galata (1832), Mendicant (1846), Governess (1858), Reine (1872), Spinaway (1875), Camélia (1876, dead-heat in Oaks), Wheel of Fortune (1879), Thebais (1881), Busybody (1884), Miss Jummy (1886), Rêve d'Or (1887), Mimi (1891), Amiable (1894), Cherry Lass (1905), Jest (1913), Princess Dorrie (1914), Saucy Sue (1925), Exhibitionnist (1937), Rockfel (1938), Galatea (1939), Godiva (1940), Sun Stream (1945), Imprudence (1947), Musidora (1949), Bella Paola (1958), Petite Etoile (1959), Never Too Late (1960), Sweet Solera (1961), Altesse Royale (1971), Mysterious (1973), Midway Lady (1986)

1000 Guineas, St Leger

Impérieuse (1857), Achievement (1867), Tranquil (1923), Herringbone (1943)

Derby, Oaks

Eleanor (1801), Blink Bonny (1857), Signorinetta (1908), Fifinella (1916)

Derby, St Leger

Champion (1800), Surplice (1848), The Flying Dutchman (1849), Voltigeur (1850), Blair Athol (1864), Silvio (1877), Iroquois (1881), Melton (1885), Donovan (1889), Sir Visto (1895), Persimmon (1896), Coronach (1926), Trigo (1929), Hyperion (1933), Windsor Lad (1934), Airborne (1946), Tulyar (1952), Never Say Die (1954), St Paddy (1960), Reference Point (1987)

Oaks, St Leger

Queen of Trumps (1835), Marie Stuart (1873), Jannette (1878), Seabreeze (1888), Memoir (1890), Dunfermline (1977), Sun Princess (1983)

CLASSIC-WINNING SIBLINGS

A total of 71 mares have produced individual winners of more than one Classic:

3 – **Penelope** (1798)
Whalebone (by Waxy) 1810 Derby
Whisker (by Waxy) 1815 Derby
Whizgig (by Rubens) 1822 1000 Guineas
3 – **Pope Joan** (1809)
Tontine (by Election) 1825 1000 Guineas (walk-over)
Turcoman (by Selim) 1827 2000 Guineas
Turquoise (by Selim) 1828 Oaks
3 – **Fillagree** (1815)
Cobweb (by Phantom) 1824 1000 Guineas, Oaks
Charlotte West (by Tramp) 1830 1000 Guineas
Riddlesworth (by Emilius) 1831 2000 Guineas
3 – **Unnamed Rubens mare** (1819)
May-day (by Lamplighter) 1834 1000 Guineas
Phosphorus (by Lamplighter) 1837 Derby
Firebrand (by Lamplighter) 1842 1000 Guineas
3 – **Cobweb** (1821)
Bay Middleton (by Sultan) 1836 2000 Guineas, Derby
Achmet (by Sultan) 1837 2000 Guineas
Clementina (by Venison) 1847 1000 Guineas
3 – **Araucaria** (1862)
Camélia (by Macaroni) 1876 1000 Guineas, dead-heat Oaks
Chamant (by Mortemer) 1877 2000 Guineas
Rayon d'Or (by Flageolet) 1879 St Leger
3 – **Set Free** (1964)
Juliette Marny (by Blakeney) 1975 Oaks
Julio Mariner (by Blakeney) 1978 St Leger
Scintillate (by Sparkler) 1979 Oaks
2 – **Virago** (1764)
Saltram (by Eclipse) 1783 Derby
Annette (by Eclipse) 1787 Oaks
2 – **Flora** (1768)
Spadille (by Highflyer) 1787 St Leger
Young Flora (by Highflyer) 1788 St Leger
2 – **Flyer** (1777)
Rhadamanthus (by Justice) 1790 Derby
Daedalus (by Justice) 1794 Derby
2 – **Horatia** (1778)
Archduke (by Sir Peter Teazle) 1799 Derby
Paris (by Sir Peter Teazle) 1806 Derby
2 – **Unnamed Highflyer mare** (1784)
Caelia (by Volunteer) 1793 Oaks
Unnamed colt (by Fidget) 1797 Derby
2 – **Unnamed Highflyer mare** (1785)
Spread Eagle (by Volunteer) 1795 Derby
Didelot (by Trumpator) 1796 Derby
2 – **Violet** (1787)
Symmetry (by Delpini) 1798 St Leger
Theophania (by Delpini) 1803 Oaks
2 – **Prunella** (1788)
Pelisse (by Whiskey) 1804 Oaks
Pope (by Waxy) 1809 Derby
2 – **Woodbine** (1791)
Music (by Waxy) 1813 Oaks
Minuet (by Waxy) 1815 Oaks
2 – **Arethusa** (1792)
Ditto (by Sir Peter Teazle) 1803 Derby
Pan (by St George) 1808 Derby
2 – **Marianne** (1798)
Octavius (by Orville) 1812 Derby
Caroline (by Whalebone) 1820 Oaks
2 – **Mandane** (1800)
Manuella (by Dick Andrews) 1812 Oaks
Altisidora (by Dick Andrews) 1813 St Leger
2 – **Parasol** (1800)
Pindarrie (by Phantom) 1820 2000 Guineas
Pastille (by Rubens) 1822 2000 Guineas, Oaks
2 – **Goosander** (1805)
Shoveler (by Scud) 1819 Oaks
Sailor (by Scud) 1820 Derby
2 – **Zaida** (1806)
Zeal (by Partisan) 1821 1000 Guineas
Zinc (by Woful) 1823 1000 Guineas, Oaks
2 – **Cressida** (1807)
Antar (by Haphazard) 1819 2000 Guineas
Priam (by Emilius) 1830 Derby

2 – **Miss Wasp** (1807)
Manfred (by Election) 1817 2000 Guineas
Vespa (by Muley) 1833 Oaks
2 – **Prudence** (1811)
Rowena (by Haphazard) 1820 1000 Guineas
Reginald (by Haphazard) 1821 2000 Guineas
2 – **Unnamed Canopus mare** (1812)
Lap-dog (by Whalebone) 1826 Derby
Spaniel (by Whalebone) 1831 Derby
2 – **Unnamed Rubens mare** (1813)
Augusta (by Woful) 1821 Oaks
Patron (by Partisan) 1829 2000 Guineas
2 – **Unnamed Phantom mare** (1820)
Ibrahim (by Sultan) 1835 2000 Guineas
The Princess (by Slane) 1844 Oaks
2 – **Arcot Lass** (1821)
St Giles (by Tramp) 1832 Derby
Bloomsbury (by Mulatto) 1839 Derby
2 – **Emma** (1824)
Mündig (by Catton) 1835 Derby
Cotherstone (by Touchstone) 1843 Derby, St Leger
2 – **Mustard** (1824)
Preserve (by Emilius) 1835 1000 Guineas
Mango (by Emilius) 1837 St Leger
2 – **Banter** (1826)
Touchstone (by Camel) 1834 St Leger
Launcelot (by Camel) 1840 St Leger
2 – **Beeswing** (1833)
Nunnykirk (by Touchstone) 1849 2000 Guineas
Newminster (by Touchstone) 1851 St Leger
2 – **Barbelle** (1836)
Van Tromp (by Lanercost) 1847 St Leger
The Flying Dutchman (by Bay Middleton) 1849 Derby, St Leger
2 – **Unnamed Laurel mare** (1840)
Rhedycina (by Wintonian) 1850 Oaks
Governess (by Chatham) 1858 1000 Guineas, Oaks
2 – **Cinizelli** (1842)
Marchioness (by Melbourne) 1855 Oaks
The Marquis (by Stockwell) 1862 2000 Guineas, St Leger
2 – **Ellerdale** (1844)
Ellington (by The Flying Dutchman) 1856 Derby
Summerside (by West Australian) 1859 Oaks
2 – **Hybla** (1846)
Mincemeat (by Sweetmeat) 1854 Oaks
Kettledrum (by Rataplan) 1861 Derby
2 – **Paradigm** (1852)
Lord Lyon (by Stockwell) 1866 2000 Guineas, Derby, St Leger
Achievement (by Stockwell) 1867 1000 Guineas, St Leger
2 – **Queen Bertha** (1860)
Spinaway (by Macaroni) 1875 1000 Guineas, Oaks
Wheel of Fortune (by Adventurer) 1879 1000 Guineas, Oaks
2 – **Mineral** (1863)
Wenlock (by Lord Clifden) 1872 St Leger
Kisber (by Buccaneer) 1876 Derby
2 – **Devotion** (1869)
Thebais (by Hermit) 1881 1000 Guineas, Oaks
St Marguerite (by Hermit) 1882 1000 Guineas
2 – **Lily Agnes** (1871)
Farewell (by Doncaster) 1885 1000 Guineas
Ormonde (by Bend Or) 1886 2000 Guineas, Derby, St Leger
2 – **Quiver** (1872)
Memoir (by St Simon) 1890 Oaks, St Leger
La Flèche (by St Simon) 1892 1000 Guineas, Oaks, St Leger
2 – **Mint Sauce** (1875)
The Lambkin (by Camballo) 1884 St Leger
Minthe (by Camballo) 1889 1000 Guineas
2 – **Pilgrimage** (1875)
Canterbury Pilgrim (by Tristan) 1896 Oaks
Jeddah (by Janissary) 1898 Derby
2 – **Thistle** (1875)
Common (by Isonomy) 1891 2000 Guineas, Derby, St Leger
Throstle (by Petrarch) 1894 St Leger
2 – **Mowerina** (1876)
Donovan (by Galopin) 1889 Derby, St Leger
Semolina (by St Simon) 1890 1000 Guineas
2 – **Illuminata** (1877)
Ladas (by Hampton) 1894 2000 Guineas, Derby
Chélandry (by Goldfinch) 1897 1000 Guineas
2 – **Vista** (1879)
Bona Vista (by Bend Or) 1892 2000 Guineas
Sir Visto (by Barcaldine) 1895 Derby, St Leger

2 – **Perdita** (1881)
Persimmon (by St Simon) 1896 Derby, St Leger
Diamond Jubilee (by St Simon) 1900 2000 Guineas, Derby,
St Leger
2 – **Morganette** (1884)
Galtee More (by Kendal) 1897 2000 Guineas, Derby, St Leger
Ard Patrick (by St Florian) 1902 Derby
2 – **Yours** (1894)
Our Lassie (by Ayrshire) 1903 Oaks
Your Majesty (by Persimmon) 1908 St Leger
2 – **Rhoda B.** (1895)
Orby (by Orme) 1907 Derby
Rhodora (by St Frusquin) 1908 1000 Guineas
2 – **Doris** (1898)
Sunstar (by Sundridge) 1911 2000 Guineas, Derby
Princess Dorrie (by Your Majesty) 1914 1000 Guineas, Oaks
2 – **Galicia** (1898)
Bayardo (by Bay Ronald) 1909 St Leger
Lemberg (by Cyllene) 1910 Derby
2 – **Donnetta** (1900)
Diadem (by Orby) 1917 1000 Guineas
Diophon (by Grand Parade) 1924 2000 Guineas
2 – **Gondolette** (1902)
Ferry (by Swynford) 1918 1000 Guineas
Sansovino (by Swynford) 1924 Derby
2 – **Absurdity** (1903)
Jest (by Sundridge) 1913 1000 Guineas, Oaks
Black Jester (by Polymelus) 1914 St Leger
2 – **Maid of the Mist** (1906)
Sunny Jane (by Sunstar) 1917 Oaks
Craig an Eran (by Sunstar) 1921 2000 Guineas
2 – **Popingaol** (1913)
Pogrom (by Lemberg) 1922 Oaks
Book Law (by Buchan) 1927 St Leger

2 – **Scapa Flow** (1914)
Fairway (by Phalaris) 1928 St Leger
Fair Isle (by Phalaris) 1930 1000 Guineas
2 – **Waffles** (1917)
Manna (by Phalaris) 1925 2000 Guineas, Derby
Sandwich (by Sansovino) 1931 St Leger
2 – **Ranai** (1925)
Watling Street (by Fairway) 1942 Derby
Garden Path (by Fairway) 1944 2000 Guineas
2 – **Drift** (1926)
Tide-way (by Fairway) 1936 1000 Guineas
Sun Stream (by Hyperion) 1945 1000 Guineas, Oaks
2 – **Rosy Legend** (1931)
Dante (by Nearco) 1945 Derby
Sayajirao (by Nearco) 1947 St Leger
2 – **Crepuscule** (1948)
Honeylight (by Honeyway) 1956 1000 Guineas
Crepello (by Donatello) 1957 2000 Guineas, Derby
2 – **Review** (1951)
Pourparler (by Hugh Lupus) 1964 1000 Guineas
Fleet (by Immortality) 1967 1000 Guineas
2 – **Libra** (1956)
Ribocco (by Ribot) 1967 St Leger
Ribero (by Ribot) 1968 St Leger
2 – **Windmill Girl** (1961)
Blakeney (by Hethersett) 1969 Derby
Morston (by Ragusa) 1973 Derby
2 – **Glass Slipper** (1969)
Light Cavalry (by Brigadier Gerard) 1980 St Leger
Fairy Footsteps (by Mill Reef) 1981 1000 Guineas

King George VI and Queen Elizabeth Stakes

At Ascot, Berkshire. Weight-for-age, 3-year-olds and
upwards. 1 mile 4 furlongs.

Year	Winner, age	Trainer	Jockey
1951	**Supreme Court**, 3	E Williams	E C Elliott
1952	**Tulyar**, 3	M Marsh	C Smirke
1953	**Pinza**, 3	N Bertie	Sir G Richards
1954	**Aureole**, 4	C Boyd-Rochfort	E Smith
1955	**Vimy**, 3	A Head	R Poincelet
1956	**Ribot**, 4	V U Penco	E Camici
1957	**Montaval**, 4	G Bridgland	F Palmer
1958	**Ballymoss**, 4	M V O'Brien	A Breasley
1959	**Alcide**, 4	C Boyd-Rochfort	W H Carr
1960	**Aggressor**, 5	J Gosden	J Lindley
1961	**Right Royal**, 3	E Pollet	R Poincelet
1962	**Match**, 4	F Mathet	Y Saint-Martin
1963	**Ragusa**, 3	P J Prendergast	G Bougoure
1964	**Nasram**, 4	E Fellows	W Pyers
1965	**Meadow Court**, 3	P J Prendergast	L Piggott
1966	**Aunt Edith**, 4	C F N Murless	L Piggott
1967	**Busted**, 4	C F N Murless	G Moore
1968	**Royal Palace**, 4	C F N Murless	A Barclay
1969	**Park Top**, 5	B van Cutsem	L Piggott
1970	**Nijinsky**, 3	M V O'Brien	L Piggott
1971	**Mill Reef**, 3	I Balding	G Lewis
1972	**Brigadier Gerard**, 4	W R Hern	J Mercer
1973	**Dahlia**, 3	M Zilber	W Pyers
1974	**Dahlia**, 4	M Zilber	L Piggott
1975	**Grundy**, 3	P Walwyn	P Eddery
1976	**Pawneese**, 3	A Penna	Y Saint-Martin
1977	**The Minstrel**, 3	M V O'Brien	L Piggott
1978	**Ile de Bourbon**, 3	R F Johnson Houghton	J Reid
1979	**Troy**, 3	W R Hern	W Carson
1980	**Ela-Mana-Mou**, 4	W R Hern	W Carson
1981	**Shergar**, 3	M Stoute	W R Swinburn
1982	**Kalaglow**, 4	G Harwood	G Starkey
1983	**Time Charter**, 4	H Candy	J Mercer
1984	**Teenoso**, 4	G Wragg	L Piggott
1985	**Petoski**, 3	W R Hern	W Carson
1986	**Dancing Brave**, 3	G Harwood	P Eddery
1987	**Reference Point**, 3	H Cecil	S Cauthen
1988	**Mtoto**, 5	A Stewart	M Roberts
1989	**Nashwan**, 3	W R Hern	W Carson

Prix de l'Arc de Triomphe

At Longchamp, Bois de Boulogne, Paris. Weight-for-age, 3-year-olds and upwards. 2,400 metres (2,300 metres 1943–1944).

Year	Winner, age	Trainer	Jockey
1920	**Comrade**, 3	P P Gilpin	F Bullock
1921	**Ksar**, 3	W R Walton	G Stern
1922	**Ksar**, 4	W R Walton	F Bullock
1923	**Parth**, 3	J H Crawford	F O'Neill
1924	**Massine**, 4	E Cunnington	A Sharpe
1925	**Priori**, 3	P Carter	M Allemand
1926	**Biribi**, 3	J Torterolo	D Torterolo
1927	**Mon Talisman**, 3	F Carter	C H Semblat
1928	**Kantar**, 3	R Carver	A Esling
1929	**Ortello**, 3	W Carter	P Caprioli
1930	**Motrico**, 5	M d'Okhuysen	M Fruhinsholtz
1931	**Pearl Cap**, 3	F Carter	C H Semblat

Italian champion Tony Bin (John Reid) holds the fast-finishing Mtoto in the 1988 Prix de l'Arc de Triomphe. (Gerry Cranham)

Year	Winner, age	Trainer	Jockey
1932	**Motrico**, 7	M d'Okhuysen	C H Semblat
1933	**Crapom**, 3	F Regoli	P Caprioli
1934	**Brantôme**, 3	L Robert	C Bouillon
1935	**Samos**, 3	F Carter	W Sibbritt
1936	**Corrida**, 4	J E Watts	E C Elliott
1937	**Corrida**, 5	J E Watts	E C Elliott
1938	**Eclair au Chocolat**, 3	L Robert	C Bouillon
1939–1940 no race			
1941	**Le Pacha**, 3	J Cunnington	P Francolon
1942	**Djebel**, 5	C H Semblat	J Doyasbère
1943	**Verso**, 3	C Clout	G Duforez
1944	**Ardan**, 3	C H Semblat	J Doyasbère
1945	**Nikellora**, 3	R Pelat	W R Johnstone
1946	**Caracalla**, 4	C H Semblat	E C Elliott
1947	**Le Paillon**, 5	W Head	F Rochetti
1948	**Migoli**, 4	Frank Butters	C Smirke
1949	**Coronation**, 3	C H Semblat	R Poincelet
1950	**Tantième**, 3	F Mathet	J Doyasbère
1951	**Tantième**, 4	F Mathet	J Doyasbère
1952	**Nuccio**, 4	A Head	R Poincelet
1953	**La Sorellina**, 3	E Pollet	M Larraun
1954	**Sica Boy**, 3	P Pelat	W R Johnstone
1955	**Ribot**, 3	V U Penco	E Camici
1956	**Ribot**, 4	V U Penco	E Camici
1957	**Oroso**, 4	D Lescalle	S Boullenger
1958	**Ballymoss**, 4	M V O'Brien	A Breasley
1959	**Saint Crespin**, 3	A Head	G Moore
1960	**Puissant Chef**, 3	C W Bartholomew	M Garcia
1961	**Molvedo**, 3	A Maggi	E Camici
1962	**Soltikoff**, 3	R Pelat	M Depalmas
1963	**Exbury**, 4	G Watson	J Deforge
1964	**Prince Royal**, 3	G Bridgland	R Poincelet
1965	**Sea-Bird**, 3	E Pollet	T P Glennon
1966	**Bon Mot**, 3	W Head	F Head
1967	**Topyo**, 3	C W Bartholomew	W Pyers
1968	**Vaguely Noble**, 3	E Pollet	W Williamson
1969	**Levmoss**, 4	S McGrath	W Williamson

Year	Winner, age	Trainer	Jockey
1970	**Sassafras**, 3	F Mathet	Y Saint-Martin
1971	**Mill Reef**, 3	I Balding	G Lewis
1972	**San San**, 3	A Penna	F Head
1973	**Rheingold**, 4	B Hills	L Piggott
1974	**Allez France**, 4	A Penna	Y Saint-Martin
1975	**Star Appeal**, 5	T Grieper	G Starkey
1976	**Ivanjica**, 4	A Head	F Head
1977	**Alleged**, 3	M V O'Brien	L Piggott
1978	**Alleged**, 4	M V O'Brien	L Piggott
1979	**Three Troikas**, 3	Mme C Head	F Head
1980	**Detroit**, 3	O Douieb	P Eddery
1981	**Gold River**, 4	A Head	G W Moore
1982	**Akiyda**, 3	F Mathet	Y Saint-Martin
1983	**All Along**, 4	P Biancone	W R Swinburn
1984	**Sagace**, 4	P Biancone	Y Saint-Martin
1985	**Rainbow Quest**, 4	A J Tree	P Eddery
1986	**Dancing Brave**, 3	G Harwood	P Eddery
1987	**Trempolino**, 3	A Fabre	P Eddery
1988	**Tony Bin**, 5	L Camici	J Reid
1989	**Carroll House**, 4	M Jarvis	M Kinane

Irish Derby

At The Curragh, Newbridge, County Kildare. For 3-year-olds. 1 mile 4 furlongs.

Year	Winner	Trainer	Jockey
1866	**Selim**	—	C Maidment
1867	**Golden Plover**	—	C Maidment
1868	**Madeira**	—	D Wynne
1869	**The Scout**	—	W Miller
1870	**Billy Pitt**	T Connolly	W Canavan
1871	**Maid of Athens**	P Doucie	T Broderick
1872	**Trickstress**	W Miller	T Moran
1873	**Kyrle Daly**	P Doucie	T Broderick
1874	**Ben Battle**	T Connolly	E Martin
1875	**Innishowen**	J Toon	G Ashworth
1876	**Umpire**	J French	P Lynch
1877	**Redskin**	D Broderick	F Wynne
1878	**Madame Dubarry**	F Martin	F Wynne
1879	**Soulouque**	T Connolly	J Connolly
1880	**King of the Bees**	D Broderick	F Wynne
1881	**Master Ned**	P Doucie	T Broderick

Year	Winner	Trainer	Jockey
1882	**Sortie**	P Doucie	N Behan
1883	**Sylph**	J Dunne	J Connolly
1884	**Theologian**	W Behan	J Connolly
1885	**St Kevin**	J Dunne	H Saunders
1886	**Theodemir**	G Moore	J Connolly
1887	**Pet Fox**	H E Linde	T Kavanagh
1888	**Theodolite**	G Moore	W Warne
1889	**Tragedy**	T G Gordon	Mr T Beasley
1890	**Kentish Fire**	R Meredith	M Dawson
1891	**Narraghmore**	C Archer	Mr T Beasley
1892	**Roy Neil**	R Meredith	M Dawson
1893	**Bowline**	R Meredith	M Dawson
1894	**Blairfinde**	S Darling	W T Garrett
1895	**Portmarnock**	S C Jeffery	W Clayton
1896	**Gulsalberk**	S C Jeffery	A Aylin
1897	**Wales**	W P Cullen	T Fiely
1898	**Noble Howard**	R Exshaw	T Moran
1899	**Oppressor**	S C Jeffery	A Anthony
1900	**Gallinaria**	D McNally	Mr G W Lushington
1901	**Carrigavalla**	D McNally	A Anthony
1902	**St Brendan**	M Dawson	D Condon
1903	**Lord Rossmore**	J Fallon	J Dillon
1904	**Royal Arch**	M Dawson	F Morgan
1905	**Flax Park**	J Dunne	P Hughes
1906	**Killeagh**	M Dawson	C Aylin
1907	**Orby**	F F MacCabe	W Bullock
1908	**Wild Bouquet**	J Dunne	P Hughes
1909	**Bachelor's Double**	M Dawson	A Sharples
1910	**Aviator**	P Behan	John Doyle
1911	**Shanballymore**	J Dwyer	John Doyle
1912	**Civility**	B Kirby	D Maher
1913	**Bachelor's Wedding**	H S Persse	S Donoghue
1914	**Land of Song**	H S Persse	S Donoghue
1915	**Ballaghtobin**	J Hunter	W Barrett
1916	**Furore**	V Tabor	H Robbins
1917	**First Flier**	J J Parkinson	W Barrett
1918	**King John**	P P Gilpin	H Beasley
1919	**Loch Lomond**	J J.Parkinson	E M Quirke
1920	**He Goes**	J·Butters	F Templeman
1921	**Ballyheron**	J Hunter	M Wing
1922	**Spike Island**	P P Gilpin	G Archibald
1923	**Waygood**	W Halsey	M Wing
1924	{ **Haine**	C Davis	Jos Canty
	Zodiac	P P Gilpin	G Archibald
1925	**Zionist**	R C Dawson	H Beasley
1926	**Embargo**	C Bartholomew	S Donoghue
1927	**Knight of the Grail**	R J Farquharson	M Beary
1928	**Baytown**	N Scobie	F Fox
1929	**Kopi**	W Earl	F Winter
1930	**Rock Star**	W Nightingall	M Wing
1931	**Sea Serpent**	P Behan	Jos Canty
1932	**Dastur**	Frank Butters	M Beary
1933	**Harinero**	R C Dawson	C Ray
1934	{ **Primero**	R C Dawson	C Ray
	Patriot King	F C Pratt	G Bezant
1935	**Museum**	J T Rogers	S Donoghue
1936	**Raeburn**	J Lawson	T Burns
1937	**Phideas**	J T Rogers	S Donoghue
1938	**Rosewell**	A J Blake	M Wing
1939	**Mondragon**	Jas Canty	Jos Canty
1940	**Turkhan**	Frank Butters	C Smirke
1941	**Sol Oriens**	A J Blake	G Wells
1942	**Windsor Slipper**	M Collins	M Wing
1943	**The Phoenix**	F S Myerscough	Jos Canty
1944	**Slide On**	R Fetherstonhaugh	J Moylan
1945	**Piccadilly**	R Fetherstonhaugh	J Moylan
1946	**Bright News**	D Rogers	M Wing
1947	**Sayajirao**	F Armstrong	E Britt
1948	**Nathoo**	Frank Butters	W R Johnstone
1949	**Hindostan**	Frank Butters	W R Johnstone
1950	**Dark Warrior**	P J Prendergast	J W Thompson
1951	**Fraise du Bois**	H Wragg	C Smirke
1952	**Thirteen of Diamonds**	P J Prendergast	J Mullane
1953	**Chamier**	M V O'Brien	W Rickaby
1954	**Zarathustra**	M Hurley	P Powell, jr
1955	**Panaslipper**	S McGrath	J Eddery
1956	**Talgo**	H Wragg	E Mercer
1957	**Ballymoss**	M V O'Brien	T P Burns

Year	Winner	Trainer	Jockey
1958	**Sindon**	M Dawson	L Ward
1959	**Fidalgo**	H Wragg	J Mercer
1960	**Chamour**	A S O'Brien	G Bougoure
1961	**Your Highness**	H L Cottrill	Hbt Holmes
1962	**Tambourine**	E Pollet	R Poincelet
1963	**Ragusa**	P J Prendergast	G Bougoure
1964	**Santa Claus**	J M Rogers	W Burke
1965	**Meadow Court**	P J Prendergast	L Piggott
1966	**Sodium**	G Todd	F Durr
1967	**Ribocco**	R F Johnson Houghton	L Piggott
1968	**Ribero**	R F Johnson Houghton	L Piggott
1969	**Prince Regent**	E Pollet	G Lewis
1970	**Nijinsky**	M V O'Brien	L Ward
1971	**Irish Ball**	P Lallié	A Gibert
1972	**Steel Pulse**	A Breasley	W Williamson
1973	**Weavers' Hall**	S McGrath	G McGrath
1974	**English Prince**	P Walwyn	Y Saint-Martin
1975	**Grundy**	P Walwyn	P Eddery
1976	**Malacate**	F Boutin	P Paquet
1977	**The Minstrel**	M V O'Brien	L Piggott
1978	**Shirley Heights**	J Dunlop	G Starkey
1979	**Troy**	W R Hern	W Carson
1980	**Tyrnavos**	B Hobbs	A Murray
1981	**Shergar**	M Stoute	L Piggott
1982	**Assert**	D V O'Brien	C Roche
1983	**Shareef Dancer**	M Stoute	W R Swinburn
1984	**El Gran Senor**	M V O'Brien	P Eddery
1985	**Law Society**	M V O'Brien	P Eddery
1986	**Shahrastani**	M Stoute	W R Swinburn
1987	**Sir Harry Lewis**	B W Hills	J Reid
1988	**Kahyasi**	L Cumani	R Cochrane
1989	**Old Vic**	H Cecil	S Cauthen

US Triple Crown races

Kentucky Derby

At Churchill Downs, Louisville, Kentucky. For 3-year-olds. 1 mile 2 furlongs (1 mile 4 furlongs to 1895).

Year	Winner	Trainer	Jockey
1875	**Aristides**	A Anderson	O Lewis
1876	**Vagrant**	J Williams	R Swim
1877	**Baden Baden**	E Brown	W Walker
1878	**Day Star**	L Paul	J Carter
1879	**Lord Murphy**	G Rice	C Shauer
1880	**Fonso**	T Hutsell	G Lewis
1881	**Hindoo**	J Rowe	J McLaughlin
1882	**Apollo**	G B Morris	B Hurd
1883	**Leonatus**	J McGinty	W Donohoe
1884	**Buchanan**	W Bird	I Murphy
1885	**Joe Cotton**	A Perry	E Henderson
1886	**Ben Ali**	J Murphy	P Duffy
1887	**Montrose**	J McGinty	I Lewis
1888	**Macbeth**	J Campbell	G Covington
1889	**Spokane**	J Rodegap	T Kiley
1890	**Riley**	E Corrigan	I Murphy
1891	**Kingman**	D Allen	I Murphy
1892	**Azra**	J H Morris	A Clayton
1893	**Lookout**	W McDaniel	E Kunze
1894	**Chant**	E Leigh	F Goodale
1895	**Halma**	B McClelland	J Perkins
1896	**Ben Brush**	H Campbell	W Simms
1897	**Typhoon**	J C Cahn	F Garner
1898	**Plaudit**	J E Madden	W Simms
1899	**Manuel**	R J Walden	F Taral
1900	**Lieut. Gibson**	C H Hughes	J Boland
1901	**His Eminence**	F B Van Meter	J Winkfield
1902	**Alan-A-Dale**	T C McDowell	J Winkfield
1903	**Judge Himes**	J P Mayberry	H Booker
1904	**Elwood**	C E Durnell	F Prior
1905	**Agile**	R Tucker	J Martin
1906	**Sir Huon**	P Coyne	R Troxler
1907	**Pink Star**	W H Fizer	A Minder
1908	**Stone Street**	J W Hall	A Pickens
1909	**Wintergreen**	C Mack	V Powers

Year	Winner	Trainer	Jockey
1910	Donau	G Ham	F Herbert
1911	Meridian	A Ewing	G Archibald
1912	Worth	F M Taylor	C H Shilling
1913	Donerail	T P Hayes	R Goose
1914	Old Rosebud	F D Weir	J McCabe
1915	Regret	J Rowe	J Notter
1916	George Smith	H Hughes	J Loftus
1917	Omar Khayyam	C T Patterson	C Borel
1918	Exterminator	H McDaniel	W Knapp
1919	Sir Barton	H G Bedwell	J Loftus
1920	Paul Jones	W Garth	T Rice
1921	Behave Yourself	H J Thompson	C Thompson
1922	Morvich	F Burlew	A Johnson
1923	Zev	D J Leary	E Sande
1924	Black Gold	H Webb	J D Mooney
1925	Flying Ebony	W B Duke	E Sande
1926	Bubbling Over	H J Thompson	A Johnson
1927	Whiskery	F Hopkins	L McAtee
1928	Reigh Count	B S Michell	C Lang
1929	Clyde Van Dusen	C Van Dusen	L McAtee
1930	Gallant Fox	J Fitzsimmons	E Sande
1931	Twenty Grand	J Rowe, jr	C Kurtsinger
1932	Burgoo King	H J Thompson	E James
1933	Brokers Tip	H J Thompson	D Meade
1934	Cavalcade	R A Smith	M Garner
1935	Omaha	J Fitzsimmons	W Saunders
1936	Bold Venture	M Hirsch	I Hanford
1937	War Admiral	G Conway	C Kurtsinger
1938	Lawrin	B A Jones	E Arcaro
1939	Johnstown	J Fitzsimmons	J Stout
1940	Gallahadion	R Waldron	C Bierman
1941	Whirlaway	B A Jones	E Arcaro
1942	Shut Out	J M Gaver	W Wright
1943	Count Fleet	G D Cameron	J Longden
1944	Pensive	B A Jones	C McCreary
1945	Hoop Jr	I H Parke	E Arcaro
1946	Assault	M Hirsch	W Mehrtens
1947	Jet Pilot	T Smith	E Guerin
1948	Citation	B A Jones	E Arcaro
1949	Ponder	B A Jones	S Brooks
1950	Middleground	M Hirsch	W Boland
1951	Count Turf	S Rutchick	C McCreary
1952	Hill Gail	B A Jones	E Arcaro
1953	Dark Star	E Hayward	H Moreno
1954	Determine	W Molter	R York
1955	Swaps	M A Tenney	W Shoemaker
1956	Needles	H L Fontaine	D Erb
1957	Iron Liege	H A Jones	W Hartack
1958	Tim Tam	H A Jones	I Valenzuela
1959	Tomy Lee	F Childs	W Shoemaker
1960	Venetian Way	V J Sovinski	W Hartack
1961	Carry Back	J A Price	J Sellers
1962	Decidedly	H A Luro	W Hartack
1963	Chateaugay	J P Conway	B Baeza
1964	Northern Dancer	H A Luro	W Hartack
1965	Lucky Debonair	F Catrone	W Shoemaker
1966	Kauai King	H Forrest	D Brumfield
1967	Proud Clarion	L Gentry	R Ussery
1968	Forward Pass	H Forrest	I Valenzuela
1969	Majestic Prince	J Longden	W Hartack
1970	Dust Commander	D Combs	M Manganello
1971	Canonero	J Arias	G Avila
1972	Riva Ridge	L Laurin	R Turcotte
1973	Secretariat	L Laurin	R Turcotte
1974	Cannonade	W C Stephens	A Cordero
1975	Foolish Pleasure	L Jolley	J Vasquez
1976	Bold Forbes	L S Barrera	A Cordero
1977	Seattle Slew	W H Turner	J Cruguet
1978	Affirmed	L S Barrera	S Cauthen
1979	Spectacular Bid	G G Delp	R J Franklin
1980	Genuine Risk	L Jolley	J Vasquez
1981	Pleasant Colony	J P Campo	J Velasquez
1982	Gato Del Sol	E Gregson	E Delahoussaye
1983	Sunny's Halo	D C Cross	E Delahoussaye
1984	Swale	W C Stephens	L Pincay
1985	Spend a Buck	C Gambolati	A Cordero
1986	Ferdinand	C Whittingham	W Shoemaker
1987	Alysheba	J C Van Berg	C McCarron
1988	Winning Colors	D W Lukas	G Stevens
1989	Sunday Silence	C Whittingham	P Valenzuela

Preakness Stakes

At Pimlico, Baltimore, Maryland. For 3-year-olds. 1 mile 1½ furlongs (1 mile 4 furlongs to 1888; 1 mile 2 furlongs 1889; 1 mile 110 yards 1894–1900 and 1908; 1 mile 70 yards 1901–1907; 1 mile 1909–1910; 1 mile 1 furlong 1911–1924).

Year	Winner	Trainer	Jockey
1873	Survivor	A D Pryor	G Barbee
1874	Culpepper	H Gaffney	M Donohue
1875	Tom Ochiltree	R W Walden	L Hughes
1876	Shirley	W Brown	G Barbee
1877	Cloverbrook	J Walden	C Holloway
1878	Duke of Magenta	R W Walden	C Holloway
1879	Harold	R W Walden	L Hughes
1880	Grenada	R W Walden	L Hughes
1881	Saunterer	R W Walden	T Costello
1882	Vanguard	R W Walden	T Costello
1883	Jacobus	R Dwyer	G Barbee
1884	Knight of Ellerslie	T B Doswell	S Fisher
1885	Tecumseh	C Littlefield	J McLaughlin
1886	The Bard	J Huggins	S Fisher
1887	Dunboyne	W Jennings	W Donohue
1888	Refund	R W Walden	F Littlefield
1889	Buddhist	J Rogers	W Anderson
1890–1893 no race			
1894	Assignee	W Lakeland	F Taral
1895	Belmar	E Feakes	F Taral
1896	Margrave	B McClelland	H Griffin
1897	Paul Kauvar	T P Hayes	C Thorpe
1898	Sly Fox	H Campbell	W Simms
1899	Half Time	F McCabe	R Clawson
1900	Hindus	J H Morris	H Spencer
1901	The Parader	T J Healey	F Landry
1902	Old England	G B Morris	L Jackson
1903	Flocarline	H C Riddle	W Gannon
1904	Bryn Mawr	W F Presgrave	E Hildebrand
1905	Cairngorm	A J Joyner	W Davis
1906	Whimsical	T J Gaynor	W Miller
1907	Don Enrique	J Whalen	G Mountain
1908	Royal Tourist	A J Joyner	E Dugan
1909	Effendi	F C Frisbee	W Doyle
1910	Layminster	J S Healy	R Estep
1911	Watervale	J Whalen	E Dugan
1912	Colonel Holloway	D Woodford	C Turner
1913	Buskin	J Whalen	J Butwell
1914	Holiday	J S Healy	A Schuttinger
1915	Rhine Maiden	F Devers	D Hoffman
1916	Damrosch	A G Weston	L McAtee
1917	Kalitan	W J Hurley	E Haynes
1918*	War Cloud	W B Jennings	J Loftus
	Jack Hare, Jr	F D Weir	C Peak
1919	Sir Barton	H G Bedwell	J Loftus
1920	Man o' War	L Feustel	C Kummer
1921	Broomspun	J Rowe	F Coltiletti
1922	Pillory	T J Healey	L Morris
1923	Vigil	T J Healey	B Marinelli
1924	Nellie Morse	A B Gordon	J Merimee
1925	Coventry	W B Duke	C Kummer
1926	Display	T J Healey	J Maiben
1927	Bostonian	F Hopkins	A Abel
1928	Victorian	J Rowe, jr	R Workman
1929	Dr Freeland	T J Healey	L Schaefer
1930	Gallant Fox	J Fitzsimmons	E Sande
1931	Mate	J W Healey	G Ellis
1932	Burgoo King	H J Thompson	E James
1933	Head Play	T P Hayes	C Kurtsinger
1934	High Quest	R A Smith	R Jones
1935	Omaha	J Fitzsimmons	W Saunders
1936	Bold Venture	M Hirsch	G Woolf
1937	War Admiral	G Conway	C Kurtsinger
1938	Dauber	R E Handlen	M Peters
1939	Challedon	L Schaefer	G Seabo
1940	Bimelech	W J Hurley	F A Smith
1941	Whirlaway	B A Jones	E Arcaro
1942	Alsab	A Swenke	B James
1943	Count Fleet	G D Cameron	J Longden
1944	Pensive	B A Jones	C McCreary

Year	Winner	Trainer	Jockey
1945	**Polynesian**	M Dixon	W D Wright
1946	**Assault**	M Hirsch	W Mehrtens
1947	**Faultless**	H A Jones	D Dodson
1948	**Citation**	H A Jones	E Arcaro
1949	**Capot**	J M Gaver	T Atkinson
1950	**Hill Prince**	J H Hayes	E Arcaro
1951	**Bold**	P M Burch	E Arcaro
1952	**Blue Man**	W C Stephens	C McCreary
1953	**Native Dancer**	W C Winfrey	E Guerin
1954	**Hasty Road**	H Trotsek	J Adams
1955	**Nashua**	J Fitzsimmons	E Arcaro
1956	**Fabius**	H A Jones	W Hartack
1957	**Bold Ruler**	J Fitzsimmons	E Arcaro
1958	**Tim Tam**	H A Jones	I Valenzuela
1959	**Royal Orbit**	R Cornell	W Harmatz
1960	**Bally Ache**	H J Pitt	R Ussery
1961	**Carry Back**	J A Price	J Sellers
1962	**Greek Money**	V W Raines	J Rotz
1963	**Candy Spots**	M A Tenney	W Shoemaker
1964	**Northern Dancer**	H A Luro	W Hartack
1965	**Tom Rolfe**	F Y Whiteley	R Turcotte
1966	**Kauai King**	H Forrest	D Brumfield
1967	**Damascus**	F Y Whiteley	W Shoemaker
1968	**Forward Pass**	H Forrest	I Valenzuela
1969	**Majestic Prince**	J Longden	W Hartack
1970	**Personality**	J W Jacobs	E Belmonte
1971	**Canonero**	J Arias	G Avila
1972	**Bee Bee Bee**	D W Carroll	E Nelson
1973	**Secretariat**	L Laurin	R Turcotte
1974	**Little Current**	L Rondinello	M Rivera
1975	**Master Derby**	W E Adams	D McHargue
1976	**Elocutionist**	P T Adwell	J Lively
1977	**Seattle Slew**	W H Turner	J Cruguet
1978	**Affirmed**	L S Barrera	S Cauthen
1979	**Spectacular Bid**	G G Delp	R Franklin
1980	**Codex**	D W Lukas	A Cordero
1981	**Pleasant Colony**	J P Campo	J Velasquez
1982	**Aloma's Ruler**	J J Lenzini	J Kaenel
1983	**Deputed Testamony**	W J Boniface	D Miller
1984	**Gate Dancer**	J C Van Berg	A Cordero
1985	**Tank's Prospect**	D W Lukas	P Day
1986	**Snow Chief**	M Stute	A Solis
1987	**Alysheba**	J C Van Berg	C McCarron
1988	**Risen Star**	L Roussel	E Delahoussaye
1989	**Sunday Silence**	C Whittingham	P Valenzuela

* Run in 2 divisions in 1918.

Belmont Stakes

At Belmont Park, Elmont, New York. 1 mile 4 furlongs (1 mile 5 furlongs 1867–1873; 1 mile 2 furlongs 1892–1895, 1904–1905; 1 mile 1 furlong 1893–1894; 1 mile 3 furlongs 1896–1903, 1906–1910, 1913–1925).

Year	Winner	Trainer	Jockey
1867	**Ruthless**	A J Minor	J Gilpatrick
1868	**General Duke**	A Thompson	R Swim
1869	**Fenian**	J Pincus	C Miller
1870	**Kingfisher**	R Colston	E Brown
1871	**Harry Bassett**	D McDaniel	W Miller
1872	**Joe Daniels**	D McDaniel	J Rowe
1873	**Springbok**	D McDaniel	J Rowe
1874	**Saxon**	W Prior	G Barbee
1875	**Calvin**	A Anderson	R Swim
1876	**Algerine**	T W Doswell	W Donohue
1877	**Cloverbrook**	J Walden	C Holloway
1878	**Duke of Magenta**	R W Walden	W Hughes
1879	**Spendthrift**	T Puryear	G Evans
1880	**Grenada**	R W Walden	T Costello
1881	**Saunterer**	R W Walden	T Costello
1882	**Forester**	L Stuart	J McLaughlin
1883	**George Kinney**	J Rowe	J McLaughlin
1884	**Panique**	J Rowe	J McLaughlin
1885	**Tyrant**	C Claypool	P Duffy
1886	**Inspector B.**	F McCabe	J McLaughlin
1887	**Hanover**	F McCabe	J McLaughlin
1888	**Sir Dixon**	F McCabe	J McLaughlin
1889	**Eric**	J Huggins	W Hayward
1890	**Burlington**	A Cooper	S Barnes
1891	**Foxford**	M Donovan	E Garrison
1892	**Patron**	L Stuart	W Hayward
1893	**Comanche**	G Hannon	W Simms
1894	**Henry of Navarre**	B McClelland	W Simms
1895	**Belmar**	E Feakes	F Taral
1896	**Hastings**	J J Hyland	H Griffin
1897	**Scottish Chieftain**	M Byrnes	J Scherrer
1898	**Bowling Brook**	R W Walden	F Littlefield
1899	**Jean Bereaud**	S C Hildreth	R Clawson
1900	**Ildrim**	H E Leigh	N Turner
1901	**Commando**	J Rowe	H Spencer
1902	**Masterman**	J J Hyland	J Bullman
1903	**Africander**	R O Miller	J Bullman
1904	**Delhi**	J Rowe	G Odom
1905	**Tanya**	J W Rogers	E Hildebrand
1906	**Burgomaster**	J W Rogers	L Lyne
1907	**Peter Pan**	J Rowe	G Mountain
1908	**Colin**	J Rowe	J Notter
1909	**Joe Madden**	S C Hildreth	E Dugan
1910	**Sweep**	J Rowe	J Butwell
1911–1912 no race			
1913	**Prince Eugene**	J Rowe	R Troxler
1914	**Luke McLuke**	J F Schorr	M Buxton
1915	**The Finn**	E W Heffner	G Byrne
1916	**Friar Rock**	S C Hildreth	E Haynes
1917	**Hourless**	S C Hildreth	J Butwell
1918	**Johren**	A Simons	F Robinson
1919	**Sir Barton**	H G Bedwell	J Loftus
1920	**Man o' War**	L Feustel	C Kummer
1921	**Grey Lag**	S C Hildreth	E Sande
1922	**Pillory**	T J Healey	C H Miller
1923	**Zev**	S C Hildreth	E Sande
1924	**Mad Play**	S C Hildreth	E Sande
1925	**American Flag**	G R Tompkins	A Johnson
1926	**Crusader**	G Conway	A Johnson
1927	**Chance Shot**	P Coyne	E Sande
1928	**Vito**	M Hirsch	C Kummer
1929	**Blue Larkspur**	C Hastings	M Garner
1930	**Gallant Fox**	J Fitzsimmons	E Sande
1931	**Twenty Grand**	J Rowe, jr	C Kurtsinger
1932	**Faireno**	J Fitzsimmons	T Malley
1933	**Hurryoff**	H McDaniel	M Garner
1934	**Peace Chance**	P Coyne	W D Wright
1935	**Omaha**	J Fitzsimmons	W Saunders
1936	**Granville**	J Fitzsimmons	J Stout
1937	**War Admiral**	G Conway	C Kurtsinger
1938	**Pasteurized**	G Odom	J Stout
1939	**Johnstown**	J Fitzsimmons	J Stout
1940	**Bimelech**	W J Hurley	F A Smith
1941	**Whirlaway**	B A Jones	E Arcaro
1942	**Shut Out**	J M Gaver	E Arcaro
1943	**Count Fleet**	G D Cameron	J Longden
1944	**Bounding Home**	M Brady	G L Smith
1945	**Pavot**	O White	E Arcaro
1946	**Assault**	M Hirsch	W Mehrtens
1947	**Phalanx**	S E Veitch	R Donoso
1948	**Citation**	H A Jones	E Arcaro
1949	**Capot**	J M Gaver	T Atkinson
1950	**Middleground**	M Hirsch	W Boland
1951	**Counterpoint**	S E Veitch	D Gorman
1952	**One Count**	O White	E Arcaro
1953	**Native Dancer**	W C Winfrey	E Guerin
1954	**High Gun**	M Hirsch	E Guerin
1955	**Nashua**	J Fitzsimmons	E Arcaro
1956	**Needles**	H L Fontaine	D Erb
1957	**Gallant Man**	J A Nerud	W Shoemaker
1958	**Cavan**	T J Barry	P Anderson
1959	**Sword Dancer**	J E Burch	W Shoemaker
1960	**Celtic Ash**	T J Barry	W Hartack
1961	**Sherluck**	H Young	B Baeza
1962	**Jaipur**	W F Mulholland	W Shoemaker
1963	**Chateaugay**	J P Conway	B Baeza
1964	**Quadrangle**	J E Burch	M Ycaza
1965	**Hail to All**	E Yowell	J Sellers
1966	**Amberoid**	L Laurin	W Boland
1967	**Damascus**	F Y Whiteley	W Shoemaker
1968	**Stage Door Johnny**	J M Gaver	H Gustines
1969	**Arts and Letters**	J E Burch	B Baeza

Year	Winner	Trainer	Jockey
1970	**High Echelon**	J W Jacobs	J L Rotz
1971	**Pass Catcher**	E Yowell	W Blum
1972	**Riva Ridge**	L Laurin	R Turcotte
1973	**Secretariat**	L Laurin	R Turcotte
1974	**Little Current**	L Rondinello	M Rivera
1975	**Avatar**	A T Doyle	W Shoemaker
1976	**Bold Forbes**	L S Barrera	A Cordero
1977	**Seattle Slew**	W H Turner	J Cruguet
1978	**Affirmed**	L S Barrera	S Cauthen
1979	**Coastal**	D A Whiteley	R Hernandez
1980	**Temperence Hill**	J B Cantey	E Maple
1981	**Summing**	L Barrera	G Martens
1982	**Conquistador Cielo**	W C Stephens	L Pincay
1983	**Caveat**	W C Stephens	L Pincay
1984	**Swale**	W C Stephens	L Pincay
1985	**Creme Fraiche**	W C Stephens	E Maple
1986	**Danzig Connection**	W C Stephens	C McCarron
1987	**Bet Twice**	W A Croll	C Perret
1988	**Risen Star**	L Roussel	E Delahoussaye
1989	**Easy Goer**	C McGaughey	P Day

Arlington Million

At Arlington Park, Chicago, Illinois (at Woodbine, Toronto in 1988). Weight-for-age, 3-year-olds and upwards.

Year	Winner, age	Trainer	Jockey
1981	**John Henry**, 6	R McAnally	W Shoemaker
1982	**Perrault**, 5	C Whittingham	L Pincay
1983	**Tolomeo**, 3	L Cumani	P Eddery
1984	**John Henry**, 9	R McAnally	C McCarron
1985	**Teleprompter**, 5	J W Watts	T Ives
1986	**Estrapade**, 6	C Whittingham	F Toro
1987	**Manila**, 4	L Jolley	A Cordero
1988	**Mill Native**, 4	A Fabre	C Asmussen
1989	**Steinlen**, 6	D W Lukas	J A Santos

Breeders' Cup races

A series of international quasi-championship events, staged in the United States every November. Flat races run in 1984 and 1987 at Hollywood Park, Inglewood, California; in 1985 at Aqueduct, Jamaica, New York; in 1986 at Santa Anita Park, Arcadia, California; in 1988 at Churchill Downs, Louisville, Kentucky; and in 1989 at Gulfstream Park, Miami, Florida. The steeplechase event has been run at Fair Hill, Maryland, from 1986 to 1988, and at Far Hills, New Jersey, in 1989.

Juvenile Stakes

For 2-year-old colts and geldings. 1 mile 110 yards.

	Winner	Trainer	Jockey
1984	**Chief's Crown**	R Laurin	D MacBeth
1985	**Tasso**	N Drysdale	L Pincay
1986	**Capote**	D W Lukas	L Pincay
1987	**Success Express**	D W Lukas	J A Santos
1988	**Is It True**	D W Lukas	L Pincay
1989	**Rhythm**	C McGaughey	C Perret

Juvenile Fillies Stakes

For 2-year-old fillies. 1 mile 110 yards.

	Winner	Trainer	Jockey
1984	**Outstandingly**	F Martin	W Guerra
1985	**Twilight Ridge**	D W Lukas	J Velasquez
1986	**Brave Raj**	M Stute	P Valenzuela
1987	**Epitome**	P Hauswald	P Day
1988	**Open Mind**	D W Lukas	A Cordero
1989	**Go for Wand**	W Badgett	R Romero

Sprint Stakes

For 3-year-olds and upwards. 6 furlongs.

	Winner, age	Trainer	Jockey
1984	**Eillo**, 4	B Lepman	C Perret
1985	**Precisionist**, 4	L Fenstermaker	C McCarron
1986	**Smile**, 4	F S Schulhofer	J Vasquez
1987	**Very Subtle**, 3	M Stute	P Valenzuela
1988	**Gulch**, 4	D W Lukas	A Cordero
1989	**Dancing Spree**, 4	C McGaughey	A Cordero

Mile Stakes

For 3-year-olds and upwards. 1 mile on grass.

	Winner, age	Trainer	Jockey
1984	**Royal Heroine**, 4	J Gosden	F Toro
1985	**Cozzene**, 5	J H Nerud	W Guerra
1986	**Last Tycoon**, 3	R Collet	Y Saint-Martin
1987	**Miesque**, 3	F Boutin	F Head
1988	**Miesque**, 4	F Boutin	F Head
1989	**Steinlen**, 6	D W Lukas	J A Santos

Distaff Stakes

For fillies, 3-year-olds and upwards. 1 mile 1 furlong (1 mile 2 furlongs 1984–87).

	Winner, age	Trainer	Jockey
1984	**Princess Rooney**, 4	N Drysdale	E Delahoussaye
1985	**Life's Magic**, 4	D W Lukas	A Cordero
1986	**Lady's Secret**, 4	D W Lukas	P Day
1987	**Sacahuista**, 3	D W Lukas	R Romero
1988	**Personal Ensign**, 4	C McGaughey	R Romero
1989	**Bayakoa**, 5	R McAnally	L Pincay

Turf Stakes

For 3-year-olds and upwards. 1 mile 4 furlongs on grass.

	Winner, age	Trainer	Jockey
1984	**Lashkari**, 3	A de Royer-Dupré	Y Saint-Martin
1985	**Pebbles**, 4	C Brittain	P Eddery
1986	**Manila**, 3	L Jolley	J A Santos
1987	**Theatrical**, 5	W Mott	P Day
1988	**Great Communicator**, 5	T Ackel	R Sibille
1989	**Prized**, 3	N Drysdale	E Delahoussaye

Open Mind (Angel Cordero) wins the 1988 Breeders' Cup Juvenile Fillies. The following year she landed the Triple Tiara, America's version of the fillies' Triple Crown. (All-Sport)

Classic Stakes

For 3-year-olds and upwards. 1 mile 2 furlongs.

	Winner, age	Trainer	Jockey
1984	**Wild Again**, 4	V Timphony	P Day
1985	**Proud Truth**, 3	J M Veitch	J Velasquez
1986	**Skywalker**, 4	M Whittingham	L Pincay
1987	**Ferdinand**, 4	C Whittingham	W Shoemaker
1988	**Alysheba**, 4	J C Van Berg	C McCarron
1989	**Sunday Silence**, 3	C Whittingham	C McCarron

Steeplechase Stakes

For 3-year-olds and upwards. Steeplechase over 16 fences. 2 miles 5 furlongs on grass (2 miles 3 furlongs in 1986).

	Winner, age	Trainer	Jockey
1986	**Census**, 8	Janet Elliot	J Teter
1987	**Gacko**, 6	X Guignand	R Duchene
1988	**Jimmy Lorenzo**, 6	J Sheppard	G McCourt
1989	**Highland Bud**, 4	J Sheppard	R Dunwoody

W S Cox Plate

At Moonee Valley, Melbourne, Victoria, Australia. Weight-for-age, 3-year-olds and upwards. 2,050 metres (1 mile 1½ furlongs to 1942, 1 mile 2 furlongs 1943–1971, 2,000 metres 1972–73).

Year	Winner, age	Trainer	Jockey
1922	**Violoncello**, 6	C H Bryans	J King
1923	**Easingwold**, 5	J Holt	G Harrison
1924	**The Night Patrol**, 7	J Scobie	G Young
1925	**Manfred**, 3	H McCalman	F Dempsey
1926	**Heroic**, 5	J Holt	H Cairns
1927	**Amounis**, 5	F McGrath	J Toohey
1928	**Highland**, 7	J Holt	W Duncan
1929	**Nightmarch**, 4	A McAulay	R Reed
1930	**Phar Lap**, 4	H R Telford	J Pike
1931	**Phar Lap**, 5	H R Telford	J Pike
1932	**Chatham**, 4	F Williams	J Munro
1933	**Rogilla**, 6	L Haigh	D Munro
1934	**Chatham**, 6	F Williams	S Davidson
1935	**Garrio**, 3	L Robertson	K Voitre
1936	**Young Idea**, 4	J Holt	H Skidmore
1937	**Young Idea**, 5	J Holt	D Munro
1938	**Ajax**, 4	F Musgrave	H Badger
1939	**Mosaic**, 4	J H Abbs	D Munro
1940	**Beau Vite**, 4	F McGrath	E McMenamin
1941	**Beau Vite**, 5	F McGrath	D Munro
1942	**Tranquil Star**, 5	R Cameron	K Smith
1943	**Amana**, 4	R J Shaw	A Dewhurst
1944	**Tranquil Star**, 7	R Cameron	A Breasley
1945	**Flight**, 5	F Nowland	J O'Sullivan
1946*	**Flight**, 6	F Nowland	J O'Sullivan
	Leonard, 4	L Robertson	W Briscoe
1947	**Chanak**, 3	J Holt	H Badger
1948	**Carbon Copy**, 3	D S McCormick	H Badger
1949	**Delta**, 3	M McCarten	N Sellwood
1950	**Alister**, 3	H Wolters	J Purtell
1951	**Bronton**, 3	R Sinclair	J Purtell
1952	**Hydrogen**, 4	E Hush	D Munro
1953	**Hydrogen**, 5	E Hush	W Williamson
1954	**Rising Fast**, 5	I J Tucker	J Purtell
1955	**Kingster**, 3	J Green	W Camer
1956	**Ray Ribbon**, 5	G S Barr	J Purtell
1957	**Redcraze**, 7	T J Smith	G Moore
1958	**Yeman**, 6	H Wiggins	L Whittle
1959	**Noholme**, 3	M McCarten	N Sellwood
1960	**Tulloch**, 6	T J Smith	N Sellwood
1961	**Dhaulagiri**, 5	B Courtney	G Lane
1962	**Aquanita**, 6	R J Shaw	F Moore
1963	**Summer Regent**, 5	R T Cotter	N Riordan
1964	**Sir Dane**, 4	R J Shaw	R Higgins

Year	Winner, age	Trainer	Jockey
1965	**Star Affair**, 3	A Armanasco	P Hyland
1966	**Tobin Bronze**, 4	H G Heagney	J Johnson
1967	**Tobin Bronze**, 5	H G Heagney	J Johnson
1968	**Rajah Sahib**, 3	T W Hill	G Moore
1969	**Daryl's Joy**, 3	S A Brown	W D Skelton
1970	**Abdul**, 3	G T Murphy	P Jarman
1971	**Tauto**, 6	R Agnew	L Hill
1972	**Gunsynd**, 5	T J Smith	R Higgins
1973	**Taj Rossi**, 3	J B Cummings	S Aitken
1974	**Battle Heights**, 7	R T Douglas	G Willetts
1975	**Fury's Order**, 5	L J Gestro & W McEwan	B Thomson
1976	**Surround**, 3	G T Murphy	P Cook
1977	**Family of Man**, 4	G M Hanlon	B Thomson
1978	**So Called**, 4	C S Hayes	B Thomson
1979	**Dulcify**, 4	C S Hayes	B Thomson
1980	**Kingston Town**, 4	T J Smith	M Johnston
1981	**Kingston Town**, 5	T J Smith	R Quinton
1982	**Kingston Town**, 6	T J Smith	P Cook
1983	**Strawberry Road**, 4	D R Bougoure	L Dittman
1984	**Red Anchor**, 3	T J Smith	L Dittman
1985	**Rising Prince**, 5	Mrs D L Stein	K Langby
1986	**Bonecrusher**, 4	F T Richie	G Stewart
1987	**Rubiton**, 4	P C Barns	H White
1988	**Poetic Prince**, 4	J R Wheeler	N Harris
1989	**Almaarad**, 7	C Hayes	M Clarke

* Run in 2 divisions in 1946.

Melbourne Cup

At Flemington, Melbourne, Victoria, Australia. Handicap for 3-year-olds and upwards. 3,200 metres (2 miles to 1971).

Year	Winner, age, weight	Trainer	Jockey
1861	**Archer**, 5, 9st 7lb	E de Mestre	J Cutts
1862	**Archer**, 6, 10st 2lb	E de Mestre	J Cutts
1863	**Banker**, 3, 5st 4lb	S Waldock	H Chifney
1864	**Lantern**, 3, 6st 3lb	S Mahon	S Davis
1865	**Toryboy**, 8, 7st 0lb	P Miley	E Cavanagh
1866	**The Barb**, 3, 6st 11lb	J Tait	W Davis
1867	**Tim Whiffler**, 5, 8st 11lb	E de Mestre	J Driscoll
1868	**Glencoe**, 4, 9st 1lb	J Tait	C Stanley
1869	**Warrior**, 6, 8st 10lb	R Sevoir	J Morrison
1870	**Nimblefoot**, 7, 6st 3lb	W Lang	J Day
1871	**The Pearl**, 5, 7st 3lb	J Tait	J Cavanagh
1872	**The Quack**, 6, 7st 10lb	J Tait	W Enderson
1873	**Don Juan**, 4, 6st 12lb	J Wilson	W Wilson
1874	**Haricot**, 4, 6st 7lb	S Harding	P Piggott
1875	**Wollomai**, 6, 7st 8lb	S Moon	R Batty
1876	**Briseis**, 3, 6st 4lb	J Wilson	P St Albans
1877	**Chester**, 3, 6st 12lb	E de Mestre	P Piggott
1878	**Calamia**, 5, 8st 2lb	E de Mestre	T Brown
1879	**Darriwell**, 5, 7st 4lb	W E Dakin	S Cracknell
1880	**Grand Flaneur**, 3, 6st 10lb	T Brown	T Hales
1881	**Zulu**, 4, 5st 10lb	T Lamond	James Gough
1882	**The Assyrian**, 5, 7st 13lb	J E Savill	C Hutchens
1883	**Martini Henry**, 3, 7st 5lb	M Fennell	Williamson
1884	**Malua**, 5, 9st 9lb	I Foulsham	A Robertson
1885	**Sheet Anchor**, 7, 7st 11lb	T Wilson	M O'Brien
1886	**Arsenal**, 4, 7st 5lb	H Rayner	W English
1887	**Dunlop**, 5, 8st 3lb	J Nicholson	T Sanders
1888	**Mentor**, 4, 8st 3lb	W S Hickenbotham	M O'Brien
1889	**Bravo**, 6, 8st 7lb	T Wilson	J Anwin
1890	**Carbine**, 5, 10st 5lb	W S Hickenbotham	R Ramage
1891	**Malvolio**, 4, 8st 4lb	J Redfearn	G Redfearn
1892	**Glenloth**, 5, 7st 13lb	M Carmody	G Robson
1893	**Tarcoola**, 7, 8st 4lb	J Cripps	H Cripps
1894	**Patron**, 4, 9st 3lb	R Bradfield	H Dawes
1895	**Auraria**, 3, 7st 4lb	J H Hill	J Stevenson
1896	**Newhaven**, 3, 7st 13lb	W S Hickenbotham	H J Gardiner
1897	**Gaulus**, 6, 7st 8lb	W Forrester	S Callinan
1898	**The Grafter**, 5, 9st 2lb	W Forrester	John Gough
1899	**Merriwee**, 3, 7st 6lb	J Wilson, jr	V Turner
1900	**Clean Sweep**, 3, 7st 0lb	J Scobie	A Richardson
1901	**Revenue**, 5, 7st 10lb	H Munro	F Dunn
1902	**The Victory**, 4, 8st 12lb	R Bradfield	R Lewis
1903	**Lord Cardigan**, 3, 6st 8lb	A E Cornwell	N D Godby

Year	Winner, age, weight	Trainer	Jockey
1904	**Acrasia**, 7, 7st 6lb	A E Wills	T Clayton
1905	**Blue Spec**, 6, 8st 0lb	W S Hickenbotham	F Bullock
1906	**Poseidon**, 3, 7st 6lb	I Earnshaw	T Clayton
1907	**Apologue**, 5, 7st 9lb	I Earnshaw	W Evans
1908	**Lord Nolan**, 3, 6st 10lb	E A Mayo	J Flynn
1909	**Prince Foote**, 3, 7st 8lb	F McGrath	W H McLachlan
1910	**Comedy King**, 4, 7st 11lb	J Lynch	W H McLachlan
1911	**The Parisian**, 6, 8st 9lb	C Wheeler	R Cameron
1912	**Piastre**, 4, 7st 9lb	R O'Connor	A Shanahan
1913	**Posinatus**, 5, 7st 10lb	J Chambers	A Shanahan
1914	**Kingsburgh**, 4, 6st 12lb	I Foulsham	G Meddick
1915	**Patrobas**, 3, 7st 6lb	C Wheeler	R Lewis
1916	**Sasanof**, 3, 6st 12lb	M Hobbs	F Foley
1917	**Westcourt**, 5, 8st 5lb	J Burton	W H McLachlan
1918	**Night Watch**, 5, 6st 9lb	R Bradfield	W Duncan
1919	**Artilleryman**, 3, 7st 6lb	P T Heywood	R Lewis
1920	**Poitrel**, 6, 10st 0lb	H J Robinson	K Bracken
1921	**Sister Olive**, 3, 6st 9lb	J Williams	E O'Sullivan
1922	**King Ingoda**, 4, 7st 1lb	J Scobie	A Wilson
1923	**Bitalli**, 5, 7st 0lb	J Scobie	A Wilson
1924	**Backwood**, 6, 8st 2lb	R Bradfield	P Brown
1925	**Windbag**, 4, 9st 2lb	G Price	J Munro
1926	**Spearfelt**, 5, 9st 3lb	V O'Neill	H Cairns
1927	**Trivalve**, 3, 7st 6lb	J Scobie	R Lewis
1928	**Statesman**, 4, 8st 0lb	W Kelso	J Munro
1929	**Nightmarch**, 4, 9st 2lb	A McAulay	R Reed
1930	**Phar Lap**, 4, 9st 12lb	H R Telford	J E Pike
1931	**White Nose**, 5, 6st 12lb	E J Hatwell	N Percival
1932	**Peter Pan**, 3, 7st 6lb	F McGrath	W Duncan
1933	**Hall Mark**, 3, 7st 8lb	J Holt	J O'Sullivan
1934	**Peter Pan**, 5, 9st 10lb	F McGrath	D Munro
1935	**Marabou**, 4, 7st 11lb	L Robertson	K Voitre
1936	**Wotan**, 4, 7st 11lb	J Fryer	O Phillips
1937	**The Trump**, 5, 8st 5lb	S W Reid	A Reed
1938	**Catalogue**, 8, 8st 4lb	A W McDonald	F Shean
1939	**Rivette**, 6, 7st 9lb	H Bamber	E Preston
1940	**Old Rowley**, 7, 7st 12lb	J A Scully	A Knox
1941	**Skipton**, 3, 7st 7lb	J Fryer	W Cook
1942	**Colonus**, 4, 7st 2lb	F Manning	H McCloud

Year	Winner, age, weight	Trainer	Jockey
1943	**Dark Felt**, 6, 8st 4lb	R Webster	V Hartney
1944	**Sirius**, 4, 8st 5lb	E Fisher	D Munro
1945	**Rainbird**, 4, 7st 7lb	S Evans	W Cook
1946	**Russia**, 6, 9st 0lb	E Hush	D Munro
1947	**Hiraji**, 4, 7st 11lb	J W McCurley	J Purtell
1948	**Rimfire**, 6, 7st 2lb	S Boyden	R Neville
1949	**Foxzami**, 4, 8st 8lb	D Lewis	W Fellows
1950	**Comic Court**, 5, 9st 5lb	J M Cummings	T P Glennon
1951	**Delta**, 5, 9st 5lb	M McCarten	N Sellwood
1952	**Dalray**, 4, 9st 8lb	C C McCarthy	W Williamson
1953	**Wodalla**, 4, 8st 4lb	R Sinclair	J Purtell
1954	**Rising Fast**, 5, 9st 5lb	I J Tucker	J Purtell
1955	**Toparoa**, 7, 7st 8lb	T J Smith	N Sellwood
1956	**Evening Peal**, 4, 8st 0lb	E D Lawson	G Podmore
1957	**Straight Draw**, 5, 8st 5lb	J M Mitchell	N McGrowdie
1958	**Baystone**, 6, 8st 9lb	J Green	M Schumacher
1959	**MacDougal**, 6, 8st 11lb	R W Roden	T P Glennon
1960	**Hi Jinx**, 5, 7st 10lb	T H Knowles	W A Smith
1961	**Lord Fury**, 4, 7st 8lb	F B Lewis	R Selkrig
1962	**Even Stevens**, 5, 8st 5lb	A McGregor	L Coles
1963	**Gatum Gatum**, 5, 7st 12lb	H G Heagney	J Johnson
1964	**Polo Prince**, 6, 8st 3lb	J P Carter	R W Taylor
1965	**Light Fingers**, 4, 8st 4lb	J B Cummings	R Higgins
1966	**Galilee**, 4, 8st 13lb	J B Cummings	J Miller
1967	**Red Handed**, 5, 8st 9lb	J B Cummings	R Higgins
1968	**Rain Lover**, 4, 8st 2lb	M L Robins	J Johnson
1969	**Rain Lover**, 5, 9st 7lb	M L Robins	J Johnson
1970	**Baghdad Note**, 5, 8st 7lb	R Heasley	E J Didham
1971	**Silver Knight**, 4, 8st 9lb	E Templeton	R B Marsh
1972	**Piping Lane**, 6, 48kg	G M Hanlon	J Letts
1973	**Gala Supreme**, 4, 49kg	R J Hutchins	F Reys
1974	**Think Big**, 4, 53kg	J B Cummings	H White
1975	**Think Big**, 5, 58.5kg	J B Cummings	H White
1976	**Van Der Hum**, 5, 54.5kg	L H Robinson	R J Skelton
1977	**Gold and Black**, 5, 57kg	J B Cummings	J Duggan
1978	**Arwon**, 5, 50.5kg	G M Hanlon	H White
1979	**Hyperno**, 6, 56kg	J B Cummings	H White
1980	**Beldale Ball**, 5, 49.5kg	C S Hayes	J Letts
1981	**Just a Dash**, 4, 53.5kg	T J Smith	P Cook
1982	**Gurner's Lane**, 4, 56kg	G T Murphy	L Dittman
1983	**Kiwi**, 6, 52kg	E S Lupton	J Cassidy
1984	**Black Knight**, 5, 50kg	G M Hanlon	P Cook
1985	**What a Nuisance**, 7, 52.5kg	J F Meagher	P Hyland
1986	**At Talaq**, 6, 54.5kg	C S Hayes	M Clarke
1987	**Kensei**, 5, 51.5kg	L J Bridge	L Olsen
1988	**Empire Rose**, 6, 53.5kg	L K Laxon	T Allan
1989	**Tawrrific**, 5, 54 kg	D L Freedman	R Dye

Trainer Bart Cummings is the Melbourne Cup king, having won Australia's most famous race a record 7 times. (Gerry Cranham)

Champion Hurdle

At Prestbury Park, Cheltenham, Gloucestershire. Hurdle race over 8 obstacles. 2 miles.

Year	Winner, age	Trainer	Jockey
1927	**Blaris**, 6	W Payne	G Duller
1928	**Brown Jack**, 4	A Hastings	L B Rees
1929	**Royal Falcon**, 6	R Gore	F B Rees
1930	**Brown Tony**, 4	J Anthony	T Cullinan
1931	no race		
1932	**Insurance**, 5	A B Briscoe	T E Leader
1933	**Insurance**, 6	A B Briscoe	W Stott
1934	**Chenango**, 7	I Anthony	D Morgan
1935	**Lion Courage**, 7	F Brown	G Wilson
1936	**Victor Norman**, 5	M Blair	H Nicholson
1937	**Free Fare**, 9	E Gwilt	G Pellerin
1938	**Our Hope**, 9	R Gubbins	Capt R Harding
1939	**African Sister**, 7	C Piggott	K Piggott
1940	**Solford**, 9	O Anthony	S Magee
1941	**Seneca**, 4	V Smyth	R Smyth
1942	**Forestation**, 4	V Smyth	R Smyth
1943	no race		
1944	no race		
1945	**Brains Trust**, 5	G Wilson	T F Rimell
1946	**Distel**, 5	M Arnott	R O'Ryan
1947	**National Spirit**, 6	V Smyth	D Morgan
1948	**National Spirit**, 7	V Smyth	R Smyth

Year	Winner, age	Trainer	Jockey	Year	Winner, age	Trainer	Jockey
1949	**Hatton's Grace**, 9	M V O'Brien	A Brabazon	1956	**Doorknocker**, 8	W A Hall	H Sprague
1950	**Hatton's Grace**, 10	M V O'Brien	A Brabazon	1957	**Merry Deal**, 7	A W Jones	G Underwood
1951	**Hatton's Grace**, 11	M V O'Brien	A Brabazon	1958	**Bandalore**, 7	J S Wright	G Slack
1952	**Sir Ken**, 5	W Stephenson	T Molony	1959	**Fare Time**, 6	H R Price	F Winter
1953	**Sir Ken**, 6	W Stephenson	T Molony	1960	**Another Flash**, 6	P Sleator	H Beasley
1954	**Sir Ken**, 7	W Stephenson	T Molony	1961	**Eborneezer**, 6	H R Price	F Winter
1955	**Clair Soleil**, 6	H R Price	F Winter	1962	**Anzio**, 5	F Walwyn	G W Robinson
				1963	**Winning Fair**, 8	G Spencer	Mr A Lillingston
				1964	**Magic Court**, 6	T Robson	P McCarron
				1965	**Kirriemuir**, 5	F Walwyn	G W Robinson
				1966	**Salmon Spray**, 8	A R Turnell	J Haine
				1967	**Saucy Kit**, 6	M H Easterby	R Edwards
				1968	**Persian War**, 5	C H Davies	J Uttley
				1969	**Persian War**, 6	C H Davies	J Uttley
				1970	**Persian War**, 7	C H Davies	J Uttley
				1971	**Bula**, 6	F Winter	P Kelleway
				1972	**Bula**, 7	F Winter	P Kelleway
				1973	**Comedy of Errors**, 6	T F Rimell	W Smith
				1974	**Lanzarote**, 6	F Winter	R Pitman
				1975	**Comedy of Errors**, 8	T F Rimell	K B White
				1976	**Night Nurse**, 5	M H Easterby	P Broderick
				1977	**Night Nurse**, 6	M H Easterby	P Broderick
				1978	**Monksfield**, 6	D McDonogh	T Kinane
				1979	**Monksfield**, 7	D McDonogh	D T Hughes
				1980	**Sea Pigeon**, 10	M H Easterby	J J O'Neill
				1981	**Sea Pigeon**, 11	M H Easterby	J Francome
				1982	**For Auction**, 6	M Cunningham	Mr C Magnier
				1983	**Gaye Brief**, 6	Mrs M Rimell	R Linley
				1984	**Dawn Run**, 6	P Mullins	J J O'Neill
				1985	**See You Then**, 5	N Henderson	S Smith Eccles
				1986	**See You Then**, 6	N Henderson	S Smith Eccles
				1987	**See You Then**, 7	N Henderson	S Smith Eccles
				1988	**Celtic Shot**, 5	F Winter	P Scudamore
				1989	**Beech Road**, 7	G B Balding	R Guest

Above *At Talaq, a high-class stayer who won the Grand Prix de Paris at Longchamp in 1984 and the Melbourne Cup at Flemington in 1986. (All-Sport)*

Below *See You Then (Steve Smith Eccles) parades at Cheltenham in March 1987 before scoring his third consecutive Champion Hurdle victory. (Gerry Cranham)*

Cheltenham Gold Cup

At Prestbury Park, Cheltenham, Gloucestershire. Steeplechase over 22 fences. About 3 miles 2 furlongs.

Year	Winner, age	Trainer	Jockey
1924	**Red Splash**, 5	F E Withington	F B Rees
1925	**Ballinode**, 9	F Morgan	T E Leader
1926	**Koko**, 8	A Bickley	J H Hamey
1927	**Thrown In**, 11	O Anthony	Mr H Grosvenor
1928	**Patron Saint**, 5	H S Harrison	F B Rees
1929	**Easter Hero**, 9	J Anthony	F B Rees
1930	**Easter Hero**, 10	J Anthony	T Cullinan
1931	no race		
1932	**Golden Miller**, 5	A B Briscoe	T E Leader
1933	**Golden Miller**, 6	A B Briscoe	W Stott
1934	**Golden Miller**, 7	A B Briscoe	G Wilson
1935	**Golden Miller**, 8	A B Briscoe	G Wilson
1936	**Golden Miller**, 9	O Anthony	E Williams
1937	no race		
1938	**Morse Code**, 9	I Anthony	D Morgan
1939	**Brendan's Cottage**, 9	G Beeby	G R Owen
1940	**Roman Hackle**, 7	O Anthony	E Williams
1941	**Poet Prince**, 9	I Anthony	R Burford
1942	**Médoc**, 8	R Hobbs	H Nicholson
1943	no race		
1944	no race		
1945	**Red Rower**, 11	Lord Stalbridge	D L Jones
1946	**Prince Regent**, 11	T Dreaper	T Hyde
1947	**Fortina**, 6	H Christie	Mr R Black
1948	**Cottage Rake**, 9	M V O'Brien	A Brabazon
1949	**Cottage Rake**, 10	M V O'Brien	A Brabazon
1950	**Cottage Rake**, 11	M V O'Brien	A Brabazon
1951	**Silver Fame**, 12	G Beeby	M Molony
1952	**Mont Tremblant**, 6	F Walwyn	D V Dick
1953	**Knock Hard**, 9	M V O'Brien	T Molony
1954	**Four Ten**, 8	J F Roberts	T Cusack
1955	**Gay Donald**, 9	J J Ford	A Grantham
1956	**Limber Hill**, 9	W P Dutton	J Power
1957	**Linwell**, 9	I Herbert	M Scudamore
1958	**Kerstin**, 8	C Bewicke	S Hayhurst
1959	**Roddy Owen**, 10	D Morgan	H Beasley
1960	**Pas Seul**, 7	A R Turnell	W Rees
1961	**Saffron Tartan**, 10	D Butchers	F Winter
1962	**Mandarin**, 11	F Walwyn	F Winter
1963	**Mill House**, 6	F Walwyn	G W Robinson
1964	**Arkle**, 7	T Dreaper	P Taaffe
1965	**Arkle**, 8	T Dreaper	P Taaffe
1966	**Arkle**, 9	T Dreaper	P Taaffe
1967	**Woodland Venture**, 7	T F Rimell	T W Biddlecombe
1968	**Fort Leney**, 10	T Dreaper	P Taaffe
1969	**What a Myth**, 12	H R Price	P Kelleway
1970	**L'Escargot**, 7	D L Moore	T Carberry
1971	**L'Escargot**, 8	D L Moore	T Carberry
1972	**Glencaraig Lady**, 8	F Flood	F Berry
1973	**The Dikler**, 10	F Walwyn	R Barry
1974	**Captain Christy**, 7	P Taaffe	H Beasley
1975	**Ten Up**, 8	J Dreaper	T Carberry
1976	**Royal Frolic**, 7	T F Rimell	J Burke
1977	**Davy Lad**, 7	M O'Toole	D T Hughes
1978	**Midnight Court**, 7	F Winter	J Francome
1979	**Alverton**, 9	M H Easterby	J J O'Neill
1980	**Master Smudge**, 8	A Barrow	R Hoare
1981	**Little Owl**, 7	M H Easterby	Mr A J Wilson
1982	**Silver Buck**, 10	M Dickinson	R Earnshaw
1983	**Bregawn**, 9	M Dickinson	G Bradley
1984	**Burrough Hill Lad**, 8	Mrs J Pitman	P Tuck
1985	**Forgive 'N Forget**, 8	J G FitzGerald	M Dwyer
1986	**Dawn Run**, 8	P Mullins	J J O'Neill
1987	**The Thinker**, 9	W A Stephenson	R Lamb
1988	**Charter Party**, 10	D Nicholson	R Dunwoody
1989	**Desert Orchid**, 10	D Elsworth	S Sherwood

Desert Orchid (Simon Sherwood) on his way to victory in the Gainsborough Handicap Chase at Sandown Park in February 1989. (Popperfoto)

Grand National

At Aintree, Liverpool, Merseyside. Handicap steeplechase over 30 fences. About 4½ miles.

Year	Winner, age, weight	Trainer	Jockey
1839	**Lottery**, 9, 12-0	G Dockeray	J Mason
1840	**Jerry**, 10, 12-0	—	Mr B Bretherton
1841	**Charity**, 11, 12-0	—	H N Powell
1842	**Gaylad**, 8, 12-0	—	T Oliver
1843	**Vanguard**, 8, 11-10	—	T Oliver
1844	**Discount**, 6, 10-12	—	H Crickmere
1845	**Cure-all**, a, 11-5	—	Mr W Loft
1846	**Pioneer**, 6, 11-12	—	W Taylor
1847	**Mathew**, 9, 10-6	J Courtenay	D Wynne
1848	**Chandler**, 12, 11-12	—	Mr J Little
1849	**Peter Simple**, 11, 11-0	T Cunningham	T Cunningham
1850	**Abd-el-Kader**, 8, 9-12	—	Mr C Green
1851	**Abd-el-Kader**, 9, 10-4	—	T Abbott
1852	**Miss Mowbray**, 8, 10-4	G Dockeray	Mr A Goodman
1853	**Peter Simple**, 15, 10-10	T Oliver	T Oliver
1854	**Bourton**, a, 11-12	H Wadlow	Tasker
1855	**Wanderer**, 10, 9-8	—	J Hanlon
1856	**Freetrader**, 7, 9-6	W Holman	G Stevens
1857	**Emigrant**, a, 9-10	C Boyce	C Boyce
1858	**Little Charley**, 10, 10-7	W Holman	W Archer
1859	**Half Caste**, 6, 9-7	C Green	C Green
1860	**Anatis**, 10, 9-10	W Holman	Mr T Pickernell
1861	**Jealousy**, 7, 9-12	C Balchin	J Kendall
1862	**Huntsman**, 9, 11-0	H Lamplugh	H Lamplugh
1863	**Emblem**, 7, 10-10	E Weever	G Stevens
1864	**Emblematic**, 6, 10-6	E Weever	G Stevens
1865	**Alcibiade**, 5, 11-4	Cornell	Capt H Coventry
1866	**Salamander**, 7, 10-7	J Walters	Mr A Goodman
1867	**Cortolvin**, 8, 11-13	H Lamplugh	J Page
1868	**The Lamb**, 6, 10-7	B Land	Mr G Ede

Year	Winner, age, weight	Trainer	Jockey	Year	Winner, age, weight	Trainer	Jockey
1869	**The Colonel**, 6, 10-7	R Roberts	G Stevens	1928	**Tipperary Tim**, 10, 10-0	J Dodd	Mr W Dutton
1870	**The Colonel**, 7, 11-12	R Roberts	G Stevens	1929	**Gregalach**, 7, 11-4	T R Leader	R Everett
1871	**The Lamb**, 9, 11-5	C Green	Mr T Pickernell	1930	**Shaun Goilin**, 10, 11-7	F Hartigan	T Cullinan
1872	**Casse Tête**, 7, 10-0	Cowley	J Page	1931	**Grakle**, 9, 11-7	T Coulthwaite	R Lyall
1873	**Disturbance**, 6, 11-11	J M Richardson	Mr J M Richardson	1932	**Forbra**, 7, 10-7	T R Rimell	J H Hamey
1874	**Reugny**, 6, 10-12	J M Richardson	Mr J M Richardson	1933	**Kellsboro' Jack**, 7, 11-9	I Anthony	D Williams
1875	**Pathfinder**, 6, 10-11	W Reeves	Mr T Pickernell	1934	**Golden Miller**, 7, 12-2	A B Briscoe	G Wilson
1876	**Regal**, 5, 11-3	J Cannon	J Cannon	1935	**Reynoldstown**, 8, 11-4	N Furlong	Mr F Furlong
1877	**Austerlitz**, 5, 10-8	R I'Anson	Mr F Hobson	1936	**Reynoldstown**, 9, 12-2	N Furlong	Mr F Walwyn
1878	**Shifnal**, 9, 10-12	J Nightingall	J Jones	1937	**Royal Mail**, 8, 11-13	I Anthony	E Williams
1879	**The Liberator**, 10, 11-4	J Moore	Mr G Moore	1938	**Battleship**, 11, 11-6	R Hobbs	B Hobbs
1880	**Empress**, 5, 10-7	H Linde	Mr T Beasley	1939	**Workman**, 9, 10-6	J Ruttle	T Hyde
1881	**Woodbrook**, 7, 11-3	H Linde	Mr T Beasley	1940	**Bogskar**, 7, 10-4	Lord Stalbridge	M Jones
1882	**Seaman**, 6, 11-6	J Jewitt	Lord Manners	1941–1945 no race			
1883	**Zoëdone**, 6, 11-0	W H P Jenkins	Graf K Kinsky	1946	**Lovely Cottage**, 9, 10-8	T Rayson	Capt R Petre
1884	**Voluptuary**, 6, 10-5	W Wilson	Mr E P Wilson	1947	**Caughoo**, 8, 10-0	H McDowell	E Dempsey
1885	**Roquefort**, 6, 11-0	A Yates	Mr E P Wilson	1948	**Sheila's Cottage**, 9, 10-7	N Crump	A P Thompson
1886	**Old Joe**, 7, 10-9	G Mulcaster	T Skelton	1949	**Russian Hero**, 9, 10-8	G R Owen	L McMorrow
1887	**Gamecock**, 8, 11-0	Jordan	W Daniels	1950	**Freebooter**, 9, 11-11	R Renton	J Power
1888	**Playfair**, 7, 10-7	T Cannon	G Mawson	1951	**Nickel Coin**, 9, 10-1	J O'Donoghue	J A Bullock
1889	**Frigate**, 11, 11-4	M Maher	Mr T Beasley	1952	**Teal**, 10, 10-12	N Crump	A P Thompson
1890	**Ilex**, 6, 10-5	J Nightingall	A Nightingall	1953	**Early Mist**, 8, 11-2	M V O'Brien	B Marshall
1891	**Come Away**, 7, 11-12	H Beasley	Mr H Beasley	1954	**Royal Tan**, 10, 11-7	M V O'Brien	B Marshall
1892	**Father O'Flynn**, 7, 10-5	—	Capt R Owen	1955	**Quare Times**, 9, 11-0	M V O'Brien	P Taaffe
1893	**Cloister**, 9, 12-7	A Yates	W Dollery	1956	**E.S.B.**, 10, 11-3	T F Rimell	D V Dick
1894	**Why Not**, 13, 11-13	W Moore	A Nightingall	1957	**Sundew**, 11, 11-7	F Hudson	F Winter
1895	**Wild Man from Borneo**, 7, 10-11	J Gatland	Mr J Widger	1958	**Mr What**, 8, 10-6	T Taaffe	A Freeman
1896	**The Soarer**, 7, 9-13	W Moore	Mr D Campbell	1959	**Oxo**, 8, 10-13	W Stephenson	M Scudamore
1897	**Manifesto**, 9, 11-3	W McAuliffe	T Kavanagh	1960	**Merryman**, 9, 10-12	N Crump	G Scott
1898	**Drogheda**, 6, 10-12	R C Dawson	J Gourley	1961	**Nicolaus Silver**, 9, 10-1	T F Rimell	H Beasley
1899	**Manifesto**, 11, 12-7	W Moore	G Williamson	1962	**Kilmore**, 12, 10-4	H R Price	F Winter
1900	**Ambush**, 6, 11-3	J Hunter	A Anthony	1963	**Ayala**, 9, 10-0	K Piggott	P Buckley
1901	**Grudon**, 11, 10-0	B Bletsoe	A Nightingall	1964	**Team Spirit**, 12, 10-3	F Walwyn	G W Robinson
1902	**Shannon Lass**, 7, 10-1	J Hackett	D Read	1965	**Jay Trump**, 8, 11-5	F Winter	Mr C Smith
1903	**Drumcree**, 9, 11-3	Sir C Nugent	P Woodland	1966	**Anglo**, 8, 10-0	F Winter	T Norman
1904	**Moifaa**, 8, 10-7	W Hickey	A Birch	1967	**Foinavon**, 9, 10-0	J H Kempton	J Buckingham
1905	**Kirkland**, 9, 11-5	E Thomas	F Mason	1968	**Red Alligator**, 9, 10-0	D Smith	B Fletcher
1906	**Ascetic's Silver**, 9, 10-9	A Hastings	Mr A Hastings	1969	**Highland Wedding**, 12, 10-4	G B Balding	E P Harty
1907	**Eremon**, 7, 10-1	T Coulthwaite	A Newey	1970	**Gay Trip**, 8, 11-5	T F Rimell	P Taaffe
1908	**Rubio**, 10, 10-5	F Withington	H Bletsoe	1971	**Specify**, 9, 10-13	J E Sutcliffe	J Cook
1909	**Lutteur**, 5, 10-11	H Escott	G Parfrement	1972	**Well To Do**, 9, 10-1	T Forster	G Thorner
1910	**Jenkinstown**, 9, 10-5	T Coulthwaite	R Chadwick	1973	**Red Rum**, 8, 10-5	D McCain	B Fletcher
1911	**Glenside**, 9, 10-3	R Collis	Mr J Anthony	1974	**Red Rum**, 9, 12-0	D McCain	B Fletcher
1912	**Jerry M**, 9, 12-7	R Gore	E Piggott	1975	**L'Escargot**, 12, 11-3	D L Moore	T Carberry
1913	**Covertcoat**, 7, 11-6	R Gore	P Woodland	1976	**Rag Trade**, 10, 10-12	T F Rimell	J Burke
1914	**Sunloch**, 8, 9-7	T Tyler	W Smith	1977	**Red Rum**, 12, 11-8	D McCain	T Stack
1915	**Ally Sloper**, 6, 10-6	A Hastings	Mr J Anthony	1978	**Lucius**, 9, 10-9	G W Richards	B R Davies
1916*	**Vermouth**, 6, 11-10	J Bell	J Reardon	1979	**Rubstic**, 10, 10-0	S J Leadbetter	M Barnes
1917*	**Ballymacad**, 10, 9-12	A Hastings	E Driscoll	1980	**Ben Nevis**, 12, 10-12	T Forster	Mr C Fenwick
1918*	**Poethlyn**, 8, 11-6	H Escott	E Piggott	1981	**Aldaniti**, 11, 10-13	J Gifford	R Champion
1919	**Poethlyn**, 9, 12-7	H Escott	E Piggott	1982	**Grittar**, 9, 11-5	F Gilman	Mr C R Saunders
1920	**Troytown**, 7, 11-9	A Anthony	Mr J Anthony	1983	**Corbière**, 8, 11-4	Mrs J Pitman	B de Haan
1921	**Shaun Spadah**, 10, 11-7	G Poole	F B Rees	1984	**Hallo Dandy**, 10, 10-2	G W Richards	N Doughty
1922	**Music Hall**, 9, 11-8	O Anthony	L B Rees	1985	**Last Suspect**, 11, 10-5	T Forster	H Davies
1923	**Sergeant Murphy**, 13, 11-3	G Blackwell	Capt G Bennet	1986	**West Tip**, 9, 10-11	M Oliver	R Dunwoody
1924	**Master Robert**, 11, 10-5	A Hastings	R Trudgill	1987	**Maori Venture**, 11, 10-13	A Turnell	S C Knight
1925	**Double Chance**, 9, 10-9	F Archer	Maj J Wilson	1988	**Rhyme 'N' Reason**, 9, 11-0	D Elsworth	B Powell
1926	**Jack Horner**, 9, 10-5	H Leader	W Watkinson	1989	**Little Polveir**, 12, 10-3	G B Balding	J Frost
1927	**Sprig**, 10, 12-4	T R Leader	T E Leader				

* *Substitute races run at Gatwick.*

Index